America Now

Short Readings from Recent Periodicals

America Now

Short Readings from Recent Periodicals
Third Edition

Edited by

ROBERT ATWAN

Exercises prepared with the assistance of

Mark Bellomo
State University of New York, New Paltz

Jennifer Ivers
Boston University

Bedford / St. Martin's   Boston   New York

For Bedford / St. Martin's
Developmental Editor: Aron Keesbury
Production Editor: Sherri Frank
Production Supervisor: Catherine Hetmansky
Marketing Manager: Karen Melton
Editorial Assistant: Ellen Thibault
Production Assistant: Helaine Denenberg
Copyeditor: Rosemary Winfield
Text Design: Jean Hammond
Cover Design: Hannus Design Associates
Cover Photograph: Martin Paul, Ltd.
Composition: Pine Tree Composition, Inc.
Printing and Binding: Haddon Craftsmen, Inc.

President: Charles H. Christensen
Editorial Director: Joan E. Feinberg
Director of Editing, Design, and Production: Marcia Cohen
Managing Editor: Elizabeth M. Schaaf

Library of Congress Catalog Card Number: 98–87519

Manufactured in the United States of America.

3   2   1   0   9
f   e   d   c   b   a

For information, write: Bedford / St. Martin's, 75 Arlington Street, Boston,
MA 02116 (617-426-7440)

ISBN: 0–312–19182–0

Acknowledgments

Teresa Allen, "A Voice from Death Row," *Grand Street*, Fall 1997. Excerpted from
Honey, This Ain't No Country Club: Women Doing Hard Time by Teresa Allen,
to be published in 1999 by Columbia University Press. Reprinted by permission
of Teresa Allen, an Associate Professor of Journalism at Boston University.

*Acknowledgments and copyrights are continued at the back of the book on
pages 340–43, which constitute an extension of the copyright page. It is a
violation of the law to reproduce these selections by any means whatsoever
without the written permission of the copyright holder.*

Preface for Instructors

The Book

People write for many reasons, but one of the most compelling is to express their views on matters of current public interest. Browse any newsstand or library magazine rack and you'll find an overabundance of articles, features, and opinion columns written in response to current issues or events. Even personal and reflective essays on subjects that aren't necessarily timely are often pegged (sometimes ingeniously) to a current issue or trend.

The third edition of *America Now*, like its predecessors, is designed to involve introductory writing students in the give-and-take of current public discussion and to activate reading, thinking, discussion, and writing. The overriding instructional principle — which informs everything from the choice of selections and topics to the design of apparatus — is that participation in informed discussion will stimulate and improve student writing. The book encourages both instructors and students to view reading, thinking, discussion, and writing as closely interrelated activities. It assumes that: (1) attentive reading and reflection will lead to informed discussion; (2) participation in open and informed discussion will result in a broadening of viewpoints; (3) an awareness of different viewpoints will stimulate additional reflection; and (4) this process in turn will lead to thoughtful compositions.

The Selections

The Main Selections. The book's fifty-three main selections — all new to this edition — are drawn from forty-four recent periodicals, ranging from such literary and intellectual magazines as *The Atlantic Monthly* and *The New Yorker* to such popular periodicals as *Mademoiselle* and *Glamour*. With its emphasis on public discourse, this collection draws a generous sampling of material from America's leading political magazines, both left and right. In general, the selections illustrate the variety of personal, informative, and persuasive writing read daily by millions of Americans. In addition to their range and interest, the selections are short — most under three pages, and some no longer than a page — to keep student interest and to serve as models for students' own writing, generally assigned to be about the same length.

The Student Writing. In fact, *America Now* retains the strong presence of student writing that marked the second edition. The collection now features twenty published student essays, almost all of which appeared in college newspapers across the country available on the Internet. These recent student essays reveal student writers confronting, in a public forum, the same topics and issues that challenge some of our leading social critics and commentators and show how student writers can enter into and influence public discussion. In this way, *America Now* encourages students to view the act of writing as a form of personal and public empowerment. Too frequently, students see the writing they do in a composition class as having little connection with real-world problems and issues. The student selections prove that writing can make a difference, and they are sure to spark lively and interesting class discussions.

The Role of the Internet. As in the second edition, nearly all of the student pieces were located on the Internet. *America Now* was the first composition reader to draw heavily on this rapidly expanding resource for readers, writers, and anyone interested in discussion of current political and cultural affairs. As Web pages, chat rooms, on-line forums, and other discussion sites proliferate, students will find a wide-open environment for sharing information, opinions, and concerns. All kinds of public forums are quickly growing more convenient and accessible; most periodicals, for example, now welcome e-mail responses, and today, student writers can enter the public sphere as never before.

The Themes

Student essays not only make up a large percentage of this edition, but they also shape the volume's contents. At Bedford / St. Martin's, as we monitored the broad spectrum of college newspapers available on the Internet, and reviewed hundreds of student essays, we found the most commonly discussed campus issues and topics. Certain issues, such as affirmative action, cloning, free speech, and capital punishment, have provoked so much recent student response that they could have resulted in several single-topic collections. Many college papers do not restrict themselves to news items and editorial opinion but make room for personal essays as well. Some popular student topics were self-image, group identity, and clothing, all of which are reflected in *America Now*'s table of contents.

To facilitate group discussion and in-class work, *America Now* features bite-sized units. These tightly focused units permit instructors to cover a broad range of themes and issues in a single semester. Each unit can be conveniently handled in one or two class periods. The units move from accessible, personal topics (for example, names, self-image, and style of dress) to more complex public issues, thus accommodating teachers who prefer to start with personal writing and gradually progress to exposition, analysis, and argument.

The Editorial Apparatus

Before, During, and After Reading. The apparatus of *America Now* supports both discussion-based instruction as well as more individualized approaches to reading and writing. Taking into account the increasing diversity of students (especially the growing number of non-native speakers) in today's writing programs, the apparatus offers extensive help with college-level vocabulary and features a "Words to Learn" list preceding each selection. This vocabulary list with brief definitions will allow students to spot ahead of time some of the words they may find difficult; encountering the word later in context will help lock it in memory. It's unrealistic, however, to think students will acquire a fluent knowledge of new words by memorizing a list. Therefore, the apparatus following each selection includes additional exercises under the headings "Vocabulary/Using a Dictionary" and "Responding to Words in Context." These sets of questions introduce students to prefixes, suffixes, connotations, denotations, tone, and etymology.

To help promote reflection and discussion, this edition includes a prereading assignment for each main selection. These "Before You Read" suggestions provide students with the opportunity to explore a few of the avenues that lead to fruitful discussion and interesting papers. A full description of the advantages gained by linking reading, writing, and classroom discussion can be found in my introduction to the instructor's manual.

Linking Reading, Thinking, Discussion, and Writing. Along with the discussion of vocabulary, the incrementally-structured questions following individual selections emphasize reading comprehension ("Discussing Main Point and Meaning") and important elements of writing ("Examining Sentences, Paragraphs, and Organization"). In addition, the selection apparatus includes "In-Class Writing Activities" and "Thinking Critically," a set of questions that encourages students to take a critical stance toward the essay. As instructors well know, beginning students can sometimes be too trusting of what they see in print, especially in textbooks. Therefore, the "Thinking Critically" questions invite students to take a more skeptical attitude toward their reading and to form the habit of challenging a selection from both an analytical and an experiential point of view.

In addition to the selection apparatus, *America Now* also contains end-of-unit questions designed to stimulate further discussion and writing. The unit apparatus approaches the reading material from topical and thematic angles with an emphasis on group discussion. The introductory comments to each unit highlight the main discussion points and the way selections are linked together. These points and linkages are then reintroduced at the end of the unit through three sets of interlocking study questions and tasks: (1) a suggested topic for discussion; (2) questions and ideas to help students prepare for class discussion; and (3) several writing assignments that ask students to move from discussion to composition — that is, to develop papers out of the ideas and opinions expressed in class discussion and debate. Finally, instructors with highly diverse writing classes may find "Topics for Cross-Cultural Discussion" a convenient way to encourage an exchange of perspectives and experiences that could also generate ideas for writing.

New to This Edition

Why a new edition of *America Now* after only two years? The reason is simple: to keep the selections as fresh and topical as possible. Any instructor who wants to use reading material that reflects recent controversies and trends knows how quickly issue-oriented anthologies become dated. Having mostly been published within a year or two of the book's publication, all of the material in *America Now* is truly contemporary with respect to the lives and experiences of students. In addition to new selections and themes, this edition of *America Now* also contains a number of unique features designed for the changing trends in America.

- **What America Is Discussing Right Now.** *All of the essays and most of the unit themes are new.* Every single selection in the book is new, and of the fifteen units, eleven are new to this edition. The units address some of the most controversial issues of the day: affirmative action, free speech, cloning, gender differences, negative stereotypes, the national dialogue on race, and the resurgence of capital punishment. Other units focus on controversial personal topics — names, clothing, self-image, and identity, for example. Because composition courses naturally emphasize issues revolving around language and the construction of meaning, this edition now includes several units designed to encourage students to consider the powerful influence of words and symbols. Language issues surface in the units on names, words, free speech, and the flag.

- **The New Visual Focus of Public Discussion.** The persuasive power of language and image, furthermore, is the main point of another new unit, "Can 'Op-Ads' Change Your Mind?" Responding to the growing presence of advertising in public discussion, this unit invites students to uncover the visual and verbal "tactics" of "opinion advertising" commonly used by various advocacy groups to influence the consciousness and ideology of large audiences.

- **New Cultural Contexts for Public Discussion.** Each unit of this edition now contains a brief selection drawn from an important and provocative current book, often from nonfiction best-sellers such as Mary Pipher's *Reviving Ophelia* and Sister Helen Prejean's *Dead Man Walking*. These "From the Bookshelf" excerpts address a unit's central theme and frequently speak directly to the main selections. Brief enough to be assigned for in-class reading and writing, the "Bookshelf" selections introduce students to some serious recent books and can be used to initiate further reading and research.

- **New Focus on Opposing Viewpoints.** For instructors who want to concentrate on argumentative skills, the book now features two sets of "Opposing Views," one on a controversial incident in women's basketball, the other on racial stereotyping. In addition, two concluding units contain student debates on affirmative action and capital punishment.

- **The Questions' New Focus.** Three new question sets have been added following each selection. Picking up on the vocabulary lists preceding each selection, a new question set, "Responding to Words in Context," supplements the existing "Vocabulary / Using a Dictionary" questions and asks students to use what they have learned from the dictionary exercises and vocabulary lists.

Following the vocabulary questions, the new "Discussing Main Point and Meaning" and "Examining Sentences, Paragraphs, and Organization" questions help guide students step-by-step through the reading process, culminating in the new "Thinking Critically" questions and the "In-Class Writing Activities."

- **The New Workbook.** *Exploring* America Now, Third Edition: *Exercises in Vocabulary, Reading, and Grammar*, by professors John Een and Leila May-Landy of the American Language Program at Columbia University, will expand the instructional possibilities of *America Now*. This workbook — which follows *America Now* unit-by-unit and selection-by-selection — helps students improve their grammar, vocabulary, and reading skills. Each of *America Now*'s selections has in this workbook a corresponding set of vocabulary and reading comprehension exercises and each unit a corresponding grammar section. Also included are activities to generate thoughtful, coherent paragraphs and essays. This workbook is an enormously useful addition to the *America Now* composition package.

The Instructor's Manual

Jennifer Ivers of Boston University and Mark Bellomo of the State University of New York at New Paltz prepared the instructor's manual, bringing to the task not only a familiarity with the text but years of classroom experience at all levels of composition instruction. The manual contains an essay for each unit, offering suggestions for teaching the selections in the unit together and separately; and suggested answers and possible discussion topics based on every question posed in the text. Anyone using *America Now* should be sure to consult the manual before designing a syllabus, framing a discussion topic, or even assigning an individual selection. Liz deBeer of Rutgers University also contributes to the instructor's manual a helpful essay on designing student panels ("Forming Forums") and advice on using the book's apparatus in both developmental and mainstream composition classes.

Acknowledgments

While putting together the third edition of *America Now* I was fortunate to receive the assistance of many talented individuals. In addition to their work on the instructor's manual, Mark Bellomo, Jennifer Ivers, and Liz deBeer offered many useful suggestions for the book's instructional apparatus. The work of John Een and Leila

May-Landy on the new ESL and developmental workbook deserves many thanks.

To revise a text is to entertain numerous questions: What kind of selections work best in class? What types of questions are most helpful? How can reading, writing, and discussion be most effectively intertwined? This edition profited immensely from the following instructors who generously took the time to respond to the first edition: Nancy Canavera, Charleston Southern University; Linda Currivan, University of Hawaii-Leeward Community College; Sheri Divers, Georgia Southern University; Mary M. Dossim, SUNY-Plattsburgh; John Gibney, Landmark College; Peggy Kocoras, Assumption College; Dawn L. Leonard, Charleston Southern University; Mark Lindemer, College of Southern Idaho; Nancy McCabe, University of Nebraska; Edward Mack, Sullivan County Community College; Alison McNeal, Slippery Rock University; Frank Noji, Kapiolani Community College; Mary J. Page, San Jose City College; William Roney, Rutgers University-New Brunswick; Natasha Saltrup, Rutgers University-Newark; Robin Schore, Mercer County College; and Warren B. Seekamp, University of Louisville; and the following instructors who responded to the second edition: Carlo Anese, Bergen Community College; Mark Bellomo, SUNY, New Paltz; Jannelle Boucher, SUNY, New Paltz; Christopher Carolei, SUNY, New Paltz; Ursula Crabtree-DeNatale, California State University, Sacramento; Chris Hartley, SUNY, New Paltz; Ronnie Kaufman, Passaic County Community College; Elizabeth Levi, Passaic County Community College; Ruggerio Manente, Passaic County Community College; Elizabeth Marsh, Bergen Community College; Michael Orlando, Bergen Community College; Brad Saenz, Pasadena City College; Donya Samara, Fresno City College; Mark Scamahorn, Santa Barbara City College; James C. Schneider, University of La Verne; and Susan Zimmerman, City College of San Francisco.

Other people helped in various ways. I'm indebted to Barbara Gross of Rutgers University (Newark) for her excellent work in preparing the instructor's manual for the first edition. Two good friends, Charles O'Neill and Jack Roberts, both of St. Thomas Aquinas College, went over my early plans for the book and offered many useful suggestions. I appreciate the advice and suggestions of: Mary Ann Ardeline, Northampton Community College; Nancy Bailey, Metropolitan State College; David Borofsky, Northampton Community College; Mary Ann Hofer, University of Findlay; Kate Mangelsdorf, University of Texas–El Paso; Evelyn J. Posey, University of

Texas–El Paso; Barbara Rayman, Arapahoe Community College; Ann Rohovec, Dona Ana College; Nancy Troutman, Northampton Community College; and Janet Vucinich, Santa Fe Community College. Many of the comments they offered during the last edition's planning stages remain relevant.

As always, it was a pleasure to work with the superb staff at Bedford / St. Martin's. *America Now* began with Bedford's associate publisher, Joan E. Feinberg, who conceived of the idea — and I thank her for it. Jane Betz, my editor on the first edition, shaped the book in lasting ways and helped with the planning of the revision. Of all the people acknowledged, I owe the most gratitude to this edition's developmental editor, Aron Keesbury. His insightful suggestions, remarkable good sense, and uncanny ability to keep track of so many minute details made this collection a pleasure to work on from start to finish. I appreciate, too, the efforts of Ellen Thibault, who tackled a variety of editorial tasks. Donna Ashley cleared permissions under a tight deadline. Sherri Frank guided the book through production with patience and care, staying on top of many details; Helaine Denenberg provided production assistance; and Elizabeth Schaaf managed the production process with her usual attentiveness. I was fortunate to receive the careful copyediting of Rosemary Winfield. In the advertising and promotion department, manager Jeannie Tarkenton as well as Patricia Lang and Jill Chmelko, deserve warm thanks for their work.

Finally, I would like to thank Bedford's publisher, Charles H. Christensen, for his deep and abiding interest in college composition. It is a great pleasure and privilege to work with him.

R. A.

Contents

xiii

to be fashionable? A popular newspaper columnist wonders why women have such fondness for uncomfortable and hazardous high-heel shoes. ... During spring break, a student tries on some very unstylish clothing and discovers the social consequences. ... Do public-school dress codes help improve the quality of education or rob students of their individuality? asks a San Diego State University psychology major.

3 Body Image: Why Is It a Serious Issue?   41

Opinion polls show that most Americans are discontent with their appearances. Usually, women want to lose pounds, and men want to gain muscle in the hope of achieving their "ideal" body images. Yet how attainable are these ideals? Tired of measuring herself against an impossible physical standard, a young woman decides to fight back. ... Are girls really influenced by the way Barbie Dolls look? a Tufts University newspaper columnist wonders. Doesn't everyone know they're just dolls? ... How can we resist the myth of the ideal body? An Illinois State University student offers some suggestions.

4   Who Has It Tougher — Boys or Girls?   59

Do males and females really behave as though they came from different planets? Can gender differences be bridged by mutual understanding, or are they so innate that a communications gap between men and women will always remain? Are girls given fewer opportunities in our society than boys? A philosophy professor disputes the idea that American girls represent a disadvantaged group. . . . True maleness means showing emotions, claims a University of Nebraska English and speech communications major. . . . A *New York Times* editorial features conflicting opinions on a controversial incident in women's basketball.

5   How Important Is Group Identity?   78

Do you ever see yourself as a representative of an ethnic, racial, or political group? How important is group membership to your sense of identity? If you see yourself only as a representative of some category, warns a *Newsweek* columnist, your leaders will so treat you. . . . A Yale University student feels very much at home with his friends in New York City's Chinatown. . . . Is it possible, a mother wonders, to persuade today's diversity-minded educators that her child's ethnic identity is simply "American"?

6   What Good Are Role Models?   99

Does everyone grow up with heroes and role models? Can you judge a society by the kinds of individuals its young decide to imitate? A media scholar believes a popular British singing group may be helping to empower their young female fans. . . . It's a waste of time to expect athletes to be socially responsible role models, argues a noted African American political scientist. . . . Maybe it's time, says a University of Nebraska student, to abandon our need for heroes.

9   Free Expression: How Much Should We Tolerate?   166

Is our right to free speech limited or unlimited? What kinds of restraint can be placed on speech, and who decides what can or cannot be expressed? A best-selling author and social critic reminds students who are too easily offended that "the art of giving and taking offense is an art of citizenship in a free society." . . . Two professors of education believe that big business hides behind free-speech issues in targeting media violence to children. . . . An Iowa State University journalism student investigates the sources of intolerance.

10   Do Words Matter?   185

"Sticks and stones may break my bones, but names will never hurt me" — is the old childhood rhyme true? Or can words seriously injure? Does what we call something make a difference in the way we think about it? Can words have serious consequences? Can they determine an identity? "Having a word for what you're being makes being it easier," suggests a magazine writer as she searches for a label that's more relaxed than "woman" and more grown-up than "girl." ... An African American essayist offers both blacks and whites some advice about using the "N-Word." ... The "next time someone calls me a *radical*, I will accept that label with pride," says a student at Franklin and Marshall College.

11   Race Relations: Is Dialogue Possible?   206

When President Clinton established an Initiative on Race to encourage a national dialogue on the topic, he may have underes-
timated the difficulties that people of different races and political views would encounter in trying to talk to each other. One
of the first problems went to the heart of the issue: Is free and
open discussion even possible? It isn't, claims a prominent author, unless blacks and whites take the trouble to "examine and
question" their own perspectives. . . . One of the nation's outstanding legal scholars reports on her efforts to find a better
method of conducting multiracial discussion. . . . If we want to
encourage a dialogue on race, then we first need to "stop the
lies," argues an award-winning poet and essayist. . . . In a more
just and equitable society, a Wayne State University student
contends, a Black History Month would be unnecessary.

12   The Flag: What Does It Symbolize?   233

Many Americans would agree that the flag has special meaning
and anyone who destroys or defaces it should be punished. For
years, Congress has threatened to pass laws that would protect
the flag from desecration. But do such laws violate the Constitution? And if burning the American flag is protected by the First
Amendment, then why do some groups protest the display of the
Confederate flag? Isn't the expressive use of that flag — or any

flag — also protected by the First Amendment? If you destroy the picture of a flag on a postage stamp would you then be subject to prosecution, asked a noted historian who raises a few key questions about what the flag means. . . . A political commentator thinks it's about time we retired that old song about the flag, the national anthem. . . . The Confederate flag may symbolize a forgotten way of life, argues a Harvard student, but the cost of flying it far outweighs any advantages. . . . A cartoonist satirically depicts the American flag of the year 2022.

13   Cloning: Is It Inevitable?   255

When a Scottish scientist successfully cloned a sheep in 1997, the experiment prompted world-wide discussion about the next step: Should we begin funding research to clone human beings? Should human cloning be altogether prohibited? A science magazine reminds us that even if it were technologically possible to clone human beings, we are still "more than our genes." . . . Why do people today feel so pressured to reproduce themselves biologically? asks a prominent political philosopher. . . . The editors of Southern Illinois University at Carbondale's newspaper believe we might miss some of cloning's medical benefits if we remain blinded by irrational fears.

14   Is Affirmative Action Still Needed?   274

Affirmative action, a hotly debated topic in the late 1970s when
courts were supporting admission policies that assisted minority
applicants, is once again an urgent issue. Will California's Proposition 209 banning affirmative action in its public colleges effectively end the policy everywhere? Or will legislators and administrators find ways to sustain it? Speaking from personal
experience, a University of Wisconsin freshman urges that admission and employment decisions be based exclusively on merit and
qualifications. . . . But *merit* is an "amorphous" term, claims an
Emory University sophomore, who believes affirmative action is
the only way to correct decades of racial and gender discrimination. . . . An African American columnist views the recent attack
on affirmative action in light of our nation's history and worries
that it is a serious step backward for racial progress.

15   Is the Death Penalty Necessary?   293

Currently, over three thousand convicts are on death row as the national rate of executions steadily climbs. Is the death penalty the only way to deal with convicted murderers? Why is the issue so divisive? Are there alternatives that could satisfy both proponents and opponents of capital punishment? A convicted serial killer in Connecticut explains why he raped and murdered eight women.... From a Florida prison cell, a woman on death row describes her life behind bars.... An Oklahoma State University student witnesses an execution and wonders afterward why she feels no emotion.... There *are* humane alternatives to the death penalty, argues a student from Virginia Tech.... Those who carry out death sentences, claims the editorial board of the Northern Illinois University newspaper, are murderers themselves.

Introduction:
The Empowered Writer

How to Read this Book

America Now collects recent articles carefully selected to stimulate reading, discussion, and writing. The articles come from two main sources — popular periodicals and college newspapers available on the Internet. Written by journalists and columnists, public figures and activists, as well as professors and students from all over the country, the selections illustrate the types of material read by millions of Americans every day. The book covers fifteen of today's most widely discussed issues and topics. In reading, discussing, and writing about the selections, you will be actively taking part in some of the major controversies of our time.

Participation is the key to this collection. I encourage you to view reading and writing as a form of participation. I hope you will read the selections attentively, think about them, be willing to discuss them in class, and use what you've learned from your reading and discussion as the basis for your papers. If you do these things, you will develop three skills necessary for successful college work: the ability to read critically, to discuss topics intelligently, and to write persuasively.

America Now invites you to see reading, discussion, and writing as closely related activities. As you read a selection, imagine that you have entered into a discussion with the author. Take notes as you read. Question the selection. Challenge its point of view or its evidence. Compare your experience with the author's. Consider how different economic classes or other groups are likely to respond.

Remember, just because something appears in a newspaper or book doesn't make it true or accurate. Form the habit of challenging what you read. Don't be persuaded by an opinion simply because it appears in print or because you believe you should accept it. Trust your own observations and experiences. Though logicians never say so, personal experiences and keen observations often provide the basis of our most convincing arguments.

When your class discusses a selection, be especially attentive to what others think of it. It's always surprising how two people can read the same article and reach two entirely different interpretations. Observe the range of opinion. Try to understand why and how people arrive at different conclusions. Do some seem to be missing the point? Do some distort the author's ideas? Have someone's comments forced you to rethink the selection? Keep a record of the discussion in your notebook. Then, when you begin to draft your paper, consider your essay as an extension of both your imaginary conversation with the author and the actual class discussion. If you've taken detailed notes of your own and the class's responses to the selection, you should have more than enough information to get started.

Participating in Class Discussion: Six Basic Rules

Discussion is a learned activity. It requires a variety of essential academic skills: speaking, listening, thinking, and preparing. The following six basic rules are vital to healthy and productive discussion.

1. *Take an active speaking role.* Good discussion demands that everyone participates, not (as so often happens) just a vocal few. Many students remain detached from discussion because they are afraid to speak in a group. This fear is quite common — so common that psychological surveys show that speaking in front of a group is generally one of our worst fears. A leading communication consultant suggests that people choke up because they are more worried about how others will respond than about what they themselves have to say. It helps to remember that most people will be more interested in *what* you say than in how you say it. Once you get over the initial fear of speaking in public, your speech skills will improve with practice.

2. *Listen attentively.* No one can participate in group discussion who doesn't listen attentively. This may sound obvious, but just think of how many senseless arguments you've had because either you or the person with whom you were talking completely misunderstood what was said. A good listener not only hears what someone is saying but understands why he or she is saying it. One of the most important things about listening is that it leads to one element that lively discussion depends on: good questions. When the interesting questions begin to emerge, you know good discussion has truly begun.

3. *Examine all sides of an issue.* Good discussion requires that we be patient with complexity. Difficult problems rarely have obvi-

ous and simple solutions, nor can they be easily summarized in popular slogans. Complex issues demand to be turned over in our minds so that we can see them from a variety of angles. Group discussion will broaden our perspective and deepen our insight into difficult issues and ideas.

4. *Suspend judgment.* Class discussion is best conducted in an open-minded and tolerant spirit. To fully explore ideas and issues, you will need to be receptive to the opinions of others even when they contradict your own. Remember, discussion is not the same as debate. Its primary purpose is communication, not competition. In discussion you are not necessarily trying to win everyone over to your point of view. The goal of group discussion should be to open up a topic so that everyone in the group will be exposed to a spectrum of attitudes. Suspending judgment does not mean you shouldn't hold a strong belief or opinion about an issue; it means that you should be willing to take into account rival beliefs or opinions. An opinion formed without an awareness of other points of view — one that has not been tested against contrary ideas — is not a *strong* opinion but merely a stubborn one.

5. *Avoid abusive or insulting language.* Free and open discussion can only occur if we respect the beliefs and opinions of others. If we speak in ways that fail to show respect for differing viewpoints — if we resort to name-calling or use demeaning and malicious expressions, for example — we not only embarrass ourselves but we close off the possibility for an intelligent and productive exchange of ideas. Contrary to what you might gather from some popular radio and television talk shows, shouting insults and engaging in hate-speech are signs of verbal and intellectual bankruptcy. They are usually the last resort of someone who has nothing to say.

6. *Come prepared.* Discussion is not merely random conversation. It demands a certain degree of preparation and focus. To participate in class discussion, you must consider assigned topics beforehand and read whatever is required. You should develop the habit of reading with pen in hand, underlining key points and jotting down questions, impressions, and ideas in your notebook. The notes you bring to class will be an invaluable aid in group discussion.

Group Discussion as a Source of Ideas

Group discussion can stimulate and enhance your writing in several important ways. First, it supplies you with ideas. Let's say that you are participating in a discussion about how we express group identities (see Chapter 5). One of your classmates mentions some of the problems a mixed ethnic background can cause. But suppose you also come from a mixed background, and, when you think about it, you believe that your mixed heritage has given you more advantages than disadvantages. Hearing her viewpoint may inspire you to express your differing perspective on the issue. Your perspective could lead to an interesting personal essay.

Suppose you now start writing that essay. You don't need to start from scratch and stare at a blank piece of paper or computer screen for hours. Discussion has already given you a few good leads. First, you have your classmate's opinions and attitudes to quote or summarize. You can begin your paper by explaining that some people view a divided ethnic identity as a psychological burden. You might expand on your classmate's opinion by bringing in additional information from other student comments or from your reading to show how people often focus on only the negative side of mixed identities. You can then explain your own perspective on this topic. Of course, you will need to give several examples showing *why* a mixed background has been an advantage for you. The end result can be a first-rate essay, one that takes other opinions into account and demonstrates a clearly established point of view. It is personal, and yet it takes a position that goes beyond one individual's experiences.

Whatever the topic, your writing will benefit from reading and discussion, which will give your essays a clear purpose or goal. In that way, your papers will resemble the selections found in this book: They will be a *response* to the opinions, attitudes, experiences, issues, ideas, and proposals that inform current public discourse. This is why most writers write; this is what most newspapers and magazines publish; this is what most people read. *America Now* consists entirely of such writing. I hope you will read the selections with enjoyment, discuss the issues with an open mind, and write about the topics with purpose and enthusiasm.

The Practice of Writing

Suppose you wanted to learn to play the guitar. What would you do first? Would you run to the library and read a lot of books on music? Would you then read some instructional books on guitar playing? Might you try to memorize all the chord positions? Then would you get sheet music for songs you liked and memorize them? After all that, if someone handed you an electric guitar, would you immediately be able to play like Jimi Hendrix or Eric Clapton?

I don't think you would begin that way. You would probably start out by strumming the guitar, getting the feel of it, trying to pick out something familiar. You would probably want to take lessons from someone who knows how to play. And you would practice, practice, practice. Every now and then your instruction book would come in handy. It would give you basic information on frets, notes, and chord positions, for example. You might need to refer to that information constantly in the beginning. But knowing the chords is not the same as knowing how to manipulate your fingers correctly to produce the right sounds. You need to be able to *play* the chords, not just know them.

Learning to read and write well is not that much different. Though instructional books can give you a great deal of advice and information, the only way anyone really learns to read and write is through constant practice. The only problem, of course, is that nobody likes practice. If we did, we would all be good at just about everything. Most of us, however, want to acquire a skill quickly and easily. We don't want to take lesson after lesson. We want to pick up the instrument and sound like a professional in ten minutes.

Wouldn't it be a wonderful world if that could happen? Wouldn't it be great to be born with a gigantic vocabulary so we instantly knew the meaning of every word we saw or heard? We would never have to go through the slow process of consulting a dictionary whenever we stumbled across an unfamiliar word. But, unfortunately, life is not so easy. To succeed at anything worthwhile requires patience and dedication. Watch a young figure skater trying to perfect her skills and you will see patience and dedication at work; or watch an accident victim learning how to maneuver a wheelchair so he can begin again an independent existence; or observe a new American struggling to learn English. None of these skills is quickly and easily acquired. Like building a vocabulary, they all take time and effort. They all require practice. And they require something even more important: the willingness to make mistakes. Can someone learn to skate without taking a spill? Or learn a new language without mispronouncing a word?

Writing as a Public Activity

Many people have the wrong idea about writing. They view writing as a very private act. They picture the writer sitting all alone and staring into space waiting for ideas to come. They think that ideas come from "deep" within and only reach expression after they have been fully articulated inside the writer's head.

These images are part of a myth about creative writing and, like most myths, are sometimes true. A few poets, novelists, and essayists do write in total isolation and search deep inside themselves for thoughts and stories. But most writers have far more contact with public life. This is especially true of people who write regularly for magazines, newspapers, and professional journals. These writers work within a lively social atmosphere in which issues and ideas are often intensely discussed and debated. Nearly all the selections in this book illustrate this type of writing.

As you work on your own papers, remember that writing is very much a public activity. It is rarely performed alone in an "ivory tower." Writers don't always have the time, the desire, the opportunity, or the luxury to be all alone. They may be writing in a newsroom with clacking keyboards and noise all around them; they may be writing at a kitchen table, trying to feed several children at the same time; they may be writing on subways or buses. The great English novelist D. H. Lawrence grew up in a small coal miner's cottage with no place for privacy. It turned out to be an enabling experience. Throughout his life he could write wherever he happened to be; it didn't matter how many people or how much commotion surrounded him.

There are more important ways in which writing is a public activity. Much writing is often a response to public events. Most of the articles you encounter every day in newspapers and magazines respond directly to timely or important issues and ideas, topics that people are currently talking about. Writers report on these topics, supply information about them, discuss and debate the differing viewpoints. The units in this book all represent topics now regularly discussed on college campuses and in the national media. In fact, all of the topics were chosen because they emerged so frequently in college newspapers.

When a columnist decides to write on a topic like affirmative action, she willingly enters an ongoing public discussion about the issue. She didn't just make up the topic. She knows that it *is* a serious issue, and she is aware that a wide variety of opinions have been expressed about it. She has not read everything on the subject but usually knows enough about the different arguments to state her own position or attitude persuasively. In fact, what helps make her writing persuasive is that she takes into account the opinions of others. Her own essay, then, becomes a part of the continuing debate and discussion, one that you in turn may want to join.

Such issues are not only matters for formal and impersonal debate. They also invite us to share our *personal* experiences. Many of the selections in this book show how writers participate in the discussion of issues by drawing on their experiences. For example, the essay by Chicago journalist Bennie M. Currie, "The N-Word and How to Use It," is based almost entirely on Currie's observations and personal experience, though the topic — hate speech and racist language — is one widely discussed and debated by educators and civil-liberties advocates. Nearly every unit of *America Now* contains a selection that illustrates how you can use your personal experiences to discuss and debate a public issue.

Writing is public in yet another way. Practically all published writing is reviewed, edited, and re-edited by different people before it goes to press. The author of a magazine article has most likely discussed the topic at length with colleagues and publishing professionals and may have asked friends or experts in the field to look it over. By the time you see the article in a magazine, it has gone through numerous readings and probably quite a few revisions. Though the article is credited to a particular author, it was no doubt read and worked on by others who helped with suggestions and improvements. As a beginning writer, it's important to remember that most of what you read in newspapers, magazines, and books has gone through a writing process that involves the collective efforts of several people besides the author. Students usually don't have that advantage and should not feel discouraged when their own writing doesn't measure up to the professionally edited materials they are reading for a course.

What Is "Correct English"?

One part of the writing process may seem more difficult than others — correct English. Yes, nearly all of what you read will be written in relatively correct English. Or it's probably more accurate to say "corrected" English, since most published writing is revised or "corrected" several times before it appears in print. Even skilled professional writers make mistakes that require correction.

Most native speakers don't actually *talk* in "correct" English. There are numerous regional patterns and dialects. As the Chinese American novelist Amy Tan says, there are "many Englishes." What we usually consider correct English is a set of guidelines developed over time to help standardize written expression. This standardization — like any agreed-upon standards such as weights and measures — is a matter of use and convenience. Suppose you went to a vegetable stand and asked for a pound of peppers and the storekeeper gave you a half pound but charged you for a full one. When you complained, he said, "But that's what *I* call a pound." What if you next bought a new compact disc you've been waiting for, and when you tried to play it you discovered it wouldn't fit your CD player. Life would be very frustrating if everyone had a different set of standards: Imagine what would happen if some places used a red light to signal "go" and a green one for "stop." Languages are not that different. In all cultures, languages — especially written languages — have gradually developed certain general rules and principles to make communication as clear and efficient as possible.

You probably already have a guidebook or handbook that systematically sets out certain rules of English grammar, punctuation, and spelling. Like our guitar instruction book, these handbooks serve a very practical purpose. Most writers — even experienced authors — need to consult them periodically. Beginning writers may need to rely on them far more regularly. But just as we don't learn how to play chords by merely memorizing finger positions, we don't learn how to write by memorizing the rules of grammar or punctuation.

Writing is an activity, a process. Learning how to do it — like learning to ride a bike or prepare a tasty stew — requires *doing* it. Correct English is not something that comes first. We don't need to know the rules perfectly before we can begin to write. As in any activity, corrections are part of the learning process. You fall off the bike and get on again, trying to "correct" your balance this time. You sample the stew and "correct" the seasoning. You draft a paper about the neighborhood you live in and as you (or a classmate or teacher) read it over, you notice that certain words and expressions could stand some improvement. And step by step, sentence by sentence, you begin to write better.

Writing as Empowerment

Writing is one of the most powerful means of producing social and political change. Through their four widely disseminated gospels, the first-century evangelists helped propagate Christianity throughout the world; the writings of Adam Smith and Karl Marx determined the economic systems of many nations for well over a century; Thomas Jefferson's Declaration of Independence became a model for countless colonial liberationists; the books and essays of numerous feminists have altered twentieth-century consciousness. In the long run, many believe, "the pen is mightier than the sword."

Empowerment does not mean instant success. It does not mean that your opinion or point of view will suddenly prevail. It does mean, however, that you have made your voice heard, that you have given your opinions wider circulation, that you have made yourself and your position a little more visible. And sometimes you get results: a newspaper prints your letter; a university committee adopts your suggestion; people visit your Web site. Throughout this collection you will encounter writing specifically intended to inform and influence a wide community.

Such influence is not restricted to professional authors and political experts. This collection features a large number of student writers who are actively involved with the same current topics and issues that engage the attention of professionals — affirmative action, group identity, capital punishment, free speech, gender differences, labeling and stereotyping, and so on. The student selections, all of them previously published, are meant to be an integral part of each unit, to be read in conjunction with the professional essays, and to be criticized and analyzed on an equal footing. The student writing holds up.

The student essays were written for a variety of reasons — some personal, some public. A San Diego State University student, Hobi Reader, set down her objections to dress codes (see p. 33) in protest after the schools her children attended adopted uniforms. Covering an execution for her college paper, Abbie Gibbs, an Oklahoma State University communications major, unexpectedly wound up as an actual witness to the execution (see p. 310). Do composition papers have a publishing future? Most students would say no, yet Henry Han Xi Lau originally wrote his essay — which appeared in the prestigious *New York Times Magazine* — for his Yale freshman writing course (see p. 86). Sara Ziegler, an Iowa State University junior, felt a need to speak out in favor of tolerance (see p. 179) after reading a letter to the editor that attacked homosexuals. Andy Miller's essay on affirmative action (see p. 275) grew out of a University of Wisconsin sociology course. And Benson Cohen, a sophomore at Emory University in Atlanta, wrote his essay (see p. 282) in response to a campus speech by anti-affirmative action activist Ward Connerly, whose views Cohen found politically offensive. Although all of these writers hoped to inform or influence a particular audience, none of them ever expected their work to be selected for a college text and to be read by students throughout the country.

America Now urges you to voice your ideas and opinions — in your notebooks, in your papers, in your classrooms, and, most importantly, on your campus and in your communities. Reading, discussing, and writing will force you to clarify your observations, attitudes, and values, and as you do so you will discover more about yourself and the world you live in. These are exciting times. Don't sit on the sidelines of controversy. Don't retreat into invisibility and silence. Jump in and confront the ideas and issues currently shaping America.

1

What's in a Name?

"What's in a name?" asks Shakespeare's Juliet. "That which we call a rose / By any other word would smell as sweet." Yet not everyone has agreed with Juliet's widely quoted remark. For a large number of Americans, personal names are a matter of vital importance. Names can suggest family origins, social position, racial and ethnic identity, or religious affiliation. In "What's in a Name?" Lini S. Kadaba looks at the growing trend away from English-sounding names toward those that reflect a person's ancestry and heritage. Names are not chosen because they are attractive or fashionable but because they say something about who the person is. As Kadaba sees it, the "very notion of what it means to be American is changing."

Most people today agonize over the names they give their children. Denise Sherer Jacobson's essay "David" brings a different twist to this common problem. She and her husband were born with cerebral palsy, and speech for them can be difficult at times. As Jacobson puts it, they "approached the task of baby naming with an added consideration most couples don't worry about — choosing a name that would be easy to say."

The last essay looks at personal names from a political angle. Is it wrong to name schools and buildings after past leaders or heroes who today may not seem to deserve the honor? Should schools not be named after George Washington or Thomas Jefferson because both men — though considered outstanding presidents — once owned slaves? In "What's in a Name? Revisionist History Revisted," Iowa

1

State student Robert Zeis confronts an issue about personal names in which the stakes are far greater than personal identity.

LINI S. KADABA

What's in a Name?

[THE PHILADELPHIA INQUIRER / December 7, 1997]

Before You Read

People change their names for many different reasons. How many can you think of? Which reasons do you most approve of? Are there name changes you disapprove of? Would you change your name? Why? What new name would you choose?

Words to Learn

smorgasbord (para. 4): wide variety (n.)

ethnic (para. 4): referring to a specific culture, background, origin, or culture (adj.)

appellations (para. 4): name or title (n.)

assimilation (para. 4): becoming part of a larger group (n.)

expunge (para. 4): remove completely (v.)

onomastics (para. 4): study of the origins of names (n.)

ingenuity (para. 4): creativity, cleverness (n.)

ambiguous (para. 5): having two or more possible meanings (adj.)

Journalist LINI S. KADABA (b. 1961), a graduate of the University of Kentucky (B.A.) and Northwestern University (M.S.), writes for the Philadelphia Inquirer *on a variety of subjects including health, the workplace, lifestyle trends, and ethnic and immigration issues. She has published articles in* Boston *magazine,* Woman's World, *and* Technology Review *and is a recipient of the Keystone Press Award, a finalist for the Livingston Awards for Young Journalists, and a fellow of the Knight Center for Specialized Journalism in the Race, Class, and Ethnicity program.*

lore (para. 5): knowledge, especially of tradition (n.)
dashiki (para. 12): bright-colored robe of African origin (n.)
impetus (para. 12): motive (n.)
manifest (para. 15): list of cargo or passengers (n.)
catchall (para. 17): phrase covering a variety of situations (n.)
inexorable (para. 17): inability to be changed or stopped (adj.)

mecca (para. 18): center of an activity (n.)
pluralism (para. 19): coexistence of many different identities and individuals (n.)
homogeneity (para. 19): state of being similar (n.)
melange (para. 20): mixture (n.)

In his homeland of Greece, the grandfather was a solid Papanastasiou — a name rooted in a centuries-old culture. But when he came to America in the early 1900s, his name, like his life, changed. The grandfather became Annas — a short, easy-to-say, straightforward name. *Annas,* surely that was a good American name.

Names connect us to family. Names influence others' perception of us. Names mark us.

It was good enough, too, for grandson Christopher Angelo Annas of South Philadelphia, until recently. The thirty-nine-year-old optometrist and second-generation Greek American, in large part, wanted to preserve — and reclaim — his heritage. In March, he legally switched his name to Christopher Angelo Anastasiou, almost all the way back to the original. "I could have changed it to Smith or Andrews — that would be easier to say — but I didn't want to do that," he said.

There was another reason Annas wanted to change his name. His grandfather, in his rush to Americanize his name, was unaware that, mispronounced, his new name sounded in English all too much like a certain part of anatomy. "I started to get a complex," said the grandson. He is now Dr. Anastasiou, though his diplomas on his office wall still bear his old identity. It is not a short name; it could span an ocean. It is not an easy name to say. Some patients call him Dr. Anesthesia now, but the grandson says he doesn't mind.

Like Anastasiou, other Americans are trading in their melting-pot names for a smorgasbord of ethnic appellations. In short, American names don't have to be white-bread names; they can be as ethnic as moussaka, tacos, or pita pockets, all of which have become, by some estimates, as American as apple pie. "We have gone from a general notion of assimilation and expunging of foreignness to an identification and affirmation of it," said Edward Callary, editor of *Names: A Journal of Onomastics* and a professor of English at Northern Illinois University. "I'm Hungarian. I'm Polish. These are my roots. . . . We all like to look at ourselves as a continuation of some line." And so Annas becomes Anastasiou, a name that embraces ethnicity but still offers a nod to the land of Yankee ingenuity. The original Papanastasiou — a wide load at thirteen letters — was too much for the grandson, and so he dropped *Pap*. Besides, he wanted to make sure his name still started with an *A,* because as a doctor, and no doubt a shrewd businessman, he wanted to remain first on the list of medical providers.

Jane Komarov, thirty-four, a composer who lives in Greenwich   5
Village in New York, changed her name in 1991. She was Jane Komaro*w*. "It's only a change by one letter, but the pronunciation is remarkable. *Komarow*. It's very ambiguous. *Komarov*. It has a very distinctive Russian sound," she said with pride. According to family lore, the name was misspelled at Ellis Island. Her grandparents accepted the misnomer as their name. For Komarov, the return to the correct spelling — and pronunciation — connects her with a richer, more obvious ethnic heritage, she said, noting her name means mosquito. "It describes me better," she said, "although I hope I'm not a mosquito."

The melting pot, it seems, has become more of a stew or goulash   6
or curry as ethnic pride moves to the front burner and we discover our deep ethnic roots in many ways. We are studying our mother tongues. We are dancing to folk tunes. We are climbing our family trees.

Pediatrician Andres Valdes-Dapena, forty-five, of Media, Penn-   7
sylvania, recently completed a ten-week Spanish class at the Berlitz Language Center, in large part, he said, to affirm his heritage. "I have a name that reeks Spanish," he said. But Valdes-Dapena grew up in a "very American household," with little exposure to the language of his Cuban father. Now, the study of Spanish has become a family affair: His wife, though non-Spanish, also took a Berlitz class, and the couple's three children all study the language in school, with the eldest, a college student, planning to major in it.

At the Adam Mickiewicz Polish Language School in the Far   8
Northeast, principal Debbie Majka said the forty students, ages four to fourteen, spend Saturday mornings learning the language, folk dances, and customs of Poland, another generation sustaining its history. "There's a value in knowing your heritage, who and what you

are, where you come from," she said. The same surely holds true for
Italian Americans or Jewish Americans.

Others celebrate their roots by tracing it generations back. Ac-   9
cording to a 1995 survey for *American Demographics* magazine, 42
million Americans have joined the genealogy hunt. But nothing, perhaps, heralds ethnicity more than a name.

"Names have more than simple label value," said biographer   10
Justin Kaplan, coauthor with his wife, novelist Anne Bernays, of the
1997 *The Language of Names: What We Call Ourselves and Why It
Matters* [See "From the Bookshelf," p. 9]. "They carry the freight of
historical association and personal association."

Names connect us to family. Names influence others' perception   11
of us. Names mark us. In *The Language of Names,* Kaplan and
Bernays write that "names are profoundly linked to identity and to
private as well as public declarations of self and purpose; they have
considerable affective power and, however unacknowledged in daily
usage, a magical role as well, the power to change people's lives."
Said Kaplan, "When you take away a person's name, it's a little like
you're taking a person's soul."

Who can forget the scene from Alex Haley's *Roots* of the young   12
slave Kunte Kinte refusing, even under the scourge of a whip, to give
up his African name? He knew to do so would enslave him all the
more. "I always felt an anger ever since I found out the history of
America and slavery. That anger just melted away once I changed the
name," said a fifty-year-old engineer who lives near Atlanta. It was
the 1970s. "It was the great dashiki era," he said, when many blacks
took African or Islamic names. The engineer had another impetus:
He was expecting his first child.

After much consideration, he created a surname by perusing a   13
map of Africa, picking Kenya as the heart of the continent and
adding *ada,* a common ending for East African names. In 1975, he
filed a petition in court to legally change his name to Richard
Kenyada, citing his "cultural, ethnic and social heritage." Since then,
he has never spoken or written his other name. At first, his relatives
disliked the new name. "They thought it was a slight against the family." But Kenyada won them over. He named his son Kareem
Kenyada. "He came up with a strong identity," the father said.

Lois Fernandez, a founder of the popular Odunde Festival, at   14
times uses the name Omi Yori, her spiritual name given to her in
1994 when she was initiated into Yoruba, a religion and culture
found in Nigeria. Earlier this year, the sixty-one-year-old South

Philadelphian visited the African country and was given the title *Iyagbogbo Agbaye,* meaning "Chief Mother of the World." The African name grounds her, she said. "We did not come through Ellis Island," she said. "We came here involuntarily. We were stripped of our language, our culture, our names. We had to go back and fetch it."

For others, their names changed as they moved through Ellis Island's bureaucracy. By some accounts, many newcomers were rechristened with supposedly American names during the heyday of immigration at the turn of the century. Officials at the Ellis Island Immigration Museum, however, dispute such stories, blaming ship captains who routinely shortened or simplified names on manifests to ease passage through immigration.

Other changes occurred freely, a desire by the immigrant to fit the American mold, "right from your scalp to your toes, and that includes your name," Bernays said. In still other cases, it was a practical necessity in a country that didn't always welcome its newest arrivals with open arms. Whatever the reason, Yitzchak became Hitchcock; Harlampoulas, Harris; Warschawsky, Ward.

Smith, the most common American surname, serves as a linguistic catchall, taking in everything from Schmidt to McGowan, all of which, in their original language, mean someone who works with metal, according to *The Language of Names.* The case of Smith illustrates "the inexorable Americanization of foreign names . . . [that] yield their roughness and irregularity to the tidal wash of American convenience and usage." Pfoersching turns into Pershing; Huber, Hoover; Bjorkegren, Burke. "Often, all that survived of a surname was its initial letter," write Kaplan and Bernays.

By the 1960s, the pressure or desire to assimilate lessened. Take Hollywood — the mecca of name changes, once upon a time. These days, an actor or actress can gain fame with a name as ethnic as Arnold Schwarzenegger, John Travolta, or Richard Dreyfuss. Other well-known people began to take back their ethnic names. David, the son of Irving Wallace, the late best-selling author, discarded his surname in favor of the ethnic original, Wallechinsky.

The very notion of what it means to be American is changing. "American identity is increasingly defined by pluralism rather than by homogeneity," said Henry Giroux, a professor of education and cultural studies at Pennsylvania State University. That shift could lead to a national debate on ways to connect different ethnic groups, or it could create a tribalism, each hyphenated American out for himself. "I think it's a very dangerous time," he said.

While a new poll by Princeton Survey Research Associates 20
showed a drop in anti-immigrant feelings since 1993, the nation still
grapples with its ethnic melange, evidenced by rollbacks in affirmative action and calls to limit social services to immigrants. At the
same time, none of us can escape our past or, apparently, want to.
Whatever our race or ethnicity, we continue to dig for our roots and
then, with great pride, proclaim the findings to all the world.

Tim Self, fifty-six, a retired carpenter who lives in Quail Valley in 21
Southern California, is president of the Self Seekers, the Self Family
Association, which has a Web site dedicated to genealogy. Self traced
his name back to the Viking name Saewulf. In the mid-1980s, he
stated using the name Tim Seawolf, adopting the modern spelling.
"Names get Americanized and shorter," he said. "I thought it would
be nice to stretch it back out, give it more depth."

Vocabulary/Using a Dictionary

1. How is the term *ingenuity* (para. 4) similar to *ingenious?*

2. What are some locations people identify as a *mecca* (para. 18)?
   For what reason? What is the term's origin?

3. What is the origin of the term *melange* (para. 20)? How does the
   term relate to the ethnicity in America?

Responding to Words in Context

1. *Anesthesia* (para. 3), a word similar to Dr. Anastasiou's changed
   last name, is used in many medical procedures and contexts,
   from performing heart surgery to filling teeth. What is anesthesia? What are some other forms of the word?

2. Kadaba refers to names getting "Americanized and shorter"
   (para. 21) in today's society. What other names, places, and
   foods can you think of that have been Americanized?

Discussing Main Point and Meaning

1. For what reason are more and more people choosing not to
   change their names into something a little more English-
   sounding?

2. Why doesn't Dr. Anastasiou change his name entirely back to the original (paras. 2–4)?

3. What does the author mean by stating that "the very notion of what it means to be American is changing" (para. 19)? How does Kadaba characterize this change? Why do you agree or disagree?

Examining Sentences, Paragraphs, and Organization

1. Kadaba begins the first three sentences of paragraph 11 with the word *names*. What effect does this have on these sentences? Why does the author do this?

2. Many of this essay's paragraphs include quotations. What do they contribute to the credibility of the paragraphs? Do they make the writer's point more believable?

3. The author organizes her essay by introducing specific individuals and discussing their experiences with name changing. How does this organization contribute to the success or failure of this essay?

Thinking Critically

1. The author states that the "melting pot . . . has become more of a stew or goulash . . . as ethnic pride moves to the front burner and we discover our deep ethnic roots in many ways" (para. 6). Why do you agree or disagree with this statement?

2. Do you agree with Kadaba's notion that "none of us can escape our past" (para. 20)? How should today's Americans view their ancestry?

In-Class Writing Activities

1. Form a group and list all your last names. Break them down into their root words and discuss their possible origins and meanings. How many ethnic backgrounds have you found? What does this suggest about the makeup of your class? Your community?

2. Make a family tree listing your birthplace along with that of your siblings, your parents, grandparents, and so on. Did any of your relatives pass through Ellis Island? What route did they travel to America, and how has their route affected your name and self-identity?

From the Bookshelf

Justin Kaplan and Anne Bernays, *The Language of Names*

Did you know that the name Wendy was invented by the Englishman who wrote Peter Pan? *Would you have guessed that the current most popular name for Hispanic and Asian infant boys in New York City and San Francisco is Kevin? For anyone curious about human names — what they mean and why they seem so important —* The Language of Names: What We Call Ourselves and Why It Matters *will be an illuminating and fascinating study. Packed with information on celebrities, history, class, race, and ethnicity, this entertaining book is written for the general reader, as shown by the following excerpt from Justin Kaplan and Anne Bernays's chapter on "New Names, New Identities."*

Justin Kaplan is a Pulitzer Prize–winning author who has written biographies of Mark Twain and Walt Whitman. He is also general editor of the famous reference book Bartlett's Familiar Quotations. *Anne Bernays is the author of eight novels (including the award-winning* Growing Up Rich *and* Professor Romeo). *She has also coauthored a popular and highly recommended book on creative writing —* What If? Writing Exercises for Fiction Writers. *The two authors have been married since 1954.*

New Names, New Identities

Every American citizen, and every applicant for citizenship under the immigration laws, has a common-law, free-speech, and pursuit-of-happiness right to take and use a new name so long as it isn't offensive, confusing, inciting to violence and racial hatred, or taken for some unlawful purpose such as fraud, flight from the law, evasion of debt or bankruptcy, or the commission of a crime. So long as it isn't also a number, a hieroglyph, or a visual symbol, the new name becomes as legal as if it had been given at birth. Americans don't need formal permission of the court to rename themselves, but many nevertheless submit a petition. They want to assert continuity of identity and property rights, make the change a matter of public record, and dispel any lingering qualms they feel about sailing under false colors. "If you change your name with or without legal recourse," *The Amy Vanderbilt Complete Book of Etiquette* counseled, "you may send out an announcement card to friends and relatives." And Emily Post told you how to word it: "Mr. and Mrs. John Original-Name announce that . . . they and their children have taken the family name of Miller."

continued on next page

continued from previous page

The formal requirements, procedures, and waiting periods vary from state to state, especially in the case of married or divorced women who want to go back to using their original names. The reasons applicants give for taking a new name range from habitual usage, marital breakup, embarrassing mispronunciation, religious conversion (frequently to Islam), and ethnic pride to aesthetic and idiosyncratic considerations and just plain convenience (as in the case of the Michigan man who in 1935 took the name Pappas in place of the original thirty-seven-letter Pappatheodorokomoundoronicolucopoulos). Apparently, assuming good faith on the part of the petitioner, almost any reason is as good as any other, and few petitions for name changes are denied. Each year for the past decade or so, about three hundred people in New York City have filed an application to the Civil Court, supplied a birth certificate, paid a $50 filing fee, and sat tight for eight weeks after publishing formal notice of the intended change in a newspaper. "I am an incest survivor," one woman wrote in her application. "I never want my father to find me." Another beneficiary of the Civil Court is the former Hassan Romieh, a publisher and twice self-nominated presidential candidate. He's now known as George Washington America. This may not get him elected and his wife may never be First Lady, but, he says, at least she can "be called Mrs. America without having to go to Atlantic City."

Kaplan, Justin, and Anne Bernays. *The Language of Names: What We Call Ourselves and Why It Matters.* New York: Simon & Schuster, 1997.

DENISE SHERER JACOBSON

David

[MAINSTREAM / March 1998]

Before You Read

People who are expecting a baby often spend a great deal of time deciding on a name for the child. How do you think most naming decisions are made? What boys and girls names do you think are most popular today? Would you make your choice based on popularity alone? What other factors would go into your decision?

Words to Learn

resonate (para. 4): vibrate, echo, continue to make a sound (v.)

resound (para. 4): bounce with exaggerated volume, sound repeatedly (v.)

morph (para. 4): alter, change form (v.)

exert (para. 4): put forth energy or influence (v.)

eccentric (para. 6): unusual in a quirky way (adj.)

fastidious (para. 7): paying close attention to detail (adj.)

grueling (para. 10): exhausting (adj.)

embellishment (para. 10): fanciful addition, ornament (n.)

enunciate (para. 11): say clearly (v.)

dote (para. 20): pay close, loving attention to (v.)

magnanimity (para. 21): generosity (n.)

DENISE SHERER JACOBSON *(b. 1950) was born in the Bronx, New York. She received her B.A. in sociology and journalism from Long Island University and her M.A. in family life education from New York University. Her work has appeared in two anthologies,* Prejudice *(1995) and* The Adoption Reader *(1995), and in numerous newspapers and literary magazines. "David" is based on an excerpt from Jacobson's book* The Question of David *(1998).*

"David, it's time to get ready. The carpool will be here any   1
minute," I yelled, rolling from the kitchen through the living room,
on my way to the bedroom where I could hear the pipe organ music,
bleeps, and bonks from his Sega game.

"David, did you hear me? You've still got to put on your shoes   2
and finish packing your backpack, David." Another bleep.

"David!"   3

It was times like these I had in mind when I first suggested the   4
name to my husband Neil for our infant son ten years ago. Like any
mother-to-be, I had my preferences when it came to choosing a name;
I wanted one that would resonate with dignity, resound with melodic
rhythm, and avoid being morphed into some horrendous nickname.
My top priority, however, went to selecting a name that Neil and I
could clearly pronounce, since we both often exerted a fair amount of
effort spitting out our own names.

Neil and I approached the task of baby naming with an added consideration most couples don't worry about — choosing a name that would be easy to say.

Our parents, of course, had named   5
each of us in infancy, at the time not
knowing we had been born with cerebral
palsy, a permanent (but not life-threaten-
ing) disability that interferes with the messages sent from the brain hub to control
voluntary movements. One of those voluntary movements affected, in both of us,
involves speech.

From the time I was four until I grad-   6
uated to high school, I endured speech
therapy three times a week with Mrs. Bo-
brick, an eccentric, gray-haired woman who had pursed red lips and
wore paper hats on her head. I had to sit in front of the large rectan-
gular mirror making faces at myself during warm-up exercises to
work on breath control and tongue coordination.

Fastidious Mrs. Bobrick timed me with a stopwatch while I'd   7
take deep breaths and hold each vowel sound as long as I could.
She would also hold a candied tongue depressor an inch or so
from my lips while my uncooperative tongue tried reaching it in all
directions — north, south, east, and west.

Sometimes, she'd stick peanut butter on the roof of my mouth so   8
I would have to nudge it off with the tip of my tongue; I cheated with
my finger when she wasn't looking. I hated peanut butter!

Mrs. Bobrick drilled me on *l* sounds and *s* sounds and those hor-   9
rible *th*, *ks*, and *sh* combinations.

I suspected Neil had gone through similar oral aerobics when he   10
was young, and though I hate to admit it, those grueling workouts did
pay off. We have the ability, now, to pronounce most words as distinctly as Lily Tomlin's Ernestine, the phone operator (without her annoying nasal embellishments), yet our words have that unhurried
flow, perhaps half a beat slower than someone with a southern drawl.

Yet, for both Neil and me, speaking clearly and fluidly involves   11
more than the ability to enunciate. It has a lot to do with energy and
anxiety. When Neil gets tired, his rich, gravelly voice digresses into a
mumble. When I'm wiped out at the end of the day, my words swirl
into each other like ingredients blended together in a malted milk.

Nervousness will cause Neil to stutter and stammer at the begin-   12
ning of a sentence, or with words starting with vowels, while when
I'm anxious, my breath constricts in my chest so tightly that it barely
allows my words to escape.

Introducing ourselves seems to create a nervous tension in both   13
of us, making us wish, for that moment, we had names that would
just trip off our tongues as easily as water overflowing into a spill-
way. Both our names contain a combination of sounds that require
quick, subtle tongue dips and rolls.

Ironically, Neil and I can say each other's name without diffi-   14
culty, but not our own; in person, we introduce one another — the
definitive movements of our lips are a visual aide.

It's harder on the phone. Whenever we call to make restaurant   15
reservations, Neil becomes a "Bob," while I change into a "Debra,"
just to keep it simple. I always hope we won't run into anyone we
know in the presence of the maitre d' or hostess. It would surely
cause us one of those embarrassing moments.

So Neil and I approached the task of baby naming with an added   16
consideration most couples don't worry about — choosing a name
that would be easy to say. We couldn't ignore sentimentality, either;
Neil and I have Jewish roots, and according to tradition, a baby is
named after a deceased relative to carry on that person's memory.

We weren't lacking in dead relatives — my mother and Neil's fa-   17
ther among them — but all the names I could think of did not fit the
practical requirements or my particular preferences.

I gave it some thought while we were undressing for bed one   18
night, since undressing gives me a lot of time to think. I hooked my
index finger inside the collar of my turtleneck and stretched it up over
my chin and grabbed a handful of the knitted material from behind
then yanked it over my head. Shivering from the chilly air, I gave an

involuntary snort and clamped my upper arms to my sides, bringing my wrist up to my mouth so I could grasp the knitted cuff with my teeth. I slid out one arm, and then the other. I let the turtleneck drop to the floor. I was hard on clothes!

Aunt Dinah!   19

My Great Aunt Dinah had lived across the courtyard from us   20
when I was growing up and never had children of her own. She would dote on my sister and me as if we were little princesses, buying us fancy dresses with crinoline petticoats, tiny pinky rings with ruby and diamond chipped birthstones, and Betsy Wetsy dolls.

Yet with all her magnanimity, Aunt Dinah was a little hard to   21
take; her love was, literally, suffocating. Her fleshy arms always engulfed us, pressing our faces into her oversized, braless bosom while she planted kisses in triplicate on top of our heads.

She reeked of the perfume she wore to mask, in vain, the stale   22
odor of her incontinence. My sister and I would squirm away in loud protests, always bringing a teary, hurtful look to the old woman's hound dog eyes. All poor Aunt Dinah wanted from us was a little warmth and affection, yet it was so hard to give because she wanted it too much.

"My Aunt Dinah had no children," I said, looking at Neil in the   23
mirror as I reached for my flannel nightgown. "She had a generous soul. . . . Maybe we could name the baby after her."

Neil raised his eyebrows. "You want to name him Dinah?"   24

"No," I laughed, "but we just have to come up with a name that   25
begins with D. . . . Maybe David?"

"David," Neil repeated without a stammer or a stutter. He   26
grinned. "David. I like it."

David, a nice, solid name: the name of a great biblical hero and   27
king — who even slew a giant.

"David," I echoed easily. I pictured Aunt Dinah smiling down on   28
me with tears in her eyes. I appeased a small amount of my childhood guilt.

Over the years, Neil and I have said *David* in myriad vocal tones   29
emoting frustration, enchantment, annoyance, anger, exhaustion, and love. We've had no difficulty introducing him to teachers, doctors, acquaintances, and new playmates in the park.

Whenever we make dinner reservations, now, we give David's   30
name, even when he doesn't come along. I'm no longer worried about running into someone we know. I have a simple explanation: "David's our son," I'd say. "We keep him in mind wherever we go."

Vocabulary/Using a Dictionary

1. How does the word *sound* in *resound* (para. 4) contribute to the term's meaning?

2. Do you know someone who is *eccentric* (para. 6)? In what ways are you eccentric?

3. Do you have a relative who *dotes* on you (para. 20)? In what ways?

Responding to Words in Context

1. Jacobson comments that "ironically, Neil and I can say each other's name without difficulty" (para. 14). Why is this ironic?

2. Jacobson characterizes her Aunt Dinah's love as *suffocating* (para. 21). How can love be suffocating? Can you think of a similar example with someone you know?

Discussing Main Point and Meaning

1. From the title, what did you expect from this essay? What else might the writer have used as a title?

2. Why do Jacobson and her husband experience a "nervous tension" (para. 13) when they introduce themselves? Would you feel nervous under similar circumstances? Why or why not?

3. Why does the author feel that naming her child David "appeased a small amount of . . . childhood guilt" (para. 28)? Does this seem justified to you? In what way?

Examining Sentences, Paragraphs, and Organization

1. Why are the first two sentences of this essay quotes? What effect does this have on your reading? Why?

2. The author introduces this essay's first three paragraphs with the word *David*. What is the effect of this repetition?

3. What would happen to the essay if the last paragraph was switched with the first paragraph? Why?

Thinking Critically

1. In paragraph 5, Jacobson brings up the fact that both she and her husband have cerebral palsy. How did you react when this information was revealed? What hints were given about their condition?

2. Jacobson comments that David is "a nice, solid name: the name of a great biblical hero and king — who even slew a giant" (para. 27). How does this comment relate to her essay? To her life?

In-Class Writing Activities

1. Discuss the significance of your name. Why did your parents choose it? Does it have biblical or religious ties? If not, what ties to history or culture does it have?

2. The pronunciation of a name may seem like a trivial matter to many people, yet to the Jacobsons it was not. Write a paragraph in which you describe a few other difficulties they had to cope with in their daily lives.

ROBERT ZEIS

What's in a Name? Revisionist History Revisited

[THE IOWA STATE DAILY, IOWA STATE UNIVERSITY / January 20, 1998]

Before You Read

Naming buildings and places after famous people can often result in controversy. Do you think schools named after George Washington or Thomas Jefferson should be changed because these early presidents owned slaves? Do you think it is fair to judge what people did hundreds of years ago by using current moral and legal standards? How would you resolve such controversies?

Words to Learn

crystallize (para. 2): make clear, take on a definite form (v.)

caveat (para. 4): warning (n.)

subhuman (para. 4): less than human (adj.)

shortsighted (para. 6): unable to think ahead (adj.)

litmus test (para. 6): assessing acids and bases by noting whether a chemically treated paper turns red or blue; assessing a person's entire belief system by noting his or her stand on a single issue (n.)

revisionist (para. 7): relating to using current social conditions to reinterpret past events (adj.)

ROBERT ZEIS (b. 1974), a native of Des Moines, Iowa, is a senior majoring in finance with a minor in political science at Iowa State University. Following his graduation in 1999, Zeis plans to attend the United States Naval Academy, where he will be an officer candidate. He is the winner of Iowa State Daily's Columnist of the Year Award for 1997–1998.

There is a growing controversy surrounding the naming of various schools, monuments, and public buildings across America. The debate involves examining the actions of the people that public facilities were named after and then deciding whether to change the facility's name based on those behaviors.

Two recent examples crystallize this argument. The first involves the George Washington School in New Orleans. The school board there voted to change the name of the school based on the historical fact that George Washington owned slaves during his life. The board went on to decide that no school in New Orleans could be named after any person who had ever owned slaves.

The other case involves the Forrest School in Gadsen, Alabama. The high school is named after Nathan Bedford Forrest, a Confederate general who helped found the Ku Klux Klan following the Civil War.

Should the namesakes of our public facilities be judged on the standards and norms of current society? Clearly no, but let me add a caveat to that response. If the person for whom a building is named made few contributions to society in his or her own era, then maybe that person should not be honored. This is the case with the Forrest School in Alabama. There should ordinarily be no problem with honoring a Confederate general. Many of those who fought bravely for the South did so because they wanted to preserve the rights of states, not slavery. Nathan Bedford Forrest was not in that group, however. He believed that the black population was subhuman and that whites were a superior race. He also helped start the KKK in the Reconstruction-era South and saw to the murders of countless black citizens. Clearly, it was a foolish idea to name a school after an obviously evil person.

If we cannot honor heroes like Washington or Jefferson, who can we honor?

Unfortunately, the New Orleans School Board went too far in changing the name of the Washington School. Washington is the man who led the Continental Army to victory over the British, giving us the freedom we celebrate every year on July 4. In 1788, he was elected the first president of the United States and set a standard for the chief executive that few have been able to imitate. It is true, however, that Washington did own a small number of slaves at his home in Mount Vernon. Though it was commonplace for wealthy white men to own slaves, and his slaves were treated very well, it was still inexcusable. It was not mentioned by the board, though, that Washington's dying wish was that those slaves be freed. They were released following the death of his wife only a few years later.

The decision by the shortsighted individuals on the school board   6
prevents them from honoring great Americans like Thomas Jefferson, James Madison, and Robert E. Lee, who all owned slaves. The era of slavery was a frightful time, not only in this nation's history but in the history of the world. The notion of owning our fellow man is a chilling concept that few today can comprehend. How, though, can we judge those who owned slaves when it was commonplace? The immense contributions made by many in history cannot be erased based on one flaw in their character. That is the real issue at stake here — not whether a person owned slaves but whether we should be judging a historically significant person's shortcomings based on an arbitrary litmus test of current societal norms.

This is known as revisionist history, and it opens a Pandora's   7
box[1] for the future. If we cannot honor heroes like Washington or Jefferson, who can we honor? We might as well grind away the faces on Mount Rushmore and demolish the thousands of monuments we've constructed for our leaders. Let's be realistic about the flaws of those we admire. We know they were not perfect and shouldn't expect them to be. Remember, though, that the accomplishments of those people far outweigh their shortcomings. We would be foolish to cast those contributions away for want of perfection.

Vocabulary/Using a Dictionary

1. How does the word *crystal* in *crystallize* (para. 2) suggest the term's meaning? How do the author's examples make his argument clearer?

2. What are some ways an individual can be *shortsighted* (para. 6)? Do you consider yourself shortsighted? In what ways?

3. Have you ever performed a *litmus test* (para. 6) in a science class? How does the author's use of this term relate to the test you performed?

---

[1]*Pandora's box:* In Greek mythology, a box that contained all human evils, given to Pandora with instructions to keep it sealed. Out of curiosity, Pandora opened the box and released the evils into the world.

Responding to Words in Context

1. Zeis makes reference to "the standards and norms of current society" (para. 4) and "current societal norms" (para. 6). If a norm is a standard, what are some representations of norms in our current society? In your class? On your campus? In your life?

2. Zeis suggests that the accomplishments of those we admire "far outweigh their shortcomings" (para. 7). What is a shortcoming? Can you think of a few shortcomings in people you admire? In yourself?

Discussing Main Point and Meaning

1. What does the author's title suggest? What do you expect from the title?

2. Why does Zeis believe "it was a foolish idea to name a school after an obviously evil person" (para. 4)? Do you believe it was foolish to name the Forrest School in Alabama after Nathan Bedford Forrest? Why or why not?

3. What is the author's main point in his last paragraph? How would you rephrase that point?

Examining Sentences, Paragraphs, and Organization

1. The author begins two sentences in paragraph 4 with the word *Clearly*. Why? What is the effect of this strategy?

2. Does the content of the last paragraph effectively conclude the author's argument? Why or why not?

3. Why does the author wait in his essay until paragraph 6 before addressing "the real issue at stake"? What is the effect of this organizational strategy?

Thinking Critically

1. Do you agree with Zeis's notion of "revisionist history" (para. 7)? How is he using the concept? Is revising our knowledge of history automatically wrong?

2. Consider Zeis's statement that "if we cannot honor heroes like Washington or Jefferson, who can we honor?" (para. 7). Do you

agree with him? How should we judge historically significant individuals today?

In-Class Writing Activities

1. Make a list of Americans that you consider historically significant. Identify what you know of their positive as well as negative contributions to society. Do the positives outweigh the negatives? Why or why not? Would you name a school, monument, or public building after them?
2. Draft a letter to a college official giving reasons for naming or renaming a building on campus after a significant individual.

Discussing the Unit

Suggested Topic for Discussion

Each of the three authors in this unit focuses on different types of names that are important in society. Lini S. Kadaba writes about the personal importance of family names; Denise Sherer Jacobson examines the importance of how a name fits into one's daily routine; and Robert Zeis discusses the importance of historical names given to public places and institutions. What other kinds of names affect our understanding of ourselves and the world around us? How do those names affect us and in what areas of our lives? Would you change those names if you could? Why or why not?

Preparing for Class Discussion

1. Each selection in this unit suggests the significance names play in our lives — the public institutions and buildings we enter, our ethnic background, the names we give our children. Consider how names affect your daily choices. What names have you encountered today? This week? How have those names affected your decision-making process? Why?
2. Compare the similarities and differences in choosing names in "David" (p. 11), "What's in a Name?" (p. 2), and "New Names, New Identities" (p. 9). How do some of the attitudes reflect cul-

tural awareness? How do individuals' personal backgrounds affect their choices in names?

From Discussion to Writing

1. Which of the three essays in this unit do you think raises the most important issues about the choices and opinions individuals have about names? In an essay, summarize the main point of the selection, and explain why you find the author's ideas significant.

2. All three of the essays in this unit acknowledge the significance history plays in the names we use and see on a daily basis. What is your conclusion about this sense of history? Write an essay in which you address one author's main ideas about the significance of history, expressing your agreement or disagreement with his or her opinion.

3. Two of this unit's essays share the same title: "What's in a Name?" Write your own similarly titled essay in which you discuss the significance you find in names.

Topics for Cross-Cultural Discussion

1. Lini S. Kadaba and Denise Sherer Jacobson both discuss the origin of personal names in America — both for very different reasons. How are names decided on in your culture? Do they have specific meanings or origins? What significance do names have in your culture?

2. Make a list of named institutions or objects in your culture, such as schools, roads, and parks. How do these differ from those in America? How does your culture arrive at or decide on the names for these institutions?

2

Our Clothing: Does It Matter What We Wear?

Does what we wear reflect our own individuality, or does it merely reflect our conformity with fashion trends? When we buy a new article of clothing, are we thinking of its comfort and durability, or are we picturing how it will make us look? In "High Heels: What a Pain!" noted newspaper columnist Susan Estrich confronts her conflict about trendy shoes and challenges the conventional notion that "women are slaves to the male-dominated, model-obsessed fashion culture." But what happens if you dress entirely at odds with fashionable expectations? "It was stigma time," Kathleen Carlin writes in "You Become What You Wear," as she discovers that society is all too ready to judge people by what they wear.

What happens, then, when we insist everyone dress alike? Does it lead to more equality, more sensible fashions, and less wasteful competition? In "Identity through Clothing," a San Diego State University psychology major criticizes mandatory school uniforms as needlessly dictatorial and counterproductive to individual development. For a different view of uniforms, see "From the Bookshelf," page 37.

SUSAN ESTRICH

High Heels: What a Pain!

[BOSTON HERALD / October 21, 1997]

Before You Read

It is said that clothing is a language like any other and that certain items and combinations mean something just the way our words and sentences do. What meanings might we find in women's high-heel shoes? Jot down a few words that come to mind. Do you think the meanings are the same for both men and women? Do you think they are the same for all cultures?

Words to Learn

podiatrist (para. 5): doctor who specializes in the care and treatment of feet (n.)

stiletto (para. 7): shoe with a thin high heel (n.)

succumb (para. 12): yield to a stronger force (v.)

SUSAN ESTRICH (b. 1945) is a professor of law and political science at the University of Southern California, specializing in criminal law, gender discrimination, and election law. She received her B.A. at Wellesley College and her J.D. at Harvard University, where she has also taught. She is the author of many scholarly publications on politics and crime and has served as special assistant to Senator Edward M. Kennedy and as staff counsel and special assistant to the chief counsel for the U.S. Senate Judiciary Committee. In 1988 she was the national campaign manager for Dukakis-Bentsen. Estrich is also a columnist for USA Today, *a contributing editor for the* Los Angeles Times, *and a radio talk-show host.*

They are wearing high heels this year. 1

Are you? 2

Since I was a little girl, I've been trying to figure out exactly who 3
they are and why the rest of us are supposed to dress just like *them*.
The chubbier I was, the more I would taunt my sister and mother for
their striving. Don't you have any taste of your own?

But even I was interested in what shoes they were wearing. 4
Everyone likes shoe-shopping. Your size isn't your fault. There's
nothing you can do about it. And at least in theory, anyone can wear
any shoe: That's why they come in so many sizes.

As podiatrists will tell you, shoes can be dangerous to your feet. 5
The thinner and higher the heel, the greater the risks of bunions,
hammertoes, back pain, corns, and calluses. Standing in high heels inevitably hurts after an hour or more because you're putting pressure
on the ball of your foot, which results in aches and pains.

It gets worse. The popularity of tennis shoes has led women's 6
feet literally to get bigger — especially
wider — but the sizing of shoes hasn't
changed. Women's feet are getting bigger,
but shoes aren't. Most women wear ill-
fitting shoes, usually ones that are too
small, which adds pinching to high-heel
hell.

> *The conventional
> critique is that women
> are slaves to the male-
> dominated, model-
> obsessed fashion
> culture.*

So why do we do it? The conventional 7
critique is that women are slaves to the
male-dominated, model-obsessed fashion
culture, leading us to sacrifice our toes and our checkbooks to satisfy
some man's idea of sexy shoes. Much of the coverage of this year's
return to stilettos as high as 6 inches focuses on the shoes and the
short skirts that go with them as a statement by women of their sexiness, voluptuousness, and femininity. Supposedly, wearing high heels
pushes your breasts out by changing your center of gravity. In Flo-
rence and Milan, men were reportedly salivating.

In the Bloomingdale's shoe department, all the salivating was 8
done by women, myself included. Strictly as research, of course, I
tried on shoes and observed other women doing the same. Almost
everyone is trying on the new higher heels. We strut around. We
throw our heads a little, and laugh.

Feet look smaller in high heels. Most women in America have big 9
feet. Believe it or not, 9½ is the most popular size. It isn't just you.
And it isn't just feet. High heels make a woman's leg look longer, and

everyone looks better with longer legs. There is a story that holds that high heels were first brought to America by a famous New Orleans madam who discovered that she could charge twice as much when a woman wore high heels.

In fact, none of the women I talked to were buying shoes to   10 please the men in their lives. "My husband won't even notice the shoes," a woman told me. More than one said husbands or boy-friends wouldn't like her because they'd make her too tall. Most men seem to prefer keeping the height advantage to heels, pushed-out breasts notwithstanding. The higher the heels get, the more men who face the tradeoff.

No one pretends high heels are as comfortable as flats. It's what   11 they do to your head, not your feet. That's what makes women walk different and look different in high heels.

I almost succumbed, but they cost too much, and how often can I   12 wear them? Not sensible. Not practical. Definitely not right for work and kids.

But the next day in Loehmann's, on sale yet, I find a pair that are   13 just as good. Now I just have to get invited somewhere in my high heels.

Vocabulary/Using a Dictionary

1. A *stiletto* (para. 7) is also a dagger. Compare the two definitions, and discuss what attributes they share.

2. To what other things might a person *succumb* (para. 12) besides the urge to buy? What is the difference between *succumbing* and *being defeated*?

3. The root of *podiatry* (para. 5) is *pod,* an organism with feet. Why do you think *podium* shares the same root as *tripod?*

Responding to Words in Context

1. Estrich discusses the way that high heels and short skirts can be interpreted as "a statement by women of their sexiness, volup-tuousness, and femininity" (para. 7). What does the context (the sentence in which it is found) of the word *voluptuousness* tell you about its meaning? Can anyone be voluptuous?

2. Try to describe the differences between *bunions, hammertoes,* and *corns* (para. 5). Then look up the words in a dictionary. How close were you? What hints tipped you off?

Discussing Main Point and Meaning

1. Why does "everyone like shoe-shopping," according to Estrich (para. 4)?
2. Does this essay praise or criticize high heels? Show evidence from the text to support your answer.
3. Do you agree that high heels are popular because of what they do to the wearer's head (see para. 11)? What, precisely, does Estrich mean by this claim?
4. What is the tone of the last sentence? How does it affect your understanding of the main point?

Examining Sentences, Paragraphs, and Organization

1. How does the second sentence — "Are you?" — establish Estrich's target audience?
2. Discuss the effectiveness of the transition between paragraphs 7 and 8, which centers on the word *salivating.* How does it mark a shift in the content of the essay?
3. Why does the first half of the essay focus on the opinions of others (podiatrists, men, the media) and the second half focus on the opinions of women who wear high heels? Is this an effective organizing structure?

Thinking Critically

1. Many women's fashions seem to constrain or contort women's bodies. List as many examples as you can. Men's fashions, on the other hand, seem to emphasize comfort. What do you make of this difference? Are you troubled by it? Why or why not?
2. Estrich seems content to accept the fact that there are many more reasons *not* to wear high heels than reasons to wear them. Does this makes her a hypocrite?

In-Class Writing Activities

1. Pick another article of clothing or fashion trend (such as neckties or haircoloring), and write a similar essay, attempting to rationalize the popularity and persistence of the trend despite its drawbacks.

2. Write two short speeches on high heels, each for a different audience. Write the first speech to aspiring models, extolling the virtues of high heels; write the second to a group of young feminist women, arguing for a boycott of high heels. Avoid using parody (negative imitation) and sarcasm.

KATHLEEN CARLIN

You Become What You Wear

[COMMONWEAL / June 1, 1996]

Before You Read

How important do you think clothing is as a sign of social class? What clothes do you identify with poor or homeless people? How do you know that someone wearing shabby, wrinkled, or torn clothing isn't an affluent person dressing down? Consider your own responses to people who have high and low social status. To what extent are your responses affected by what those people are wearing?

KATHLEEN CARLIN *was born in Elyria, Ohio. She worked as a surgical nurse before returning to school in 1990 to earn a B.A. in English and a B.S. in sociology and anthropology from Rocky Mountain College in Billings, Montana, graduating* summa cum laude. *She is a member of Americorps and Volunteer Montana!, serving at the Family Support Network where she works with families in which the abuse and neglect of children is an issue, and she is also a volunteer at the office of the Yellowstone County Sheriff, where she works with victims of crime.*

Words to Learn

truism (para. 1): statement of an obvious truth (n.)

unkempt (para. 2): untidy (adj.)

stigma (para. 3): mark of disgrace (n.)

histrionics (para. 3): theatrical behaviors calculated to cause emotional effect (n.)

gig (para. 4): planned performance or job, for musicians or other entertainers (n.)

incredulous (para. 5): skeptical, disbelieving (adj.)

derision (para. 6): ridicule (n.)

civility (para. 7): courtesy, politeness (n.)

inherent (para. 7): essential (adj.)

internalize (para. 9): make external values or thoughts a part of one's thinking (v.)

prevail (para. 9): triumph, be common (v.)

A standard criticism of sociological research projects is that they go to great lengths to prove what most people with common sense already know. Without exactly taking sides for or against that criticism, I want to describe a sociological exercise that might seem to validate it — except that, for me and a classmate (and maybe for some who read this account), the experience made a truism come alive.

> *Some of the children we encountered stared, pointed, and laughed; adults gave us long, incredulous looks.*

What we did: During spring break from a local college, my friend and I went downtown to shop. First, however, we made ourselves virtually unrecognizable to our friends and even to our families. We wore clothing slightly inappropriate for the weather, clean but wrinkled, clearly out of sync with the styles worn by most visitors to the area. We carried plastic bags of nameless possessions. Both of us were slightly unkempt. My friend wore a faded flannel shirt and T-shirt, a wrinkled skirt over sweat pants. I wore a wool hat that concealed my hair, an unfashionable coat and scarf, and glasses with clip-on sun shades.

The aim was to look like street people and to observe what difference that made in the way other people responded to us — whether the appearance of poverty would place a stigma on us. We were also prepared to act out some mildly unusual behaviors that might speak of some emotional disabilities, without appearing seriously disturbed or dangerous. As it turned out, there was no need for histrionics; people turned us off or tuned us out on the basis of appearance alone.

Our first stop (after parking our cars near the railroad tracks)   4
was in the bargain store of a local charity, where we politely asked
access to a bathroom and were refused. Next we entered the lobby of
a large hotel, where we asked for a coffee shop and a bathroom. The
bellhop said, "You must go to the twentieth floor." We weren't up to
trying our gig at an exclusive restaurant, so we wandered around the
first floor and left. From there we went to a pawnshop, where we
more or less blended with the patrons, and then on to the upper-scale
stores and coffee shops during the lunch hour.

It was stigma time. Some of the children we encountered stared,   5
pointed, and laughed; adults gave us long, incredulous looks. Clerks
in stores followed us around to watch our every move. In a lunch-
room a second assistant hurried to the side of the cashier, where they
took my $2 check without asking for an ID; it seemed worth that
price to have us out the door. At one doorway a clerk physically
blocked the entrance apparently to discourage our entry.

We had money to cover small purchases, and, apart from wear-   6
ing down-scale clothing, we did nothing in any of these settings to
draw attention to ourselves; we merely shopped quietly in our accustomed manner. At one establishment we did blow our cover when we
ordered croissants with a latté and an espresso; that may have been
too far out of character for "bag ladies." Elsewhere we encountered
derision, mockery, distrust, and rude stares.

So what did we learn? Mostly what we expected, what everybody   7
knows: people judge by appearances. Just looking poor brings with it
a stigma, accompanied by the withdrawal of much of the social civility most of us take for granted. Lacking the culturally acceptable
symbols of belonging in this milieu, we became, to a degree, objects,
with less inherent dignity as persons.

There was, however, one surprise — more accurately, a shock. It   8
became clear most strongly at the shop I mentioned earlier, the one
where a clerk conspicuously positioned herself in the entryway on
seeing us. I had just noticed the place and had turned to my companion, saying, "I've never seen this store. Let's go in." She looked at me
with dismay: "You're not really going in there, are you?"

I knew what she meant and shared her feeling. The place felt   9
out of bounds for us. In a very few hours, we found ourselves
accepting and internalizing the superficial and biased judgments
of ourselves that prevailed among the people we met; we stigmatized ourselves. It's a good lesson to learn, maybe especially for
sociologists.

Vocabulary/Using a Dictionary

1. Something considered historic has innate importance. What role does importance play in *histrionics* (para. 3)? How does a historic event differ from an experience of histrionics?

2. Some people have astigmatisms — floating spots in their fields of vision — in their eyes. How are *stigma* (para. 3) and *astigmatism* alike?

3. What is the relationship between *civility* (para. 7) and *civilization?* Would an uncivilized person necessarily lack civility?

Responding to Words in Context

1. How is the author using the word *become* in the title? How is it used with respect to someone's clothing?

2. Do you think the author uses the word *histrionics* (para. 3) fairly, given its context — criticism of prejudice against the homeless?

3. Look at the last sentence in paragraph 6. Try to pinpoint and describe the subtle differences between "derision, mockery, distrust, and rude stares."

4. *Stigma* (paras. 3, 5, 7, 9) is used several times in the essay. What effect does this repetition have?

Discussing Main Point and Meaning

1. Why do Carlin and her partner park their car "near the railroad tracks" (para. 4)?

2. Why does Carlin think that she and her partner blew their "cover" in the coffee shop (para. 6)?

3. What is the "shock" that Carlin describes in paragraph 8? How does it relate to the title of the article?

Examining Sentences, Paragraphs, and Organization

1. How do the first and last sentences relate to each other?

2. Paragraph 5 resembles a list. How does the list — rather than a fuller description of each experience — affect your understanding of what happened that day?

3. Carlin alludes to her main point in the last sentence of the first paragraph, when she says that a "truism [came] alive," but waits until the second-to-last paragraph to address that point directly. Would the article have been more or less effective if she had placed the main point clearly in the first paragraph? Why?

Thinking Critically

1. Do you have any reason to question Carlin's insistence that she and her friend were met with stares, points, laughs, and "long, incredulous looks" (para. 5)?

2. Carlin states that her sociological exercise "made a truism come alive" (para. 1). How is this different from proving "what most people with common sense already know" (para. 1)?

In-Class Writing Activities

1. Freewrite about an experience that made you feel stigmatized. Discuss how your experience was similar to, or different from, this author's experience. Do you think you internalized any "biased judgments" (para. 9) as a result?

2. Make a list of the places you frequent and the activities you do regularly. Write about how the quality of your life would change if you were suddenly excluded from doing those things.

HOBI READER

Identity through Clothing

[THE DAILY AZTEC, SAN DIEGO STATE UNIVERSITY / September 29, 1997]

Before You Read

How do you respond to dress codes? Do you think school uniforms strip students of their individuality, creativity, and diversity? Would you say the same of military uniforms or the standard scrubs worn by hospital doctors and nurses? What about athletic uniforms? Before you read, carefully consider what makes a uniform. Could a classroom of children all wearing jeans, tennis shoes, and t-shirts be considered to be in uniform?

Words to Learn

implementation (para. 4): placement of a rule or plan into action (n.)

elitist (para. 7): having a sense of belonging to a superior group (adj.)

adage (para. 10): tested proverb or well-known saying (n.)

albeit (para. 10): although (conj.)

dictate (para. 11): issue orders or commands, say something for another to write (v.)

Picture a sea of people clothed only in navy blue and white. Their identities have been lost, and sameness is required. Other colors are not an option. Shirts with collars must be tucked in, and no jeans are allowed. Skirts can be no shorter than two inches above the knee. No web belts are allowed, and no clothing may be worn too large.   1

HOBI READER *(b. 1956) is a native of La Mesa, in San Diego County, California, who returned to school after a twenty-one-year break and earned her B.A. in psychology at San Diego State University in August 1998. Reader is currently at work there on a self-designed master's degree in interdisciplinary studies; her thesis is on cultural influences on development. Her essays have been published in* Free Falling and Other Student Essays *(1997) and in SDSU's student newspaper, the* Daily Aztec.

Material is to be made of stiff cotton. Long shorts and headgear are not allowed. All people must look alike in order for learning to take place at optimum levels. Uniqueness is disallowed. Any breaking of these rules will result in stiff penalties.

Sound like a new science fiction novel? Or perhaps a list of dress codes at Folsom Prison? No, this is the dress code for many of San Diego County's primary, middle, and junior high schools. The school district has come up with this plan in order to keep the kids more focused on school. But it's a mystery to some how clothing can be an obstacle if teachers are doing a good job.

One argument is that uniforms will eliminate gang identification. But the uniforms have not helped gang members forget who they are. Parents who have been unable or unwilling to prevent their children from being in a gang or from wearing gang clothing will not instantly become more responsible now that their children are wearing the uniforms. They still have subtle identifiers — the painted faces, the greased-back hair, the tattoos, and that look of recognition they give one another.

Picture a sea of people clothed only in navy blue and white.

There was a dress code at most schools before the implementation of uniforms. It varied from school to school but was pretty basic as far as proper school attire goes. Instead of sending the few offenders home to change or putting them in detention, the schools chose to punish everyone, even those in complete compliance — better to make it really difficult for everyone.

The schools told the parents that the uniforms would help save them lots of money when purchasing school clothes. Parents of teenagers know how fashion conscious they can be, and now with the limited color choices and the stores sold out of anything "cool," parents spend hours and hours shopping all over town because of the dress code limits. But what are the parents to do with all of the other clothes that can't be worn to school? Why do children have to suffer because of the need for control among the school staff? The staff is not required to wear uniforms.

The children and parents were involved in a vote about the uniforms. This was done democratically. Parents were mailed ballots and asked to vote. The school then informed parents the vote was overwhelmingly in favor of the uniforms. No count was given, at least from Chula Vista Junior High School. Parents were not given any other specifics of the vote. The kids were given two color choices for

2

3

4

5

6

the uniforms so they could be involved. Funny how they just happened to pick the same colors as every other uniformed public school in the district.

The administration fed the public the sob story that the poor kids 7 will now look just like the rich kids. Do you think the poor kids will forget they are poor just because they are dressed like everyone else? And what about the real world? There are rich, and there are poor. Are we planning to just surprise the kids with this truth? Furthermore, those kids wearing the $60 designer shorts are certainly aware of their elitist roles, just as the other kids are.

Most parents involved with their children rarely found them to be 8 dressed distastefully. Children should always be encouraged to be individuals. This new power play on the part of the schools forced many children to change schools so they would not be subjected to uniforms. It's wonderful that some kids chose to "just say no" to uniforms.

When these children grow up, they will still have to decide what 9 to wear. The real world has required dress codes for some jobs, but for the most part, people can wear what they want.

What skills will the children lose by being told what to wear for 10 so many years? Will they forget what they once enjoyed wearing? Aren't the clothes we wear an expression of ourselves? What about the old adage (albeit sexist) "clothes make the man"? Will the kids still know who they are?

How can public schools dictate to the students like that? Isn't 11 this just teaching them that being the same as everyone else is good? Will it kill the flame of uniqueness budding in some of these young men and women? If all of us were the same, what would the world be like? There is concern it will be just like a science fiction story.

The next Albert Einstein may at this moment be drowning in a 12 sea of navy blue and white clothing.

Vocabulary/Using a Dictionary

1. Why might it be redundant to use adjectives like *old* or *familiar* to modify *adage* (para. 10)?

2. Why would a top athlete or other professional not mind being called *elite* yet be offended if called *elitist* (para. 7)?

3. In paragraph 4, Reader could have just written, "There was a dress code at most schools before uniforms." Why does she add the phrase "the implementation of"?

Responding to Words in Context

1. Analyze the use of the idiomatic *sob story* in paragraph 7. How does it add to the overall tone of the article?
2. Reader calls the uniform policy a "power play" (para. 8). Why might the school administrators reject this characterization? How does the phrase contribute to the overall representation of the schools involved in this controversy?

Discussing Main Point and Meaning

1. What are Reader's main objections to school uniforms? What are her criticisms of those who favor uniforms?
2. To what two other environments or contexts does Reader compare the atmosphere at Chula Vista Junior High School since the appearance of uniforms? Do you think the comparisons are reasonable? Why or why not?
3. Why is it ironic that some students chose to "just say no" (para. 8) to uniforms?
4. What effect is the image of "the next Albert Einstein . . . drowning in a sea of navy blue and white" supposed to have (para. 12)? Would your response change if you found out that as a student, Einstein had worn school uniforms? Why or why not?

Examining Sentences, Paragraphs, and Organization

1. There is no active subject in the sentence "There is concern it will be just like a science fiction story" (para. 11). To whose concern do you think Reader is referring?
2. Paragraphs 10 and 11 ask readers a lot of questions. What is the purpose of these questions? Is asking questions an effective stylistic device? Why or why not?
3. Reader is a college psychology student. Do you think her approach to this argument is psychologically informed? Why or why not?

Thinking Critically

1. Do you think that choosing what clothing to wear is the most significant means of self-expression for young people? In what other ways do kids express themselves?

2. The author argues that "poor kids" and "rich kids" are still "aware of their . . . roles" (para. 7), despite the uniforms. What do you think? Can uniformity in dress promote social equality in public schools? Do public schools have a responsibility to minimize class differences?

In-Class Writing Activities

1. Write a letter of response to the author from the point-of-view of the parents who apparently voted for the uniform policy. Try to answer each of Reader's specific criticisms.

2. Think about Reader's science fiction analogy (paras. 2 and 11). Many science fiction stories include an emphasis on uniform dress and appearances. Write a paragraph explaining why you think that science fiction often associates the future with uniformity.

From the Bookshelf

Anne Hollander, *Sex and Suits*

An art historian, Anne Hollander has written two stimulating and informative books about clothing, presenting it as an art form similar to painting or sculpture that has evolved over centuries. Her first book, Seeing Through Clothes *(1978), comprehensively examines the way different styles of clothing contribute to our understanding of the human body as well as human nature. In her recent award-winning book,* Sex and Suits: The Evolution of Modern Dress, *she focuses on the evolution of modern fashion. For anyone interested in how t-shirts and blue jeans became fashionable or how our choice of clothing reveals our personalities,* Sex and Suits *will be a difficult book to put down. In the following brief excerpt, Hollander explains why people — despite what they might say — really like uniforms.*

Uniform Fashions

It's in fact clear that "uniforms," so vigorously despised in much current rhetoric about clothes, are really what most people prefer to wear, garments in which they feel safely similar to their fellows. Once in uniform, they can choose their personal details, feel unique, and then sneer at the members of other tribes who all seem ridiculously

continued on next page

continued from previous page

alike in their tribal gear. For the past two centuries, men have dreaded looking like fools much more than women have; and so the dress of the male tribe has had a somewhat stronger uniform quality than the female one. Women have envied that very thing about it — and sneered at it, too.

One known reason for fashion's deep appeal is the way it provides the ability to look like everyone else, in the ancient tribal way; but at the same time, it provides a choice of tribes. Beyond that, fashion delightfully invites risky indulgence in private fantasy with a host of variations and details, offered in a context of complete and perhaps confusing and deceptive freedom of choice. Seen in one way, fashion makes many look remarkably alike; seen in another way, fashion permits each to look excitingly unique. Guilt and fear about this uneasy combination never seem to lessen; it is a responsibility.

Hollander, Anne. *Sex and Suits: The Evolution of Modern Dress.* New York: Alfred A. Knopf, 1994. Paperback by Kodansha Globe 1995.

Discussing the Unit

Suggested Topic for Discussion

All three authors in this unit discuss clothing and how it shapes our perceptions of ourselves and others. Susan Estrich writes about the popularity of high heels; Kathleen Carlin examines how our clothing affects the impressions people form about us; and Hobi Reader discusses negative reactions to public-school uniforms. In what ways do your clothes alter the way you feel about yourself? Do you consider these changes when you decide what to wear? Does how you dress affect more than just how you feel about yourself and how your day will go?

Preparing for Class Discussion

1. Both Kathleen Carlin and Hobi Reader's titles ("You Become What You Wear" and "Identity through Clothing") suggest that

clothing is essential to identity construction, though for slightly different reasons. Carlin suggests that the way outsiders react to one's clothing can determine one's identity, and Reader insists that if one is denied freedom of dress, one will lose any sense of individuality. Where does Susan Estrich fall on this issue? Where do you place yourself? Do you dress for yourself, for others, or both? What most motivates your clothing choice? What should?

2. Clothing is particularly important to teenagers. It causes conflicts with parents, competition among peers, and self-esteem problems for many teens. If, as Hobi Reader states, uniforms are not the answer, and if, as Susan Estrich implies, we seem destined to be a fashion-conscious society despite all of the drawbacks, what suggestions can you make to those teens struggling with their self-image through clothing? Do you agree with Anne Hollander (see "From the Bookshelf," p. 37) that uniforms and fashion are not always in opposition?

From Discussion to Writing

1. Each author in this unit describes the way a particular population is affected by the language of clothes. Susan Estrich discusses the contradictions some women face in choosing to dress fashionably; Kathleen Carlin argues that street people are denied respect because of their clothing and general appearance; Hobi Reader attempts to protect the right of students to express themselves through clothing. Try to think of other populations who are affected by specific clothing issues — people who are hard to fit, nudists, punk rockers, and so on. Write an essay about one of those populations, appealing to the reader to be more understanding of their predicament of living in such a clothing-conscious society.

2. At what age were you first allowed to dress yourself? How much did your parents influence your clothing choice while you were in high school? Who had the final say? Think about why the clothes a child wears might be important to a parent. Write a short article for a parenting magazine describing how parents should intervene in the way their children dress. Remember that you are trying to be helpful to the audience (parents) and not critical of them.

3. On some college campuses, pajama bottoms and sweatshirts are the most common outfit. At other schools, students go to class "dressed to the nines." To which category does your school belong? Or does it fall somewhere in the middle? Write an open letter to the student body, appealing to them to change their stylish (or unstylish) ways, as an experiment to promote more social and personal awareness.

Topics for Cross-Cultural Discussion

1. Are the clothing customs of your culture gender-based? Class-based? Religiously inspired? Or is clothing in your native culture merely functional?

2. Describe a special article of clothing from your native culture. Explain what it represents or symbolizes, and describe any controversy it inspires.

3

Body Image:
Why Is It a Serious Issue?

Are you content with the way you look? Opinion polls show that most Americans are not and that females are in general less content with their appearance than males. As individual self-esteem grows increasingly dependent on body image, every year many young people go to extreme measures to alter their looks through drugs, radical diets, or cosmetic surgery (see "From the Bookshelf," p. 56).

A large part of women's struggle with self-image comes from their daily exposure to the impossible physical ideals displayed on television, and in movies, magazines, and all kinds of advertisements. In "Caught with a Centerfold," one young woman, Jennifer Silver, valiantly fights back after she discovers her boyfriend's infatuation with *Playboy* magazine: "Yes, the real reason I hated *Playboy*," she admits, "was that the models established a standard I could never attain without the help of implants, a personal trainer, soft lighting, a squad of makeup artists and hairdressers, and air-brushing."

Another one of the unattainable images to which young girls may aspire is the ever-popular Barbie doll. In "I'm a Barbie Girl," Tufts University student Karen Epstein acknowledges the influence "the shapely Barbie" icon exerts on the physical expectations of young girls, but she also wonders how anyone can delude themselves into seeing Barbie as anything other than a doll, an "unanatomically correct piece of plastic with a ridiculously extensive wardrobe." Still, fantasy or not, images like Barbie's help create what a psychology graduate student from Illinois State University calls "the myth of the ideal body." It is a physical standard, Karlene Robinson reminds us in "In Pursuit of the Impossible Body Image," that millions of college students find extremely hard to ignore.

JENNIFER SILVER

Caught with a Centerfold

[MADEMOISELLE / January 1997]

Before You Read

What is your feeling about magazines like *Playboy* that feature naked female models in sexually provocative poses? Are these magazines harmless, or do they offer a distorted image of women? Can someone be a feminist and still enjoy such magazines?

Words to Learn

fledgling (para. 1): young and inexperienced (adj.)

innocuous (para. 1): harmless (adj.)

titanic (para. 3): huge (adj.)

diabolical (para. 6): devilish (adj.)

throes (para. 6): condition of agonizing struggle (n.)

grave (para. 9): extremely serious (adj.)

abashed (para. 11): embarrassed, ashamed (adj.)

vehemence (para. 11): intense emotional force (n.)

prudish (para. 11): excessively modest (adj.)

visceral (para. 11): related to the body, especially the abdomen (adj.)

JENNIFER SILVER *(b. 1969) was born in Los Angeles, California, and since then, by her latest calculations, has moved twenty-three times. She has worked as a technical writer, army officer, legal assistant, omelet chef, ESL instructor, bookkeeper, grocery store cashier, nanny, and unpublished novelist, among other things. She now teaches English in a private girls' school in New York City and hopes to stay there for a good long time.*

spoiling for (para. 12): craving
(adj.)

graciously (para. 17): courteously,
compassionately (adv.)

Last year I moved in with my boyfriend, and for a few months 1
we were in that blissful state of fledgling domesticity so sickening to
friends and family; sooner or later, there had to be a rude shock. And
there was: Like Bluebeard's wife, I found something I wished I
hadn't. It *looked* innocuous enough — a piece of scrap paper on the
floor — until I picked it up.

You know those subscription cards that flutter out every time 2
you open a magazine? Well, this one had fluttered out of *Playboy*.
Gentle reader, I *freaked*.

And thus my true love and I began a battle of truly titanic 3
proportions.

"I thought you were a feminist!" I 4
yelled.

I didn't want my boyfriend buying into Playboy's definition of sexuality.

"I can't talk to you when you get this 5
emotional!" he screamed back.

It certainly didn't help that, by some 6
diabolical coincidence, the magazine arrived every month while I was in the
throes of PMS — which in my book
stands for "paranoid and miserable situation."

My boyfriend began to get defensive. "Subscribing to *Playboy* 7
doesn't mean anything," he claimed. "Men are visually stimulated,
that's all."

"Oh. *Well.* Then you won't mind if I start going out for coffee 8
with some of the men from my writing class? You know, it won't
mean anything — I'm *conversationally* stimulated, that's all."

That gave him pause. But still the damn magazine kept coming, 9
and even I was taken aback by how furious it made me. I've never
been uptight about porn. I don't think it's one of the world's graver
problems, and I don't believe it needs to be censored unless it has
children or violence or degradation in it. So why was I feeling so
threatened?

His Fantasy Was My Nightmare

I started polling my friends, hoping I'd find people to back me 10
up — and I did, in abundance. Many of them agreed they'd be out-
raged if their boyfriends got *Playboy*.

And yet, like me, my friends were slightly abashed by the vehe-   11
mence of their feelings about porn. It didn't feel "cool" to get so
upset; it felt prudish. Yet we knew we weren't prudish, and our visceral reaction was baffling to us.

Part of the reason had to be political. I'll admit that my feelings   12
about *Playboy* sometimes got mixed in with a general rage about the
way women are treated in society. I'd listen to a friend's ongoing
problems with sexism in her office, I'd hear some of Pat Robertson's
Neanderthal comments on the radio, or I'd see a beer commercial on
TV that portrayed women as dumb bimbos — and I'd come home
spoiling for a fight. And there was *Playboy*!

But part of my reaction was very definitely personal — and the   13
most obvious explanation, jealousy, just didn't wash. Did I want him
to fantasize about no one but me? No. In fact, having a great relationship and still being able to fantasize about others is a natural, eat-
your-cake-and-have-it-too kind of pleasure.

How about insecurity, though? Ah.   14

Measuring Myself against an Impossible Ideal

Yes, the real reason I hated *Playboy* was that the models estab-   15
lished a standard I could never attain without the help of implants, a
personal trainer, soft lighting, a squad of makeup artists and hairdressers, and air-brushing. It's a standard that equates sexuality with
youth and beauty. I didn't want my boyfriend buying into *Playboy*'s
definition of sexuality. I was planning a future with this man, and I
wanted to feel secure in the knowledge that, even after two kids and
twenty years, he would still find me sexy.

After sorting all this out in my mind, I leveled with my boy-   16
friend. I told him that he wasn't doing something bad, but that it
made me *feel* bad. Rational or not, justified or not, I didn't like having *Playboy* in my house. Having to confront my insecurities once
a month was not the worst thing in the world, but I could live without it.

When he understood how I felt, he kindly and graciously can-   17
celed his subscription. It was a relief not to have to open our mail-
box and find that magazine anymore — but, more important, it reminded me that just because my boyfriend got *Playboy* didn't mean
he was the enemy. He was willing to look at the world through *my*
eyes.

Not Hugh Hefner's.   18

Vocabulary/Using a Dictionary

1. Discuss how the above definition of *grave* (para. 9) is similar to the use of *grave* as a noun.

2. To be graceful is to move beautifully. Both *graceful* and *graciously* (para. 17) come from the same root (*grace*). How are beautiful movement and compassion or courtesy similar?

3. A *fledgling* (para. 1) is literally a bird that has just become able to fly out of the nest. The word comes from *fledge* — "having the ability to fly." Why does the metaphoric use seem to emphasize inexperience (inability) rather than ability?

Responding to Words in Context

1. Silver creates her own interpretation of the acronym *PMS:* instead of *premenstrual syndrome,* she calls it "paranoid and miserable situation" (para. 6). Does this detail affect Silver's main point? Should it?

2. Silver writes that she has "never been uptight about porn" (para. 9) but then goes on to discuss her discomfort with "*Playboy's* definition of sexuality" (para. 15). What does *uptight* mean if not uncomfortable? Explain whether these two assertions conflict with each other.

Discussing Main Point and Meaning

1. Though Silver's article begins and ends with a discussion about her relationship with her boyfriend, what is the main point she is trying to make?

2. Through her use of a sectional format, Silver separates jealousy and insecurity as two distinct possible causes for her discomfort with *Playboy.* Can jealousy and insecurity be so easily separated in this case? Doesn't jealousy often come out of insecurity? Explain why or why not.

3. *Playboy's* models, according to this author, establish "a standard that equates sexuality with youth and beauty" (para. 15), which she rejects. How does Silver explain what she means when she says that she does not want her boyfriend "buying into" (para.

15) that standard? Do you think her explanation is adequate? Why or why not?

Examining Sentences, Paragraphs, and Organization

1. When she addresses her audience as "Gentle reader" (para. 2), Silver is imitating the polite conventions of nineteenth-century writers. How does the second half of that sentence reveal her twentieth-century sensibilities?

2. Though sexism and pornography are political issues in our society, Silver devotes only one full paragraph to politics. Identify that paragraph, and analyze its effectiveness.

3. Silver responds to her boyfriend's logic that "Men are visually stimulated" (para. 7) with the claim that she is *"conversationally stimulated"* (para. 8). In doing this she suggests that her boyfriend's use of *Playboy* would compare to her having coffee with men from her writing class. Do you agree with the comparison? Why or why not?

Thinking Critically

1. Do you believe Silver's claim that she is "*not* uptight" (para. 9) about porn? Do you believe that she does *not* want her boyfriend to fantasize only about herself (para. 13)? Why or why not? Use other statements from the text to support your answer.

2. Why do you think Silver restricts her critique to *Playboy*? If her boyfriend regularly received a women's lingerie or swimwear catalog do you think she would be equally upset? Should she be criticizing all unreasonable representations of female sexuality? Why or why not?

In-Class Writing Activities

1. People interpret the word *pornography* in many different ways. Develop your own definition in an essay, and discuss the values that you think it expresses about our society.

2. Why is the audience for pornography overwhelmingly male? Are men taught to be interested in pornography by society, or are they, as Silver's boyfriend argues, just "visually stimulated" (para. 7)? Try to imagine a media industry whose audience is

overwhelmingly female. Compare and contrast the two media, and in a one- to two-page essay analyze what you perceive to be the causes of these trends.

KAREN EPSTEIN

I'm a Barbie Girl

[THE TUFTS DAILY ONLINE, TUFTS UNIVERSITY / November 21, 1997]

Before You Read

How can a little plastic doll influence a girl's self-image? Do you believe that by playing with a Barbie doll a young girl develops an unrealistic image of what she should look like in the future?

Words to Learn

curvaceous (para. 1): shapely, full (adj.)

hail (para. 3): praise enthusiastically (v.)

cannibalistic (para. 4): feeding on one's own kind (adj.)

delude (para. 4): deceive the mind or judgment of (v.)

anatomically (para. 9): related to the structure of the human body (adv.)

KAREN EPSTEIN (b. 1976) of Tappan, New York, graduated magna cum laude *with a B.A. in English from Tufts University in May 1998. She is a member of the Golden Key National Honor Society. Actively involved with the student-run* Tufts Daily *for all four years of her undergraduate studies, Epstein earned the position of editor in chief in the fall of 1997. Since its publication in the* Tufts Daily *in November 1997, her article has inspired students to share with her their opinions on Barbie. Says Epstein, "Most women [have] agreed with me that Barbie is, after all, a doll and not the root cause of image problems in our society."*

It wasn't her curvaceous hips. Or her Scarlett O'Hara–esque   1
waist. Or even her unnaturally voluptuous bustline. The only things
that bothered me were her feet. Those tiny little plastic feet were bent
up in this permanent high-heel position that was extremely aggravat-
ing because I could never get those itsy-bitsy high-heel pumps to stay
on. Ah, but the handsome Ken: he had these big, wide, "manly" feet
that were perfectly flat. Those sensible shoes never fell off. Poor Barbie, on the other hand, never got to wear shoes in my house.

To my dismay, the Mattel toy company has not yet announced   2
whether they will bring in their podiatry experts to examine thirty-
eight-year-old Barbie's feet before her upcoming surgery. Earlier this
week, the company told the world that the shapely Barbie is scheduled for some extensive nips and tucks — a wider waist, slimmer
hips, and a smaller bustline. She's even getting a new face, minus the
toothy grin.

There is no one cause of the obsession with body image in this country and the rampant eating disorders young girls and women develop.

Many who felt that the pop icon Bar-   3
bie doll upheld an unrealistic standard of
beauty are hailing Mattel's decision to
make her look more like a real woman.
And her highly unrealistic 38-18-34 figure (according to some estimates) gives
girls a negative body ideal from a young
age. "I actually think it's healthy because
we are surrounded by cultural icons that
create unrealistic expectations in adult
women. . . . Barbie's change is a wholesome step in the right direction," retired plastic surgeon Sharon Webb told the *Boston Globe*.

I don't know about you, but for me, Barbie was always, well, a   4
doll. When Barbie's skinny plastic legs popped out of their sockets, I
knew she wasn't real. When my friend Lauren's bratty, semicannibal-
istic six-year-old neighbor chewed off Barbie's foot, and Barbie kept
up that same cheery grin, I knew she wasn't real. I never deluded
myself into thinking we little girls were supposed to grow up to have
38-18-34 figures. My mom didn't look like that. My teenage sisters
didn't look like that. NO women I knew looked like Barbie. She was
fun. She was a fantasy. And she sure did have some nice clothes.

I've always been a big fan of Barbie. I'm not alone. According to   5
M. G. Lord, the author of *Forever Barbie*, the average American girl
owns eight Barbie dolls — eight gals, that is, to "one pathetic,
overextended Ken," she says. That was the case with me, although I
think the number far exceeded eight. I don't remember all of their

official names anymore, but I remember many in the lineup: there was punk-rocker Barbie, bride Barbie, "day-to-night" Barbie (her outfit converted from a work suit to evening wear, tres yuppie 1980s), the Barbie that came with an assortment of "fashion wigs," the Barbie with the funky hair-curler, birthday Barbie, ballerina Barbie, and, my favorite, permanently puckered kissing Barbie, who, at the push of a button on her back, would give Ken a big smooch. I was very upset when Barbie's kissing button stopped working. Looking back on it, I realize perhaps she just didn't like Ken anymore.

My Ken was a busy fella. He was forced to play the boyfriend, brother, father, husband, "insert male role here" role in every one of my Barbies' adventures. What a nice guy. And, oh, those adventures. I could dress her in fancy clothes and send her on a romantic date with Ken, give her a bath in my Barbie bubble bath, put her to bed in the Barbie dream house (I didn't actually have one, but I could pretend). It was a fantasy. "I mean, they say Barbie is unrealistic. But she's got a Ferrari, a Malibu dream house, and big plastic boobs. Here in LA, you can't get more realistic than that," said late-night TV host Jay Leno earlier this week.

Don't get me wrong. I do understand the concern many have with Barbie's current look. And, although her incredibly unrealistic body image did not affect me consciously as a child, there is a good chance it did affect me unconsciously. There is no one cause of the obsession with body image in this country and the rampant eating disorders young girls and women develop. While I place more of the blame on unattainable images of sickly thin women in advertising, movies, and television for the perpetuation of unrealistic standards of beauty, I must say that, despite my love for the Barbie I grew up with, Mattel is making the right move. If it helps one girl to not internalize the ridiculous ideal of big-busted thinness as perfection, it's worth it. But I'll never forget my Barbie.

Even Christina Hoff Sommers, the author of a book entitled *Who Stole Feminism,* told the *Boston Globe,* "The new Barbie is more attractive, and she did need a makeover. But I didn't mind the fact that the older one reflected earlier ideals of feminine beauty. I liked Barbie as a child. She was glamorous. And part of being a child is fantasy and play, not an exercise in self-esteem."

In the end, she's a doll. A fantasy. An unanatomically correct piece of plastic with a ridiculously extensive wardrobe. And funny feet.

Vocabulary/Using a Dictionary

1. *Delude* (para. 4) and *illusion* come from the same Latin root for *play*. What kind of play might be involved in a delusion?

2. The Greek for *cutting up* is the root for *anatomically* (para. 9). Discuss how the study of human anatomy (the separate — cut up — parts of the human body) might be different from the study of human physiology (human life processes).

3. Christopher Columbus coined the term *cannibal* (a flesh-eating person) (para. 4) as a Spanish variant of the West Indian *Galibi* (strong men, which is what they called themselves). Explain how the context of Columbus's voyage could explain the significant difference between these related terms.

Responding to Words in Context

1. Epstein uses a lot of informal language: "itsy-bitsy" (para. 1), "nips and tucks" (para. 2), "gals" (para. 5), "funky" (para. 5), "smooch" (para. 5), and "fella" (para. 6), for example. How do examples like these contribute to the overall tone of Epstein's article? Are they appropriate given the subject matter?

2. "Real" (para. 4), "unrealistic" (paras. 3, 6–7), "fantasy" (paras. 4, 6), and "ideal" (para. 7) are employed in this article, though Epstein never really defines the terms. Develop your own definitions of the words with the help of Epstein's usage. Is there any place for fantasy in real life? Is there any element of realism in fantasy?

Discussing Main Point and Meaning

1. Epstein insists that Barbie is just a "fantasy" (paras. 4, 6). How does she then justify her support for Mattel's decision to redesign Barbie so that girls won't "internalize the ridiculous ideal of big-busted thinness as perfection" (para. 7)?

2. In addition to the discussion about Barbie, this essay makes several references to Ken as well. Summarize some of those references, and describe how they contribute to Epstein's main point.

3. In paragraph 5, Epstein describes all the different kinds of Barbies she had as a child. List the Barbies Epstein mentions, and add some examples of your own. How does the variety of types and themes contribute to Epstein's argument?

4. Why didn't Epstein think that she was supposed to grow up to look like Barbie?

Examining Sentences, Paragraphs, and Organization

1. "Poor Barbie," Epstein writes, "never got to wear shoes in my house" (para. 1). In this sentence, how is the author's point of view revealed?

2. It's not until paragraph 7 that Epstein expresses her direct support for Mattel's plans to redesign Barbie's appearance. Were you surprised by it? How did it affect your impression of Epstein and of the issue in general?

3. The essay begins and ends with a focus on Barbie's feet. Given that Barbie's feet are neither the focus of a feminist critique of Barbie's appearance nor important evidence for Epstein's claim about fantasy, why do you think she does this? Is this an effective way to frame the issues raised by the article? Why or why not?

Thinking Critically

1. On the one hand, Epstein is critical of, even condescending to, those who think that children's play is anything more than fantasy. On the other hand, she clearly supports the toy company's decision to change Barbie's looks for the psychological benefit of young girls. Can she have it both ways? Does she address these contradictory positions fully in your opinion?

2. "NO women I knew looked like Barbie," Epstein says (para. 4). Think carefully about this statement. Is this a more significant point than even Epstein realizes? To Epstein, the statement supports her theory that children's fantasies are only play and thus that they cannot compete with reality (that is, her mother and teenage sisters' appearances). But isn't she missing a crucial point about Barbie's looks, which resemble no living woman?

In-Class Writing Activities

1. Pick a boy's toy that encourages an unrealistic image of masculinity. Write an imitative essay that critiques the toy in a fashion similar to Epstein's essay. Call for specific changes that

would help to prevent boys from internalizing a harmful image or standard.

2. Write a letter from Barbie to her critics in which she defends her appearance and her effects on the children who play with her.

KARLENE J. ROBINSON

In Pursuit of the Impossible Body Image

[THE DAILY VIDETTE ONLINE, ILLINOIS STATE UNIVERSITY / February 18, 1998]

Before You Read

What do you think is more important to a person's self-esteem — how good one looks or how much one has achieved? If you had to choose between looking like a top film star or graduating with four years of straight As, which would you choose? Why?

Words to Learn

negate (para. 2): invalidate, nullify (v.)

integration (para. 2): wholeness (n.)

disown (para. 2): refuse ownership (v.)

anorexia nervosa (para. 4): disease characterized by self-starvation (n.)

bulimia nervosa (para. 4): disease characterized by binge eating and weight loss measures such as self-induced vomiting or laxative abuse (n.)

KARLENE J. ROBINSON *(b. 1965) grew up in the Jamaican West Indies and moved to Lockport, New York, with her family when she was seventeen. Robinson holds a B.A. and M.A. in psychology, is the recipient of the EOP Academic Achievement Award, and is a member of several honor societies. As a graduate student in counseling psychology at Southern Illinois University at Carbondale, Robinson is concerned by the extent to which "individuals' self-concepts are wrapped up in their body images." Robinson wrote this article when she was studying at Illinois State University.*

Millions of college students pursue an impossible body image.   1
Their self-acceptance is based on having the perfect body, the ideal
size, and the ideal weight and disappears once the extra pounds return. They also have trouble believing other people can accept them
without that ideal body.

In their pursuit of the ideal body, they devalue the body they   2
have and negate their unique sense of self. Their body images get in
the way of their liking who they are. They do not feel a sense of integration and acceptance. You may know of friends, family members,
or acquaintances who disowned their bodies. Even if they do not reject their bodies entirely, they may hate certain parts of their bodies.
For instance, we often hear someone say, "I hate my legs" or "I hate
my nose."

Both men and women, but more so women, have gone to great   3
lengths to transform themselves to meet society's expectations of
the ideal body. The image of the culturally desirable body is pro-
jected in the media via TV, the movies,
magazines, and billboards. Women are
expected to be thin, and men are expected to be muscular. The implication in
the media is that to have the ideal body is
to be attractive, powerful, witty, and self-
controlled. The ideal body defines individual self-worth and identity.

*The ideal body defines
individual self-worth
and identity.*

Given that most people's bodies do not naturally fit the physical   4
ideal, the pursuit can lead to years of dieting, eating disorders (such
as anorexia nervosa and bulimia nervosa), self-esteem issues, and an
obsessive preoccupation with body image. Dieting is a health hazard.
The never-ending battle with weight gain, weight loss, and an unstable weight can be very stressful. We also lose control of our lives
when we rely on external forces to validate our sense of worth and
define our identity.

How do we not accept the myth of the ideal body? To do that   5
we need to seriously think about how we feel about our bodies, what
we believe about our bodies, and why we feel or believe that way. It
is important to attend to one's thoughts and feelings and note any
association with eating habits. Do not use food to mask problems
that you are avoiding or problems that are too painful for you to
face. Eat a well-balanced diet regularly without feeling guilty, and
have food become a normal part of life, rather than the focus of your
life.

Vocabulary/Using a Dictionary

1. *Integration* (para. 2) and *integrity* (adherence to a strong behavioral or moral code) share the same Latin root for "make whole." What does wholeness have to do with a behavioral code? How might these issues also be related to the more common use of *integrate* in a racial or cultural sense?

2. The original meanings of *anorexia* and *bulimia* (para. 4) are, respectively, "without appetite or hunger" and "huge appetite or hunger." They become pathologies (diseases) when attached to *nervosa* (coming from the nervous system). Look up *nervous* in the dictionary, and discuss how its definitions inform your understandings of the two diseases.

3. Can you think of an antonym for *negate* (para. 2)? What would be the opposite of negating the "sense of self" that Robinson discusses?

Responding to Words in Context

1. Robinson uses the term *ideal* in every paragraph in her essay. Though ideals are often thought to be good things to have, it is difficult to discern whether Robinson would think so. Do you think she is critical of ideals in general, or is she merely attempting to question the validity of one particular ideal? Use evidence from the text to support your answer.

2. Robinson often uses the first-person plural pronoun (*we*) to refer to her subject (young women). How does this choice define the article's point of view and therefore affect its target audience?

Discussing Main Point and Meaning

1. Robinson focuses her argument on college students. Why?

2. What is wrong with the way that the media portray "society's expectations of the ideal body" (para. 3), according to this article?

3. How is the psychological problem of disowning one's body (para. 2) related to the physical problem of having an eating disorder (para. 4), according to Robinson?

4. What are some of Robinson's suggestions for addressing destructive self-images? Is her list sufficient? What other suggestions would you add?

Examining Sentences, Paragraphs, and Organization

1. Why does Robinson quote people who have expressed hatred for specific body parts (para. 2)? Would the point have been more or less successful if she had paraphrased instead or just ended after the statement that many "may hate certain parts of their bodies"?

2. Until the last paragraph, the essay is focused on highly psychological problems. The solutions Robinson provides in the last paragraph are more behavioral in nature. Why do you think the author makes this switch? Do you find it effective?

3. "Dieting is a health hazard" (para. 4) is reminiscent of what other health warning? Is the sentence effective in this context?

Thinking Critically

1. Robinson blames society for the pressure many feel to pursue the ideal body, but she puts the burden on individuals to defend against this problem by changing their own behavior. Shouldn't she be suggesting ways to relieve the social pressures in the first place? Isn't prevention a more productive approach than treatment after the fact?

2. Many experts say that eating disorders are at least partially chemically related. In other words, although most women may feel the social pressure to be thin, only some develop the serious diseases of anorexia and bulimia. How could this distinction be better drawn in Robinson's article? Why is it important to draw this distinction?

In-Class Writing Activities

1. Robinson writes in largely general terms. List specific situations that could trigger the kinds of self-esteem problems she is talking about, and, in the spirit of her last paragraph, provide more specific behavioral solutions.

2. Think about the way ideal body images affect students at your college or university. In a letter to the administrative officer of your choice (such as the director of student life, health services, residence life, or food services), describe the specific problems at your school, and make concrete suggestions for helping alleviate those problems.

From the Bookshelf

Naomi Wolf, *The Beauty Myth*

One of the important feminist books of the 1990s is Naomi Wolf's *The Beauty Myth: How Images of Beauty Are Used Against Women.* "No other work," claimed the New York Times in a review, has "so honestly depicted the confusion of accomplished women who feel emotionally and physically tortured by the need to look like movie stars." Educated at Yale University and Oxford University, where she was a Rhodes scholar, Naomi Wolf has contributed essays to a wide range of national magazines. In the following passage she describes the incredibly profitable new business of cosmetic surgery.

Selling Ugliness

If women suddenly stopped feeling ugly, the fastest-growing medical specialty would be the fastest dying. In many states of the United States, where cosmetic surgeons (as opposed to plastic surgeons, who specialize in burns, trauma, and birth defects) can be any nonspecialist M.D., it would be back to mumps and hemorrhoids for the doctors, conditions that advertising cannot exacerbate. They depend for their considerable livelihood on selling women a feeling of terminal ugliness. If you tell someone she has cancer, you cannot create in her the disease and its agony. But tell a woman persuasively enough that she is ugly, you do create the "disease," and its agony is real. If you wrap up your advertisement, alongside an article promoting surgery, in a context that makes women feel ugly and leads us to believe that other women are competing in this way, then you have paid for promoting a disease that you alone can cure.

This market creation seems not to be subject to the ethics of the genuine medical profession. Healing doctors would be discredited if they promoted behavior that destroyed health in order to profit from the damage: hospitals are withdrawing investment from tobacco and alcohol companies. The term for this practice, *ethical investing,* recognizes that some medical profit relationships are unethical. Hospitals can afford such virtue, since their patient pool of the sick and dying is always naturally replenished. But cosmetic surgeons must create a patient pool where none biologically exists. So they take out full-page ads in the *New York Times* — showing a full-length image of a famous model in a swimsuit, accompanied by an offer of easy credit

and low monthly terms, as if a woman's breasts were a set of consumer durables — and make their dream of mass disease come true.

Wolf, Naomi. *The Beauty Myth: How Images of Beauty Are Used Against
Women*. New York: Anchor-Doubleday, 1991.

Discussing the Unit

Suggested Topic for Discussion

The authors in this unit are concerned with the concept of the ideal
body and how it is connected to one's self-image or self-esteem. Jennifer Silver resists *Playboy*'s standards of the female body and sexuality; Karen Epstein wonders if Barbie's "incredibly unrealistic body
image" really has any effect on girls; and Karlene J. Robinson warns
against letting the ideal body define our worth and identities. Do you
define yourself by your physical image? Do you consider yourself to
be obsessed or preoccupied with your own body? Do you have
friends who are? How else should we define ourselves, if not by our
physical appearance? How might we begin to change our society's
obsession with body image?

Preparing for Class Discussion

1. Though there is no reference to gender in the title of this unit, it
   is clear from the focus of these three essays that women are most
   affected by the body image ideals of our society. Do you think
   there is pressure on men to achieve a specific body ideal (Karlene
   J. Robinson suggests there is in para. 3 of her essay)? What is
   that ideal? Women turn to dieting, exercise, cosmetic surgery,
   and consumerism in response to the pressure they feel to be
   young, thin, and yet voluptuous. How do you think men respond
   to the pressure to adhere to the masculine ideal?

2. Some would argue that ideals of thinness and youth are preferable
   to their opposite. What do you think? How do you think each of
   the authors in this unit would respond to the idea that society is
   better off prizing youth and thinness than age and obesity?

From Discussion to Writing

1. Jennifer Silver, Karen Epstein, and Karlene J. Robinson all place the blame for women's body image problems on unrealistic ideals of beauty. Are they really talking about ideals? Aren't ideals by definition unrealistic? Brainstorm a list of other unattainable ideals that exist in our culture. Discuss whether those ideals are as harmful as the body-image ideals.

2. A role model, unlike an ideal, is something people can be reasonably expected to follow or imitate. Epstein explains that she had the models of her mother's and sisters' bodies with which to contrast the ideal of Barbie (para. 4). Try to come up with a realistic model of beauty for women. What specific characteristics — physical, intellectual, spiritual, emotional — do you think are achievable for any woman?

3. Assume that you will one day be the parent of a daughter. Write a letter to her describing the problems that the authors in this unit detail, which will most certainly affect your daughter's self-image. Advise her about how she can develop positive feelings about her body and how she can guard against the social pressure to criticize or disown her body. Quote the authors in this unit where appropriate. Alternatively, write a letter to a future son, encouraging him not to buy into the standard of beauty this culture sets for women. Teach him how to value qualities that are not a part of the current feminine beauty ideal, again using the authors in this unit, where appropriate.

Topics for Cross-Cultural Discussion

1. What are the overall body ideals in your native culture? Describe the size, shape, and features that are thought attractive in that culture and how they differ from those described in these essays.

2. Does the burden of body image ideals fall more or less on the shoulders of women in your native culture than it does on American women? Why do you think this is so? Is cosmetic surgery (see "From the Bookshelf," p. 56) as common in your native culture as it is in the United States?

4

Who Has It Tougher — Boys or Girls?

The latest dispute in the nation's ongoing gender wars has raised a question concerning the relative difficulties of boyhood versus girlhood. The quick question is, Which is harder — being a boy or being a girl? And like most quick questions, there appear to be only slow answers. In "The 'Fragile American Girl' Myth," noted philosopher Christina Hoff Sommers wonders how anyone ever got the idea that girls are "an underprivileged class." As she argues: "To the extent that there is a gender gap among youth, it is boys who turn out to be on the fragile side."

Although boys, too, may have it tough, they bring on some of their own problems, suggests student Mark Zmarzly, a columnist for the *Daily Nebraskan,* who claims in "Boys Don't Cry" that males have "become so accustomed to masking their true emotions that it seems like second nature."

Along with other differences, do boys and girls also grow up with different attitudes about competitiveness that show up later in college sports? Dorothy J. Samuels and Gail Collins disagree in a *New York Times* editorial about a controversial incident in a women's basketball game.

CHRISTINA HOFF SOMMERS

The "Fragile American Girl" Myth

[AMERICAN ENTERPRISE / May–June 1997]

Before You Read

Recent sociological studies showing that girls are an "underprivileged group" have been contested by new studies suggesting that boys actually have tougher lives. Before you read, make two brief lists of what you consider to be the major problems faced by boys and girls. Compare your list to the problems mentioned in the following selection.

Words to Learn

redress (para. 1): compensation for injury (n.)

drove (para. 2): flock, pack, large number (n.)

rig (para. 9): fix, manipulate, set up dishonestly (v.)

unduly (para. 12): excessively, too much (adv.)

advocacy (para. 13): active support of a cause (n.)

mendacious (para. 14): false (adj.)

Did you know that the United States Congress now categorizes   1
American girls as "a historically underserved population"? In a recent education statute, girls are classified with African Americans, Native Americans, the physically handicapped, and other disadvantaged minorities as a group in need of special redress. Programs to

CHRISTINA HOFF SOMMERS *(b. 1950) is an associate professor of philosophy at Clark University who specializes in contemporary moral theory. Her articles have appeared in publications such as the* New Republic, *the* Wall Street Journal, *the* Chicago Tribune, *and the* New England Journal of Medicine, *among others. She has edited two ethics textbooks, has published numerous professional papers, and is the author of* Who Stole Feminism? *published in 1994. This selection is adapted from her remarks at a December 1996 American Enterprise Institute conference.*

help girls who have allegedly been silenced and demoralized in the nation's sexist classrooms are now receiving millions of federal dollars. At the United Nations women's conference in Beijing, the alleged silencing and short-changing of American schoolgirls was treated as a pressing human rights issue.

Several popular books have appeared in recent years to build up 2
the notion that ours is a "girl-poisoning culture." The phrase is Dr. Mary Pipher's, and her book, *Reviving Ophelia: Saving the Selves of Adolescent Girls,* has been at the top of the *New York Times* bestseller list. According to Pipher, "Something dramatic happens to girls in early adolescence. Just as planes and ships disappear mysteriously into the Bermuda Triangle, so do the selves of girls go down in droves. They crash and burn." [See "From the Bookshelf," p. 74.]

Where did she get this idea? Where did the United States Con- 3
gress get the idea that girls are a victim group? How did the "silencing" of American schoolgirls become an international human rights issue?

Where did the United States Congress get the idea that girls are a victim group?

To answer that, consider some high- 4
lights of what might be called the myth of the incredible shrinking girl. The story epitomizes what is wrong with the contemporary women's movement. First, a few facts.

The U.S. Department of Education 5
keeps records of male and female school achievement. They reveal that girls get better grades than boys. Boys are held back more often than girls. Significantly fewer boys than girls go on to college today. Girls are a few points behind in national tests of math and science, but that gap is closing. Meanwhile, boys are *dramatically* behind in reading and writing. We never hear about that gap, which is not shrinking.

Many more boys than girls suffer from learning disabilities. In 6
1990, three times as many boys as girls were enrolled in special education programs. Of the 1.3 million American children taking Ritalin, the drug for hyperactivity, three-quarters are boys. More boys than girls are involved in crime, alcohol, drugs.

Mary Pipher talks about the "selves" of girls going down in 7
flames. One effect of a crashing self is suicide. *Six times* as many boys as girls commit suicide. In 1992, fully 4,044 young males (ages fifteen to twenty-four) killed themselves. Among same-age females, there were 649 suicides. To the extent that there is a gender gap among youth, it is boys who turn out to be on the fragile side.

This is not to deny that some girls are in serious trouble or that   8
we can't do better by girls, educationally and otherwise. What I am
saying is you cannot find any responsible research that shows that
girls, as a group, are worse off than boys or that girls are an underprivileged class. So where did that idea come from? Therein lies a
tale.

The reality is the contemporary women's movement is obsessed   9
with proving that our system is rigged against women. No matter
what record of success you show them, they can always come up with
some example of oppression. Never is good news taken as real evidence that things have changed. The women's movement is still fixated on victimology. Where they can't prove discrimination, they in-
vent it.

I, for one, do not believe American women are oppressed. It is   10
simply irresponsible to argue that American women, as a gender, are
worse off than American men.

More women than men now go to college. Women's life ex-   11
pectancy is seven years longer than men's. Many women now find
they can choose between working full-time, part-time, flex-time, or
staying home for a few years to raise their children. Men's choices are
far more constricted. They can work full-time. They can work full-
time. Or they can work full-time.

The reason we hear nothing about men being victims of society   12
or boys suffering unduly from educational and psychological deficits
is because the feminist establishment has the power to shape national
discussion and determine national policy on gender issues.

Feminist research is advocacy research. When the American As-   13
sociation of University Women released a (badly distorted) survey in
1991 claiming that American girls suffer from a tragic lack of self-
esteem, a *New York Times* reporter got AAUW President Sharon
Shuster to admit that the organization commissioned the poll to get
data into circulation that would support its officers' belief that
schoolgirls were being short-changed. Usually, of course, belief
comes after, not before, data gathering. But advocacy research
doesn't work that way. With advocacy research, first you believe,
and then you gather figures you can use to convince people you are
right.

The myth of the short-changed schoolgirl is a perfect example of   14
everything that's gone wrong with contemporary feminism. It's all
there — the mendacious advocacy research, the mean-spiritedness to

men that extends even to little boys, the irresponsible victimology, the outcry against being "oppressed," coupled with massive lobbying for government action.

The truth is, American women are the freest in the world. Any- 15
one who doesn't see this simply lacks common sense.

Vocabulary/Using a Dictionary

1. Based on the meaning of *advocacy* (para. 13), in what fields do you think professionals are sometimes referred to as *advocates?*

2. *Duly* means "in a proper manner" or "at the expected time." Is *unduly* (para. 12) an exact antonym? Why or why not?

3. *Mendacious* (para. 14) and *mend* ("fix, remove faults") are ultimately related to the same Latin root. Try to explain what the connection between the words might be. Then look up the words in the dictionary to test your hypothesis.

Responding to Words in Context

1. Look up *victimology* (para. 14) in the dictionary. If you cannot find it, try to develop a definition by examining its use in this essay, by looking up related words, and by thinking about other *ologies* with which you are familiar.

2. If *underprivileged* (para. 8) were changed to *unprivileged,* how would the meaning of the word change?

Discussing Main Point and Meaning

1. Does this article argue *for* or *against* something? Explain your answer, citing evidence from the text.

2. Explain the meaning of the essay's title. What is a myth? What does Hoff Sommers want the reader to do with the myth she names?

3. Does this article contain a feminist argument, in your opinion? Why or why not?

4. What does Hoff Sommers argue the women's movement should examine with its resources? Does that argument make sense to you? Why or why not?

Examining Sentences, Paragraphs, and Organization

1. Examine the author's last statement. How is it connected to her main point? Is there sufficient evidence to support its claim?

2. Hoff Sommers mentions Mary Pipher's thesis that girls lose themselves in adolescence and asks, "Where did she get this idea?" (para. 3). Does she want an answer to this question? Why or why not?

3. At the bottom of paragraph 11, Hoff Sommers writes: "Men's choices are far more constricted. They can work full-time. They can work full-time. Or they can work full-time" (para. 11). What tone does this repetition convey? Is it effective?

Thinking Critically

1. Does Hoff Sommers generalize fairly about "the contemporary women's movement" (para. 4)? She really cites only two specific pieces of feminist research. Is it appropriate to develop theories based on a couple of examples?

2. Examine paragraphs 5 to 7, which describe the areas where boys supposedly "suffer" more than girls, according to Hoff Sommers. Is there any problem in the logic that Hoff Sommers is trying to develop here? Is the list of boys' vulnerabilities she provides evidence enough to prove that girls are indeed *not* an "underserved population" (para. 1)?

In-Class Writing Activities

1. Freewrite about your own educational experiences. Do you think your gender affected your progress in certain ways? Explain your answer with specific anecdotes or by quoting from the text.

2. Working in groups, develop strategies for addressing the fragility of both boys and girls in school. Write a report for your local school committee, making suggestions that would bridge the gender gap in education from both directions.

MARK ZMARZLY

Boys Don't Cry

[THE DAILY NEBRASKAN, UNIVERSITY OF NEBRASKA–LINCOLN / January 26, 1998]

Before You Read

Many boys grow up believing that emotional or sensitive behavior makes them look weak or unmasculine. Why do you think this is the case? Do you think that girls would prefer boys to be more emotional, or do you think girls actually encourage boys to suppress their emotions?

Words to Learn

complement (para. 1): provide with a counterpart, make whole (v.)
abound (para. 1): become great in number, be plentiful (v.)
execution (para. 9): performance (n.)
flourish (para. 10): thrive or grow, flower (v.)

As children, most of us were taught that God created man and woman. God created them in his own likeness to complement each other and produce offspring. God provided Adam with no handbook or lecture on masculinity, and thus emotion and procreation abounded. 1

Imagine the same story set in the modern day. God created man and woman. Man felt an obligation from society to display the true essence of masculinity and male responsibility. Man guarded his emotions and never allowed himself to care for woman. Along the way were one-night stands, broken promises, a pass at woman's best friend, and in the end, no man at all. 2

MARK ZMARZLY (b. 1975) was a senior at the University of Nebraska at Lincoln when he wrote this essay, the first of sixteen opinion articles that he penned as a columnist for the Daily Nebraskan *in the spring of 1998. Zmarzly has since graduated with a B.A. in English and speech communications.*

Somewhere since the beginning of life, things have changed in the   3
male world. The first man in history was never told that if he displayed emotion he would be looked down on. His life was one of
emotion and love. To be a man in today's society is difficult. A male
must be successful in work and family. To be masculine is to be physically and emotionally strong. Somewhere along these guidelines,
emotional strength became emotional suppression.

Let's take a survey to prove my point. I want everyone who has   4
cried in the last year to raise his or her hands. (For those of you who
have actually raised your hand, this is a rhetorical thing. Put them
down.)

Why aren't there more males represented? Two simple reasons: 5
guys rarely cry, and those who do, don't want the ridicule of their
friends. Crying is just an obvious emotional expression. The thing
that most concerns me is the loss of the ability to express oneself
emotionally, especially to a woman.

> Males become so accustomed to masking their true emotions that it seems like second nature.

Males become so accustomed to   6
masking their true emotions that it seems
like second nature. At this point, the male
behavior goes from unhealthy to dangerous. You begin to not care about women
and finally fail to see them as people. It is
easier to use a woman for physical means
as opposed to actually caring for one. This
behavior is common among males, but the effect is amplified when in
a primarily male setting, such as a fraternity.

I love my fraternity and always will. Joining was the best decision   7
I have ever made, and I will always cherish the memories I have there
and the experience I will take away from it. That said, fraternity life
can lead to the destructive lifestyle that I have described above.

For those of you who are now marching up Greek row trying to   8
close down the remaining fraternities, allow me to clarify my position. A fraternity is not a breeding ground for guys who use women.
Some of my closest brothers have been with the same woman all
though college and are getting married in the summer.

On the other hand, some of my closest brothers never last more   9
than two weeks with the same woman, but these behaviors stem from
personal choice, not group affiliation. As a group, fraternities attempt
to teach respect toward women. I don't think you will find one
pledge program on campus where this is not a goal, but somewhere

between group execution and individual attitude, this goal falls short. In the end, the fraternity simply provides males with the opportunity to use women, in the way of social functions, social skills, and ample occasions to meet women.

The sad truth of the situation is that this type of behavior can   10
flourish in any primarily male group. Let me give you an example. Let's say five guys are sitting around in a room. One has a drinking problem, one comes from a broken family, one is getting kicked out of the university with a 0.6, one works in a porn shop, and one has a girlfriend. Which one gets made fun of the most?

Obviously, the one with the girlfriend will be the target. He will   11
receive taunts and whipping sounds from his friends. A male's tendency toward treating women poorly does increase when faced day in and day out with this kind of pressure. You lose sight of the fact that this friend of yours truly cares for a woman, and all you see is a "whipped little boy."

For those men out there who are frantically writing a response to   12
my column to prove to women that all guys aren't bastards, please grant me a small favor. Go take a close look in the mirror and ask yourself some questions. Have you ever dogged on one of your friends for being "whipped"? Have you made yourself emotionally available to every woman that you've dated? Have you ever made a degrading remark about a woman? Ask yourself these questions, and then pick that pen back up if you think I'm wrong.

This is not an attempt to condone or justify this type of behavior.   13
Males, myself included, have fallen off of the path of good intentions and must try to correct this behavior. It would be nice to say that there is a cure or a method to stop this destructive behavior, but there is no such twelve-step program. If the men out there can look at this as a warning and not a how-to guide, then I think it's a step in the right direction. The only real cure for this behavior is a woman.

One day all of the guarding will cease, and a woman will be al-   14
lowed in to see what true masculinity should be.

Vocabulary/Using a Dictionary

1. The words *complement* (para. 1) and *compliment* are often confused, perhaps because they do come from the same Latin word — a word that means "fill up, finish, or fulfill." In what

ways do *complement* ("make whole") and *compliment* ("praise") fulfill or fill up something or someone?

2. Discuss the irony of Zmarzly's use of the word *flourish* (para. 10), which is a synonym for "flower." Do you think the irony was intended?

3. What other definition of *execution* (para. 9) do you know of? How do you think the two meanings are connected?

Responding to Words in Context

1. Can you define *ridicule* based on Zmarzly's use of it in paragraph 5?

2. Zmarzly uses the noun form of *males* to describe men (paras. 3, 5, 6, 9, 11, 13) but never *females* to describe women. What do you think is the reason for this difference? What is the effect of it?

Discussing Main Point and Meaning

1. What biblical story does Zmarzly use to begin his article? Why do you think he chose to begin this way?

2. What point is Zmarzly trying to make about men and emotion?

3. According to Zmarzly, if five young men, all with different notable characteristics, were in the same room, which one would get "made fun of the most" (para. 10)? Why?

4. What is Zmarzly's solution to men's inability to express their emotions?

Examining Sentences, Paragraphs, and Organization

1. How does the last sentence in paragraph 9 clarify the point Zmarzly makes about fraternities?

2. How does Zmarzly anticipate and address possible objections to his argument in paragraph 12? Does he do this effectively?

3. Why does Zmarzly feel the need to write, in paragraph 13, that his is "not an attempt to condone or justify this behavior"?

4. In this article, Zmarzly moves from modern definitions of masculinity to the effect of peer pressure on men to a call for change. Is the structure effective? Why or why not?

Thinking Critically

1. This article is almost wholly directed toward the behavior of men, but in the final sentence of paragraph 13, Zmarzly writes that "the only real cure for this behavior is a woman." How is the reader to interpret this statement? Does it follow logically from the previous arguments? Why or why not?

2. Why, according to this author, is emotional expression more healthy than emotional suppression? Do you agree? Why or why not?

In-Class Writing Activities

1. In small groups, prepare a short skit that illustrates an emotionally "healthy" conversation among several young men about their girlfriends or between a couple about their relationship.

2. Pick a characteristic often thought to be undesirable in women (for example, aggression or competitiveness) in the way that emotionality is thought to be undesirable in men. Write a similar plea to women for change, expressing both sympathy for and criticism of women who conform to limiting social expectations.

_____

OPPOSING VIEWS

When Coaches Conspire to Set a Record

Before You Read

On February 22, 1998, an incident on a basketball court made front-page national news. Nykesha Sales, an injured star player for the University of Connecticut women's team, was allowed an uncontested basket by the opposing team so that she could break the school's scoring record. Before you read the following opposing views on the controversial play, consider this question: Do gender differences cause male and female athletes to compete differently?

Words to Learn
[Samuels]

endemic (para. 2): particular to (adj.)
credence (para. 3): belief in, acceptance of (n.)

Words to Learn
[Collins]

arbiter (para. 1): judge, one in charge of decision-making (n.)

patronizing (para. 2): condescendingly complimentary, looking down on (adj.)

paternalistic (para. 2): providing for needs without giving responsibility to (adj.)

muss (para. 2): make untidy (v.)

ad hoc (para. 2): improvised, designed for the situation at hand (adj.)

DOROTHY J. SAMUELS

A Shot Against Women's Sports

[THE NEW YORK TIMES / February 27, 1998]

Nykesha Sales is a terrific basketball player and, by all accounts,   1
a terrific person. But that hardly justifies the elaborate rigging that allowed Ms. Sales, the University of Connecticut's injured star forward, to limp down the court to score an uncontested basket during a game on Tuesday with Villanova, thereby breaking her school's scoring record. Some record. It will go down as a two-point shot that set back women's sports. The only record broken was for poor judgment.

Sure, it was sad when it looked as if a ruptured Achilles tendon   2
would end Ms. Sales's college playing career just one point shy of the school record. But disappointments are endemic to competition, and learning to roll with them is an important lesson sports can teach.

DOROTHY J. SAMUELS (b. 1951), a graduate of Bryn Mawr College and Northeastern University School of Law, is a member of the New York Times Editorial Board. She resides in New York City with her husband and three sports-minded children.

Clearly the opposing coaches, players, referees and officials who conspired to let Ms. Sales score meant well. But by handing her a tainted record, they managed to detract from her impressive accomplishments and gave fresh credence to harmful stereotypes just as women's sports are beginning to get more respect. 3

Some record. It will go down as a two-point shot that set back women's sports.

"Males are made up differently from women," said Michael Tranghese, commissioner of the Big East Conference, to explain why he had approved the gift point to Ms. Sales, though he would not have approved the same thing for a male athlete. Unlike men, he explained, "women break down" and "get emotional." That kind of "sensitivity" should be outmoded by now — and not only on the basketball court. 4

GAIL COLLINS

A Sweet Moment of Teamwork

[THE NEW YORK TIMES / February 27, 1998]

College basketball, at least as played by women, is still school sports — athletics as part of the learning experience. One lesson it teaches is that the score is a stern arbiter that does not always give worthy players their just rewards. But another is that individual achievement is useless without cooperation. Nykesha Sales is a notably unselfish player. Had she hogged the ball more often, she could undoubtedly have broken the record before she was injured. 1

Journalist GAIL COLLINS *was a financial reporter at United Press International and a columnist at* New York Newsday *and the* New York Daily News *before joining the editorial board at the* New York Times *in 1995. Collins is the recipient of an Associated Press award for commentary, and her articles have appeared in* New York Magazine, The Nation, Ladies' Home Journal, *and* Ms. *She is the author of* Scorpion Tongues: Gossip, Celebrity, and American Politics *(1998).*

In organizing a special opportunity for her to sink one final basket, her coach and teammates paid tribute to the importance of teamwork.

Part of the reaction against the incident has to do with the fact   2
that it involves women and that giving a female player an extra shot somehow seems patronizing. Certainly the conference's commissioner could not have sounded more paternalistic if he had instituted a penalty for hair-mussing. But male players have also arranged to let a much-admired teammate set a much-deserved record — usually in ad hoc efforts by an individual player, like the time Denny McClain set up Mickey Mantle for a record home run.

> It was a once-in-a-lifetime gesture, a sweet moment of teamwork to celebrate a team player.

In Ms. Sales's case, everyone worked together. Even the former holder of the UConn record gave her blessing.

Letting Nykesha Sales win her school's scoring title is not going   3
to turn the Eastern Conference into the World Wide Wrestling Federation. It was a once-in-a-lifetime gesture, a sweet moment of teamwork to celebrate a team player.

Vocabulary/Using a Dictionary

1. A patron is a sponsor, benefactor, or customer. How do you think the current use of *patronizing* (Collins, para. 2) developed?

2. Is a paternal parent a mother or a father? How is this meaning related to the adjective form *paternalistic* (Collins, para. 2)?

3. Look up *credo* and *credibility*. How are they related to *credence* (Samuels, para. 3)?

Responding to Words in Context

1. In her second paragraph, Collins moves from describing the conference commissioner as *patronizing* to calling him *paternalistic*. How does this shift amplify Collins's meaning?

2. How would you have discerned the meaning of *endemic* (Samuels, para. 2) if you had not been provided with its definition? What is the root of the word? What other words share the same root?

Discussing Main Point and Meaning

1. What problem almost prevented Nykesha Sales from breaking UConn's scoring record?

2. How did the Big East basketball commissioner explain his decision to approve the uncontested basket?

3. What does Collins argue was the point in organizing the opportunity for Sales to break the record?

4. What is the other example Collins gives of a record-breaking set-up by male athletes? Why does she give this example?

Examining Sentences, Paragraphs, and Organization

1. How does Samuels compliment Sales in her opening statement? What effect does the compliment have on your understanding of the essay?

2. Samuels quotes Michael Tranghese (para. 4), but Collins gives only a descriptive paraphrase of his statements (para. 2). Why do you think the authors use the same material differently?

3. Compare and contrast the two authors' final paragraphs in terms of tone.

Thinking Critically

1. Samuels argues that the Sales episode will give "fresh credence to harmful stereotypes" (para. 3) of women as emotional and non-competitive. Do emotionality and generosity necessarily have negative connotations? Is the substance of those stereotypes harmful, or is it just the interpretation of that substance that is harmful?

2. "Even the former holder of the UConn record gave her blessing," Collins explains. If the issue in the Sales case is fair competition, is the former record holder's opinion valid evidence?

In-Class Writing Activities

1. Pick an issue similar to the one at the heart of this controversy — an issue related to fairness. For example, think about how teachers often let students drop their lowest grade or how prisoners

sometimes get early release for good behavior. Write two paragraphs about the issue — one supporting the adherence to rules and requirements at all costs and one arguing that exceptions are occasionally appropriate.

2.   Neither of these viewpoints really addresses the opposing team's (Villanova's) cooperation in Sales's uncontested basket. Write a statement for the press from the opposing team, explaining its position on the issue.

From the Bookshelf

Mary Pipher, *Reviving Ophelia*

Not all books that reach number one on the New York Times *bestseller list are thrillers, diet plans, or celebrity profiles. Sometimes a serious study captures the attention of millions of readers. A recent example of such a book is Mary Pipher's* Reviving Ophelia: Saving the Selves of Adolescent Girls, *a moving account of the special difficulties faced by today's adolescent girl. From years of clinical experience, Pipher has concluded that we live in a "girl-poisoning" society that stifles and undervalues young women. In* Reviving Ophelia *she adroitly weaves together the personal voices of the many girls she has interviewed with her own cultural and sociological commentary. Although her account is not a happy one, Pipher offers a number of insightful strategies that will enable girls to develop their capabilities and reach their full potential as human beings. Mary Pipher holds a Ph.D. in psychology and is a clinical psychologist with a practice in Lincoln, Nebraska. She is also the author of* Hunger Pains: The American Woman's Tragic Quest for Thinness *(1985) and* The Shelter of Each Other: Rebuilding Our Families *(1997).*

What Happens to Adolescent Girls?
Something dramatic happens to girls in early adolescence. Just as planes and ships disappear mysteriously into the Bermuda Triangle, so do the selves of girls go down in droves. They crash and burn in a social and developmental Bermuda Triangle. In early adolescence, studies show that girls' IQ scores drop and their math and science scores plummet. They lose their resiliency and optimism and become less curious and inclined to take risks. They lose their assertive, ener-

getic, and "tomboyish" personalities and become more deferential, self-critical, and depressed. They report great unhappiness with their own bodies.

Psychology documents but does not explain the crashes. Girls who rushed to drink in experiences in enormous gulps sit quietly in the corner. Writers such as Sylvia Plath, Margaret Atwood, and Olive Schreiner have described the wreckage. Diderot, in writing to his young friend Sophie Volland, described his observations harshly: "You all die at 15."

Fairy tales capture the essence of this phenomenon. Young women eat poisoned apples or prick their fingers with poisoned needles and fall asleep for a hundred years. They wander away from home, encounter great dangers, are rescued by princes, and are transformed into passive and docile creatures.

Pipher, Mary. *Reviving Ophelia: Saving the Selves of Adolescent Girls.* New York: G. P. Putnam, 1994. Ballantine Books Paperback, 1995.

Discussing the Unit

Suggested Topic for Discussion

The essays in this unit offer different opinions on the ways that men and women are treated and behave in our society. Christina Hoff Sommers argues that young women aren't in as much trouble as some feminist scholars say they are, whereas Mark Zmarzly holds that men are worse off than they're allowed to admit. Dorothy Samuels and Gail Collins weigh in on a controversial incident in women's basketball. Do you think that male and female behaviors are judged by different standards in our society? Do you expect women to behave differently than men? How so? Describe an experience in which you felt that your behavior was judged by gender alone.

Preparing for Class Discussion

1. None of the essays in this unit seems to question the assumption that men and women are inherently different in their behavior. Mark Zmarzly argues that men and women should try to be more alike in some ways; Christina Hoff Sommers, Dorothy J. Samuels, and Gail Collins all examine how society interprets male and female differences. Do you think that gender differences should be given automatic credence? Are individual personality differences more significant than generalized gender distinctions?

2. Only Mark Zmarzly argues that being emotional (having more traditionally feminine traits) is a positive and enriching human characteristic. Why is emotion often considered to be inferior to logic, rationality, or empirical evidence as a way of knowing? Do you think that emotion is as valid as rationality?

From Discussion to Writing

1. Make a list of your major personality traits — both positive and negative. Then assign each of those traits a gender — that is, decide whether each trait is considered more masculine or more feminine by society. Do you generally fall into one category or another? Do most of the items on your list match your actual gender?

2. The media, especially the television and film industries, are often accused of exploiting all kinds of stereotypes. Pick a favorite television show or movie, and write a comparative character analysis, choosing one male character and one female character. Use the articles in this unit as source material or to help you establish a vocabulary for your analysis.

3. Some feminists and cultural critics argue that gender is learned — that babies are taught from a young age to be boys or girls and do not have innate gendered tendencies. Others argue that biology determines gender and that males and females become who they are because of natural instincts. Write an essay defending one of these positions, using your own experiences for illustration. Feel free to bring in outside knowledge from psychology, sociology, or other fields related to this question.

Topics for Cross-Cultural Discussion

1. In some cultures it is perfectly acceptable for men to show emotion and even to cry in public. Do you know of any examples? Does your family come from a tradition that has absolute gender roles or that allows more gender variability? Discuss how cultural expectations or values contribute to gender differences, in your own culture as well as others you know about.

2. Do you think that American culture is more fixated on gender differences or on ethnic and racial differences? In your experience, are you more often treated in a way that is based on assumptions about your gender or about your ethnic background? Why do think this is so? Do you think answers to these questions will vary from person to person? Why or why not?

5

How Important Is
Group Identity?

How important is race, gender, class, age, ethnic heritage, or sexual orientation to someone's sense of self? Aren't we all separate individuals first, with our own complicated personal histories, and group members second? And since each of us belongs to more than one group, how do we determine which groups matter most to our identity? Imagine, for example, an affluent retired female African American trial lawyer who is the grandmother of eight, maintains close ties to the Baptist church, is active in the Democratic Party, and is president of her local gardener's club. How might she rank her various identities in order of importance? Is it even possible to do so?

In "Kicking Away Your Freedom," the *Newsweek* columnist Meg Greenfield wonders why so many people seem eager to surrender their individuality and conform to group stereotypes. As she argues: "To let yourself be transformed into the emblem of some cause, any cause, or demographic category and to draw your identity and take your marching orders from it is to kick away your freedom, your independence, and your individuality." Yet can't group identities also be liberating and fun? Yale student Henry Han Xi Lau thinks so in "I Was a Member of the Kung Fu Crew." "Chinatown is ghetto, my friends are ghetto, I am ghetto," he claims as he celebrates a particular culture and a community.

Is it possible to resist group classification entirely? In "They've Got to Be Carefully Taught," Susan Brady Konig offers a humorous

78

look at her daughter's preschool "Cultural Diversity Month," where ethnic diversity is insisted on: "Then I get up to teach the children an indigenous folk tune from the culture of Sarah's people, passed down through the generations from her grandparents to her parents and now to Sarah — a song called 'Take Me Out to the Ballgame.'"

MEG GREENFIELD

Kicking Away Your Freedom

[NEWSWEEK / March 23, 1998]

Before You Read

What do you think it means to represent a particular group of people? For example, if you are African American, does that mean that all other African Americans think, believe, and behave exactly as you do? If that doesn't seem possible, then can you explain how any individual (such as a blue-collar worker, a woman, or a disabled person) can be said to *represent* any large group of people?

Words to Learn

embodiment (para. 1): bodily form (n.)
reflexive (para. 3): directed or turned back on itself (adj.)
indignant (para. 3): feeling strong displeasure at something considered unjust (adj.)

advocacy (para. 3): support (n.)
manifesto (para. 3): public declaration of intentions, opinions, or purposes (n.)
recourse (para. 4): source of help or protection (n.)

MEG GREENFIELD *(b. 1930), a native of Seattle who lives in Washington, D.C., has been with the* Washington Post *since 1968, and is its editorial page editor. Greenfield writes a weekly national news column at the* Post *and also contributes a biweekly column at* Newsweek. *She has won a Pulitzer Prize for editorial writing.*

inexorable (para. 4): unyielding, unalterable (adj.)

anthropological (para. 4): pertaining to the science of human beings (adj.)

idiosyncratic (para. 4): having a habit peculiar to an individual (adj.)

constituency (para. 5): voters in an electoral district (n.)

emblem (para. 6): symbol, badge (n.)

demographic (para. 6): relating to the statistical study of the human population (adj.)

automaton (para. 7): robot (n.)

The 1960s civil rights legislation and court rulings were meant 1
to end official segregation and discourage discrimination against individuals on the basis of their group characteristics, principally race and gender but eventually other characteristics as well. A lot of this has been accomplished. What is odd is that over precisely the same time period and in part as a consequence of the change, more and more people seem to be regarding themselves and behaving as embodiments of one of these groups, rather than as individual free agents who put things together in their own unique, unpredictable, unprogrammed way. Their moral outlook, their understanding of their obligations and entitlements and interests in life, and their notions of how they should be treated are more and more determined by what they now see themselves as *representing* rather than by their own individual instincts and tastes.

> To let yourself be transformed into the emblem of some cause . . . and to draw your identity and take your marching orders from it is to kick away your freedom.

Family, clan, and tribal loyalty are, of course, as old as human 2
history. And so, too, is the inclination to form secret orders, exclusive organizations, fraternal lodges, and the rest that create fierce new allegiances and ideas of who one is and, accordingly, what rights and duties (and licenses to assault or repress) flow from that. As long ago as the Roman Empire, teams of young men competing at sports in the Hippodrome and designated the Blues and the Greens generated such intense support from the populace that long after their days of competition had ended, large parts of the citizenry continued to identify themselves as either Blues or Greens and battled each other as "civic factions." People would claim to be either one or the other and may not even have known the origin of the sides.

As reflexive as this is, it seems to me as nothing to the instinctive, 3
mindless, instantaneous re-creation of the individual as the representative of a group (generally oppressed) that sillies up our public relationships today. I think of the day I was backing my car out of the
garage and looked first to the right and then to the left, where an indignant seventeen- or eighteen-year-old jogger was glaring into the
open window and clearly trying to tell me that I was a careless old
fool who could have hit him. If only he had said that, I would have
known how to respond, a simple apology; we'd have had a proper
reckoning between two actual people. But this is what he said, in a
resentful, snappish sort of way: "You know, people coming down the
street on *this* side of your garage are entitled to consideration, too."
What? Who were these people? There was no one in sight for blocks.
Did they have an advocacy group? Did they meet at night and draft
manifestos? What was I supposed to reply? "Well, you people coming down the street from east to west are getting way *out of line*"? I
just smiled in a pained sort of way and let him mutter off to resume
his morning run.

This was in the 1980s. What had become by then so ingrained a 4
habit of mind that even a teenage twerp had instant recourse to it got
its start in the late 1960s, I think, for a combination of reasons. One
obvious one was that the necessary mechanics of trying to achieve integration of institutions previously segregated by race inevitably involved making judgments based on race so as to measure progress,
spot obstruction, and so forth. But I think at least as important was
the gradual but inexorable recasting of so much of what had once
been private experience as public experience. Relationships between
men and women that were once interpreted in personal terms were
now interpreted politically or in a kind of coldly clinical, anthropological way. Everything was now an "issue" to be debated and resolved, an "issue" that was presumed to be common to all such relationships, not an idiosyncratic, special thing.

There is a terrible draining of vitality and mutual respect from all 5
relationships that give way to this temptation to stereotype, and it is
worsened when both parties indulge it — as distinct from one of
them doing the stereotyping and the other protesting it. I'm not
thinking so much of all the one-on-one personal or workplace connections now as of the essential connection of political leader to constituency. If you see yourself primarily as a representative of some
category of persons and that category takes precedence over all else,
you will be so treated by your bosses and political leaders. They will

know exactly what it takes to appease you. They will know exactly how they can "deliver" you, and generally they will be right.

To let yourself be transformed into the emblem of some cause, any cause, or demographic category and to draw your identity and take your marching orders from it is to kick away your freedom, your independence, and your individuality. It is to suspend all these and basically to lose your influence over events that matter to you. You will find you have forgotten how to speak out with views that do not conform to those of the group or that you will have been led not to trust such views. You will see life through a very narrow lens and be very much in the control of those who do the defining of the group interest. Our society and our political culture are mired in a lot of this right now. For it is not just ourselves that we tend to think of as mainly representative of some group. We have also allowed others to revise our history and philosophy and literature by the same standard. The principles of representation of a faction or a side or a group take precedence.

The Blues versus the Greens. My side, right or wrong. We don't break with the party line. Even a little bit. It would endanger our side. When people in this country reverse the trend of thinking of themselves as embattled and victimized representatives of pedestrians traversing the street from left to right — or was it right to left? — they will have time to recall and recapture the pleasures of thinking and judging and reacting for themselves, and seeing others as they are as well, not as automatons predictably representing this group or that. They will complicate and probably improve the politicians' behavior by doing so. There's nothing so dangerous for manipulators as people who think for themselves.

Vocabulary/Using a Dictionary

1. What word is *manifesto* (para. 3) similar to? What is the origin of the word? What was the original meaning of the word?

2. In paragraph 4, the author speaks of "an 'issue' that was presumed to be common to all relationships, not an idiosyncratic, special thing." What does *idiosyncratic* mean? What is an idiosyncrasy? How does Greenfield apply it to human relationships?

3. Several difficult vocabulary terms come together when Greenfield writes "the necessary mechanics of trying to achieve integration of institutions previously segregated by race inevitably involved

making judgments based on race so as to measure progress" (para. 4). Can you rephrase the author's statement in simpler terms?

Responding to Words in Context

1. You probably won't find *sillies* (para. 3) in the dictionary. What does it mean? What word is it formed from? Can you substitute a different word with a similar meaning? Have you experienced something that sillies up a relationship in your own life?

2. Greenfield writes that "our society and our political culture are mired" (para. 6) in a struggle between the independence of the individual and those people who do the defining of the group interest. Looking at the word *mired* in this context, what do you believe it means?

Discussing Main Point and Meaning

1. What is the problem that Greenfield argues can "kick away your freedom" (para. 6)?

2. How does the author's use of the example of the Hippodrome help illustrate her point that in modern America, the individual is re-created as the representative of a group (para. 2)?

3. The author "smiled in a pained sort of way" (para. 3) at the jogger who said, "You know, people coming down the street on *this* side of your garage are entitled to consideration, too" (para. 3). Why did she respond in this way? In what way does the jogger's comment illustrate Greenfield's main point?

4. Looking at the concluding paragraphs of the essay, do you feel that Greenfield includes herself as a person who lets herself "be transformed into the emblem of some cause, any cause, or demographic category" (para. 6)?

Examining Sentences, Paragraphs, and Organization

1. What is the topic sentence in paragraph 5? In this paragraph, to whom do the repeated pronouns *them* and *they* refer?

2. Is there a change in the writer's tone between the first paragraph and the last one? If so, how would you characterize the change?

3. Greenfield repeats in almost every paragraph the idea that people see themselves "behaving as embodiments of . . . groups." How does the author change the style in which she relates this idea to the reader?

Thinking Critically

1. Do you agree with Greenfield's statement that in modern America, individuals are being re-created "as the representative of a group" (para. 3)? Why or why not? Support your argument.

2. "There's nothing so dangerous for manipulators as people who think for themselves," Greenfield declares in the last sentence of the essay. Do you agree with this motto? Do you feel that you are in danger of being manipulated by politicians? Are people who think for themselves considered dangerous by politicians?

In-Class Writing Activities

1. We classify and categorize others every day according to where they come from and how they talk, walk, look, and speak. Often we do not recognize ourselves as being representative of stereotypical categories. Take a close look at yourself, brainstorm, and list the different groups you belong to.

2. In this essay, Greenfield discusses the negative aspects of adopting a group identity, stating that "to let yourself be transformed into the emblem of some cause . . . and to draw your identity and take your marching orders from it is to kick away your freedom" (para. 6). Write a short essay describing a time you stood up for a cause you believed in, and explain whether you felt a loss of freedom or liberty because of the stand you took.

From the Bookshelf

Henry Louis Gates Jr., Colored People

"I am not Everynegro," says Henry Louis Gates Jr. in his award-winning memoir, Colored People. *"I am not native to the great black metropolises: New York, Chicago, or Los Angeles, say. Nor can I claim to be a 'citizen of the world.' I am from and of a time and place — Piedmont, West Virginia — and that's a world apart, a world of difference." In this highly celebrated childhood autobiography, one of America's most prominent literary critics revisits his roots and commemorates a now largely vanished community. In doing so, Gates sensitively explores the complexity of an African American identity, as can be observed in the following brief excerpt from the book's preface, which is addressed to his two young daughters.*

A summa cum laude graduate of Yale University in history who also holds a Ph.D. in English from Cambridge University, Henry Louis Gates Jr. is currently the W.E.B. Du Bois Professor of the Humanities and Chair of the Department of Afro-American Studies at Harvard University. The author of several books of criticism, Gates writes frequently for The New Yorker *magazine.*

A Conflict of Identity

I want to be able to take special pride in a Jessye Norman aria, a Muhammad Ali shuffle, a Michael Jordan slam dunk, a Spike Lee movie, a Thurgood Marshall opinion, a Toni Morrison novel, James Brown's Camel Walk. Above all, I enjoy the unself-conscious moments of a shared cultural intimacy, whatever form they take, when no one else is watching, when no white people are around. Like Joe Louis's fights, which my father still talks about as part of the fixed repertoire of stories that texture our lives. You've seen his eyes shining as he describes how Louis hit Max Schmeling so many times and so hard, and how some reporter asked him, after the fight: "Joe, what would you have done if that last punch hadn't knocked Schmeling out?" And how ole Joe responded, without missing a beat: "I'da run around behind him to see what was holdin' him up!"

Even so, I rebel at the notion that I can't be part of other groups, that I can't construct identities through elective affinity, that race must be the most important thing about me. Is that what I want on my gravestone: Here lies an African American? So I'm divided. I want to be black, to know black, to luxuriate in whatever I might be calling blackness at any particular time — but to do so in order to come out the

continued on next page

---

continued from previous page

other side, to experience a humanity that is neither colorless nor re-
ducible to color. Bach *and* James Brown. Sushi *and* fried catfish. Part of
me admires those people who can say with a straight face that they have
transcended any attachment to a particular community or group . . . but
I always want to run around behind them to see what holds them up.

Gates, Henry Louis Jr. *Colored People: A Memoir.* New York: Knopf, 1994.

HENRY HAN XI LAU

I Was a Member of the Kung Fu Crew

[THE NEW YORK TIMES MAGAZINE / October 19, 1997]

Before You Read

In what ways can group identity be liberating and empowering? In
what ways does it encourage uniformity and conformity? In what
ways can it set different groups at odds with each other?

Words to Learn

ghetto (para. 1): section of a city
inhabited predominantly by
members of a minority
group (n.)

kung fu (para. 1): Chinese martial
art based on the use of fluid
movements of the arms and
legs (n.)

karaoke (para. 3): singing along to
prerecorded music (n.)

amble (para. 4): go at a slow, easy
pace (v.)

asymmetrical (para. 5): lacking correspondence in size, form, and
arrangement of parts (adj.)

HENRY HAN XI LAU *(b. 1978) grew up in New York City's Chinatown
and now lives in Sunset Park, Brooklyn. He is a junior at Yale University,
where he is majoring in history and international studies. Lau wrote this
piece, which is part of a longer essay, for his freshman composition course at
Yale. This is his first publication.*

stalemate (para. 8): deadlock, situation permitting no further
progress (v.)

articulate (para. 10): express
clearly (v.)

Chinatown is ghetto, my friends are ghetto, I am ghetto. I went   1
away to college last year, but I still have a long strand of hair that
reaches past my chin. I need it when I go back home to hang with the
K.F.C. — for Kung Fu Crew, not Kentucky Fried Chicken. We all
met in a Northern Shaolin kung fu class years ago. Our *si-fu* was
Rocky. He told us: "In the early 1900s in China, your grand master
was walking in the streets when a foreigner riding on a horse disre-
spected him. So then he felt the belly of the horse with his palms and
left. Shortly thereafter, the horse buckled and died because our grand
master had used *qi-gong* to mess up the horse's internal organs."
Everyone said, "Cool, I would like to do that." Rocky emphasized,
"You've got to practice really hard for a long time to reach that level."

By the time my friends and I were in the eighth grade, we were   2
able to do twenty-plus pushups on our knuckles and fingers. When
we practiced our crescent, roundhouse, and tornado kicks, we had
10-pound weights strapped to our legs. Someone once remarked,
"Goddamn — that's a freaking mountain!" when he saw my thigh
muscles in gym class.

Most Chinatown kids fall into a few general categories. There are   3
pale-faced nerds who study all the time to get into the Ivies. There are
the recent immigrants with uncombed hair and crooked teeth who
sing karaoke in bars. There are the punks with highlighted hair who
cut school and the gangsters, whom everyone else avoids.

Then there is the K.F.C. We work hard like the nerds, but we   4
identify with the punks. Now we are reunited, and just as in the old
days we amble onto Canal Street, where we stick out above the older
folks, elderly women bearing leaden bags of bok choy and oranges.
As an opposing crew nears us, I assess them to determine whether to
grill them or not. Grilling is the fine art of staring others down and
trying to emerge victorious.

How the hair is worn is important in determining one's order on   5
the streets. In the 1980s, the dominant style was the mushroom cut,
combed neatly or left wild in the front so that a person can appear
menacing as he peers through his bangs. To gain an edge in grilling
now, some kids have asymmetrical cuts, with long random strands
sprouting in the front, sides, or back. Some dye their hair blue or
green, while blood red is usually reserved for gang members.

Only a few years ago, examination of the hair was sufficient. But   6
now there is a second step: assessing pants. A couple of years ago,
wide legs first appeared in New York City, and my friends and I
switched from baggy pants. In the good old days, Merry-Go-Round
in the Village sold wide legs for only $15 a pair. When Merry-Go-
Round went bankrupt, Chinatown kids despaired. Wide-leg prices at
other stores increased drastically as they became more popular. There
are different ways of wearing wide legs. Some fold their pant legs in-
ward and staple them at the hem. Some clip the back ends of their
pants to their shoes with safety pins. Others simply cut the bottoms
so that fuzzy strings hang out.

We grill the opposing punks. I untuck my long strand of hair so   7
that it swings in front of my face. Nel used to have a strand, but he
chewed it off one day in class by accident. Chu and Tom cut their
strands off because it scared people at college. Jack has a patch of
blond hair, while Tone's head is a ball of orange flame. Chi has gelled
short hair, while Ken's head is a black
mop. As a group, we have better hair than
our rivals. But they beat us with their
wide legs. In our year away at college,
wide legs have gone beyond our 24-inch
leg openings. Twenty-six to 30-inch jeans
are becoming the norm. If wide legs get any bigger, they will start flying up like a skirt in an updraft.

> Chinatown is ghetto, my
> friends are ghetto, I am
> ghetto.

We have better accessories, though. Chi sports a red North Face   8
that gives him a rugged mountain-climber look because of the jungle
of straps sprouting in the back. Someone once asked Chi, "Why is the
school bag so important to one's cool?" He responded, "Cuz it's the
last thing others see when you walk away from them or when they
turn back to look at you after you walk past them." But the other
crew has female members, which augments their points. The encounter between us ends in a stalemate. But at least the K.F.C. members are in college and are not true punks.

In the afternoon, we decide to eat at the Chinatown McDonald's   9
for a change instead of the Chinese bakery Maria's, our dear old hang-
out spot. "Mickey D's is good sit," Nel says. I answer: "But the Whopper gots more fat and meat. It's even got more bun." Nel agrees. "True
that," he says. I want the Big Mac, but I buy the two-cheeseburger meal
because it has the same amount of meat but costs less.

We sit and talk about ghettoness again. We can never exactly ar-   10
ticulate what being ghetto entails, but we know the spirit of it. In
Chinatown toilet facilities we sometimes find footprints on the seats

because F.O.B.'s (fresh off the boats) squat on them as they do over the holes in China. We see alternative brand names in stores like Dolo instead of Polo, and Mike instead of Nike.

We live by ghettoness. My friends and I walk from 80-something   11
Street in Manhattan to the tip of the island to save a token. We gorge ourselves at Gray's Papaya because the hot dogs are 50 cents each. But one cannot be stingy all the time. We leave good tips at Chinese restaurants because our parents are waiters and waitresses, too.

We sit for a long time in McDonald's, making sure that there is   12
at least a half-inch of soda in our cups so that when the staff wants to kick us out, we can claim that we are not finished yet. Jack positions a mouse bite of cheeseburger in the center of a wrapper to support our claim.

After a few hours, the K.F.C. prepares to disband. I get in one of   13
the no-license commuter vans on Canal Street that will take me to Sunset Park in Brooklyn, where my family lives now. All of my friends will leave Chinatown, for the Upper East Side and the Lower East Side, Forest Hills in Queens and Bensonhurst in Brooklyn. We live far apart, but we always come back together in Chinatown. For most of us, our homes used to be here and our world was here.

Vocabulary/Using a Dictionary

1. What is the function of the letter *a* in *asymmetrical* (para. 5)? Name a few other words that use this prefix in a similar way.

2. Describe what singing *karaoke* (para. 3) means. What language does it come from? What is the origin of the term?

3. *Kung fu* (para. 1) and *karaoke* come from different languages. What language does *kung fu* come from? How was the word formed?

Responding to Words in Context

1. The word *ghettoness* (para. 10, 11) appears in the essay. What do you think the writer means when he uses the term? What clues can you find in the essay that will support your conclusion?

2. Lau relates a second step involved in *grilling* (para. 4) other "punks" on the street — *assessing* pants. By looking at how Lau describes the experience, what do you think is the definition of the word *assessing*?

Discussing Main Point and Meaning

1. What did the title suggest to you before reading the essay? After finishing the essay and on reflection, do you interpret the title any differently?

2. How does the author describe the category that his K.F.C. (para. 1) belongs to in Chinatown? What other kinds of groups are there? Do you think Lau believes his group is superior to the others? Why or why not?

3. How does Lau describe the conditions in Chinatown? How does Chinatown affect the identity of the K.F.C. (para. 1)?

4. What does the author mean in the last sentence of his final paragraph? Try putting his thoughts into your own words.

Examining Sentences, Paragraphs, and Organization

1. Why does Lau begin the essay with a story related by his *si-fu* Rocky? What effect does this narrative have on our understanding of the author's experience?

2. Throughout the essay, why does the author repeat phrases such as "We all met" (para. 1), "we practiced" (para. 2), "We work hard," "we are reunited," "we amble onto," and "we stick out" (all para. 4)? Why does Lau constantly refer to himself in the plural?

3. Why does the author include the short biographical account of his trip to a McDonald's restaurant toward the end of the essay? How does this anecdote help to reinforce Lau's main idea?

Thinking Critically

1. In paragraph 11 the author states "We live by ghettoness." Do you think that Lau's essay accurately defines what he refers to as *ghettoness?*

2. Do you agree with the behavioral code that is exemplified throughout the essay by Lau and his Kung Fu Crew?

In-Class Writing Activities

1. Lau hints that Chinatown is a place that he can return to and be reminded of his roots — to become closer to a place that helped

shape his identity when he was younger. Do you have a place like this you can visit? Write a short essay in which you discuss a place that shaped your identity and define the sense of self it helped to create.

2. The author does not experience his return to Chinatown alone because he is always accompanied by the Kung Fu Crew. Throughout the essay Lau shows to his crew in Chinatown the importance of having a group identity (specifically paragraphs 5 to 8). Do you think that having a group identity is necessary in some communities? Write a brief essay stating how you feel about this idea, supporting your opinion with examples from your own life.

SUSAN BRADY KONIG

They've Got to Be Carefully Taught

[NATIONAL REVIEW / September 15, 1997]

Before You Read

Do you think the broad national emphasis on cultural and ethnic diversity can backfire and separate people rather than bring them together? Do you think it would be a good idea to begin ignoring differences and to start celebrating similarity? What would be the social benefits? What would be the disadvantages?

SUSAN BRADY KONIG *(b. 1962) was born in Paris, France, and raised in* New York City. *She received her B.A. in English from Georgetown University, her M.A. in English and American literature from New York University, and her M.F.A. in creative writing from Vermont College. Konig has been a writer for the* Washington Post *Style section and an editor at* Seventeen *magazine. She has published articles in* Ladies' Home Journal, Travel & Leisure, Us, The National Review, *and other periodicals. She currently writes an opinion column for the* New York Post *and lives in New York City.*

Words to Learn

diverse (para. 2): of various kinds, varied (adj.)

decidedly (para. 14): unquestionably, certainly (adv.)

culmination (para. 21): climax, summit (n.)

disparity (para. 21): inequality, difference (n.)

indigenous (para. 22): having originated in a particular region or environment, native (adj.)

concerted (para. 24): performed together in cooperation (adj.)

At my daughter's preschool it's time for all the children to learn that they are different from one another. Even though these kids are at that remarkable age when they are thoroughly color blind, their teachers are spending a month emphasizing race, color, and background. The little tots are being taught in no uncertain terms that their hair is different, their skin is different, and their parents come from different places. It's Cultural Diversity Month. 1

> *The little tots are being taught in no uncertain terms that their hair is different, their skin is different, and their parents come from different places. It's Cultural Diversity Month.*

I hadn't really given much thought to the ethnic and national backgrounds of Sarah's classmates. I can guarantee that Sarah, being two and a half, gave the subject absolutely no thought. Her teachers, however, had apparently given it quite a lot of thought. They sent a letter asking each parent to contribute to the cultural-awareness effort by "providing any information and/or material regarding your family's cultural background. For example: favorite recipe or song." All well and good, unless your culture isn't *diverse* enough. 2

The next day I take Sarah to school and her teacher, Miss Laura, anxious to get this Cultural Diversity show on the road, begins the interrogation. 3

"Where are you and your husband from?" she cheerily demands. 4

"We're Americans," I reply — less, I must confess, out of patriotism than from sheer lack of coffee. It was barely 9:00 A.M. 5

"Yes, of course, but where are you *from?*" I'm beginning to feel like a nightclub patron being badgered by a no-talent stand-up comic. 6

"We're native New Yorkers."   7

"But where are your *people* from?"   8

"Well," I dive in with a sigh, "my family is originally Irish on   9
both sides. My husband's father was from Czechoslovakia and his
mother is from the Bronx, but her grandparents were from the
Ukraine."

"Can you cook Irish?"   10

"I could bring in potatoes and beer for the whole class."   11

Miss Laura doesn't get it.   12

"Look," I say, "we're Americans. Our kids are Americans. We   13
tell them about American history and George Washington and apple
pie and all that stuff. If you want me to do something American, I
can do that."

She is decidedly unexcited.   14

A few days later, she tells me that she was trying to explain to   15
Sarah that her dad is from Ireland.

"Wrong," I say, "but go on."   16

"He's *not* from Ireland?"   17

No, I sigh. He's from Queens. I'm from Ireland. I mean I'm   18
Irish — that is, my great-grandparents were. Don't get me wrong, I'm
proud of my heritage — but that's entirely beside the point. I told
you we tell Sarah she's American.

"Well, anyway," she smiles, "Sarah thinks her Daddy's from *Ice-*   19
land! Isn't that cute?"

Later in the month, Miss Laura admits that her class is not   20
quite getting the whole skin-color thing. "I tried to show them how
we all have different skin," she chuckled. Apparently, little Henry
is the only one who successfully grasped the concept. He now runs
around the classroom announcing to anyone who'll listen, "I'm
white!" Miss Laura asked the children what color her own skin
was. (She is a light-skinned Hispanic, which would make her skin
color . . . what? Caramel? Mochaccino?). The kids opted for purple
or orange. "They looked at me like I was crazy!" Miss Laura said.
I just smile.

The culmination of Cultural Diversity Month, the day when the   21
parents come into class and join their children in a glorious celebration of multicultural disparity, has arrived. As I arrive I see a large
collage on the wall depicting the earth, with all the children's names
placed next to the country they are from. Next to my daughter's
name it says "Ireland." I politely remind Miss Laura that Sarah is, in

fact, from America and suggest that, by insisting otherwise, she is confusing my daughter. She reluctantly changes Sarah's affiliation to USA. It will be the only one of its kind on the wall.

The mom from Brazil brings in a bunch of great music, and the   22
whole class is doing the samba[1] and running around in a conga[2] line. It's very cute. Then I get up to teach the children an indigenous folk tune from the culture of Sarah's people, passed down through the generations from her grandparents to her parents and now to Sarah — a song called "Take Me Out to the Ballgame." First I explain to the kids that Sarah was born right here in New York — and that's in what country, Sarah? Sarah looks at me and says, "France." I look at Miss Laura, who just shrugs.

I stand there in my baseball cap and sing my song. The teacher   23
tries to rush me off. I say, "Don't you want them to learn it?" They took long enough learning to samba! I am granted permission to sing it one more time. The kids join in on the "root, root, root" and the "1, 2, 3 strikes you're out," but they can see their teacher isn't enthusiastic.

So now these sweet, innocent babies who thought they were all   24
the same are becoming culturally aware. Two little girls are touching each other's hair and saying, "Your hair is blonde, just like mine." Off to one side a little dark-haired girl stands alone, excluded. She looks confused as to what to do next. She knows she's not blonde. Sure, all children notice these things eventually, but, thanks to the concerted efforts of their teachers, these two- and three-year-olds are talking about things that separate rather than connect.

And Sarah only knows what she has been taught: Little Henry is   25
white, her daddy's from Iceland, and New York's in France.

Vocabulary/Using a Dictionary

1. What does the word *interrogation* (para. 3) suggest about Miss Laura's questions?

2. In paragraph 21, Konig describes the *culmination* of Cultural Diversity Month. What does it mean when something is a culmination?

---

[1]*samba:* Brazilian dance of African origin.
[2]*conga:* Cuban ballroom dance.

3. What is the root of the word *concerted* (para. 24)? What does Konig's use of the word *concerted* reveal about her attitude toward the efforts of Sarah's teachers?

Responding to Words in Context

1. The terms *cultural awareness* (para. 2) and *culturally aware* (para. 24) are used by the author to describe the effort that Sarah's teachers are putting toward Cultural Diversity Month. What do we mean when we use the word *culture?* Apply this definition to the term *cultural awareness.*

2. In paragraph 21, Konig makes use of the word *affiliation* to describe Sarah's relationship to the United States. Try using the word in another context. The word also has an unusual origin. What is it?

Discussing Main Point and Meaning

1. Describe what Konig suggests by the title of the essay. How would you describe her idea in your own words?

2. What is the main concern that the author had with her daughter's teacher? Was this concern well founded? In your opinion, do you believe Miss Laura deliberately confused Sarah's cultural identity?

3. Does Konig explain why Miss Laura acts the way she does? What do you suspect is the reason for the teacher's behavior?

4. How do Konig's final paragraphs convey the main point of her essay? Find the sentence that best summarizes the main point.

Examining Sentences, Paragraphs, and Organization

1. What is the topic sentence of the opening paragraph?

2. Note the divisions made between each paragraph in the essay. Hiding the numbers, try to divide the sentences into paragraphs by yourself. What are your criteria for judging where a new paragraph starts and an old paragraph ends?

3. Without her use of dialogue (conversation between two or more persons) in the essay, do you think Konig's claim would be more or less effective?

Thinking Critically

1. Do you think Konig's essay is trying to be politically correct? How do you define *political correctness?* Would you consider Konig to be a politically correct person? Is Miss Laura politically correct? Use examples from the essay to support your ideas.

2. Does Konig feel uncomfortable with the fact that her "culture isn't *diverse* enough" (para. 2)? Is she ashamed of being American and not Irish? Do you agree with the author's views about cultural awareness?

In-Class Writing Activities

1. In the essay, Konig suggests that her daughter's class was too young to grasp the concept of cultural diversity. This raises an interesting and controversial question: Is too much cultural awareness at an early age dangerous? At what age should children begin their education about cultural differences? In a brief essay, describe whether you agree or disagree with the author, drawing on both Konig's views and your own in making your case.

2. In response to the question "But where are your *people* from?" (see para. 8 of the essay), the author states: "Look, . . . we're Americans. Our kids are Americans. We tell them about American history and George Washington and apple pie and all that stuff. If you want me to do something American, I can do that" (para. 13). What does Konig mean to "do something American," to have an American identity? Can you relate to this type of group identity? Write an essay describing what you think makes up an American identity and whether you can identify with it.

Discussing the Unit

Suggested Topic for Discussion

The authors in this unit all write about a group identity and how it affects development. To what extent does our personality depend on the identity of the groups we've been members of? To what extent is our self-image dependent on group identity? One's self-image derives from assimilating many different sources — the media, the dominant culture, gender, race, class, peers, parents, and so on. Which of these sources do you think plays the biggest role in determining your identity?

Preparing for Class Discussion

1. Henry Han Xi Lau's desire to return to Chinatown even when he is attending Yale University makes an interesting statement. If "Chinatown is ghetto," the Kung Fu Crew is ghetto, and, as Lau declares, "I am ghetto," then why did he choose to move away from his home to attend university? Do we constantly desire new experiences on which to formulate our identities? Do we need to move away from places that played a great role in constituting identity in order to truly appreciate them? Do we need new places to act as modes of comparison against our personal Chinatowns that we treasure? Jot down a few thoughts on how you feel about this subject.

2. How do you think Meg Greenfield would respond to Henry Han Xi Lau's essay in this chapter? Would Greenfield accept Lau's suggestion that forming a group identity helps people to survive in modern America? What might Greenfield argue is wrong with Lau's view? How might Henry Louis Gates Jr. respond to Lau's essay (see "From the Bookshelf," p. 85)?

3. To what extent is our sense of being a representative of a group determined by the context in which we find ourselves? For example, if you are the only French student on an American campus, many people around you may interpret you and your behavior as typically French. But when you return to France, you would hardly be regarded as a representative of all French people. How does this fact affect your idea of what group identity means?

From Discussion to Writing

1. In this chapter you've read essays on how having a group identity is experienced from three different viewpoints. Using these pieces as a model, write your own essay examining the experience of having a group identity in a culture you know well.

2. Write an essay in which you describe what you are most proud of about yourself. Is it your identification with a group, a public

achievement, or a private accomplishment? Be sure to explain why you feel the way you do.

3. For Susan Brady Konig, too much cultural awareness and an uninformed push toward cultural diversity was a maddening and frustrating experience. Are you frustrated by being exposed to excessive cultural diversity? Can instructors teach excessive amounts of cultural awareness? Do you know people who are angered by too much of this instruction? Write a one-page essay discussing whether excessive cultural diversity can be maddening.

Topics for Cross-Cultural Discussion

1. Susan Brady Konig devotes considerable time in her essay to discussing her daughter's American heritage in contrast to the teacher's perception that the students' backgrounds are necessarily multinational. Does such a contradiction exist in your culture? What are the similarities and differences in Americans' ideas of cultural heritage and the ideas that exist in your culture?

2. All three authors in this chapter address the dangers or merits of identifying oneself with a group. Whereas Meg Greenfield discusses group identities more generally, Henry Han Xi Lau and Susan Brady Konig discuss groups based primarily on ethnicity. In what other ways do people group themselves? What other kinds of groups exist in your culture? Is there as much of an emphasis on group identity? More? To what do you attribute the differences?

6

What Good Are Role Models?

One of the most common characteristics of young people is their need for heroes or role models — individuals whose talents they admire and whose careers they hope to imitate. Some find their heroes on baseball fields or basketball courts; others look for them in movies and popular entertainment; and still others locate them in classrooms, courtrooms, or boardrooms.

Yet how important are role models to a young person's development? And what happens when our heroes don't turn out to be worth imitating? In "Girls 'n' Spice: All Things Nice?" Professor Susan J. Douglas takes a look at one of the world's most popular singing groups, the Spice Girls. Do they represent a mere marketing gimmick, she wonders, or does the group "help empower young girls as they enter the treacherous process of discovering their sexuality"? For almost a century, athletic heroes have been viewed as important role models, and more recently the emergence of African American superstars has placed what political science professor Adolph Reed Jr. argues are unnecessary burdens on black athletes (see "From the Bookshelf," p. 116). In "Black Athletes on Parade," Reed holds that it's "unreasonable and unfair to expect athletes to adopt any public role other than simply as athletes." Perhaps forgetting about role models and heroes altogether, suggests University of Nebraska at Omaha student Tim Mills, "gives us a chance to become heroes ourselves."

SUSAN J. DOUGLAS

Girls 'n' Spice: All Things Nice?

[THE NATION / *August 25–September 1, 1997*]

Before You Read

Why would the Spice Girls, young women in their twenties who promote an ostensibly feminist message, appeal primarily to girls between eight and fourteen? Do you think their appeal is more in their
message, their image, or their music?

Words to Learn

debunk (para. 4): expose as being
  false or exaggerated (v.)
insinuate (para. 6): suggest or hint
  at slyly (v.)
riff (para. 6): improvise (v.)
brouhaha (para. 7): uproar (n.)
obeisance (para. 7): respect, defer-
  ence (n.)
vilify (para. 8): speak ill of,
  defame (v.)
pander (para. 8): cater to low
  tastes (v.)
luminescent (para. 9): emitting light
  (adj.)

euphoria (para. 9): strong feeling of
  happiness, confidence, or well-
  being (n.)
saccharine (para. 11): excessively
  sweet or sentimental (adj.)
auspices (para. 11): sponsorship (n.)
vacuous (para. 11): empty, lacking
  contents (adj.)
demure (para. 14): shy, modest
  (adj.)
deferential (para. 14): yielding respectfully to another's opinion
  (adj.)

Susan J. Douglas *(b. 1950) is professor of communication studies at
the University of Michigan and media critic for* The Progressive. *She is the
author of* Where the Girls Are: Growing Up Female with the Mass Media
(1995). Douglas has lectured widely, written articles for such publications as
The Nation *and the* Village Voice, *and has appeared on a variety of radio
and television talk shows. Her upcoming projects include a book on the history of radio listening in America and an examination of the portrayal of
motherhood in the mass media.*

It's 8:12 A.M. The feminist mom, who looks like she just got shot   1
out of a wind turbine and has a cheap chardonnay hangover, is making pancakes for four eight-year-old girls having a sleepover party.
Let's just say that she's not in the most festive mood. Then, blasting
from the other room she hears the now-familiar faux-rap riff, "I'll tell
ya what I want, what I really really want. . . ." She peeks around the
corner to see the four girls singing and dancing with abandon, suck-
ing in "girl power" with every pore. Should she be happy that they're
listening to bustier feminism instead of watching Barbie commercials
on Saturday morning TV? Or should she run in, rip the CD out of the
player, and insist that they listen to Mary Chapin Carpenter or Ani
DiFranco instead?

Welcome to the Spice Girls debate, which has been raging in the   2
British and American press since the beginning of the year. With their Wonderbras, bare thighs, pouty lips, and top-of-the-head ponytails favored by Pebbles on
The Flintstones, the Spice Girls advocate "girl power" and demand, in their colos-
sal, intercontinental hit "Wannabe," that boys treat them with respect or take a
hike. Their boldfaced liner notes claim that "The Future is Female" and suggest
that they and their fans are "Freedom Fighters." "We're freshening up feminism for the nineties," they told *The Guardian.* "Feminism has become a dirty
word," they said. "Girl Power is just a nineties way of saying it."
New Age feminism means "you have a brain, a voice, and an
opinion."

> *When adolescent girls flock to a group, they are telling us plenty about how they experience the transition to womanhood in a society in which boys are still very much on top.*

In addition to their chart-topping CD, they have a magazine, a   3
book (*Girl Power*), fan clubs everywhere, a new ad for Pepsi with the
kind of production values previously reserved for Michael Jackson,
and plans for a movie that would be a girls' version of *A Hard Day's
Night.* They each have a nickname: Red-headed Geri is "Ginger
Spice"; Melanie C., who does backflips onstage, is "Sporty Spice";
Emma, the one with the Chatty Cathy ponytails, is "Baby Spice";
Victoria, allegedly upper class, is "Posh Spice"; and Melanie, the only
woman of color, is, you guessed it, "Scary Spice." They are twenty-
one to twenty-four years old. Their biggest fans are girls between the
ages of eight and fourteen.

Are they a group of no-talent, flash-in-the-pan bimbos whose success comes primarily from a highly calculated and cynical marketing strategy that has fused bubble-gum music with a pseudo-feminist message? Or are they a refreshing fusion of politics and music that debunks antiquated stereotypes about feminism and helps empower young girls as they enter the treacherous process of discovering their sexuality?

Not since the Beatles has a British band conquered the worldwide pop charts with such speed or thoroughness. "Wannabe," their first single, hit number two on *Billboard*'s Top Ten about fourteen minutes after its U.S. debut in January and then hit number one. The song has topped the charts in thirty-five countries across four continents, and in Britain three subsequent singles also went to number one. In a five-month period, they sold 10 million albums, grossing an estimated $165 million for Virgin records.

More than that, they insinuated themselves into British politics during the spring elections and were courted by politicians on both sides. They were in the press on a near daily basis, and reporters hung on their every word as they said they were "desperately worried about the slide to a single currency" in Europe. Tony Blair's hair was all right, one of them noted, "but we don't agree with his tax policies." By March, John Major's Chancellor of the Exchequer was quoting them in his speeches, riffing to the audiences, "I'll tell you what I want, what I really want . . . healthy sustainable growth and rising living standards for the next five years."

Their most repeated quip was that Margaret Thatcher was their hero and role model — "the first ever Spice Girl." Thatcher responded by adding them to her Christmas-card list. The Tories quickly sought to claim the girls as mascots who might achieve the improbable and make Major seem way cool, and their media strategy room was reportedly adorned with Spice Girls posters. Tony Blair, for his part, claimed that "Wannabe" was one of the records he'd most want if stranded on a desert island. A Labour M.P. invited them to join him for a tour of Parliament. There was actually a brouhaha over whom they would vote for. After a record number of women — 101 — were elected to Parliament in May, reporters asked the group if they felt that their "girl power" message had contributed to this female sweep. "This was the sort of cultural obeisance that only the Beatles have ever really managed to secure," noted *The Guardian*.

And not since New Kids on the Block has a group been so vilified for being inauthentic, manufactured, and determined to pander to

4

5

6

7

8

the most exploitable desires of preteen girls. The backlash was quick — there were the usual columns asserting that the Spice Girls were nothing more than the malleable creation of Svengali-type males and others denouncing their music as having less substance than cotton candy. By April there was the SpiceSlap Web page, in which the heads of the girls popped out of holes and your task was to slap as many of them as quickly as possible back into oblivion. *Ad Age* reported that by the end of the month, the page had gotten over 170,000 hits.

Ever since the success of girl-group music in the early sixties, 9 music that adolescent girls adore has been dismissed by music critics as inauthentic, overly commercialized trash. *The Rolling Stone History of Rock & Roll,* referring presumably to such luminescent achievements as "Will You Love Me Tomorrow," "Nowhere to Run," and "Be My Baby," put it this way: "The female group of the early 1960s served to drive the concept of art completely away from rock 'n' roll. . . . this genre represents the low point in the history of rock 'n' roll." Real rock and roll must be "authentic" — meaning it features instrumental virtuosity, original songwriting, social criticism, a stance of anger and/or alienation. We are not talking fizzy pop euphoria here. Think Pearl Jam, Nirvana, Counting Crows, Rage Against the Machine. Male standards of performance have usually defined what is truly "genuine."

But while the music industry — and music criticism — remain 10 male dominated, female performers from Chrissie Hynde to Tori Amos to Salt-N-Pepa have achieved both commercial success and critical respect. So it's not just serious boys with whom the Spice Girls are unfavorably compared. It's the new whole new spate of serious girls, many of them part of or inspired by the riot grrl movement of several years ago. The explosion of feminism-inspired rock, rap, pop — even country music — means that Spice Girls lyrics like "Come a little closer baby, get it on, get it on" seem like drivel compared with songs about date rape, abortion, and the ongoing devaluation of women in society.

And male critics are not the only ones who have dissed the Girls. 11 Feminists like Andi Zeisler have blasted their "Mattel-doll approach" in which "their saccharine image is being peddled under the auspices of female advancement." Zeisler argues that when "giggly things whose strings are pulled by their male managers" utter pro-female sentiments, it makes feminism seem vacuous and preposterous. By posing as political, they devalue politics.

In other words, it's pretty effortless, and irresistible, to dismiss   12
these girls as nothing more than the Bay City Rollers in drag. After
all, they are the most recent female singers to insist on having it both
ways — on being sex objects while simultaneously critiquing patriar-
chal ways of looking at and thinking about young women. They
swear, they smoke, they drink, they undress men with their eyes and
goosed Prince Charles at a spring benefit in Manchester. They wear
Wonderbras, bustiers, microminis, and fuck-me pumps. They try to
look like Barbie and sound like Gloria Steinem. "Don't rely on your
sexuality, but don't be afraid of it," they advise succinctly. "Girl
power," they say, "is when . . . you and your mates reply to wolf
whistles by shouting 'Get your arse out.' . . . You don't wait around
for him to call. . . . You believe in yourself."

Madonna, of course, in the early years, with her black bra straps   13
and "Boy Toy" belt, was a champ at this, and thousands of teenage
wannabes, grateful for her claim that female sexual energy was nothing to be ashamed of, helped make her a millionaire. But it was precisely because her earliest fans were adolescent girls that Madonna
was initially dismissed as a flash in the pan even though critics were
not far off the mark when they described her as sounding, as one of
them put it, "like a chipmunk on helium."

Despite all the huffing and puffing of adults, one way or the   14
other, it doesn't matter much what we think of the Spice Girls. What
matters is what they mean to their preteen fans. When adolescent girls
flock to a group, they are telling us plenty about how they experience
the transition to womanhood in a society in which boys are still very
much on top. Girls today are being urged, simultaneously, to be independent, assertive and achievement-oriented, yet also demure, attractive, soft-spoken, fifteen pounds underweight, and deferential to men.

They are told that if they aren't sexy, they are nothing, but that   15
their sexuality is dangerous to them and threatening to much of the
rest of society. Boys are supposed to want them, but they aren't supposed to want boys back — thirty years after the women's movement
began, the term *slut* is alive and well. The loss of self-esteem that all
too many teenage girls suffer — when they learn to silence themselves, to censor their real desires and aspirations — has kept Mary
Pipher's *Reviving Ophelia* (advice on how to help girls survive adolescence in a "girl hostile" environment) on the best-seller list for
more than two years. [See "From the Bookshelf," p. 74.] So along
come five feisty, outspoken, attractive young women making bouncy
dance music who assure girls that these contradictions can be fi-

nessed — that they can be, simultaneously, attractive to boys yet independent, tough, and strong — and, whammo, platinum records and a new wannabe movement.

What might singing a song like "Wannabe" at the top of your   16
lungs when you're ten years old, while reading liner notes such as "She Who Dares Wins" and "Silence Is Golden But Shouting Is Fun," mean for feminist politics ten years from now? Especially when, in just a few years, these same girls will be ready for the likes of Sleater-Kinney, Liz Phair, Melissa Etheridge, and even some golden oldies by Laura Nyro or Annie Lennox. Of course, we don't know, and music, by itself, can hardly make history.

Right now, popular music is probably the most girl-friendly   17
medium going. The movies remain dominated by hard-body, big-gun action films; the news media either ignore or trivialize issues of central importance to young women; and most TV programming aimed at teenage girls features skinny, poreless women who screw up at work and obsess about dating. Fashion magazines, despite their sometimes quasi-feminist politics, publish multipage spreads that insist girls should be preoccupied with one thing: "How to Get a Better Butt, Fast!"

But in their rooms with their boomboxes, whether they're listen   18
ing to bubble gum or punk, teenage girls can imagine a world where they can have love and respect, where boys desire them but won't mess with them. So while it's easy as pie to hold a group like the Spice Girls in contempt, we should be wary when music embraced by preteen girls is ridiculed. These girls are telling us that they want a voice, that they want someone to take them seriously, that they want to be worldly wise and optimistic at the same time. The Spice Girls tell them that feminism is necessary and fun. Hey, when I was ten we had "I Wanna Be Bobby's Girl." Crass commercial calculation and all, the Spice Girls are a decided improvement.

Vocabulary/Using a Dictionary

1. Without looking at the definition of the word *saccharine* (para. 11), what would you guess was the meaning of the word? What other word does *saccharine* look like it is related to?

2. Think of some ways to use the word *vacuous* (para. 11). How would you apply the word to a person? What does it have in common with *vacuum?*

3. Describe what being *deferential* means (para. 14). How does it relate to the word *defer*?

Responding to Words in Context

1. You may not find the word *bustier* (para. 1) in any dictionary. Look at the word in the context of the essay: "Should . . . [the feminist mom] be happy that . . . [her daughters] are listening to bustier feminism instead of watching Barbie commercials on Saturday morning TV?" Then try to figure out its definition.

2. Douglas uses the word *dissed* in the context of her essay (para. 11). As a modern slang term, you may have a different definition for this word than your instructor or a dictionary does. What does the word mean to you? Be prepared to explain your answer.

3. If someone were to say to you, "Your outfit looks antiquated!," what would they mean? What other word does *antiquated* (para. 4) look like?

Discussing Main Point and Meaning

1. What controversy does the author introduce in paragraph 4?

2. Why do you think John Major's Chancellor of the Exchequer, Margaret Thatcher, Tony Blair, and other British politicians "courted" the favor of the Spice Girls (para. 6–7)?

3. Why do you think Douglas quoted *The Guardian,* which alluded to the popularity of the Spice Girls, saying: "This was the sort of cultural obeisance that only the Beatles have ever really managed to secure" (para. 7)? What effect does this quotation have on Douglas's main point?

4. In paragraph 14, Douglas discusses how "we" should regard the Spice Girls. Does what we think matter? What conclusion does she reach?

Examining Sentences, Paragraphs, and Organization

1. Do you think Douglas's major transitions in the essay (para. 9, sentence 1; para. 11, sentence 1) are effective? What should a transition sentence do?

2. In her use of comparison and contrast as a rhetorical strategy, the author (and others who are quoted) compares the Spice Girls to

many other musical groups. What groups are they compared to? Are the comparisons favorable or unfavorable?

3. Where do you think Douglas's conclusion to her essay starts? Explain your answer.

Thinking Critically

1. "Right now, popular music is probably the most girl-friendly medium going," Douglas declares in paragraph 17. Do you agree with this statement? Is popular music girl-friendly? Are other media in society friendly toward women? Why? What are some media in society that are not so friendly toward women? Why?

2. From evidence supplied in the essay, construct your own working definition of what the Spice Girls mean by the term *girl power* (para. 1). Why do they use the word *girl* and not *woman?* Is this term synonymous with *feminism?* Explain your answers.

In-Class Writing Activities

1. Imagine that you are the host of a television show and want to schedule a program discussing the issue of women's rights with the Spice Girls. Make a list of one question that you would like to ask each member of the band if they were guests on your show. What other kinds of guests would you invite to participate in the program?

2. In paragraph 18, Douglas suggests that by listening to the Spice Girls, preteen and young teen "girls are telling us that they want a voice, that they want someone to take them seriously, that they want to be worldly wise and optimistic at the same time. The Spice Girls tell them that feminism is necessary and fun." Write a brief essay explaining whether you agree or disagree with this idea, stating reasons that support your claim.

ADOLPH REED JR.

Black Athletes on Parade

[THE PROGRESSIVE / July 1997]

Before You Read

Why would anyone think that a famous athlete has an obligation to be a role model? Do you believe that African American sports figures shoulder a greater burden of social responsibility than white athletes?

Words to Learn

canard (para. 1): false story or report (n.)

discourse (para. 2): conversation, formal discussion (n.)

flamboyantly (para. 2): in a showy manner (adv.)

affecting (para. 5): moving the emotions (adj.)

seriatim (para. 7): one after the other (adv.)

burgeon (para. 10): grow or develop quickly (v.)

deportment (para. 11): conduct, behavior (n.)

affront (para. 11): deliberate insult (n.)

loutish (para. 12). rude, crudely clumsy (adj.)

prowess (para. 15): exceptional ability or skill (n.)

malinger (para. 18): pretend illness, especially to avoid duty or work (v.)

syphilis (para. 19): an infectious, usually sexually transmitted disease caused by a spiral bacteria (n.)

quiescence (para. 20): quiet, stillness (n.)

ludicrous (para. 20): laughably absurd (adj.)

exhort (para. 20): urge, advise, or caution earnestly (v.)

fetter (para. 21): shackle, anything that confines (n.)

ADOLPH REED JR. (b. 1947) is a professor at the Department of African-American Studies at the University of Illinois at Chicago and the author of W.E.B. DuBois and American Political Thought *(1997). Reed is a regular columnist for the* Village Voice *and* The Progressive *and a frequent contributor to* The Nation.

It's difficult to be patient with the argument that the crossover 1
popularity of Tiger Woods or Michael Jordan or Bill Cosby or Oprah
Winfrey proves that racial injustice has been defeated. That reasoning
is either a straight-up rightist canard or a more or less willfully naïve,
ostrich-like evasion.

Equally frustrating is the "nothing-has-changed-since-slavery" 2
line that seems to have gained currency in black political discourse as
the realities of the Jim Crow[1] world slip out of collective memory.
Recently I was on a panel with a black political scientist who insisted
that things had gotten no better for black people in this country since
1619; several years ago I saw Derek Bell, then a tenured Harvard
Law professor, flamboyantly push a version of the same line. This is,
of course, a self-discrediting argument. How many black people were
on the Harvard Law School faculty or teaching in predominantly
white universities thirty years ago, much less earlier?

> *In a racially just world, black athletes should not be expected to hold to a higher standard of behavior than whites.*

But while there has been undeniable 3
progress, racialized expectations still prevail — especially in sports.

Tiger Woods's Masters victory made 4
him a social spokesman for black athletes.
It's a familiar pattern. Woods was not
only expected to comment on how his accomplishment, as the first black winner of
the most Southern of all PGA tournaments, related to Jackie Robinson; he also was called upon to pay
homage to Charlie Sifford, Lee Calvin Peete, Lee Elder, and other
black trailblazers on the PGA tour.

Woods's responses seemed reasonable enough and genuine. His 5
acknowledgment that he had paused on the last hole of the last Masters round to reflect that he was walking a path carved by his black
predecessors was even affecting.

By contrast, Chicago White Sox star Frank Thomas created a bit 6
of a media stir by admitting that he doesn't know much about Jackie
Robinson or his sport's racial history. The ensuing controversy
centered on Thomas's — and, by extension, other black athletes' —
larger social and racial obligations.

---

[1]*Jim Crow:* Practice of segregating or discriminating against blacks (comes from the name of an early Negro minstrel song).

This theme of special obligation also figured into the Tiger   7
Woods hype. All along he has been trumpeted as a "role model" for
black — and Asian American — kids. He's a clean-cut, articulate, and
apparently earnest young man whose public persona isn't flamboyant
or especially controversial. Nike, evoking the concluding scene from
Spike Lee's *Malcolm X*, projects Woods as such a role model in an ad
that quick-cuts to nonwhite kids all over the globe who proclaim,
seriatim: "I am Tiger Woods."

Woods now joins Michael Jordan among the company's most   8
visibly promoted human icons. Jordan has been the object of criticism for his silence about Nike's horrible labor practices in its off-
shore production operations. (The stunning fact is that Nike pays
him more than the annual payroll of its entire Indonesian workforce.)
He has been criticized as well for not speaking out or being conspicuously active on behalf of black issues and causes. Woods, similarly, has been faulted by some for not being a vocal enough race
man — though recent disclosures of racist threats and harassment
he's received on the golf circuit give those objections a strange twist.

The fact that people have such expectations of athletes like Jor-   9
dan and Woods is Jackie Robinson's ironic legacy. Robinson's star-
dom as a baseball player was inseparable from his political renown
for breaking the color bar in a very visible arena of American culture.
His views were solicited on all manner of political and social issues
that concerned black Americans. [See "From the Bookshelf," p. 116.]

This was understandable, especially at the time: Robinson sym-   10
bolically represented the goals of the burgeoning civil-rights movement and large social and political aspirations of black Americans
much more broadly. At the same time, though, the spokesman status
thrust onto him was both unfair to him (though he may not have
bristled at it) and deeply troublesome politically. After all, Jackie
Robinson had no special expertise for this role. He was a baseball
player. Nor was he accountable to any particular body to speak in
the name of black Americans.

In addition to carrying the weight of race spokesmanship,   11
Robinson also faced constant scrutiny for deportment. Indeed, he
was selected as the pathbreaker partly because of his articulate, All-
American demeanor. And his agreement not to retaliate against
affronts — no matter how bad — was a precondition of the whole
arrangement.

In a racially just world, black athletes should not be expected to   12
hold to a higher standard of behavior than whites. Nor should they

be expected to shoulder the burden of racial activism. And do we really want the likes of Charles Barkley, the NBA's most prominent black Republican, or the Philadelphia 76ers' loutish rookie of the year, Alan Iverson, declaiming on social affairs in the name of black Americans?

Sure, it would be good and useful for Michael Jordan and Tiger   13 Woods to exert pressure on Nike to clean up its dreadful labor practices. But the implication that they have some special obligation to do so because of their status as black — or in Woods's case, even Asian American — athletic icons is wrong.

Woods and Jordan have the right to be apolitical no less than   14 Larry Bird, Pete Sampras, Wayne Gretzky, or Brady Anderson. Frank Thomas has the right to have grown up playing baseball without paying much attention to the sport's history, even the history of its desegregation, from which originates his opportunity to become wealthy playing it. When you boil off the self-righteous presumptions about special racial responsibility, Thomas's ignorance about Jackie Robinson is not really different from that of many young players who don't know much about the game's history or stars of the past. Reverence for, or even interest in, a sport's lore isn't a condition for being able to play it well; nor should it be.

The presumption that black athletes should shoulder greater so-   15 cial expectations at least bears a family resemblance to the persisting myth of special black athletic prowess, which in turn, works to perpetuate the worst stereotypes and to undermine the careers of black professional athletes in general.

On the average, blacks in pro baseball and football perform   16 somewhat better statistically than their white counterparts. At first glance this fact may seem to lend confidence to the claim that blacks are more gifted. The reality, however, is quite the opposite: marginal black players are more likely than comparably talented whites to get weeded out along the way.

The myth of black athletic superiority leads scouts and coaches   17 to evaluate black athletes with higher expectations in mind. So the black player needs to exhibit a higher level of skill or performance to impress.

Black athletes who don't perform up to inflated expectations are   18 more likely to be characterized as lazy, malingering, or otherwise possessed of bad attitudes. In 1980, for example, Houston Astros' star pitcher J. R. Richard nearly died when he suffered a career-ending stroke on the field. He had been complaining of weakness for some time, but when no clear medical basis for his complaint was detected right away, the reaction of the Astros' management and the Houston media was to attack Richard for dogging it, even though Richard had been among the league's leaders in innings pitched for several years. After he collapsed, a medical exam disclosed a blood clot. Earlier treatment would probably have saved his career as the most dominating pitcher in baseball.

Frank Robinson and Roberto Clemente have been enshrined on   19
the highest echelon of Major League's pantheon of heroes, and rightly so. When they were playing, though, the story was different. The Cincinnati Reds traded Robinson, claiming he was too old at twenty-nine, because the club considered him to have a bad attitude. Pittsburgh Pirates management and the local media circulated similar complaints about Clemente. Both men were rapped as surly or moody, and both were plagued by rumors that their inevitable submission to slumps or late-season exhaustion stemmed from being weakened by the ravages of syphilis, thereby getting the black hypersexuality stereotype into the picture. What prompted these judgments? Both men simply sought to conduct themselves with a measure of dignity; they presumed a right to be treated with equal respect.

Booker T. Washington said blacks should be "patient suffering,   20
slow to anger," and that is the downside of Jackie Robinson's legacy, though it's hardly his fault. The public imagery of Jackie Robinson's accomplishment and ordeal has been used as a justification for preaching quiescence in the name of moral superiority. Robinson's "quiet dignity" was frequently invoked, for example, against more aggressive black radicalism in the 1960s. (Recently, even *The Nation*[2] — in its continuing drive to become the respectably liberal, loyal edge of Clintonism — published a ludicrous article exhorting blacks in South Carolina to draw on the race's legacy of demonstrated moral superiority and thus defuse the state's controversy over the public display of the Confederate battle flag by embracing the flag and revalorizing it as a symbol of a racially democratic New South.)

As a professional athlete and as a black person, Jackie Robinson   21
fought to bring into existence a world in which he and others would

[2]*The Nation:* Political magazine with a predominantly liberal point of view and readership. The previous selection on the Spice Girls originally appeared in *The Nation.*

be able to pursue their craft on an equal basis with everyone else, without the fetters of stereotypes or invidious, unfair expectations and double standards. A world, that is, in which a ballplayer would be simply a ballplayer. That quest — obviously just and proper in its own right — had much broader ramifications in 1947. Why? Because a dynamic political movement spurred it along.

It's not only unreasonable and unfair to expect athletes to adopt 22
any public role other than simply as athletes; it's also a waste of time.

Vocabulary/Using a Dictionary

1. "That reasoning is either a straight-up rightist canard or a more or less willfully naive, ostrich-like evasion," Reed writes in paragraph 1. Explain the author's statement in your own words.

2. What does the author mean by "black political discourse" (para. 2)? What does Reed imply by relating "the 'nothing-has-changed-since-slavery' line" to black political discourse?

3. In the essay, the words *loutish* (para. 12) and *malingering* (para. 18) are both used to describe the behavior of black athletes. Do the words have similar meanings? Would you consider the words to be antonyms?

Responding to Words in Context

1. In paragraph 20 Reed sarcastically describes how *The Nation* is urging "blacks in South Carolina to draw on the race's legacy of . . . moral superiority and thus defuse the state's controversy about the public display of the Confederate battle flag" by adopting the flag and "revalorizing it as a symbol of a radically democratic New South." What is the meaning of the complex word *revalorize*? What word does it come from? What does *The Nation* wish blacks from South Carolina to do?

2. The word *invidious* (para. 21) looks similar to the word *insidious*, but the two have different meanings. How do the meanings of the two words differ?

Discussing Main Point and Meaning

1. What does the title of the essay suggest? How is the author's intent expressed through the title "Black Athletes on Parade"?

2. Explain what Reed refers to as "the myth of black athletic superiority" (para. 17). Why does he use the word *myth?*
3. Of what importance to Reed's point is the reference to Houston Astros' star pitcher J. R. Richard's near death when he suffered a career-ending stroke on the field (para. 18)?
4. Reed concludes his essay with the sentence, "It's not only unreasonable and unfair to expect athletes to adopt any public role other than simply as athletes; it's also a waste of time." According to the author, why is it a waste of time to expect that athletes would adopt any other (public) role?

Examining Sentences, Paragraphs, and Organization

1. What is the topic sentence of paragraph 13? How do you know?
2. What would happen to this essay if the first paragraph and the last were switched? Why?
3. Cicero, a Roman statesman and orator (106–43 B.C.), held that the public speaker had three "offices" or main functions — to teach, to please, to move. If we apply Cicero's ideas about oration to writing, which of these three offices does Reed's essay seem to be an example of? Why?

Thinking Critically

1. Do you agree with the author that it is "unreasonable and unfair" and a "waste of time" for athletes "to adopt any public role other than simply as athletes" (para. 22)? Do you think Reed has provided enough evidence to support this conclusion?
2. Although Reed is a professor of political science (the study of the description and analysis of political and especially governmental institutions and processes), his essay borders on the informal in tone. He doesn't cite any expert sources and keeps his supporting bits of data short and to the point. Do you find his approach persuasive? Why do you think Reed chose the examples of Charles Barkley and Alan Iverson to contrast with Jackie Robinson? Would you trust his authority more or less if he had relied on academic research and historical data rather than using contemporary examples to prove his point?

In-Class Writing Activities

1. On May 9, 1947, two days before the first black player was to begin his Major League baseball career with the Brooklyn Dodgers, there were rumors of an alleged plot by National League players to strike against Jackie Robinson. National League President Ford Frick averted the walkout by issuing the following ultimatum:

> If you do this you will be suspended from the league. I do not care if half the league strikes. Those who do it will encounter quick retribution. . . . I don't care if it wrecks the National League for five years. This is the United States of America, and one citizen has as much right to play as another. The National League will go down the line with Robinson whatever the consequence.

Freewrite a few ideas about the above paragraph. What are your impressions about Frick's character? Would you consider Frick a role model?

2. Sometimes we have unreasonable expectations for people we hold in high esteem, and sometimes we become disappointed when these people don't live up to our expectations. For example, on the popular comedy show *Frasier*, the main character, Dr. Frasier Crane, flashes back to the first time he learned that his father wasn't perfect: When Frasier was a child and the two went out to dinner, Martin Crane (his father) couldn't add up the bill in his head. Think of a moment in your life when you held unreasonable expectations for someone you considered a role model, and discuss how you felt when you realized that you expected too much of that person.

From the Bookshelf

Arnold Rampersad, *Jackie Robinson*

*Not every athlete elected to baseball's Hall of Fame receives congratu-
lations and tributes from the nation's top political figures. But Jackie Robinson was much more than a ballplayer; he was an exceptional human being.
At a dinner in his honor several days before the 1962 induction ceremonies
took place in Cooperstown, New York, Robinson received praise from President Kennedy, Richard Nixon, Governor Nelson Rockefeller, and Martin
Luther King Jr. In the prologue to his award-winning biography, Jackie
Robinson, Princeton professor Arnold Rampersad describes the momen-
tous occasion.*

Jackie Robinson's Finest Moment

In January [1962], merit was sufficiently color blind for Robinson
to garner 124 votes, or four more than he needed for admission [to
the Baseball Hall of Fame]. With congratulations pouring in, he had
passed the months since his selection keenly anticipating this historic
moment in Cooperstown. Three days before his induction, on the
evening of July 20, he had sat in a golden haze of glory when some
nine hundred admirers, led by the governor of New York, who hailed
him as "a hero of the struggle to make American democracy a genuine reality for every American," honored him with a testimonial dinner at the Waldorf-Astoria Hotel. In an evening rich with praise,
three messages stood out. One was from Richard Nixon, the former
Vice President of the United States, whom Robinson had firmly supported in the 1960 presidential election. "There are days when I feel
a special pride simply in being American," Nixon had written Robinson when the news first broke, "and Tuesday, January 23, 1962, was
certainly one of them." The second was from John F. Kennedy, who
tuned out the persistent drumbeat of Robinson's opposition to his
presidency to offer a glowing tribute. "He has demonstrated in his
brilliant career," President Kennedy declared, that "courage, talent,
and perseverance can overcome the forces of intolerance.... The
vigor and fierce competitive spirit that characterized his performance
as an athlete are still evident in his efforts in the great battle to
achieve equality of opportunity for all people."

The most eloquent tribute had come from Dr. Martin Luther
King Jr., the central figure in the civil rights movement and the inspiration behind the testimonial dinner. King, like Kennedy and Nixon,

was absent on July 20; he was in Albany, Georgia, caught up in perhaps the most explosive crisis of the Movement to that point, as a coalition of liberal organizations confronted one of the worst strongholds of segregation, about sixty miles from the place where Robinson himself was born on a plantation in 1919. Spelling out the meaning of Jackie Robinson's example, King defended Robinson's right, challenged by some observers who saw him as a faded athlete perilously beyond his depth, to speak out on matters such as politics, segregation, and civil rights. "He has the right," King insisted stoutly, "because back in the days when integration wasn't fashionable, he underwent the trauma and the humiliation and the loneliness which comes with being a pilgrim walking the lonesome byways toward the high road of Freedom. He was a sit-inner before sit-ins, a freedom rider before freedom rides. And that is why we honor him tonight."

Praised by friend and foe alike, a hero to the heroes of a struggle inspired in many ways by his own achievements in baseball, Robinson felt a profound sense of satisfaction in what he had accomplished and was helping to accomplish. Now the vice president of a successful company, living with his handsome family in a fine home in a wealthy Connecticut town, he seemed the epitome of success. "You are the richest man I know," a friend wrote to him a few days later, "because you have *everything;* who could ask for more?"

Rampersad, Arnold. *Jackie Robinson.* New York: Random House, 1997.

TIM MILLS

Where Have All Our Heroes Gone?

[THE GATEWAY, UNIVERSITY OF NEBRASKA AT OMAHA / January 27, 1998]

Before You Read

Do you believe that young people in general are becoming cynical about heroes and role models? If someone asked you who your heroes were, what would you answer?

Words to Learn

heyday (para. 1): period of greatest vigor, success (n.)
tyrant (para. 2): absolute ruler (n.)
pharamaceutical (para. 7): related to the art and science of preparing and dispensing drugs and medicines (adj.)

Here's a word you might remember from grade school — *hero.*   1
It's rooted in days long gone. For me, its heyday was in the early 1980s. That was when I learned about people like George Washington, Christopher Columbus, Mother Theresa, Gandhi, Martin Luther King Jr., and all the other folks who dedicated their lives to make the world a little bit better place to live.

As time went on, something happened. Suddenly, no one was   2
talking about these people anymore. I found out tidbits like Washington was a tyrant, Columbus was instrumental in the slave trade, and even Santa Claus was a fake. To make things worse, the majority of people didn't pay much attention to those whose spirits remained true and whose acts really made a difference.

TIM MILLS (b. 1974) was a senior at the University of Nebraska at Omaha when he wrote this piece for the student publication The Gateway. *Mills wrote this article as a response to news of the increase in teen violence, which he attributes in part to a lack of positive role models. He graduated in May 1998 with a B.S. in journalism and lives in Omaha.*

That was all right. I still had the movies and television to provide 3
me with a new crop of heroes, people whose virtuosity we should aspire to attain and accomplishments we should strive to equal. Luke
Skywalker was flying around space saving our universe from the
forces of evil. The next thing I knew he was making headlines for
using his light saber for a lot more than battling the dark side. Many
of Hollywood's brightest stars had developed serious sinus problems,
and Pee Wee Herman . . . well, we all know that story.

Okay, I can deal with that. There's still sports, right? When all 4
was said and done, baseball's legendary Mickey Mantle wasn't much
more than a homerun-hitting distillery. There is no magic that will
save Magic Johnson (although his strength in dealing with his disease
is admirable — who aspires to be an aging basketball star with
AIDS?). And, I guess if you're a football player who's into cocaine
and prostitutes, it might be beneficial to have a coach in Dallas who
carries a gun.

**But really, who needs
heroes anyway?**

So politics, movies, and sports all 5
look pretty bleak. How about the music
business? Not much luck there, either.
Most of them are snacking on shotgun
barrels, dining on a mix of cocaine, heroin, and whiskey, and well,
frankly just aren't hero material (Marilyn Manson?).

Many of the people who are supposed to be pillars of strength 6
and icons of respectability are a bunch of disappointing fakes, myths,
and legends with closets full of skeletons. (I won't get into any of the
recent discoveries about the man we elected to lead our nation. He's
getting into plenty on his own.).

But really, who needs heroes anyway? We're doing just fine with- 7
out them, thank you very much. Divorce rates are through the roof.
Pharmaceutical companies are selling record numbers of antidepressants. Bill Gates is slowly taking over the world. Our favorite television shows feature people being chased, beaten, and arrested, cheesy
neoyuppies backstabbing their friends, and a group of animated kids
discussing anal probes and *CrackWhore* magazine. One of the poor
bastards even dies in every episode.

I suppose you could say I'm being awfully pessimistic. Look at 8
people like [the late] Princess Diana and the difference her crusade
has made in reducing the number of people having their limbs incon-
veniently removed by landmines. Or Christopher Reeve's amazing
courage proving that he truly is Superman. Colin Powell's extraordinary leadership even provides a few rays of hope in Washington.

I know there are a lot of great people out there doing plenty of   9
wonderful things for the greater good. They're risking their lives, giving up huge amounts of time, energy, and money to make our world
just. But the concept of heroes is gone. Do you ever hear anyone talking about who their heroes are? It used to be a common question. It
told you something about the person you were talking to. It gave you
a bit of insight into their values and beliefs, their goals and aspirations.

Today, most people would be hard pressed to come up with an   10
answer. We've been fooled too many times. On one hand, it's a
shame. On the other, it's liberating. Maybe, it gives us a chance to become heroes ourselves. We're no longer pressured to live up to someone else's deeds. We can accomplish our own goals, spread our own
goodness to others. We don't have to save the world. We can feel
good about just making a difference in our own little corner of the
globe. Things like opening a door for a stranger, giving a friend a
ride, and saying *please* and *thank you* will have meaning again.
Maybe if we all remembered a few of the simpler acts of heroism, we
won't need any of the heroes we don't have anyway.

Vocabulary/Using a Dictionary

1. Mills says that for him, the *heyday* (para. 1) of the word *hero*
   was in the early 1980s. What does he mean by this? Explain your
   answer.

2. What does Mills mean by *tyrant* (para. 2)? Who does he refer to
   as a *tyrant*? Why?

3. What is the origin of the word *pharamaceutical* (para. 7)? What
   does the original word mean?

Responding to Words in Context

1. In paragraph 3, Mills sarcastically states: "I still had the movies
   and television to provide me with a new crop of heroes, people
   whose virtuosity we should aspire to attain and accomplishments
   we should strive to equal." If you look up the word *virtuosity* in
   the dictionary, you probably won't find the author's meaning. What do you think Mills means when he uses the word
   virtuosity?

2. "There are a lot of great people out there . . . risking their lives,
   giving up huge amounts of time, energy, and money to make our

world just," states Mills in paragraph 9. What does he mean when he uses the word *just?* Can you find any other meanings for the word?

Discussing Main Point and Meaning

1. What do you think made the author lose his faith in heroes?
2. In paragraph 7, do you think the author means what he says when he says: "But really, who needs heroes anyway? We're doing just fine without them, thank you very much."
3. Mills concludes the essay by explaining how it is "liberating" that "today, most people would be hard pressed to come up with an answer" as to who their heroes are. What do you think he means by this opinion?

Examining Sentences, Paragraphs, and Organization

1. What is the topic sentence in paragraph 9?
2. In order to support his idea that the "new crop of heroes" is "pretty bleak" (paras. 3, 5), Mills organizes his examples according to different groups of people. What different groups does he use as support for his idea? Does he deal with the entertainment industry all at once, or does he treat them individually? Why?
3. Throughout the essay, Mills makes use of figurative language, using words for more than their literal meanings; his use of the figurative language of irony can be observed throughout the essay. Irony is the use of words to suggest the opposite of their usual sense. For example, told that the car repair would cost $2,000 and take at least two weeks, she said, "Oh, that's *wonderful!*" With this definition in mind, find a few examples where Mills uses irony in the essay.

Thinking Critically

1. Do you agree with Mills that "the concept of heroes is gone" (para. 9)? Do you ever hear anyone talking about who their heroes are? Explain.
2. Should we suppose public entertainers are to be "pillars of strength and icons of respectability" (para. 6)? How about local

politicians? What about the president? Local religious educators? How about the Pope? Explain your answers.

In-Class Writing Activities

1. The title of Mills's essay is "Where Have All Our Heroes Gone?" Reflect on the title and essay, and in your own words freewrite your ideas about where the American hero has gone (if you think he or she has gone anywhere). Support your ideas with information from your own life and American society in the late twentieth century.

2. Mills alludes to many famous people in his essay — George Washington, Christopher Columbus, Mother Theresa, Gandhi, Martin Luther King Jr., Santa Claus, Luke Skywalker, Pee Wee Herman, Mickey Mantle, Magic Johnson, coach Barry Switzer, Kurt Cobain, Marilyn Manson, President Clinton, Bill Gates, police officers from the show *Cops,* the cast of *Friends,* the cartoon characters from *South Park,* Princess Diana, Christopher Reeve, Superman, and Colin Powell. Taking two or three of these personalities, question the nature of their fame. Why are they famous? Are they famous because they are heroes? Why? Would you consider the personalities you've chosen to be positive role models? Why or why not?

Discussing the Unit

Suggested Topic for Discussion

Can the media really influence human behavior, or do the media merely reflect — rather than affect — society? Are the media responsible in their portrayal of role models? Should the media be responsible for protecting the public, especially children, from possible negative role models? If so, why? What are the benefits and drawbacks of having the media protect us from negative role models?

Preparing for Class Discussion

1. Can you think of a time when television, music, or some other medium influenced your opinion about someone you considered

a role model? How did this make you feel? Did your opinion of the person change?

2. List the traits or characteristics that you feel constitute a good role model. Do you find it easy or difficult to come up with such a list? Given the list that you've created, compare and contrast it with the lists made by others in the class, explaining your choices.

From Discussion to Writing

1. Assume that you have your own talk show. The theme of today's show is "Role Models: What Good Are They?" What three celebrities would you like to appear on your show as part of a panel discussion about the issue? Keeping the theme of the show in mind, what questions would you like to ask them? Explain your reasons for your choice of guests and questions.

2. Write an essay in which you describe some of the different (positive and negative) role models you've encountered in your life. Then formulate your own definition of *role model*, discussing how the people you've chosen fit that definition and explaining whether you think imitating their behavior made you a better person.

3. In Tim Mills's article, he states: "The concept of heroes is gone" (para. 9). He then argues that this fact "gives us a chance to become heroes ourselves. . . . We can accomplish our own goals, spread our own goodness to others." Do you think Susan Douglas would agree with this statement? Write an essay comparing and contrasting what you think the two authors' views about this statement would be, supporting your claims with information from the essays.

Topics for Cross-Cultural Discussion

1. Tim Mills suggests that American heroes come from politics, music, sports, and movies, however inadequate the heroes may be. From what public arenas does your culture draw its heroes? Are they worthier than American heroes? Why or why not?

2. Are Jackie Robinson and the Spice Girls considered heroes or role models in your culture? Explain your answer.

7

Can We Resist Stereotypes?

America has often been called a melting pot — a place where hundreds of cultures mingle together. But how well do we actually know one another? Is our understanding of other cultures and ethnic groups only skin deep? In this chapter we take a look at *stereotypes* — the standard beliefs (sometimes justified, often not) that people hold about those different from themselves and often about themselves.

One common stereotype in today's society is that of the super-achieving Asian American student, a stereotype reinforced by the high percentage of such students enrolled in prestigious colleges throughout the nation. In "The Myth of the Asian American Super-student," Edmund Lee and Kenneth Li report on new studies that dispel the stereotype and show a "vast range of Asian American educational performance."

Stereotypes are easily reinforced by the convenient — and often simplistic — labels people habitually use to describe others. In "We Are More Than Labels," Bryan Garvey, a University of Tennessee journalism major, issues a warning: "Don't let labels get in the way of who you are, whoever you may be." Garvey's suggestion, however, is easier said than done, as a Kansas State University newspaper column and its response clearly demonstrate. In "Stop Stereotyping Young Black Males," Eric Waters describes from personal experience how African American men are often perceived on college campuses. His point of view was challenged a few days later by G. Stuart Englebert, whose "Stereotyping and Racism Are Not the Same" accuses Waters of applying the term *racism* as a synonym for benign stereotyping.

EDMUND LEE AND KENNETH LI

The Myth of the Asian American Superstudent

[A. MAGAZINE / August–September 1997]

Before You Read

Before you read the selection, consider the following questions: How do you think the stereotype of Asian American superstudents got started? Do you think there is any justification for the stereotype? Is your opinion based on personal experience or images you've encountered in the mass media?

Words to Learn

discord (para. 3): conflict, lack of harmony (n.)

prodigy (para. 4): person with extraordinary talent (n.)

boilerplate (para. 4): newspaper sections, such as syndicated stories or mastheads, that are sometimes available in plate form; also used to mean standardized reports. (n.)

conspicuous (para. 5): easy to see, striking (adj.)

premium (para. 6): high value (n.)

monolithic (para. 6): having unity in purpose or structure (adj.)

bimodal (para. 7): having two statistical trends (adj.)

unprecedented (para. 8): never before seen (adj.)

disparate (para. 11): fundamentally different (adj.)

chasm (para. 12): deep crack or gap, difference of opinion (n.)

EDMUND LEE (b. 1972) is a contributing writer for the Village Voice *whose works have appeared in* A. Magazine, Inside Asian America, Go: The Guide to Asian Pop Culture, *and* Vibe *magazine. He lives in New York.*

KENNETH LI (b. 1972) was born in Kowloon, Hong Kong, and emigrated to New York City at the age of two. He received his B.A. in journalism from New York University. Li currently works as a reporter at the New York Daily News, *and is a staff writer at* A. Magazine. *His articles have also appeared in* Vibe *magazine.*

beleaguer (para. 16): surround with troops, harass (v.)

agenda (para. 17): list of priorities, to-do list (n.)

qualitative (para. 18): pertaining to the specific character or nature of something (adj.)

quantitative (para. 18): pertaining to the number or percentage of something (adj.)

stellar (para. 19): outstanding (adj.)

stratospheric (para. 19): related to a layer of the atmosphere, extremely high (adj.)

raison d'être (para. 19): reason for living (French) (n.)

laurels (para. 20): aromatic evergreen leaves, wreath conferred as mark of honor, honor won for achievement (n.)

Vincent Benitez, seventeen, a Filipino American high school senior in New Jersey, failed geometry and chemistry last year. Between going to parties and cutting class, efforts to maintain his C– grade point average are almost an afterthought. "I could do better, I could apply myself, but it's kind of hard," he explains. "I don't always pay attention, and the teachers don't help."   1

Ruby Hwong, fifteen, is a Taiwanese American sophomore at the prestigious Brooklyn Technical High School in New York City, but she is barely scraping by. "I feel left out," she says. "Like in my math class, everybody knows everything, and when I ask them for help, they sigh, 'Oh you're so stupid!'"   2

Vincent and Ruby's testimonies are hardly isolated cases. Their stories strike a sharp discord with the prevailing perception that Asian Americans wear Coke-bottle size glasses and have a genetic ability to outperform other students.   3

Americans are already too familiar with the curve-busting stereotypes. This is due, in large part, to the media's fascination with superachieving Asian Americans and to popular wishes to reaffirm the potential that the American dream bestows on immigrants. Child prodigies such as Dr. Bala Ambati, who became an M.D. at sixteen, and Wall Street wiz-kid Matt Seto, who by junior year in high school was overseeing mutual funds portfolios well over the $1 million mark, are well known and widely publicized. But although their accomplishments make great copy, their examples are extreme. People like Vincent and Ruby don't yet fit the tabloid boilerplates, but they are overlooked, invisible; in some cases, they slip between the cracks.   4

Still, it's easy to see where the perception of Asian American students comes from. In 1990, over 50 percent of all Asian Pacific Americans (APAs) ages 18 to 24 were enrolled in college, compared with 34.4 percent of the general population. Moreover, over the last ten   5 years, the Asian American portion of undergraduate and graduate student populations has been rising rapidly. At prestigious colleges throughout the nation, this trend is especially conspicuous: at Stanford University, for instance, 41 percent of the entire student body is of Asian descent.

But is the cultural and family premium on education — and the ensuing excellence among offspring — the rule? Two landmark studies, released in March and April of this year [1997], say otherwise. Their findings confirm and shed light on what some Asian American students have known all along — that the Asian Pacific American student body is hardly monolithic. Among a vast range of ethnic origins, socioeconomic status, and parental educational and occupational status, there's an equally vast range of Asian American educational performance.

The tightly wound core of popular misconceptions about Asian American students has led many beleaguered American educators to dismiss Asians as a no-need population.

"A careful analysis of the data does not support the academic success myth," writes Heather Kim in her study, the first known study of academic performance among Asian Pacific American high school seniors, which Kim conducted as part of her postdoctoral work with the Princeton, New Jersey–based Educational Testing Service (ETS). "Asian Americans represent a bimodal mixture of extremely successful higher education attainment and a large undereducated mass."

Kim's study is unprecedented in that it is one of the first scientific studies to look at Asian American students not as one group but to analyze them broken down according to different factors — and looked at in this fashion, the variation in academic performance among Asian American students is wide indeed. Drawn from statistics compiled by the U.S. Department of Education, Kim drew a sample of 961 Asian American high school seniors among six ethnic groups — Chinese, Korean, Japanese, Filipino, South Asian (Pakistani and Asian Indian), and Southeast Asian (Vietnamese, Cambodian, Laotian, Hmong, and Thai). Kim's study found that while 80 percent of South Asian high school seniors scored above the 50th percentile on standardized math and reading tests, only 38 percent of Southeast Asian high school seniors scored in the same range. Among other groups, 75 percent of Korean Americans had the same achievement, followed by 62 percent of Chinese Americans, 58 percent of Japanese Americans, and 51 percent of Filipino Americans.

Another finding: While almost all Asian American seniors in-   9
tended to at least finish high school, most South Asians and Korean Americans desired a higher educational attainment — master's degrees or Ph.D.s, while most Chinese, Filipino, and Japanese Americans considered finishing only at the college level.

Yet another study, conducted by Shirley Hune, a professor at   10
UCLA, and Kenyon S. Chan, a professor at California State University–Northridge, for the Office of Minorities in Higher Education of the American Council on Education (ACE), looks at Asian Americans in higher education on the same nationwide scale, broken down along ethnic and economic lines. Strikingly, this study's findings parallel those of Kim's. "The education of Asian Americans has been ignored for a long time," says Kenyon S. Chan. "We thought that it was important to look at the state of APAs, since many of their needs are not being met."

"The image of APAs as a 'model minority group' has underlied   11
many of American education's policies and practices toward APAs over the past three decades," the report states. "The new 'positive' image conceals disparate educational achievements within and among APA ethnic groups and ignores obstacles in their educational pipeline."

In order to understand the educational attainment chasm among   12
the ethnic groups within Asian Pacific America, it is necessary to look at the newer immigration trends. The 1975 Indochina Migration of Refugee Assistance Act and the 1980 Refugee Act helped to resettle Vietnamese, Cambodians, Hmong, and Laotians fleeing war-torn countries. This wave of Asian immigration was very different from the one brought on by the Immigration Act of 1965, which was composed largely of educated professionals, with preference given to scientists, nurses, physicians, and engineers. Among these immigrants and their children, attaining higher education was as much a given — and a privilege — as it was for generations before them.

But more recent immigrants, particularly refugees, arrived in the   13
United States with very different baggage. "You have to understand that these people come from a chaotic situation," says Kenyon S. Chan. "They are concerned with just surviving. Then, perhaps, education." About 1 million immigrants fled devastation and political instability in Indochina to settle in the United States between 1975 and 1990. Within the Southeast Asian American population, the rate of poverty is staggering — 42 percent compared to 14.1 percent for the

larger Asian American community and 13.1 percent of the total U.S. population, according to the ACE report. According to Hune and Chan's analysis, the nature of their immigrant experience, coupled with a lower standard of living, puts newer immigrants in a "high-risk" category. Large proportions of Southeast Asians have attained less than a fifth-grade education — 33.9 percent of Laotians, 40.7 percent of Cambodians, and 54.9 percent of Hmong. Among these groups another obstacle to reaching higher educational levels is linguistic isolation: Many live in communities where the use of English is limited.

But experts are quick to note that wide variations in academic   14
performance cannot be pinned to any one group. The New York City public school system, for instance, has recently seen a steady rise of immigrants from rural China. And although Chinese Americans have resided in this city for over a hundred years, these new immigrants hail from provinces with dialects different from the more often-heard clatter of Cantonese, Mandarin, and Taiwanese. "Many of the educators in the New York City public school system don't know how to deal with these new Chinese," says Caroline Yu, executive director of the Coalition for Asian American Children and Families. "There aren't many counselors, for instance, who can speak English and the newer dialects, like Fuchinese. And many of these kids have never been in a classroom. Their parents probably never went to school: They're from the laboring class."

The multi-culti fabric for which New York City is famous — and   15
the city's supposed ability to absorb many different cultures — doesn't necessarily mean that the Board of Education has developed the ability or the sensitivity to effectively respond to the needs of new immigrants. According to Yu, some of the newer immigrant students have even ended up in the special education track in the public school system. "Because they can't speak English, or because [teachers] think they can't learn English, they think they're stupid," she says. "But we've been trying to work with these educators and get these kids out of that rut."

The tightly wound core of popular misconceptions about Asian   16
American students had led many beleaguered American educators to dismiss Asians as a no-need population. But findings like those of ETS and ACE, and local observations by student advocates like Caroline Yu, point to a need for more, not less, support for Asian students. "We need, obviously, more bilingual and even multilingual, educators and counselors," says Heather Kim. "And people need to be aware and culturally sensitive."

Most of the recommendations made by the ACE report prescribe   17
similar advice: that educators must be aware of the diversity among
Asian Pacific American students and of the specific plights in Southeast Asian and Pacific Islander communities. Linda Pang, an attorney
and the Chairperson for the Asian Pacific American Advisory Council
of the New York City Public School System, has organized conferences with teachers, administrators, and students to look into the varied requirements of Asian American students. "The principals of
many of the schools in New York came, and they responded well,"
she says. "They very much appreciated our forum and the chance to
finally get a better grasp of what's going on." And yet, she admits, it
is not at the top of their agenda.

Both authors agree that their studies are just a beginning, and   18
that more research is needed, especially of a qualitative nature. A
qualitative, as opposed to a numbers-crunching quantitative study,
would involve observing a family or a particular community for a
long period to better see the lives and the situations behind the statistics. "That would be far more interesting and valuable," says Frank
Tang, a professor at New York University's School of Education.
"These studies are good, but we need to go to the next level."

For now, the "other" Asian American students remain hidden,   19
overshadowed by the conspicuous, stellar accomplishments of some
of their classmates. But the "Asian" emphasis on performance, and
the multilayered reality behind it, begs for another question. Do
young Asian Americans today consider stratospheric SAT scores and
Ivy League diplomas to be their sole raison d'être?

For Ruby and Vincent, these laurels have little to do with their   20
private wishes, which are perhaps as much ingredients of the American dream as careers in medicine, law, or engineering. Ruby, for instance, wants to be a movie star. And while school for Vincent has
been a letdown, a love for rap and a talent for writing lyrics has provided relief. "I want to be in the music industry," he exclaims. "I'm
not interested in this school stuff. I know I need to do it now, but
music is what I love. That's where I want to be."

Vocabulary/Using a Dictionary

1. How is the word *discord* (para. 3) related to music? Break the
    word down into its root and prefix to begin your answer. What
    do you think *concord* means?

2. People are often criticized for having an *agenda* (para. 17). Why do you think an agenda can carry a negative connotation? Does it in the context of this article?

3. What is the literal meaning of *laurels* (para. 20)? For what achievements do people receive actual laurels? What does the phrase *to rest on one's laurels* mean?

Responding to Words in Context

1. Why do the authors use metaphors from astronomy — *stellar* and *stratospheric* (para. 19) — to describe some Asian American students?

2. Kenyon S. Chan uses the term *pipeline* to describe education in paragraph 11. Is this an appropriate choice? What image does it create?

Discussing Main Point and Meaning

1. In what way is Heather Kim's study *bimodal* (para 7)? What two different trends or populations does her analysis reflect?

2. According to Lee and Li, how is the stereotype of the Asian American superstudent harmful to some Asian American students?

3. What historical events have played a role in determining the educational status of different Asian American populations?

4. Think about the way that the successful-Asian-student stereotype encourages generalizations about white students and minority students — that white students lose opportunities because of Asian students and that African American and Latino students just aren't trying as hard as other minority students. How does this article call those myths into question?

Examining Sentences, Paragraphs, and Organization

1. How do the testimonies in the two opening paragraphs illustrate the main point of this article? Why did Lee and Li quote students in these paragraphs? Is the introduction effective, in your opinion? Why or why not?

2. The main evidence supporting Lee and Li's argument comes from what two sources? How do the authors use this evidence — by quoting, paraphrasing, summarizing, or all these methods? Refer

to your dictionaries or language handbooks for help distinguishing among the three methods.

3. This article begins and ends with specific anecdotes about two particular students, but the body focuses on trends among different groups (though it employs the voices of many individual scholars). What are the purpose and effect of this organizing strategy? Would you have organized the article any differently? For what reasons?

4. What kind of research should educators now be conducting, according to the authors and Frank Tang, professor at New York University's School of Education (para. 18)? Why?

Thinking Critically

1. Given that Asian Pacific Americans attend college at a higher rate than the general population and that the percentage is "rising rapidly" (para. 5), are Lee and Li's concerns somewhat overstated? Should educators be more concerned with the populations who have a less than 50 percent college attendance rate? Explain your answer.

2. Could the problem causing the disparities in educational performance among Asian American groups be economics rather than stereotyping, given that Southeast Asians are generally poorer and have come from less stable socioeconomic backgrounds? Should educators or economists have the responsibility for addressing the problems of Southeast Asian Americans? Reread paragraphs 12 and 13 before you answer.

In-Class Writing Activities

1. How many Asian American students attended your high school? Write a short description of the stereotypes and the myths that were used to characterize them as a group. Then describe any ways that reading Lee and Li's article has helped you rethink those stereotypes.

2. Write a journal entry from the point of view of an Asian American student that describes the experience of the pressures that these myths must place on him or her. Describe specific situations in the classroom, at home, or in society at large that might be particularly stressful.

BRYAN GARVEY

We Are More Than Labels

[THE DAILY BEACON, UNIVERSITY OF TENNESSEE AT KNOXVILLE / October 28, 1997]

Before You Read
Try picturing yourself from a specific person's point of view. What labels might that person use to describe you? Before you read, jot down a few of the labels. How much did these labels depend on the particular type of person you imagined was observing you? Now try the experiment again, but imagine yourself observed by an entirely different type of person. Do the labels change as well?

Words to Learn

bailiff (para. 2): officer who keeps order in a courtroom (n.)

plethora (para. 4): excess (n.)

eclectic (para. 4): having elements from various sources (adj.)

inanimate (para. 5): lifeless, spiritless (adj.)

demographic (para. 6): related to human population classifications (such as age, race, sex, and residence) (adj.)

phantasm (para. 8): something without physical reality (n.)

confound (para. 9): mix up, confuse (v.)

Sometimes I wonder if I am real and everyone else is a part of a   1
crazy dream I'm having, or someone else is real and I am simply an
unknown character in their dream. Am I simply a random person in a
passing truck to them, or is that other person a nobody to me, talking
to an insignificant other on the sidewalk?

BRYAN GARVEY *(b. 1975) was a senior at the University of Tennessee at Knoxville when he wrote this piece for the university's* Daily Beacon. *He was born in Jacksonville, Florida, and raised in Kentucky and Tennessee. In May, 1998, he received his B.S. in communications with a journalism major. He lives in Knoxville.*

An old episode of *The Twilight Zone* got me thinking once about   2
perceived existences. The show began in a courtroom with a man receiving a death sentence; he was to be hanged at midnight. As he
waited in his cell, he tried to convince his lawyer that the whole scenario was simply a dream that kept repeating like a broken record,
starting over at every stroke of midnight. The only way to stop the
hellish cycle was to keep him from being hanged. Once the lawyer
was finally convinced, he rushed out to contact the governor for a
pardon. The lawyer finally contacts the governor, but right at midnight. We see the trap door of the gallows drop, but the rope is
empty. The scene immediately flashes to the courtroom again where,
once again, the same main character is being sentenced to death.
Only this time his lawyer from before is the judge, his cell mate's the
bailiff, and the judge is a juror, or something like that. Short story
long, but oh well.

The age-old point is that we may never be sure of our existence.   3
More specifically, we may never be sure of

*Don't let labels get in the
way of who you are,
whoever you may be.*

who we are. For me, "I think, therefore I
am" will suffice; I exist and I am me. But
for others it's not that easy, so a whole
elaborate system of labels has been developed.

It would be impossible to enumerate   4
even a few of the plethora of labels we use for people. Often we use
this categorization to simplify our complicated and eclectic social
world. How many times have you heard a sentence begin, "There
are two types of people in this world . . . ?" But this organizational
system is obviously quite necessary. *The Miracle Worker* taught us
that Helen Keller's world was that of a savage beast until she learned
that everything had a label. Without this system our languages
would be reduced to conjunctions and articles and the like. But
there's a sharp difference between labeling an object and labeling a
person.

Sure, a basketball is a basketball, and a long-hair is indeed some-   5
one with long hair. However, I'd like to think that people can be perceived with a little more depth than an inanimate rubber sphere. I
can't get to know a basketball to see if I like it. It either bounces and
grips right or it doesn't. To label someone for the sake of physical description is one thing, but to allow those one or two words to relay a
person's character is something else entirely.

Now stereotypes (a common form of labels for people) are not   6
always completely false. They obviously exist for a reason. As comedians have previously illuminated, perhaps many Japanese tourists
are often seen with photography equipment, and maybe some politicians aren't completely honest. Heck, I even know a couple of people
with long hair who have listened to the Grateful Dead. But we never
really know someone until we know them. My own demographic labels might put me in another part of the country working on cars and
drinking Hamm's. But as one University of Tennessee statistics professor is so fond of saying, "People are not statistics."

I am who I am because of (1) what I've experienced in life and   7
(2) my basic values and life interests. If someone doesn't know all this
information about me, then they don't know me. And even if I fit a
stereotype yesterday, I could have changed completely today. I have
the same label but a different identity, and then your concrete perception crumbles.

So why are there folks who are so ready to strictly define every-   8
one around them? They are the ones who are seeking too hard to
label themselves. They're scared to address their identity, so they
cover it with labels. Thoreau once wrote, "All men want, not something to *do with,* but something to *do,* or rather something to *be.*"
What he meant was everyone wants not labels but real identities. No
one wants to be the phantasm of someone else's dream — the lawyer
who may be the bailiff next time around.

The moral is, don't let labels get in the way of who you are, who-   9
ever you may be. Moreover, don't let them confound who anyone
else is and especially who I am. I just might leave you completely out
of my next dream. Then who would you be?

Vocabulary/Using a Dictionary

1. What does an *inanimate* (para. 5) object lack? Is a tree inanimate? Is a blood cell? Is a grasshopper?

2. Can you think of any words that sound or look like *phantasm*
   (para. 8)? How might they be similar in meaning?

3. *Demographic* (para. 6) comes from the Greek words *demos* and
   graphein, or *graphos.* If *graphein* means "write," what do you
   think *demos* means? What must be the literal meaning of *autograph? Geography? Telegraph?*

Responding to Words in Context

1. Garvey says that "there's a sharp difference between labeling an object and labeling a person" (para. 4). What does he mean by this? Does the definition of *labeling* change from case to case?

2. Why does Garvey consider the cycle of the *Twilight Zone* episode he summarizes "hellish" (para. 2)?

Discussing Main Point and Meaning

1. Does Garvey think that stereotypes are completely invalid? Why or why not?

2. What point does Garvey make with the story of Helen Keller (para. 4)?

3. What does Garvey's statistics professor say about statistics (para. 6)? How does that point reinforce Garvey's main arguments?

4. How are identities different from labels, according to this article?

Examining Sentences, Paragraphs, and Organization

1. "Heck, I even know a couple of people with long hair who have listened to the Grateful Dead," writes Garvey (para. 6). What is the point of this sentence? Describe its tone and effect on you as a reader.

2. Examine the quote from Thoreau in paragraph 8. What is the difference between *doing with, doing,* and *being?* How do those things relate to Garvey's argument?

3. Garvey's article ends in a rhetorical question. What is that question, and what is its purpose?

Thinking Critically

1. Garvey says that Rene Descartes's philosophy of "I think, therefore I am" is good enough for him (para. 3). Do you believe him? Do you feel the same way? Is simply thinking enough for anyone?

2. Is it hypocritical for Garvey to suggest that stereotypes are acceptable as jokes (para. 6) but that they are otherwise useless? If

a joke is based on misinformation (a misnomer, for example), how can it still be funny? Do you find stereotypes humorous or offensive? Explain your answer.

In-Class Writing Activities

1. Describe yourself *demographically* (para. 6). That is, list your age, sex, race, ethnic background, class, state, hobbies, intellectual interests, the languages you speak, and so on. Now list all of the possible stereotypes that could apply to you based on those demographics. Are you surprised by how many you could think of? How inadequate are they as descriptions of who you are as an individual?

2. If you were compelled to classify the "two types of people in this world" (para. 4), what types would you choose? Honest and dishonest? Active and passive? Optimists and pessimists? Left brains and right brains? Try to rationalize how your categories might determine all other characteristics of a person. Once you've fully established those categories, explain why the two types are insufficient as labels. Give examples of types that would fall between or outside of your categories.

OPPOSING VIEWS

Stereotyping and Racism

Before You Read

Can our stereotypes of particular groups be racist? If a woman walking alone at night is frightened because a black male is walking behind her, does that make her a racist? If you meet a tall African American on campus and you assume he's an athlete, does that make you a racist? Is there a difference between believing in a stereotype or holding a prejudicial attitude and being an outright racist?

Words to Learn
[Waters]

misconception (para. 2): incorrect interpretation, misunderstanding (n.)
incarcerate (para. 3): imprison, confine (v.)

Words to Learn
[Englebert]

cower (para. 1): cringe in fear (v.)
prevalent (para. 1): widely practiced (adj.)
symptomatic (para. 3): relating to symptoms (adj.)
proverbial (para. 3): as well known as a proverb because commonly referred to (adj.)

dogmatic (para. 4): authoritatively assertive about unproved beliefs (adj.)
absolutism (para. 4): form of government in which all power is vested in a single authority (n.)
slyly (para. 6): underhandedly, secretively (adv.)

ERIC WATERS

Stop Stereotyping Young Black Males

[THE COLLEGIAN, KANSAS STATE UNIVERSITY / March 14, 1996]

Prior to attending college, I was relatively optimistic about the   1
relations among different races. Having grown up in a predominantly
black environment, I looked forward to living among people who
came from a variety of backgrounds. However, I did not anticipate
dealing with the many stereotypes concerning myself and others as
black males.

Eric Waters (b. 1976), a student at Kansas State University, was inspired to write this article for The Collegian *in an effort to encourage students to "get to know an individual on a civil level" before passing judgment or forming stereotypes. Born in Venice Beach, California, and raised in Kansas City, Kansas, Waters will become the first member of his family to graduate from a major university when he receives his degree in December 1998. He is currently a senior in graphic design.*

Throughout my first semester, I came into contact with many 2
students who had many misconceptions concerning black males. A
number of students said, "So tell me: are you on the football or basketball team?" This really disturbed me because it made me think
that on a predominantly white campus when students saw a black
male they automatically perceived him to be an athlete. They imagined that if a black male is on a predominantly white college campus,
he must be either a swift runner with a football or skillful on a basketball court. They failed to realize he just might be attending college
to broaden his mind and obtain the skills necessary to become a success in life. Who knows? He may also be on a complete academic
scholarship, as I am.

Last year, a column appeared titled "Stop Perpetuating Stereo- 3
types of Black Males." Errol Williamson made a valuable statement
that many black males "are very educationally minded." However, several individuals and groups have
trouble agreeing with this statement. Why?
It is simple. They see the local news, read
the local paper, and see the statistics
showing the numbers of black males who
are without high school diplomas, incarcerated, dead, or considered dangerous
and criminally minded. After seeing these statistics, they form a negative image of black males.

> Let's face it: Many
> people are ignorant
> about other races
> outside their own.

Unfortunately, the news neglects to report the statistics on black 4
males who are not incarcerated, are leaders in high places, have graduated from high school and college, are supporting their families, are
helping others in their times of need, are alive and well, and are making a difference in their communities and making a difference in the
lives of others.

Throughout my first semester, I also learned that individuals will 5
judge people by what they hear from others and what is printed on a
piece of paper. There was a time when a rape occurred on campus.
The next day, it was in the college paper with a brief description stating the subject was a white male and so on. After that, there was not
too much more said or heard about it. A couple of weeks later, another rape occurred. This time in the college paper, there was a
sketched-out picture of the subject, description, time and place the
rape had occurred, and a lot more detailed information — all on the
front page. Students had posted the sketched photo throughout

the residence halls and across campus. Meetings were held to discuss it, campus police seemed to be watching goings and comings, and it was the center of everyone's conversation. Do you know why? The rapist was a black male.

I often see people wear shirts that say *eracism*. Yes, there is noth-   6
ing wrong with it, but tell me how you are going to erase racism when you may be a racist yourself. Let's face it: Many people are ignorant about other races outside their own. For example, take the following incident I have experienced many times on campus.

It is about 10:30 P.M., and I am walking back to my room alone.   7
My trip to the library lasted a little bit longer than I had expected. However, as I am walking along, I realize a young woman keeps looking back at me as if I am after or following her. Therefore, she begins to walk faster and faster until she finally makes a ridiculous stop at Bluemont Hall, where she waits until I am clear down the street. Now what am I supposed to think? First of all, she does not even know me. Second, she makes me feel like I am some sort of criminal on the loose who is out to harm her. Finally, she knows Bluemont is closed long before 10:30 P.M., and the only reason she stopped there was to avoid me. All this is due to her stereotype of black males. [For another view of a similar incident, see "From the Bookshelf," p. 145.]

Ignorance means not knowing, and I believe that whether we like   8
it or not many students and people in general are living in ignorance. You know who you are. If this is supposed to represent the real world, it does not represent a lot. As you are reading this, I know that I might be stepping on your toes, but that is because I am speaking the truth. And yes, the truth does hurt.

It is about time to do away with labels and misconceptions con-   9
cerning black males and whoever else that you have stereotyped. Sometimes I wonder what this world would be like if everyone were colorless. Then how would we treat one another? What would we base our judgments and stereotypes on? How would we consider one group as a threat to another? How would we consider one group as superior to another?

Think about it.   10

G. STUART ENGLEBERT

Stereotyping and Racism Are Not the Same

[THE COLLEGIAN, KANSAS STATE UNIVERSITY / March 20, 1996]

I am writing in response to Eric Waters's March 14 column. While I am in agreement with some points he hits on, I feel he has fallen into the same trap as many others have when addressing issues of racism. Once again, another brave writer has taken up the fight of explaining ignorance only to cower behind big brother racism. While I agree unfair stereotyping and discrimination are prevalent, I do not believe this constitutes racism. I write only in response to Waters and do not assume anyone else reasons as he does.

I am concerned about the ease with which he links stereotyping to racism. For someone who professes to be going to school to broaden his mind, I was shocked at his failure to distinguish between stereotyping and racism. Perhaps the linkage of stereotyping to racism was unintentional; in one short passage in his article, however, he equates the two as one.

I would not have taken offense at all to the column if he had not made this equation. However, he did, and I feel it is symptomatic of arguments made pertaining to race relations — symptomatic in the sense that anytime there is a misunderstanding, or a difference of opinion, immediately the *racism* word is thrown out. I feel that this is the proverbial cop-out for not understanding why misconceptions exist. The fact that people stereotype others does not make them racists.

I will not pretend I am free of stereotypical behavior as Waters does. I confess to holding dogmatic views of young black males and

G. Stuart Englebert (b. 1968) grew up in Winston-Salem, North Carolina, and attended high school in Clemmons. He graduated from Kansas State University in May 1997 with a degree in history and entered the University of Kansas School of Law in September 1997. He plans to graduate in May 2000. Englebert was a junior at Kansas State University when he wrote this piece for the Collegian.

all other members of society. And that includes members of my own race. I feel that people who say they do not hold stereotypes are either lying or really haven't examined themselves very closely. Stereotyping is an unavoidable and necessary element of human survival. It becomes racism only when it reaches the point of absolutism. I admit to making unfair judgments about people, but they are always from personal experience. I resent the accusation that stereotyping exists only because of misrepresentation in the media. *You* may find the answer to life's problems on television, but I do not. I base my stereotypes of people on actual life experience. Now that I have confessed to the awful crime of learning through experience, I will also point out that I can unlearn from experience. It is only those who cannot unlearn their prejudicial views who approach racism.

In his column, Waters casually asserts that stereotyping and racism are one and the same thing. I think everyone can admit to having prejudicial views, but that does not make a person a racist. As Waters points out, prejudice stems from ignorance. Or it can stem from the truth. Whatever the case may be, most of us are smart enough and flexible enough to change our views when reality clashes with our prejudice.   5

The fact that people stereotype others does not make them racists.

However, the fact that I may hold certain misconceptions about entire races does not mean I assert that my race is naturally superior to all others. That and only that is racism. This is the accusation Waters seems to make when he slyly replaces the word *stereotype* with *racism*.   6

Those are strong accusations — accusations that by your own logic also implicate you as a racist. For you are also guilty of stereotyping in your assertion that many students misjudge you just because you're black. Have you ever considered that it may be a personal character flaw? Perhaps they just don't like you because you're you.   7

Sure, stereotypes exist. That's life. You know you're guilty of them, too. How can you expect others to rid themselves of stereotypes when you can't admit you hold them? It's time to stop hiding behind that word *racism*. You wondered what it would be like if everyone were colorless. How would we base our judgments? I do not know on what our judgments would be based, but you can rest assured judgments would still exist. And you would be out of excuses.   8

Vocabulary/Using a Dictionary

1. *Misconception* (Waters, para. 2) can be broken down into the prefix *mis-* and the verb *conceive,* whose main definitions are "generate a pregnancy" or "form an idea." How are these definitions similar? What kind of idea is a misconception? If *misconception* could be applied to a pregnancy, what would it mean?

2. How does Englebert distinguish between his *dogmatic* views and *absolutism* (para. 4)? In your own words, what is the distinction? Does Englebert make it clear enough? Or does the reader need to know the definitions of the two terms to understand Englebert's meaning?

3. How does the word *cower* (Englebert, para. 1) set the tone of Englebert's article?

Responding to Words in Context

1. Englebert's criticism of Waters is the fusing of the words *stereotype* and *racism.* Locate the paragraph where Waters introduces the word *racism* in his article, and discuss whether you agree with Englebert's criticism. Do you think Waters does equate stereotyping with racism? Explain why or why not.

2. Englebert writes that Waters would be "out of excuses" (para. 8) if there were no such thing as race. What does he mean by *excuses?*

Discussing Main Point and Meaning

1. On what kind of experiences does Waters base his analysis of stereotyping on his college campus? Why was he surprised by these experiences?

2. What is the relationship between stereotyping and racism, according to each author? Who do you think is right? Why?

3. How does Englebert argue that he comes to judgments about other people? How does he suggest that people who have judged Waters may have come to those judgments?

Examining Sentences, Paragraphs, and Organization

1. Examine paragraph 3 of Englebert's article, in which he establishes the foundation of his criticism of Waters. He argues that

Waters throws out the word *racism* as a "cop-out" to avoid "understanding why misconceptions exist." How does his word choice in this paragraph try to create an image of Waters? How might that image be indirectly connected to the subject of Waters's essay?

2. "I base my stereotypes of people on actual life experience," writes Englebert (para. 4). Is this a confession? Or a boast? What do you make of this sentence, given its context?

3. What does Waters want the reader to "think about" (para. 10)? What feeling is this imperative supposed to inspire in the reader? Did you "think about it"? Why or why not?

4. Englebert uses Waters in paragraph 4 to make a point about prejudice. How does he interpret Waters's assertion that "prejudice stems from ignorance" (para. 5)? Would Waters approve of the way Englebert employs that assertion?

Thinking Critically

1. Englebert argues very strongly against one passage in Waters's essay, which he says "equates" (para. 2) stereotyping and racism. If he had addressed other parts of Waters's argument, do you think some of his criticisms might have been answered? Why does he never quote Waters when it is so clearly Waters's use of language that angers him?

2. Waters's article is largely autobiographical and anecdotal (based on real experiences of specific people). How does this description relate to Englebert's idea that "learning through experience" (para. 4) is the way to come to judgments? Don't Waters and Englebert practice the same methods? Is there any way to reconcile the two arguments?

In-Class Writing Activities

1. Brainstorm a list of stereotypical media representations of black men and women that Waters addresses (para. 2). Then see if you can make a list of stereotypical media representations of white men and women. Can you? If so, how do they compare? If not, why do you think this is?

2. Write a third piece based on the opposition between Waters and Englebert, suggesting ways that they might bring their arguments

together into a productive compromise. Also address the way the resources of their university might be used to facilitate a solution to both the stereotyping Waters criticizes and the fingerpointing that Englebert has a problem with.

From the Bookshelf

Brent Staples, *Parallel Time*

In 1986, Brent Staples published "Just Walk on By" in Ms. magazine. This reflective essay recounts the fear Staples inspired as an African American who liked to take late-night walks in his Chicago neighborhood. The essay, which offers an interesting illustration of racial stereotyping, has been widely reprinted in college anthologies. In 1994, Staples revised the essay (a sample of which follows) as part of Parallel Time: Growing Up in Black and White, an eloquent memoir that chronicles his childhood in a small Pennsylvania factory town and his gradual separation from friends and community as scholarships and a college education thrust him into a white professional world.

A member of the editorial board of the New York Times, Staples holds a Ph.D. in psychology from the University of Chicago. He has worked as a newspaper reporter, and his essays have appeared in many national magazines.

My First Victim

At night, I walked to the lakefront whenever the weather permitted. I was headed home from the lake when I took my first victim. It was late fall, and the wind was cutting. I was wearing my navy pea jacket, the collar turned up, my hands snug in the pockets. Dead leaves scuttled in shoals along the streets. I turned out of Blackstone Avenue and headed west on 57th Street, and there she was, a few yards ahead of me, dressed in business clothes and carrying a briefcase. She looked back at me once, then again, and picked up her pace. She looked back again and started to run. I stopped where I was and looked up at the surrounding windows. What did this look like to people peeking out through their blinds? I was out walking.

continued on next page

continued from previous page

But what if someone had thought they'd seen something they hadn't and called the police. I held back the urge to run. Instead, I walked south to The Midway, plunged into its darkness, and remained on The Midway until I reached the foot of my street.

I'd been a fool. I'd been walking the streets grinning good evening at people who were frightened to death of me. I did violence to them by just being. How had I missed this? I kept walking at night, but from then on I paid attention.

I became expert in the language of fear. Couples locked arms or reached for each other's hand when they saw me. Some crossed to the other side of the street. People who were carrying on conversations went mute and stared straight ahead, as though avoiding my eyes would save them. This reminded me of an old wives' tale: that rabid dogs didn't bite if you avoided their eyes. The determination to avoid my eyes made me invisible to classmates and professors whom I passed on the street.

Staples, Brent. *Parallel Time: Growing Up in Black and White.* New York: Pantheon, 1994.

Discussing the Unit

Suggested Topic for Discussion

The articles in this unit investigate three specific stereotypes based on race. Edmund Lee and Kenneth Li explore the harmful effects of a seemingly positive stereotype; Bryan Garvey points out the dangers of labels; and Eric Waters and G. Stuart Englebert disagree on the concepts of stereotyping and racism. Have you ever stereotyped others, or have you been categorized this way? How did the experience make you feel? What do you think can be done to alleviate stereotyping and its harmful effects in America?

Preparing for Class Discussion

1. Do you ever stereotype or label yourself? For example: "I'm a teenager! I'm supposed to act stupid in public!" or "All of us Italians are loud and emotional," or "I would never burp in front of anyone because girls are supposed to have better manners than boys." How is labeling yourself different from labeling another person? Can people be prejudiced against themselves?

2. When you describe someone to another person (and the two have never met), what characteristics do you mention and in what order? Do you always place demographics first? Why or why not? How would you like to be described to someone who had never met you?

From Discussion to Writing

1. Write a brief essay about your heroes or role models. Do they come from the same demographic groups you do? If so, explain whether this is a good or a bad thing. If not, explain whether their differences matter at all in your choices.

2. Some stereotypes seem harmless, especially when they are attached to a talent. For example, we might find it acceptable to expect professional hockey players to have macho attitudes, scientists to be eccentric, or book reviewers to wear glasses. Other stereotypes interpret a physical or demographic trait as negative, ignoring any talent or likable characteristic — expecting fat people to be gluttonous and undisciplined, Asian Americans to be passive and weak, welfare recipients to be lazy and dishonest, beautiful models to be empty-headed. Describe the difference in intention and in effect of these two different kinds of stereotyping. List as many of your own examples as possible in the process.

3. The media seem to be a willing conduit for stereotypes. Morning radio shows, television sitcoms and talk shows, all forms of news coverage, advertising, mail order catalogues, the Internet, the popular music industry, and the high fashion world all, in some way, use stereotyping to reach their audiences. Write an essay analyzing one specific media outlet and its use of stereotypes. Then suggest ways that that use might be decreased, explaining why the decrease might benefit not only viewers but the media itself.

Topics for Cross-Cultural Discussion

1. Are some countries more or less prone to stereotyping? Why or why not?

2. Have you ever been in, or lived in, a country where people held negative stereotypes of Americans? What were those stereotypes? What misconceptions were they based on? Were they popular beliefs? If so, why?

Can "Op-Ads" Change Your Mind?

Most of the ads we see and hear daily try to persuade us to buy consumer goods like cars, cosmetics, and candy. Yet advertising does more than promote consumer products. Every day we also encounter numerous ads that promote not things but opinions. These *opinion-advertisements* (*op-ads,* for short, since they often appear in the *opinion/editorial* or *op-ed* pages of newspapers) may take a variety of forms — political commercials, direct mail from advocacy groups seeking contributions, posters and billboards, or paid newspaper and magazine announcements.

Unlike most product advertising, which relies heavily on creating favorable images, opinion advertising — whether from the left, right, or center of the political spectrum — works mainly by rhetorical argument and persuasion. In other words, opinion-advertisements are frequently far more verbal than visual; they contain more text and require more attentive reading than almost any other type of advertising found in print. Nearly all opinion advertising also requires a catchy headline that focuses on a controversy and discloses the ideological stance of the organization that sponsored the ad.

This unit features five such advertisements, taken from the print media. Included here are ads paid for by U.S. English, supporting English-only legislation; the National Center for Tobacco-Free Kids, endorsing comprehensive antitobacco legislation; Planned Parenthood Federation of America, "promoting genuine reproductive choices for all Americans"; the American Civil Liberties Union, advocating a ban on official prayer sessions in public schools; and Negative Population Growth, inviting support for a smaller U.S. population. These selections, taken from both liberal and conservative periodicals, represent only a fraction of the advertisements designed to influence the ideas and attitudes of Americans on the many controversial cultural and political issues of the day. A careful examination of their verbal techniques — whether you agree or disagree with their messages — will help you better understand the basics of ideological persuasion.

U.S. ENGLISH

[NATIONAL REVIEW / June 16, 1997]

Before You Read

Is it necessary to make English the "official" language of the United States in order to provide an incentive for immigrants to learn the language? Should immigrants be required to speak English in schools and on the job?

Words to Learn

bilingual (para. 1): capable of using two languages with equal facility (adj.)
bureaucrat (para. 1): official who follows administrative routines in an inflexible way (n.)

Mauro E. Mujica, Architect
Chairman/CEO, U.S.English

Why An Immigrant Heads An Organization Called U.S.English.

His name is Mauro E. Mujica. He immigrated to the United States in 1965 to study architecture at Columbia University. English was not his first language then – but he is perfectly bilingual today. Learning English was never an option. It was required for success. Now he is the Chairman of U.S.ENGLISH, the nation's largest organization fighting to make English the common language of government at all levels. Why? Because English is under assault in our schools, in our courts and by bureaucrats and self-appointed leaders for immigrant groups. The whole notion of a melting pot society is threatened if new immigrants aren't encouraged to adopt the common language of this country. We're not suggesting that people shouldn't hold onto their native languages. We just don't believe the government should spend money providing services in multiple languages when money could be better used teaching new immigrants English.

Join us. Support us. Fight with us.
Because English is the key to opportunity for all new immigrants.

Speak up for America. Call 1-800-U.S.ENGLISH

1747 Pennsylvania Avenue, NW, Suite 1100
Washington, DC 20006
http://www.us-english.org

THE NATIONAL CENTER
FOR TOBACCO-FREE KIDS

[THE NEW YORK TIMES / March 11, 1998]

Before You Read

Is it the government's responsibility to keep children from smoking? And if cigarettes are so bad for kids, why are they acceptable for adults? If we want to ban cigarettes altogether, should we then focus our attention on legislation to ban other health hazards — like junk food, alcohol, excessive noise, motorcycles, and suntanning?

Words to Learn

comprehensive (para. 1): fully detailed, inclusive (adj.)
legislation (para. 1): laws (n.)

Without national tobacco legislation...
The Lives of Five Million Kids Could Go Up In Smoke

America needs comprehensive tobacco legislation to drive down tobacco use among kids, help adults quit and eliminate second-hand smoke in public places and worksites.

Congress, the Clinton Administration, our organizations and **you** – national tobacco control is everybody's responsibility.

More than five million children under 18 will die early, unless current smoking rates are reversed (Source: CDC).

American Association for Health Education; American Association of School Administrators; American Association of University Women; American Federation of Teachers; American Medical Student Association; Association of Schools of Public Health; Child Welfare League of America; Girls Incorporated; Girl Scouts, USA; National Association of Elementary School Principals; National Association of Secondary School Principals; National Education Association; National Federation of State High School Associations; The National PTA

Tobacco vs. Kids.
Where America draws the line.

CAMPAIGN for TOBACCO-FREE Kids™

To learn more, call 1-800-284-KIDS
or see our web site at www.tobaccofreekids.org

The National Center for Tobacco-Free Kids, 1707 L Street NW, Suite 800, Washington, DC 20036

PLANNED PARENTHOOD
FEDERATION OF AMERICA

[AMERICAN PROSPECT / April 1998]

Before You Read

Why do we debate the issue of abortion so ardently in this country? Should we instead discuss pregnancy prevention methods with equal passion? If more people focused their energies on issues like teen pregnancy, available and affordable contraception, and adoption, would the furor over abortion die down? Or is the real question being debated the issue of how "private" a person's body is?

Words to Learn

profound (para. 2): deep, complete (adj.)

noble (para. 4): having high hereditary rank, showing greatness (adj.)

vulnerable (para. 5): easily attacked (adj.)

contraception (para. 8): method for preventing an embryo from being formed (n.)

genuine (para. 11): authentic, honest (adj.)

Twenty-five years after *Roe v. Wade*, Planned Parenthood® gives new meaning to "choice."

Planned Parenthood, as our name suggests, has always looked to the future.

On this 25th anniversary of the Supreme Court's decision affirming a woman's right to choose whether or not to have a child, we reflect on the profound meaning of reproductive choice, the work yet to be done to assure real choices for all, and the responsibility born of our freedom to choose.

The responsibility to fulfill the vision of making every child a wanted child and every pregnancy intentional. The responsibility to respect and support women's choices about childbearing or abortion. The responsibility to keep these decisions moral and medical — not political.

A generation after *Roe v. Wade*, America has far to go to realize these noble goals. A few examples:

▶ Legislative assaults and anti-choice violence have taken away access to abortion and family planning for many, especially the vulnerable, the poor, the young, and the geographically isolated.

▶ Early medical abortion has been kept from American women.

▶ Despite all the talk about reducing the need for abortion, many health insurance plans don't cover family planning — women's most common health care need — and most fail to cover the full range of birth control options.

▶ Emergency contraception is not widely available, even though it could prevent half of all abortions.

▶ Nearly 60% of teens say they don't have enough information about birth control and 45% don't know where to get it.

Clearly, the freedom to choose whether or when to have a child is fundamental. The *right* to choose abortion must never be taken for granted. But it is not enough.

Full access to family planning and all reproductive health care, fair insurance coverage, emergency contraception, responsible sex education, early medical and surgical abortion methods, and the development of new, more reliable birth control options can give people the genuine chance to make reproductive choices freely and responsibly.

We think it's time to fulfill the promise made a generation ago. And make life better for the generations to come.

You can help by making a call and mailing the coupon below. Thank you.

Remind. your self. what choice. you. have.

Call **1-888-38 STAND UP** toll-free to learn more about Planned Parenthood's *Responsible Choices* campaign, and to be connected with your Senators in Washington. Tell them you support access to abortion and family planning.

Planned Parenthood. Responsible Choices.

AMERICAN CIVIL LIBERTIES UNION

[THE NEW YORK TIMES / March 17, 1998]

Before You Read

Do you pray? Do you think that students should pray in public schools? If you were forced to participate in official prayer sessions that did not recognize your particular religious beliefs, how would you feel? Would you just think quietly and ignore the prayer? Would you insist that your prayers be included in the session as well? Or would you complain to your school board that the practice violates the separation of church and state established in the Bill of Rights of the U.S. Constitution?

Words to Learn

official (para. 1): approved by an authority (adj.)
denominations (para. 1): classification as of currency, stamps, or religions (n.)

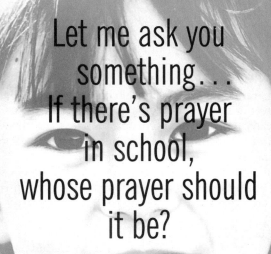

Let me ask you something... If there's prayer in school, whose prayer should it be?

Official prayer sessions in public school seem like a good idea to many Americans, provided they get to choose the prayer. But in such a diverse society, how can one prayer satisfy every religious belief? How would you feel if your child were required to say a Catholic prayer in school every day? Or a Baptist prayer or Muslim prayer? What about a Jewish prayer or a Buddhist prayer? There are over 1,500 religious denominations in America. How many of us would want our children to recite someone else's prayer? Maybe prayer is just too personal to let the government or any one particular religious group decide what prayers our children should be saying in school. Think about it.

Ira Glasser
Executive Director of the American Civil Liberties Union
125 Broad Street
New York, New York 10004
www.aclu.org

NEGATIVE POPULATION GROWTH, INC.

[THE NEW REPUBLIC / April 20, 1998]

Before You Read

Do new immigrants have as much right to come to the United States as the seventeenth-century founders of this nation did? Or do you think we already have too many people to take care of? Some argue that immigrants drain our limited economic resources; others claim that immigrants provide cheap labor that benefits the U.S. economy. What do you think that people fear more — the number of immigrants or the kinds of immigrants who migrate to the United States?

Words to Learn

heed (para. 2): pay close attention to (v.)

enact (para. 4): make into law (v.)

deport (para. 6): expel from a country (v.)

deter (para. 6): discourage (v.)

devastate (para. 8): ruin, defeat (v.)

vitally (para. 9): having a life-giving or life-sustaining quality (adv.)

sustainable (para. 10): able to be supported or continued (adj.)

sound (para. 10): free from disease or defect, firm and safe (adj.)

A Message from Negative Population Growth, Inc.

Why Does Our Government Allow Over One Million New Immigrants to Come Here Every Year?

...When a Majority of Americans Say We Should Not Admit More Than 100,000 a Year at Most!!

A recent Roper poll, sponsored by NPG, Inc., showed that a majority of Americans (54%) want immigration cut to not more than 100,000 a year. So why does our Federal Government allow more than ten times that many to come here every year?

The poll showed 70% of Americans – that's over two out of three – want immigration cut drastically to not over 300,000 a year. How in the world can our government possibly justify an immigration policy that allows four times that many to come here every year? Don't our elected representatives have an obligation to heed the clearly expressed wishes of the American public?

The poll also showed that a substantial number of Americans (20%) simply want immigration halted completely. In other words, one American in five wants no immigration at all.

We urge Congress, with the vigorous support of President Clinton, to enact legislation that would drastically reduce the present level of immigration, and thus bring our immigration policy into line with the clearly expressed wishes of the overwhelming majority of the American people.

Illegal Immigration – Out of Control

Polls have shown for years that, almost unanimously, Americans want illegal immigration stopped. Despite that, our Federal Government has done very little to reduce illegal immigration, much less stop it. An estimated 350,000 illegal aliens settle here permanently each year. That is over three times more than the 100,000 a year a majority of Americans favor for total immigration. These illegal settlers join a pool of an estimated five to six million illegal aliens who are already living here permanently in violation of our laws.

The Roper poll cited above showed that 74% of Americans (three out of every four) want illegal aliens identified and deported. So why is our government not doing just that? In 1996, only about 110,000 illegal aliens were deported. A vastly increased program of deportations would not only deter prospective illegal migrants abroad, but also motivate those already here to leave voluntarily.

The Central Issue – Overpopulation

NPG urges a drastic reduction in immigration solely because of its contribution to the disastrous growth of our U.S. population. We are on the path from our present population of 268 million to a population of nearly 500

million by 2100. More than 90% of that growth will be the direct result of post-2000 immigration.

Immigration is the driving force behind the population growth that is devastating our environment and the quality of our lives. Primarily because of immigration we are rushing at breakneck speed toward an environmental and economic disaster.

U.S. Population Size –
A Vitally Important National Issue

Other things being equal, our population size determines our impact on our already over-stressed environment and increasingly scarce resources. The size of our population is, therefore, a vitally important national issue.

If we are to have any hope at all of creating an economy that will be sustainable indefinitely, in a sound and healthy environment, with an adequate standard of living for all, we need a smaller, not a larger, U.S. population. But we will never be able to achieve a smaller population unless we reduce immigration to a small fraction of its present level. That is a simple fact.

Isn't there someone among our political leaders who is willing to recognize the need for a smaller U.S. population and for public policies to achieve it? He or she would have the support of a majority of Americans. The Roper poll cited above showed that 54% of Americans believe that our country is already overpopulated.

NPG is a nonprofit, national membership organization established in 1972. Contributions to NPG are tax-deductible to the extent the law allows.

> Yes, I want to become a member of NPG, and help you work towards a smaller U.S. population. I am enclosing my check for annual membership dues.
>
> ___ $30 ___ $50 ___ $100 ___ Other
>
> Name _____
>
> Address _____
>
> City _____ State _____ Zip _____
> Please mail to: NR-153
>
> ◤ **Negative Population Growth, Inc.**
>   1608 20th Street, NW, Washington, DC 20009

Vocabulary/Using a Dictionary

1. What role do you think *bureaucrats* play in the "assault" of English, according to U.S. English?

2. How do you think *legislation* is different from *law* (National Center for Tobacco-Free Kids, para. 1)?

3. What would be the opposite of a "genuine chance" (Planned Parenthood Federation of America, para. 11)? Why does this ad use this phrase?

4. What do you think this American Civil Liberties Union ad means by "official prayer sessions"? Do you think the ACLU would approve of unofficial prayer sessions?

5. When something is "vitally important" (Negative Population Growth, para. 9), what is it important to? What does the expression refer to as it is used in this ad?

Responding to Words in Context

1. What does U.S. English mean by "a melting pot society" (para. 1)?

2. In paragraph 2 of the National Center for Tobacco-Free Kids ad, the parties with "responsibility" are listed as "Congress, the Clinton Administration, our organizations, and *you*." Why does this ad use the second-person pronoun *you* here? Is it effective?

3. Why does the Planned Parenthood Federation of America draw a distinction between "moral and medical" decisions and "political" ones (para. 3)?

4. Why does the American Civil Liberties Union list so many different religious denominations in this ad?

5. Could Negative Population Growth switch the positions of *sustainable* and *sound* in this ad and retain the meaning of the sentence (para. 10) in which they appear? Why or why not?

Discussing Main Point and Meaning

1. What changes does U.S. English suggest should be made with respect to immigrant services and education (para. 2)?

2. Aside from stopping kids from smoking, what other purposes does the National Center for Smoke-Free Kids list (para. 1)?

3. Is Planned Parenthood's ad only about abortion rights? What other issues are addressed?

4. Who is the intended audience for the American Civil Liberties Union ad? How does the tone of the ad reflect that intention?

5. What do you think is the most urgent concern of the ad from Negative Population Growth?

Examining Sentences, Paragraphs, and Organization

1. "[English] was required for success" in Mauro E. Mujica's day, U.S. English contends (para. 1). Does the ad seem to say that English is still required for everyone's success? If so, why does this ad use the past tense?

2. What idiom is used in the ad headline for the National Center for Tobacco-Free Kids? Is it effective?

3. There are several sentence fragments in paragraph 3 of the Planned Parenthood ad. What is their purpose?

4. "Think about it" is the final sentence in the American Civil Liberties ad. What is "it"? Is this sentence effective? Why or why not?

5. Negative Population Growth employs many numbers and statistics. Is there any logic to the way these numbers are organized? How effective is the way they are used?

Thinking Critically

1. Since Mauro E. Mujica is "perfectly bilingual" according to U.S. English (para. 1), shouldn't this ad use *his* writing to send out its message?

2. Why isn't it a parent's responsibility to keep his or her child from smoking (National Center for Tobacco-Free Kids)? Is the government responsible for restricting all potentially harmful products?

3. Does Planned Parenthood fulfill its promise to "[give] new meaning to 'choice'" in this ad? Explain your answer.

4. Because many high schools are plagued by violence or have experienced occasional acts of destructive violence, how do you think the American Civil Liberties Union would respond to prayers — to help prevent violence?

5. Isn't the 54 percent majority that Negative Population Growth refers to a pretty small majority (para. 1)? Is it a big enough majority, in your opinion, to warrant a broad campaign for change?

In-Class Writing Activities

1. Describe the resources offered in your high school for nonnative speakers of English. Were they adequate? Are there changes that should be made to decrease or increase them?

2. In small groups, brainstorm a plan to cut the smoking rates at your college or university, arguing for what you think are the most effective ways to get young people to quit.

3. Write a short rebuttal to the main points Planned Parenthood makes (see the bulleted outline of points, paras. 5 to 9) from the point of view of an activist against abortion rights.

4. Write a pledge or meditation that you think could serve as an alternative to "official prayer" that might offer a compromise to the two opposing positions on the issue of prayer in public schools.

5. Rewrite Negative Population Growth's ad in one paragraph.

From the Bookshelf

Tom Shachtman, *The Inarticulate Society*

As mass advertising and political sound bites increasingly dominate the media, Americans appear to be losing the ability to discuss ideas and opinions reasonably, open-mindedly, and eloquently. This deterioration of American discourse is no accident, Tom Shachtman claims in The Inarticulate Society: Eloquence and Culture in America, *but is rather a condition actively promoted by politicians and corporate executives to prevent the public from engaging in productive discussion and debate. As a practical example of this deliberate dumbing down of public discourse, Shachtman points out that in 1963 the average news commentator drew on approximately 10,000 words to report events; today, commentators use about 5,000 words, a vocabulary barely larger than that of television shows for five-year-olds. How this debased speech threatens our democratic way of life is the central question of this provocative study, which should be of interest to anyone disturbed by the current state of American public discourse. In the book excerpt reprinted below, Shachtman looks at the ways advertising methods have corrupted political expression. Tom Shachtman is the author of numerous books of fiction and nonfiction, as well as several highly acclaimed television documentaries.*

Sound Reasoning or Sound Bites?

Today's mass market advertising believes the audience infinitely malleable, manipulates the audience's emotions, and shows contempt for the audience, in particular for its intelligence. There are few constraints on advertising's ability to twist our willingness to trust, on its appeals to our flagrant self-interest, on its predilection for giving us license, or on the ways it plays on our insufficiencies. "Advertising deals in open sores," according to Jerry della Femina, an agency founder. "Fear. Greed. Anger. Hostility. You name the dwarfs and we play on every one. We play on all the emotions and on all the problems." Pierre Martineau wrote in an advertising insider's textbook that one of advertising's "very definite purposes" is "to help the consumer become articulate about his buying choices, to put words in his mouth which sound convincing, even if they are not the right words."

As political discourse moves ever closer to advertising, it exhibits more of the same ventriloquist tendencies, the same marketing mentality, the same contempt for our intelligence, and plays on the same dwarfs that advertising does. In the 1988 campaign for the presidency, a particular success for this constellation of pandering attributes came from the "Willie Horton" television commercial, which blamed Michael Dukakis for the failures attendant on a program that let convicted murderers out on prison furlough. The commercial was apparently wildly effective in persuading voters to vote against Dukakis and for George Bush, but it was roundly derided for its nasty tone and half-truths. Vice President Bush disavowed it, and so did his campaign consultant, Roger Ailes, who went so far as to threaten lawsuits against those who said that the commercial had

continued on next page

continued from previous page

been his idea. Its success, however, has been imitated by more and more negative ads, appeals to fear, and similar strategies aimed at the audience's emotions rather than at their ability to reason.

Shachtman, Tom. *The Inarticulate Society: Eloquence and Culture in America.* New York: Free Press, 1995.

Discussing the Unit

Suggested Topic For Discussion

All of the advertisements in this unit try to convince us that a certain ideological standpoint on an important social issue is the correct one. Many other advertisements use the same tactics to convince us of different things. Consider these types of advertisements. Which techniques used by the advertisements in this unit are also used in other areas of our lives? Are these techniques effective? If you don't think so, then why do the advertisers spend so much time and money on their messages?

Preparing for Class Discussion

1. Only Negative Population Growth provides no photograph in its ad. How does this ad work differently from the others? What purpose do the photos in the other ads serve?

2. Examine the headlines for each ad. Which summarize the main points of the ads, and which are just hooks meant to grab the reader's attention?

From Discussion to Writing

1. In small groups, develop an op-ad for an issue that you think is important (getting young people to vote, for example). Employ some strategies used in these ads that you think are particularly effective.

2. Turn the ad you support most strongly into an argumentative essay.

Topics for Cross-Cultural Discussion

1. What differences do you think there are between U.S. advertising and advertising in your native culture? Is advertising a medium for political opinion in countries other than the United States?

2. Would these ads be effective in your native culture, or are their strategies inappropriate for non-American audiences? Explain your answer.

Free Expression: How Much Should We Tolerate?

Ask an average American to tell you what the Constitution's Third or Seventh Amendment says, and most likely you'll just get a blank stare. Ask that same person what the *First* Amendment guarantees, and you'll probably get an answer immediately — the right to free speech. Why is this particular right so prized in our society? And what should we do about certain kinds of speech — for instance racist, sexist, or homophobic remarks — that inflict pain and give offense?

This unit examines three important issues related to free expression. In "A Civic Duty to Annoy," a best-selling social critic and Radcliffe Public Policy Fellow, Wendy Kaminer, argues that civic life demands a great deal of give and take and that people need to be a bit less sensitive about expressions that offend them. Resisting the complaints of her Harvard students about being "marginalized" or "oppressed," she maintains that "sometimes nurturing students means challenging their complaints instead of satisfying their demands for sympathy."

Does the First Amendment protect expression that may incite violence? Looking at a recent rash of violent crimes in our schools, two professors of education, Nancy Carlsson-Paige and Diane Levin, claim that children have for years been the target of violent games and television programs designed to profit America's corporations:

"Efforts to limit violence in children's media," they contend, "never get past the violation-of-free-speech argument." Their point: Unless we find a way to control the barrage of media violence young people are exposed to daily, *real* violence in our streets and schoolyards will grow at an alarming rate.

In the final selection, Sara Ziegler, a student at Iowa State University, explores the ways our culture breeds intolerance. Responding to an antihomosexual letter to the editor, she reminds us in "How to Breed Intolerance" that intolerance, unlike reasonable disagreement, is often based on ignorance, rumor, stereotypes, and disrespect.

WENDY KAMINER

A Civic Duty to Annoy

[THE ATLANTIC MONTHLY / September 1997]

Before You Read

Have you ever been in a situation where you think someone has unjustly complained about being oppressed? Do you think that too many people these days complain about being oppressed?

WENDY KAMINER *(b. 1949), lawyer, author, and social critic, is the president of the National Coalition against Censorship, a Public Policy Fellow at Radcliffe College, and a contributing editor at* The Atlantic Monthly. *Her numerous articles and reviews have appeared in such publications as the* New York Times, The New Republic, *and* The Nation. *Kaminer's books include* True Love Waits: Essays and Criticism *(1996),* It's All the Rage: Crime and Culture *(1995), and* I'm Dysfunctional, You're Dysfunctional: The Recovery Movement and Other Self-Help Fashions *(1992). Kaminer was awarded a Guggenheim Fellowship in 1993.*

Words to Learn

devolve (para. 1): pass on to a substitute (v.)

orthodox (para. 2): conforming to traditional beliefs (adj.)

irreverence (para. 3): lack of reverence or respect (n.)

piety (para. 3): act of devoutness (n.)

solidarity (para. 3): unity within a group (n.)

scoff (para. 4): mock (v.)

proffer (para. 5): present for acceptance (v.)

promiscuously (para. 5): casually, indiscriminately (adv.)

derogatory (para. 6): belittling (adj.)

puerile (para. 6): immature, juvenile (adj.)

solicitude (para. 8): care, concern (n.)

paradigmatic (para. 10): serving as a model (adj.)

exalt (para. 10): elevate, praise (v.)

forswear (para. 11): renounce under oath (v.)

provocation (para. 11): act of inciting, something that irritates (n.)

rectitude (para. 11): moral virtue, righteousness (n.)

What is there about being in a room filled with people who   1
agree with me that makes me want to change my mind? Maybe it's
the self-congratulatory air of consensus among people who consider
themselves and one another right-thinking. Maybe it's the consistency
of belief that devolves into mere conformity. Maybe it's just that I
can no longer bear to hear the word "empower."

At self-consciously feminist gatherings I feel at home in the worst   2
way. I feel the way I do at family dinners, when I want to put my feet
up on the table and say something to provoke old Uncle George. To get George
going, I defend affirmative action or the capital-gains tax.[1] To irritate my more orthodox feminist colleagues, I disavow any personal guilt about being born white and middle-class. I scoff every time I hear a
Harvard student complain that she's oppressed.

> **We tend to forget that criticism sometimes expresses greater respect than praise.**

I'm not alone in my irreverence, but feminist pieties combined   3
with feminine courtesy keep most of us in line. Radcliffe College,
where I am based, is devoted to nurturing female undergraduates.
We're supposed to nod sympathetically, in solidarity, when a student
speaks of feeling silenced or invisible because she is female, of color,

---

[1]*capital gains tax:* Tax imposed on a profit from the sale of assets, such as bonds or
real estate.

or both. We're not supposed to point out that Harvard students are among the most privileged people in the universe, regardless of race or sex.

I don't mean to scoff at the discrimination that a young woman   4
of any color may have experienced or is likely to experience someday. I do want to remind her that as a student at Harvard/Radcliffe or any other elite university she enjoys many more advantages than a working-class white male attending a community college. And the kind of discrimination that students are apt to encounter at Harvard — relatively subtle and occasional — is not "oppression." It does not systematically deprive people of basic civil rights and liberties and is not generally sanctioned by the administration.

Besides, everyone is bound to feel silenced, invisible, or un-   5
appreciated at least once in a while. Imagine how a white male middle manager feels when he's about to be downsized. Like laments about dysfunctional families, complaints about oppression lose their power when proffered so promiscuously. Melodramatic complaints about oppression at Harvard are in part developmental: Students in their late teens and early twenties are apt to place themselves at the center of the universe. But their extreme sensitivity reflects frequently criticized cultural trends as well. An obsession with identity and self-esteem has encouraged students to assume that every insult or slight is motivated by racist, sexist, or hetero-sexist bias and gravely threatens their well-being. What's lost is a sense of perspective. If attending Harvard is oppression, what was slavery?

Sometimes nurturing students means challenging their complaints   6
instead of satisfying their demands for sympathy. I've heard female students declare that any male classmate who makes derogatory remarks about women online or over the telephone is guilty of sexual harassment and should be punished. What are we teaching them if we agree? That they aren't strong enough to withstand a few puerile sexist jokes that may not even be directed at them? That their male classmates don't have the right to make statements that some women deem offensive? There would be no feminist movement if women never dared to give offense.

When nurturing devolves into pandering, feminism gives way to   7
femininity. Recently a small group of female students called for disciplinary proceedings against males wearing "pornographic" T-shirts in a dining hall. They found it difficult to eat lunch in the presence of such unwholesome, sexist images. Should we encourage these young

women to believe that they're fragile creatures, with particularly delicate digestive systems? Should we offer them official protection from
T-shirts? Or should we point out that a group of pro-choice students
might someday wear shirts emblazoned with words or images that
pro-life students find deeply disturbing? Should we teach them that
the art of giving and taking offense is an art of citizenship in a free
society?

That is not a feminine art. Radcliffe, for example, is an unfail-   8
ingly polite institution. Criticism and dissatisfaction are apt to be expressed in a feminine mode, covertly or indirectly. It's particularly
hard for many of us not to react with great solicitude to a student
who declares herself marginalized, demeaned, or oppressed, even if
we harbor doubts about her claim. If she seeks virtue in oppression,
as so many do, we seek it in maternalism.

We tend to forget that criticism sometimes expresses greater re-   9
spect than praise. It is surely more of an honor than flattery. You
challenge a student because you consider her capable of learning. You question her premises because you think she's game enough
to re-examine them. You do need to take the measure of her self-
confidence, and your own. Teaching — or nurturing — requires that
you gain students' trust and then risk having them not like you.

Sometimes withholding sympathy feels mean, insensitive, and un-   10
caring; you acquire all the adjectives that aren't supposed to attach
to women. You take on the stereotypically masculine vices at a
time when the feminine virtue of niceness is being revived: Rosie
O'Donnell is the model talk-show host, civility the reigning civic
virtue, and communitarianism[2] the paradigmatic political theory.
Communities are exalted, as if the typical community were composed
solely of people who shared and cared about one another and never
engaged in conflict.

In fact communities are built on compromise, and compromise   11
presupposes disagreement. Tolerance presupposes the existence of
people and ideas you don't like. It prevails upon you to forswear cen-
soring others but not yourself. One test of tolerance is provocation.
When you sit down to dinner with your disagreeable relations, or
comrades who bask in their rectitude and compassion, you have a
civic duty to annoy them.

---

[2]*communitarianism:* Social organization of communities in which ownership of production and distribution of goods is held in common.

Vocabulary/Using a Dictionary

1. What does Kaminer mean when she says: "I'm not alone in my *irreverence,* but feminist *pieties* combined with feminist courtesy keep most of us in line" (para. 3)?

2. Think of some synonyms for the word *puerile* (para. 6). Do they capture all the subtleties of the word?

3. What is the root of the word *paradigmatic* (para. 10)? From what word do both terms originate?

Responding to Words in Context

1. Kaminer remarks that "it's particularly hard for many of us not to react with great solicitude to a student who declares herself *marginalized,* demeaned, or oppressed, even if we harbor doubts about her claim" (para. 8). What do you think the author means when she uses the word *marginalized?*

2. In paragraph 5, Kaminer mentions *dysfunctional* families. What do you think the prefix *dys-* indicates? What does this word mean?

Discussing Main Point and Meaning

1. According to Kaminer's title, it is our "Civic Duty to Annoy." Explain what you think she means by this. Use examples from her essay to support your opinion.

2. How is criticism expressed at Radcliffe College, the author's employer (para. 8)?

3. At the end of her essay, Kaminer discusses how she feels about "withholding sympathy" from her students (para. 10). What does she say?

Examining Sentences, Paragraphs, and Organization

1. In two different sentences of her essay, Kaminer uses the word *scoff* (a word meaning "express derision, mockery, or scorn"): "I *scoff* every time I hear a Harvard student complain that she's oppressed" (para. 2) and "I don't mean to *scoff* at the discrimination that a young woman of any color may have experienced or

is likely to experience someday" (para. 4). How does the repetition of this word help you to understand the author's tone?

2. Who do you think is Kaminer's major audience for "A Civic Duty to Annoy"? What are their ethnic, racial, gender backgrounds? Political philosophies? What is their level of education? How can you tell?

3. How are Kaminer's paragraphs organized? According to time? According to location? From general to specific? From specific to general? From least to most important? From problem to solution?

Thinking Critically

1. Do you agree with the author's statement that "teaching — or nurturing — requires that you gain students' trust and then risk having them not like you" (para. 9)? Have you ever had an experience with a teacher that was similar to this?

2. Kaminer seems to believe that our society has gone too far to protect people from criticism and disappointment in college, social groups, and other aspects of everyday life. Do you agree with her? Are we, as a society, too agreeable?

In-Class Writing Activities

1. "We tend to forget that criticism sometimes expresses greater respect than praise," declares Kaminer in paragraph 9. Think about this quote as it relates to your learning experiences. Have you ever had a teacher who gave you criticism you were thankful to receive? Did you feel a greater sense of respect between yourself and the teacher after having received the criticism? Did the criticism improve your work as a student? Freewrite some ideas about this subject.

2. Have you ever exercised your "Civic Duty to Annoy" as Kaminer did when "to irritate . . . [her] more orthodox feminist colleagues" she would "disavow any personal guilt about being born white and middle-class" and "to provoke old Uncle George" she would "defend affirmative action or the capital-gains tax" (para. 2)? If you have, write a short essay describing a time you've exercised this right.

From the Bookshelf

Richard Dooling, *Blue Streak*

Blue Streak: Swearing, Free Speech, and Sexual Harassment *is a funny and irreverent meditation of how politically correct speech regulations have gutted the spirit of the First Amendment. The book covers a number of issues regarding offensive language, such as obscenity and hate speech, as it examines our society's concern with taboo words and expressions. Those who enjoy such television shows as* Saturday Night Live, Comedy Central's The Daily Show, *or* Politically Incorrect *will almost certainly enjoy Richard Dooling's provocative defense of what he believes is an endangered First Amendment. A lawyer who specializes in employment-discrimination cases, Dooling is the author of three highly acclaimed novels,* Critical Care *(1992),* White Man's Grave *(1994), and* Brain Storm *(1998).*

The Growing List of Forbidden Words

According to an article in the *Wall Street Journal* (November 3, 1994), the Pennsylvania Association of Realtors, the Pennsylvania Newspaper Association, and the Pennsylvania Human Relations Commission recently issued guidelines against the use of certain words in real-estate ads, including: *bachelor pad, landmark, couples, newlyweds, mature, older seniors, adults, single, children, senior citizen, setting up housekeeping,* and *traditional neighborhood,* to name but a few. In Pennsylvania, it's best not to describe the neighborhood at all, because the guidelines forbid using adjectives such as *exclusive, private, integrated, established,* or *close to* any local structure (probably because it discriminates against people who are not close to the same structure).

In 1994, the Fair Housing Council of Suburban Philadelphia filed lawsuits against landlords (and ladies) and three newspapers asking for more than $1 million in damages due to discriminatory ads. An ad describing a house in Chester as a *rare find* was pulled because the house was located in a black area, which suggested that it was *rare* for blacks to live in nice houses. Describing property as having an *ocean view* or being *within walking distance* of some local landmark discriminates against disabled persons (the blind and the crippled). If you say you have a *family room* you are discriminating against homosexuals and childless couples. A *master bedroom,* a *mother-in-law suite,* or a *bachelor pad* are all hopelessly sexist and forbidden.

Dooling, Richard. *Blue Streak: Swearing, Free Speech, and Sexual Harassment.* New York: Random House, 1996.

NANCY CARLSSON-PAIGE
AND DIANE LEVIN

The Profiteering That Kills Kids

[THE BOSTON GLOBE / April 2, 1998]

Before You Read

Are children's television shows too violent? Do you remember watching any excessive violence on television as a child? Did you see any excessive violence in the media? Do you think it adversely affected you?

Words to Learn

saturate (para. 3): soak thoroughly (v.)

perpetuate (para. 4): preserve the existence of (v.)

deregulate (para. 4): remove restrictions and regulations from (v.)

gruesomely (para. 5): frightfully (adv.)

desensitization (para. 6): act of making less sensitive (n.)

NANCY CARLSSON-PAIGE (b. 1944) is a professor at Lesley College, in Cambridge, Massachusetts, where she teaches conflict resolution and peaceable schools. She has coauthored four books with Diane Levin. The most recent — Before Push Comes to Shove: Building Conflict Resolution Skills with Children (1998) — is a companion text to a children's book by Carlsson-Paige entitled Best Day of the Week (1998).

DIANE LEVIN (b. 1947) is a professor of education at Wheelock College in Boston, Massachusetts, where she teaches early childhood courses on media, violence, and play. She is the author of Remote Control Childhood: Combating the Hazards of Media Culture (1998) and Teaching Young Children in Violent Times: Building a Peaceable Classroom.

If people are shocked by the killings in Jonesboro, Arkansas, [1] which follow the killings in Stamps, Arkansas, which follow the killings in West Paducah, Kentucky, and Pearl, Mississippi, which follow on the heels of a more than doubling in violent crimes among youth since the mid-1980s, then they haven't been paying attention.

Children in the United States are swimming in a culture of vio- [2] lence that has its effects from subtle to deadly on every child. The violence comes in many forms — family abuse, violence on the streets, in the community, violence in the news. Every ten seconds a child in this country is abused or neglected. Every two hours a child is killed by a firearm.

Efforts to limit violence in children's media never get past the violation-of-free-speech argument. But whose free speech are we talking about?

And then there is entertainment vio- [3] lence — every child's automatic membership in a media-saturated popular culture that glorifies violence through images, actions, and models marketed to children via television, toys and other products, videos, video games, and Hollywood films. On TV alone, children see thirty-two acts of violence every hour and over one thousand murders a year. Teachers and researchers have been warning for more than a decade that this violent culture marketed to children has harmful effects, both in the present and for the long term.

Most people don't realize, perhaps because it could hurt the in- [4] terests of those who perpetuate and profit most from it — big business — that there is an obvious explanation for why these concerns were voiced: This situation didn't always exist. It began in 1984 when the FCC[1] deregulated children's television. With deregulation it became possible to market toys and other products with TV programs. Quickly after deregulation, the kid culture from the earliest stages of play became saturated with violence, and teachers began reporting increases in violence in children's behavior and play in the classroom. From that time, the violent culture has grown in intensity with each new marketing ploy, media-product link-up, and innovation.

---

[1]FCC: Federal Communications Commission. Their Internet address is <www.fcc.gov>.

Gruesomely violent video games and episodes of cartoons show   5
children what the world is like. Violence is fun. We do it for play. Toy
weapons add to the fun. No one gets hurt. Children take these messages
and incorporate them into their behavior and play, trying them out with
each other, using them as building blocks for their social development.

Children are innocent victims of these messages. They believe what   6
they see. In the early years, they learn from what is in front of them and
much less from what's beneath the surface. They don't easily understand logical cause and effect. They see violence glamorously portrayed
without harmful effects, and they accept it at face value. Glamorized
violence conveyed repeatedly at this developmental stage exploits their
vulnerability and establishes the roots of desensitization to violence.

Efforts to limit violence in children's media never get past the   7
violation-of-free-speech argument. But whose free speech are we talking about? Corporate America profits by the millions off children by
marketing the violence. What about the millions of parents who deplore the violent culture marketed to their children but can't find a vehicle for expression? You don't have free speech when corporations
control the air waves and the public has little or no access.

Children can't speak for themselves. They don't understand   8
about motives, profits, and corporate responsibility. They just want
the toy they saw explode on an exciting TV show or ad. Children
need protection.

Whatever special circumstances describe the lives of the youths   9
dressed in combat with real guns in Jonesboro, we need to step back
and face the fact that all children are affected by violence and that
adults have to do something to change that.

Some of the forms of violence will be very hard to change. But   10
media violence promoted to young children? That could change
quickly if people are willing to act. Corporations will never do it on
their own. Government seems paralyzed. It's the rest of us who must
demand an end to irresponsible marketing practices and profiteering
that end up hurting all of us.

Vocabulary/Using a Dictionary

1. What do the authors mean in paragraph 4 when they say that big
    business *perpetuates* entertainment violence?

2. Both *deregulated* (para. 4) and *desensitization* (para. 6) share the same prefix — *de-*. What do these words mean? What does the prefix *de-* signify?

Responding to Words in Context

1. Carlsson-Paige and Levin have titled their essay "The Profiteering That Kills Kids." After reading the essay, what do you think the word *profiteering* means?
2. What definition do the authors give for *entertainment violence* (para. 3)?

Discussing Main Point and Meaning

1. Why are the authors annoyed at the shock some people display "by the killings in Jonesboro, Arkansas, which follow the killings in Stamps, Arkansas, which follow the killings in West Paducah, Kentucky, and Pearl, Mississippi" (para. 1)?
2. What are the authors referring to with these lines: "Violence is fun. We do it for play. Toy weapons add to the fun. No one gets hurt" (para. 5)?
3. How do the authors feel about "the violation-of-free-speech argument" (para. 7) as it relates to limiting violence in the children's media?
4. Toward the end of the essay, what is the final plea of the authors? To whom are they addressing this plea?

Examining Sentences, Paragraphs, and Organization

1. Looking at the first sentences of paragraphs 3, 5, 6, 7, and 8, what do we find are the repeated concerns of Carlsson-Paige and Levin?
2. In what paragraph do the authors state their main idea? What is the main idea?
3. Does the conclusion of the essay logically follow what is introduced at the beginning? Explain.

Thinking Critically

1. Do you think that entertainment violence is the most important single factor contributing to "a more than doubling in violent crimes among youth since the mid-1980s" (para. 1)?

2. Think back to the 1980s. Do you agree that in 1984, quickly after the Federal Communications Commission deregulated children's television, "kid culture from the earliest stages of play became saturated with violence" (para. 4)? What do you personally consider to be violent?

In-Class Writing Activities

1. Does big business have a constitutional right to portray violence on television? On the radio? In video games? Do you think the warnings "Parental Advisory: Explicit Lyrics" or "This program contains graphic content" are adequate to protect children?

2. Suppose you are a lawyer for a parent who is trying to sue a television station for the damage its portrayal of violence has done over the years to his or her children, both of whom have committed violent crimes. State your case for how you would convince a jury that the television station was responsible for the crimes committed. Draw on Carlsson-Paige and Levin's views and your own in constructing your case. If you prefer, pretend you are representing the television station instead, and defend its rights and reputation.

SARA ZIEGLER

How to Breed Intolerance

[THE IOWA STATE DAILY, IOWA STATE UNIVERSITY / March 9, 1998]

Before You Read

Do you consider yourself to be a tolerant person? Have you ever been pushed beyond your limit of tolerance? For what? How did you react? Were you ashamed of yourself afterward?

Words to Learn

speculation (para. 1): consideration of an idea (n.)

intolerance (para. 1): condition of not tolerating those different from one's self, bigotry (n.)

dissenter (para. 4): one who differs from another in opinion (n.)

pedophile (para. 4): adult who has recurrent sexual urges toward children (n.)

creed (para. 6): system of religious or other belief (n.)

Know as little as possible. Rely on rumor and speculation. Ignore facts. Utilize stereotypes. Spread your views to others in the hopes that they, too, will learn to hate. This is how you breed intolerance.   1

Intolerance is the art of ignoring any views that differ from your own. It manifests itself in hatred, discrimination, prejudice, and   2

SARA ZIEGLER *(b. 1977) was a junior at Iowa State University, in Ames, Iowa when she wrote this piece. At the time, she was the opinion page editor of the* Daily Columnist, *where she is now managing editor. Ziegler wrote this piece in response to a student letter to the editor that protested a court ruling allowing homosexuals to be scoutmasters in the Boy Scouts. "I realize that many people may not embrace lifestyles and actions that are 'different,'" says Ziegler. "However, bigotry and prejudice are never acceptable." She plans to graduate in May 2000 with a degree in journalism and mass communication and political science.*

stereotypes. Once it festers in people, intolerance is nearly impossible to overcome. But why would anyone want to be labeled *intolerant?* Why would people want to be uninformed about the world around them? Why would one want to be part of the problem in America, instead of the solution?

> *Intolerance does not stem from disagreement. It stems from fear. And fear stems from ignorance.*

There are many explanations for intolerant attitudes, some dating back to childhood. It is likely that intolerant folks grew up imitating intolerant parents and the cycle of prejudice has simply continued for generations. Perhaps intolerant people are so set in their ways that they find it easier to ignore anything that might not conform to their limited view of life. Or maybe intolerant students have simply never been exposed to anyone different from themselves. But none of these reasons is an excuse for allowing the intolerance to continue.

Intolerance should not be confused with disagreement. It is, of course, possible to disagree with an opinion without being intolerant of it. If you understand a belief but still don't believe in that specific belief, that's fine. You are entitled to your opinion. In fact, knowledgeable dissenters are important for any belief. If we all believed the same things, we would never grow, and we would never learn about the world around us. Intolerance does not stem from disagreement. It stems from fear. And fear stems from ignorance. When you are ignorant about homosexuality, you will distort the facts to fit your opinions. You will discount science and say things like, "Regardless of what geneticists and researchers may say when they try to link homosexuality in some way to a biological source. . . ." You will make up nonexistent "facts" about behaviors of homosexuals, insinuating they are all pedophiles. And you will belittle an entire category of people because, ultimately, your argument consists of nothing but an irrational fear of the unknown.

To tolerate a belief or stance does not mean you share these views. In fact, *Webster's New World Dictionary* defines the verb *tolerate* as "to respect others' beliefs, practices, etc. without sharing them." When "tolerating" others, you do disagree with them. But you disagree with them while respecting their right to their own opinion.

Intolerance isn't about your personal beliefs that are contrary to others'; it's about your actions toward them and your lack of respect for their views. It is entirely appropriate to disagree with a particular creed because of religious convictions. This is not necessarily "hiding behind the Bible." Once again, believing different creeds is not intolerance; not *respecting* different creeds is intolerance. And the Bible never justifies treating anyone differently based on what they believe.

Even though intolerance is frequently a set behavior, rooted deeply in many people's lives, there are ways to change opinions and actions. If you know and associate with homosexuals, you are infinitely more likely to be tolerant of them. You will learn, your prejudice will cease, and no one will need to erect a safe zone to protect homosexuals from you.   7

All you need to do to avoid intolerance is to respect each person for who they are — something everyone should be doing anyway.   8

Vocabulary/Using a Dictionary

1. Ziegler defines *intolerance* (para. 1) as "the art of ignoring any views that differ from your own" (para. 2). What is the dictionary definition of the word?

2. In paragraph 4, Ziegler states: "In fact, knowledgeable *dissenters* are important for any belief." What do you think she is trying to say?

3. What is a *creed* (para. 6)? Can you list some synonyms for the word? How does the word differ from *religion*?

Responding to Words in Context

1. In paragraph 2 the author suggests that intolerance "*manifests* itself in hatred." What do you think is the meaning of *manifests*? What does Ziegler mean by this statement?

2. Ziegler claims that intolerance "stems from fear" and that "fear stems from *ignorance*" (para. 4). What is ignorance? Would you consider *ignorance* to be a bad word?

Discussing Main Point and Meaning

1. According to Ziegler, how do you "breed intolerance" (para. 1)?

2. What is the author's reason for using the example about homosexuality (paras. 4–5)?

3. If you "tolerate a belief or stance" (para. 5), does it mean that you share these views?

4. What does Ziegler suggest we need to do "to avoid intolerance" (para. 8)?

Examining Sentences, Paragraphs, and Organization

1. If you read the first four sentences of the essay and then stopped without looking at the rest of the composition, what would you think about the writer? Why does she use these sentences as an introduction?

2. Throughout her essay, Ziegler tries to define many different words — *intolerance* (para. 2), *disagreement* (para. 4), *ignorance* (para. 4), and *tolerance* (para. 5). Why is it useful for her to try to define these words in the context of the essay?

3. Do you think the essay suffers from a lack of specific examples to back up Ziegler's main idea? Do you think that too many generalizations are made?

Thinking Critically

1. Do you agree with Ziegler's "many explanations for intolerant attitudes" (para. 3)? Can you think of other explanations?

2. In paragraph 4, the author claims that "when you are ignorant about homosexuality, you will distort the facts to fit your opinions. You will discount science and say things like, 'Regardless of what geneticists and researchers may say when they try to link homosexuality in some way to a biological source. . . .'" Is this assertion based on the true definition of the word *ignorance,* or does it agree with the author's definition?

In-Class Writing Activities

1. Write a short essay trying to accomplish the same goal as Ziegler did — to try to explain what breeds intolerance. Making use of examples (specific or general) from your own life, use whatever tone, style, and organization you prefer to make your point. (Keep in mind the definition of the word *intolerance.*)

2. Describe the social scene at your campus. By your estimate, are certain groups intolerant of one another? Why? Do other social groups seem more likely to tolerate the presence of certain groups? Why?

Discussing the Unit

Suggested Topic for Discussion

"I can say whatever I want," argues a citizen. "I have rights." Right? Wrong. The constitutional guarantees of individual liberties are not absolute. That is, even though you have the right to freedom of speech, you do not have the right to say anything at any time. For example, you do not have the right to deliberately lie about a person. Similarly, even though you have religious freedom, you cannot commit a crime in the name of religion. Discuss how you feel about this idea.

Preparing for Class Discussion

1. In "The Profiteering That Kills Kids," Nancy Carlsson-Paige and Diane Levin complain that "efforts to limit violence in children's media never get past the violation-of-free-speech argument" (para. 7). This statement suggests that unlimited freedom of speech is wrong, even harmful. How do you think Wendy Kaminer might respond to this complaint?

2. "It is likely that intolerant folks grew up imitating intolerant parents and the cycle of prejudice has simply continued for generations," remarks Sara Ziegler in "How to Breed Intolerance" (para. 3). Explain how this statement links with the following idea discussed by Carlsson-Paige and Levin in their essay: "What about the millions of parents who deplore the violent culture marketed to their children but can't find a vehicle for expression?" (para. 7).

From Discussion to Writing

1. Pretend the authors included in this chapter comprised a guest panel on *your* talk show. Write an essay about the show, stating

the questions you would like to ask them (about freedom of expression), and suggest what *you* think their answers might be.

2. As mentioned in "Suggested Topic for Discussion," "the constitutional guarantees of individual liberties are not absolute." Keeping this fact in mind, how would you interpret this statement: "Your right to swing your fist ends where my nose begins"?

3. Describe a particular occasion when you were afraid to exercise your right to freedom of expression. Looking back now, was your fear justified?

Topics for Cross-Cultural Discussion

1. How do your rights to freedom of expression in your homeland differ from those in the United States?

2. How comfortable do you feel expressing your opinions about the United States? Do you feel Americans encourage you to share your opinions? Do you feel that what you have to say is taken seriously?

10

Do Words Matter?

How do the words we use in everyday conversation matter? Does it make any difference whether we say *girl* instead of *woman* or *colored people* instead of *people of color*? Do some words show a hostile attitude? And what happens when the right word doesn't seem to exist? as M. P. Dunleavey asks in "'Guy' Envy." Why don't females, she wonders, have a label that's more relaxed than *woman* and more grown up than *girl*? Why don't they have a word like *guy*?

In "The N-Word and How to Use It" Bennie M. Currie approaches an older word-related issue: The word *nigger* can be used as a term of endearment among blacks and as a racist epithet by whites. Many African Americans, Currie points out, have a "love/hate relationship" with the word, "one of the most complex, perplexing, and emotionally incendiary words in the American lexicon." As Currie reminds us, people often find ways to make negative or hostile labels their own. In the unit's final selection, "Radicals: Threats or Heroes?," Franklin and Marshall College student Melissa Stein wonders why so many people she knows are terrified of having the label *radical* attached to them.

M. P. DUNLEAVEY

"Guy" Envy

[GLAMOUR / May 1996]

Before You Read

How is the word *guy* different from the word *man?* Do women have a word similar to *guy* that they use to describe themselves? What type of person do you think of when you hear the word *guy?* Can women be *guys?*

Words to Learn

clout (para. 1): prestige, influence (n.)

umpteen (para. 2): innumerable, many (adj.)

dynamo (para. 3): energetic person (n.)

egalitarian (para. 4): characterized by the belief in the equality of all people (adj.)

prismatic (para. 5): refracting light as a prism, multicolored (adj.)

dialectal (para. 5): related to a regional variety of a language (adj.)

semantics (para. 9): study of meaning in language (n.)

coopt (para. 11): win over into a group (v.)

There are still a few reasons to envy men: that 74-cents-to-the-dollar thing, their choke hold on Congress, and the word *guy*. On the first two fronts — earning power and political clout — women continue to gain ground. But when it comes to calling ourselves something besides *woman,* something that captures our most laid-back, casual sense of ourselves — our *guyness,* if you will — we need a word of our own.

1

M. P. DUNLEAVEY *(b. 1965) is a staff writer at* Glamour *magazine. Her work has also appeared in the* New York Times, *the* Sunday Times Book Review, *and* New York *magazine. She is also a writer for the critically acclaimed cyberserial* The Couch *(www.thecouch.com).*

Not that there's anything wrong with *woman*. Given the   2
umpteen unwonderful alternatives (*girl, babe, chick, lady, broad,
dame, lass*), it's clear why we fought so hard for this nonpejorative
term. *Woman* is admirable. *Woman* is honorable. *Woman* speaks of
maturity, motherhood, and busting through barriers. And that's *exactly* why we need a term to give us a break from all that. A word
that would let us kick back and not shave for a couple of days. A
word like *guy*.

Guy is efficient. Think about it: "There's a new guy in market-   3
ing — he's got some great ideas." The focus completely skips over
him — his gender, his maleness — to the important stuff. That he's
a man hardly registers. We females, on the other hand, have no
shorthand that unhooks us from the biological and political implications of our sex. "We just hired a woman to run the ad-sales division and she's a dynamo." It's hard to hear that without thinking,
Oh, she's a *woman*. Is she young, cute, straight, married? Does she
market to women? Did they hire her be-
cause she's a woman? Will she fit in with
the guys?

> **What women need is a word that will let us slip into a more easygoing side of ourselves the way men can slip into guyhood.**

A few months ago, Natalie Angier, a   4
science reporter for the *New York Times,*
gave in to her own *guy* envy and confessed her longing for "a word that conveys snazziness and style, a casual term
for the double-X[1] set . . . a delicious egalitarian word like . . . *gal*."

Gal? *Gal?* Though Angier insists that "*gal* has a rich and pris-   5
matic quality to it," *The Oxford English Dictionary* strikes closer to
the vein, revealing that *gal* is nothing more than "a vulgar or dialectal
pronunciation" of *girl*. Oh, that's progress. Besides, as a friend from
Nevada points out, "*Gal* is from the heartland. *Gal* has a warm
heart, big hips, and a bad dye job."

What women need is a word that will let us slip into a more easy-   6
going side of ourselves the way men can slip into guyhood.

When men take off their uniforms, jackets, and ties, they're guys.   7
When they put them on again, they're men. In part it's an attitude

---

[1]*double-X:* Women have two X chromosomes, and men have one X and one Y chromosome. The chromosome is one of a set of threadlike structures that are composed of
DNA and a protein and that carry the genes.

thing: In the Oval Office, Bill Clinton is a man. Jogging down Pennsylvania Avenue, he's a guy. Charles Barkley is a guy, unless he's on the court; then he's a man. Of course, some males favor one side of the man/guy fence. Hawkeye is a guy. Colonel Potter is a man. Humphrey Bogart, Robert De Niro, Ronald Reagan — men. Steve Martin, Jerry Seinfeld, Spike Lee — guys.

But: Mary Tyler Moore, Rita Hayworth, Connie Chung, Hillary   8
Rodham Clinton, Whoopi Goldberg, Julia Louis-Dreyfus, Rosie Perez — all different, all women. Everyone knows that Whoopi is much more of a guy than Hillary is, but we don't have the word to say so. Meanwhile, don't even try plugging female words into classic guy phrases. Whatta *girl*! (Ugh.) She's a great *babe*. (Oh, no.) She's a *woman's woman*? From time to time we do call ourselves *guys* ("do any of you guys have a spare tampon?"), but let's not kid ourselves. We're on borrowed terminology.

This is not just semantics. Until fairly recently, women could not   9
be all that guys were and are. It may seem that we've always lived and worked and dressed as comfortably as one of the fellas, but until thirty years ago women were constrained by a standard of femininity that embraced the word *lady* right along with the wearing of gloves. In the 1950s, women didn't require a word like *guy* because acting like one wasn't written into their parts. Now our roles have changed, and it's time that language caught up.

The more traditional words that describe women do come in   10
handy; every once in a while you *want* to be a lady, a bitch, or a chick and having a word for what you're being makes being it easier. But how do you describe a woman you hang out with who is cool with herself and others, a woman you can watch the game with and whose shoulder you can cry on, knowing that she knows where you're coming from? There is no womanly translation of *guy,* and yet most women I know aspire to a certain level of guyhood. Just as our mothers longed to be ladies, this confident, centered, sympathetic yet amusing human being is who we'd like to be.

We'll always be women — no one is advocating giving that up.   11
But we need choices, and unless something better comes along we may just have to stake our own claim to *guy*. After all, we successfully coopted the original guy symbol: blue jeans. There *was* a time when women weren't supposed to touch denim unless they were washing it. Funny how things change. Right, guys?

Vocabulary/Using a Dictionary

1. What does *dialectal* mean (para. 5)? What is the origin of the word?

2. Dunleavey argues that women are "on borrowed terminology" (para. 8) and that the problem with this issue is "not just *semantics*" (para. 9). What does she mean with her use of the word *semantics?*

3. What does it mean when Dunleavey states: "After all, we successfully *coopted* the original guy symbol: blue jeans" (para. 11). Consider how *coopted* relates to other words with similar roots, like *cooperate* or *coordinate*.

Responding to Words in Context

1. In paragraph 2, Dunleavey states that "given the umpteen unwonderful alternatives (*girl, babe, chick, lady, broad, dame, lass*), it's clear why we fought so hard for . . . [the] nonpejorative term [*woman*]." Looking at the word in context, what does *nonpejorative* mean?

2. The author makes use of an illustration in paragraph 3: "females . . . have no shorthand that unhooks us from the biological and political implications of our sex. 'We just hired a woman to run the ad-sales division and she's a *dynamo*.'" What do you think Dunleavey means by the word *dynamo?*

3. "We'll always be women — no one is *advocating* giving that up," the author remarks in paragraph 11. What does Dunleavey mean by the word *advocating?* Explain the difference between *advocacy* and *advocate.*

Discussing Main Point and Meaning

1. What reason does Dunleavey give for why women have not gained ground when it comes to "calling ourselves something besides *woman*" (para. 1)?

2. Dunleavey has a problem with *New York Times* science reporter Natalie Angier's "longing for 'a word that conveys snazziness and style, a casual term for the double-X set . . . a delicious egalitarian word like . . . *gal*'" (para. 4). What is the problem?

3. What point is the author trying to make when she replaces "classic guy phrases" with "female words" such as "Whatta *girl*! . . . She's a great *babe*. . . . She's a *woman's woman*" (para. 8)?

4. Dunleavey concludes her essay by stating that "we need choices, and unless something better comes along we may just have to stake our own claim to *guy*" (para. 11). What does she mean?

Examining Sentences, Paragraphs, and Organization

1. Is the first sentence of paragraph 3 ("*Guy* is efficient.") the topic sentence? How do you know? If you disagree, then what is the topic sentence of paragraph 3?

2. In "'Guy' Envy" the author makes use of a common pattern for paragraph development, *analysis and classification*. What is being analyzed in her essay?

3. List some examples Dunleavey uses to support her main idea that women lack a word for "something that captures our most laid-back, casual sense of ourselves" (para. 1).

Thinking Critically

1. In paragraph 10, Dunleavey writes that "having a word for what you're being makes it easier." What does she mean by this? Do you agree with the author that it is harder for women to be guys because there is no word for female guyness?

2. According to Dunleavey, what exactly is a guy? Are certain men and boys, as well as women, excluded from guyness?

In-Class Writing Activities

1. Make two lists — words that describe men and words that describe women. Which words correspond fairly closely in meaning (*beefcake* and *hot babe*, for example)? Which don't seem to have a counterpart for the other gender? What about the word *fellow* or *dude*? Can these words cross the gender line? What do you suppose this says about the English language?

2. The English language is rich in synonyms, and no two synonyms mean exactly the same thing. Think of any two words

that are close in meaning (like *man* and *guy*). If you're drawing a blank, then use a thesaurus. In an essay, draw a clear distinction between these two words. Be sure to use plenty of examples.

From the Bookshelf

Richard Lederer, *Crazy English*

Although academics and critics frequently examine the political dimensions of language, it's worth remembering that words can also provide us with a great deal of fun. In his best-selling book Crazy English, *Richard Lederer, one of the nation's most entertaining writers on the subject of words, looks at the strangeness of the English language: "In what other language," he asks, "do people drive in a parkway and park in a driveway?" In the following brief sample from* Crazy English, *Lederer describes some of the ways words change their meanings over time.*

How Words Change

Like people, words grow after they are born; once created, they seldom sit still and remain the same forever. Some words expand to take over larger territories. They begin with a precise meaning, but their boundaries widen and often grow fuzzier and less definite. A fabulous example of this expansive process is the word *fabulous*. Once *fabulous* meant "resembling or based on a fable." Later came the meaning "incredible, marvelous" because fables often contained incredible and marvelous characters and events. Nowadays the word is weakening in meaning still more, and anything can be fabulous: The latest styles of blue jeans are fabulous, as is *Paradise Lost*; the latest breakthroughs in computers are fabulous, and so is the current Picasso exhibit. A *picture* was once a painted representation of something seen; now any visual representation — photograph, pen and ink, crayon — is a picture. A *holiday* first signified "a holy day," but modern holidays include secular days off like Valentine's Day and Independence Day. Not only has the *holy* part of the compound generalized, but so has the *day* part. Thus, a holiday can now last more than twenty-four hours, as in the rather British "I'm going on holiday to the Caribbean."

continued on next page

continued from previous page

Other words travel in exactly the opposite direction and narrow to acquire more specific meanings than the ones with which they started life. Once at the end of a Chinese meal, my young daughter opened a fortune cookie and read the message inside: "You are genial, clever, intellectual, and discriminating." "But," she protested, "I don't discriminate!" My perceptive child was being sensitive to the fact that *discriminate* has taken on the specialized meaning of making choices in matters of race. Much the same thing has happened to the words *segregation, colored, chauvinism, comrade, fairy, queer, queen,* and *gay.* In *Little Women* (1870), Louisa May Alcott wrote without any ambiguity whatsoever, "As Mrs. March would say, what can you do with four gay girls in the house?"

Lederer, Richard. *Crazy English.* New York: Pocket Books, 1998.

BENNIE M. CURRIE

The N-Word and How to Use It

[THE CHICAGO READER / December 19, 1997]

Before You Read

Have you ever heard the word *nigger* used as a term of affection? Have we become desensitized to the true meaning of the word? Should we use the word at all?

BENNIE M. CURRIE (b. 1961) is a freelance journalist based in Chicago whose work has appeared in American Visions, the Chicago Reader, and Emerge magazine. In addition to his experience as an investigative reporter and travel writer, Currie has worked in public and media relations and has taught journalism to high school students.

Words to Learn

perplexing (para. 8): confusing (adj.)

incendiary (para. 8): capable of causing fire or conflict (adj.)

lexicon (para. 8): dictionary, vocabulary (n.)

vexing (para. 9): irritating (v.)

query (para. 9): question (n.)

adage (para. 10): traditional saying (n.)

curator (para. 12): person in charge of a museum (n.)

epithet (para. 13): term characterizing a person or thing, abusive word (n.)

ubiquitous (para. 14): existing everywhere at the same time (adj.)

paradoxical (para. 15): self-contradictory (adj.)

disparage (para. 16): belittle (v.)

endearing (para. 16): inspiring affection (adj.)

conjure (para. 17): summon as if by magic (v.)

flak (para. 18): shells from artillery, abuse (n.)

vociferously (para. 18): noisily (adv.)

wallow (para. 19): roll about, revel (v.)

lampoon (para. 20): satire usually directed against an individual (n.)

obsolete (para. 20): out of fashion (adj.)

candidly (para. 23): impartially, openly (adv.)

N-I-G-G-E-R. I'll never forget the first time I accidentally used that word in mixed company. It was twenty years ago at the University of Missouri, and I was engaged in lighthearted chitchat with Kent, my white roommate, when I casually called him a *nigger*. 1

For a second I'd forgotten that I was not among my black friends in my old neighborhood in Saint Louis, where calling a buddy *nigger* was synonymous with calling him *brother* or *man*. It was just another way to talk cool, using a word that had become a part of our vocabulary long before we were aware of all its varied meanings and usages. 2

> *While my wife and I are readying ourselves for questions like "Where do babies come from?" I know that none will be more vexing than the first innocent query about the N-word.*

I was barely conscious of my accidental utterance, but there was nothing casual about Kent's reaction. His eyes widened, and his body flinched as though he'd just absorbed a boxer's jab. Then he snapped to an upright position on the edge of his bed, narrowed his eyes, and pointed an index finger at me. "*I'm* not a nigger," he said, his tone 3 implying that he thought *I* was a nigger. He never actually called me a nigger, but the mere suggestion was enough to put me in a fighting mood.

"Do I look like a nigger to you?" I shouted.   4

"But *you* just called *me* a nigger," he replied.   5

"Well, that's different. *You* can't call me that. Not ever."   6

Fortunately, our dorm mates stopped this exchange before I   7
could throw a punch at Kent, who probably thought I was nuts. Actually I was simply too angry to realize that I was the one at fault.

By calling Kent a nigger, I'd exposed him to what my old neigh-   8
borhood friends called a "black thing" he didn't understand. The "thing" is the love/hate relationship many black people have with *nigger,* one of the most complex, perplexing, and emotionally incendiary words in the American lexicon. And to be truthful, black people are hardly unified in their understanding or usage of this piece of slang.

There have been times in my life when I've felt very comfortable   9
using the word, but I've also struggled with its usage. And now that I'm a parent I cringe at the notion that my two children will someday have to try to understand what these six letters mean to them, their friends and foes, and the larger society. While my wife and I are readying ourselves for questions like "Where do babies come from?" I know that none will be more vexing than the first innocent query about the N-word.

I could take the easy way out and tell our kids that *nigger* is a   10
bad word that good boys and girls should never use. Or maybe I could recite the old "sticks and stones" adage and tell them it's a name that can never hurt them. But neither tactic is likely to work, especially the second, since I don't believe it myself.

If my kids are destined to be introduced to a word born of racial   11
hatred, then their parents should be the ones to do it. But television, the Internet, the school playground, and other competitors for our kids' attention may get to them first. Or a dictionary.

Last February Kathryn Williams, curator of the Museum of   12
African American History in Flint, Michigan, was asked by a little boy, "Am I a nigger because I'm black?" She told the naturally curious child that a nigger was any ignorant person, then advised him to look up the word in the dictionary for reassurance. The kid paged through the venerable *Merriam-Webster's Collegiate Dictionary,* where he found that *nigger* is a term for "a black person — usu. taken to be offensive." With only minor revisions, this definition has existed for nearly half a century.

This was a shocking revelation for Williams, who started a peti-   13
tion drive to pressure Merriam-Webster to revise the definition. Her
campaign gained momentum last September, when *Emerge* magazine
ran a brief article about it. Since then, scores of people have joined
her, many of them contending that the current definition inaccurately
explains the meaning of the word. Some of them also believe the
racial epithet is undeserving of inclusion in a dictionary and want it
deleted altogether.

I know why Williams and others like her are upset. Being called   14
nigger by a white person or a white-run institution is a slap in the
face for many blacks. It evokes thoughts of the sorry legacy of slavery
and the racism that haunts the nation. And it hurts. When I checked
out the definition in my own copy of the Collegiate edition I felt
stung — particularly since I knew that dictionaries are almost as
ubiquitous as Gideon Bibles.[1]

I don't believe the publishers of the Collegiate edition meant to   15
offend anyone. Most likely, they were simply reflecting the confusion
that stems from the paradoxical usage of the word among Americans
of all hues, cultures, and generations.

Since my dorm-room experience, several whites have told me of   16
their own struggles to understand the term — and to understand why
a word that was used for centuries by white people to disparage and
dehumanize their black slaves and today is a chief element of hate-
speak (witness the Nigger Joke Center on the World Wide Web) is
cool for blacks to use but taboo for them. They ask, How can any
self-respecting black person stand to use it? Why do black kids call
each other "my nigga" in such endearing tones, privately as well as
publicly? Is this a "self-hatred thing"?

I say no. It's what blacks have always done since we hit Amer-   17
ica's shores 400 years ago. We take what's given to us or thrown at
us, and we find a way to make it our own. Blacks melded African
rhythms and European music to create jazz, this country's only original musical art form. We took the parts of livestock whites didn't
care to eat — intestines, tongues, ears, and feet — mixed them with
our native African dishes and conjured up soul food.

In the same manner, blacks took the loaded term *nigger* and dis-   18
armed it by making it a household word. In fact, we went on to embrace it by using it to spice up poetry, rap lyrics, and many a comedy

---

[1]*Gideon Bible:* Religious book placed in hotel rooms by members of Gideons International, a Christian missionary organization.

stand-up routine. A case in point is Paul Mooney, a comedian and writer (*Saturday Night Live, Good Times,* and *In Living Color*). He doesn't just use *nigger* to accent his stand-up act. It's often the focal point of his jokes. In one bit he complains about the flak he catches from whites who sometimes object more vociferously to his liberal use of the word than do many blacks. "Make that nigger stop saying *nigger.* He's giving me a nigger headache," he jokes. "Well white folks, you shouldn't have ever made up the word. You fucked up. I say nigger 100 times every morning. It makes my teeth white."

Chris Rock, who currently hosts a weekly HBO talk show, is an-   19 other funny man at peace with his use of *nigger.* While my grand-mother has never heard of him, she and Rock assign a similar mean-ing to the term. The hot comic told *B.E.T. Weekend* magazine he uses it to describe "a certain *kind* of black person who wallows in ig-norance and likes being ignorant." During a recent HBO special, Rock expressed this point of view with these one-liners: "Niggers react to books the way vampires react to sunlight." "Niggers always want credit for something they should be doing. 'I take care of my kids.' You're *supposed* to take care of your kids!" "Black people don't give a damn about welfare reform. Niggers are shaking in their boots."

Rock, who used to lampoon CBS anchor Bryant Gumbel for   20 "talking white," recently apologized publicly for using such a label. But he doesn't plan to cut *nigger* out of his act anytime soon. "I'll stop when niggas stop," he said. "Niggas robbed my house, robbed my mother's house. Black people didn't do that." He adds, "I would love to have no reason to use the word. I'd love for it to be obsolete."

Richard Pryor, one of Rock's role models, was at the height of   21 his legendary career in 1982, when he vowed never again to use the word to refer to another black person. He said he'd had an epiphany during a visit to Africa. He didn't see any "niggers" in the mother-land and realized that blacks there had no need to use the word. Pryor shared his pledge with the audience during a stand-up routine that was later released as a feature film, *Richard Pryor Live on the Sunset Strip.* The statement inspired lots of blacks to make the same vow.

I haven't made that pledge, but before I saw Pryor's film I never   22 thought twice about why I used *nigger.* I'm less comfortable using it now, but because of my lifelong cultural association with the word, I can't foresee total avoidance. Because my kids have a different cul-ture, I've never used it around them, and I don't intend to.

Since my kids aren't going to grow up hearing *nigger* under our   23
roof, the question still remains: How should I explain this word to
them? There's only one way to do it — candidly and carefully. I'll tell
them that the word is a national shame and at times a painful reminder of their ancestors' struggle for freedom. And I'll explain that
the term has a history just as relevant as Jim Crow, the Revolutionary
War, lynching, or Watergate, which is why forcing a dictionary to
delete it would be a mistake, would be censorship.

Meanwhile the people at Merriam-Webster are busy mulling a   24
revision of their definition of *nigger,* according to spokesman Steve
Perrault. He wrote me via e-mail that it's too early to pinpoint when
or if a change will be made, but he assured me the issue will be resolved before the dictionary's next scheduled major update, in 2003.
"The problem for us is that it's not simply a matter of changing one
entry," Perrault said. "If we revise our treatment of the offensive
word, we also have to revise our treatment of the many other offensive words in the dictionary. That makes it a fairly major undertaking, and our feeling is that we want to be sure we're getting it right."

Sounds like a good idea. But does this really require much delib-   25
eration? I don't think so. The third edition of the *American Heritage
Dictionary of the English Language* already has it figured out. Its definition of *nigger* begins with the words "offensive *slang* . . . used as a
disparaging term for a black person." As an illustration, a quote from
James Baldwin follows: "You can only be destroyed by believing that
you really are what the white world calls a Negro."

This interpretation seems fair and accurate to me. It's even suit-   26
able for the eyes of a child. And it may even enlighten a confused college kid or two.

Vocabulary/Using a Dictionary

1. What other word or words look like *query* (para. 9)? What do
    the definitions of these words have in common? Do these words
    share the same origin?

2. Currie mentions that dictionaries that carry the improper defini-
    tion of the word *nigger* are as *ubiquitous* (para. 14) as Gideon
    Bibles. What does *ubiquitous* mean? What is the origin of the
    word?

3. In paragraph 18, the author refers to the comedian Paul
    Mooney's stand-up comedy act: "In one bit he [Mooney] com-

plains about the flak he catches from whites who sometimes object more *vociferously* to his liberal use of the word [*nigger*] than do many blacks." Can you think of a few synonyms for the word *vociferous?* What do you think is the root of the word?

Responding to Words in Context

1. In paragraph 2, the author reflects: "In my old neighborhood in Saint Louis . . . calling a buddy *nigger* was *synonymous* to calling him *brother* or *man*." What does the word *synonymous* mean? Use the word in a sentence.

2. Currie speaks of an "accidental utterance" (para. 3) he makes during "lighthearted chitchat" with Kent, his white roommate. Can you think of a time when you've made an "accidental utterance"?

3. In discussing the film *Richard Pryor Live on the Sunset Strip* (para. 21), Currie mentions an "epiphany" Pryor experienced during his trip to Africa, where "he didn't see any 'niggers' in the motherland and realized that blacks there had no need to use the word." What does Currie mean by his use of the term *epiphany?*

Discussing Main Point and Meaning

1. Describe what happened the first time Currie accidentally used the word *nigger* in mixed company (paras. 1–8).

2. What does the author mean when he states that "if my kids are destined to be introduced to a world born of racial hatred, then their parents should be the ones to do it" (paras. 11)?

3. Why was the curator of the Museum of African American History shocked by the definition of the word *nigger* in *Merriam-Webster's Collegiate Dictionary* (paras. 12–13)?

4. Describe how watching *Richard Pryor Live on the Sunset Strip* inspired Currie (paras. 21–22).

Examining Sentences, Paragraphs, and Organization

1. How does Currie's introduction grab your attention? What is the purpose of an introduction?

2. Where in the essay does the author make a major transition, explaining how blacks changed their opinion of the "emotionally incendiary" word *nigger* to an eventual "embrace" of the term? Is this transition effective?

3. Who is Currie's main audience? Explain your answer.

Thinking Critically

1. Currie makes use of statements from comedians Paul Mooney, Chris Rock, and Richard Pryor to support the ideas presented in his essay. Why do you think he chose comedians as a source of support for his opinions? Do you think the essay would be more effective if he had used statements from academics or other more mainstream groups?

2. Do you agree with the author's opinion that it is solely the parents' responsibility to introduce children to a world "born of racial hatred" (para. 11)? Are television, the Internet, the school playground, dictionaries, and other sources responsible for presenting children with ideas about racism?

In-Class Writing Activities

1. Currie, in paragraph 8 states that "*nigger* [is] one of the most complex, perplexing, and emotionally incendiary words in the American lexicon." In your own words, write a short essay describing why you think the word is so complicated, puzzling, and emotionally agitating.

2. Kathryn Williams, curator of the Museum of African American History, was shocked when she read the definition of the word *nigger* in *Merriam-Webster's Collegiate Dictionary* to be "a black person — usu. taken to be offensive." To research this point, look up the definition of the word *nigger* in a dictionary. Write the definition down at the top of a blank sheet of paper. Spend a few minutes freewriting about the definition. Use these questions to help start your freewrite: Do you agree with the dictionary definition? Does the definition accurately explain the meaning of the word? What population does the definition target?

MELISSA STEIN

Radicals: Threats or Heroes?

[THE COLLEGE REPORTER, FRANKLIN AND MARSHALL COLLEGE / September 22, 1997]

Before You Read

Imagine that you are going to meet a friend who wants to introduce you to someone who is supposed to be a *radical*. What do you think your friend would mean by the word *radical*? Make a quick mental list of three or four people you consider to be radicals.

Words to Learn

status quo (para. 1): existing state or condition (n.)
feminism (para. 2): belief that women should have the same rights as men (n.)
stigma (para. 2): mark of disgrace (n.)
metamorphosis (para. 3): change of form from one stage to the next (n.)

What is a radical? It seems today that people are terrified of the term, particularly of having the label attached to them. Accusing individuals or groups of being radical often serves to silence them into submission, thereby maintaining the status quo and, more important, preserving the power of a select minority (most often in Western society, wealthy white males) served by the status quo.   1

Feminism is a perfect example of this phenomenon. The women's movement has been plagued by stereotypes, misrepresentations by the media, and accusations of man-hating and radicalism, when the basic foundation of feminism is simply that women deserve equal rights in all facets of life. When faced with the threat of being labeled *radical*,   2

MELISSA STEIN *(b. 1977) was a sophomore at Franklin and Marshall College in Lancaster, Pennsylvania, when she wrote this article for the* College Reporter *in 1997. She is working toward a degree in English and history, with a minor in women's studies, and plans to graduate in 1999.*

women back down from their worthy cause and, consequently, participate in their own oppression. It has gotten to the point that many women are afraid to call themselves *feminists* because of the stigma attached to the word. If people refuse to be controlled and intimidated by stigmas, the stigmas lose all their power. Without fear on which to feed, such stigmas can only die.

To me, a radical is simply someone who rebels against the norm or 3 advocates a change in the status quo. On closer inspection, it becomes clear that the norm is constantly evolving and therefore is not a constant entity. So why then is deviation from the status quo such a threat when the status quo itself is unstable and subject to relentless metamorphosis? It all goes back to maintaining the power of those who have it and preventing the rise of those who don't.

> *It has gotten to the point that many women are afraid to call themselves* feminists *because of the stigma attached to the word.*

In fact, when we look at the word *radical* in a historical context, nearly every figure we now hold up as a hero was considered a radical in his or her time. Radicals are people who effect change; they are the people about whom history is written. Abolitionists[1] were radicals. Civil rights activists were radicals. Even the founders of our country, in their fight to win independence from England, were radicals. Their presence in history has changed the way our society functions, mainly by shifting the balance of power that previously existed. Of course, there are some radicals who have made a negative impact on humanity, but undeniably, there would simply be no progress without radicals.

That being said, the next time someone calls me a *radical*, I will 5 accept that label with pride.

Vocabulary / Using a Dictionary

1. "Accusing individuals or groups of being radical often serves to silence them into submission, thereby maintaining the *status quo*," remarks Stein in paragraph 1. What does the author mean by *status quo*? Use the word in a sentence.

---

[1]*abolitionist:* Antislavery advocate in the mid-1800s. Some abolitionists called for an immediate end to slavery everywhere in the United States, and others supported a gradual end to slavery.

2. In paragraph 2 the author states that "many women are afraid to call themselves *feminists* because of the *stigma* attached to the word. If people refuse to be controlled and intimidated by *stigmas,* the *stigmas* lose all their power. Without fear on which to feed, such *stigmas* can only die." What is a *stigma?* What point is Stein trying to make?

3. Stein describes the status quo as being "subject to relentless *metamorphosis*" (para. 3). What does Stein mean by *metamorphosis?*

Responding to Words in Context

1. What is Stein's definition for the word *radical* (para. 3)? How do you think this relates to a dictionary definition of the word?

2. Stein's essay was taken from a Web page entitled "Editorials" created by Franklin Marshall College. What is an editorial? What purpose does it serve?

3. What do you think the word *entity* means? What does Stein mean when she says that "the norm is constantly evolving and therefore is not a constant *entity*" (para. 3)?

Discussing Main Point and Meaning

1. What does the author's title suggest? What is the purpose of a title?

2. Stein comments, "It has gotten to the point that many women are afraid to call themselves *feminists*" (para. 2). What reason does she give to explain the reaction of these women?

3. What does the author mean in her last paragraph? Try rewriting her final thought in your own words.

Examining Sentences, Paragraphs, and Organization

1. Does Stein provide support for her claim that "it seems today that people are terrified of the term" *radical* (para. 1)? If so, what support does she give?

2. Stein constructs her paragraphs according to the rhetorical strategy of *definition.* Explain how you think the author employs this strategy in "Radicals: Threats or Heroes?"

Thinking Critically

1. Stein asserts "that people are terrified of the term" *radical,* "particularly having the label attached to them" (para. 1). Do you agree?

2. Do you agree with the author's declaration in paragraph 4 that "undeniably, there would simply be no progress without radicals"?

In-Class Writing Assignments

1. "To me, a radical is simply someone who rebels against the norm or advocates a change in the status quo. . . . nearly every figure we hold up as a hero was considered a radical in his or her time" (paras. 3–4), the author remarks. A radical, by definition, favors drastic political, social, and economic change. Based on this information, do you think any radicals are operating in the world today? Can you think of anyone in the modern world who fits this definition of the word *radical?* Write a short essay explaining why you think the person you chose is a radical, citing specific examples to support your claim.

2. Have you (or someone close to you) ever been involved with an activity or a group that was considered radical? Write a brief essay describing the experience.

Discussing the Unit

Suggested Topic for Discussion

All three of this unit's authors discuss the uses of words to label people — for their gender, race, or political beliefs. Bennie M. Currie and Melissa Stein both point out the problems with labels, and M. P. Dunleavey is searching for a suitable label. Are there times when labels for people are helpful? What labels do you use for other people, and what labels have been applied to you? How do these labels affect your life or the lives of those labeled?

Preparing for Class Discussion

1. Both Bennie M. Currie and M. P. Dunleavey struggle with a problem faced by both women and blacks — ownership of language. Describe what is meant by this, using points the authors have raised in their essays.

2. Melissa Stein claims that "the women's movement has been plagued by stereotypes, misrepresentations by the media, and accusations of man-hating and radicalism, when the basic foundation of feminism is simply that women deserve equal rights in all facets of life" (para. 2). Do you think Dunleavey would agree with this statement? Explain your answer.

From Discussion to Writing

1. Write an essay describing a time you learned a lesson about the power of words.

2. Based on your reading, class discussion, and personal reflections on this unit, write an essay on the question of who should be responsible for defining words in the dictionary, particularly dictionaries used in schools and colleges. Provide specific reasons why you chose the person or people you did, and support your argument with examples from your reading and personal experience.

3. G. K. Chesterton, a famous English critic and author, once wrote: "Why shouldn't we quarrel about a word? What is the good of words if they aren't important enough to quarrel over? Why do we choose one word more than another if there isn't any difference between them?" Write an essay in which you discuss the three points of Chesterton's quote, supporting your opinion with evidence and examples from your own experience and observations, the essays presented in this unit, or other sources.

Topics for Cross-Cultural Discussion

1. People in the United States often create words that represent inaccurate stereotypes of other cultures. Does your native culture

have words to describe Americans that seem inaccurate now that you have experienced life in the United States?

2. Think of your native language. Have you noticed any words that have lost their true meaning or significance over a period of time? Why do you think the meaning changed?

11

Race Relations:
Is Dialogue Possible?

In his second term, President Bill Clinton established an Initiative on Race, whose purpose was to stimulate a year-long national dialogue on race. Yet no sooner did the panels, forums, and meetings begin than the Initiative ran into some serious obstacles. Finding themselves deliberately excluded from discussion and debate, many prominent conservatives, black and white, criticized the Initiative as conducting a monologue rather than a spirited dialogue. As the Initiative soon learned, it's one thing to invite open discussion on a sensitive issue, but it's an entirely different matter to obtain it.

The authors of the following selections choose different ways to respond to the president's call for dialogue. Alex Kotlowitz, the author of a noted book on race relations, raises serious questions about the possibility of engaging in a dialogue on race. In "Colorblind," he wonders how we can have productive conversation on race when blacks and whites can see no gray. Achieving productive dialogue will be difficult, argues Lani Guinier, one of America's leading legal scholars, but she is optimistic that a method of discourse for "multiracial deliberation" can be eventually worked out. In "Finding a Space for Real Conversations on Race," she reports on her ongoing work to establish models of dialogue that will encourage "listening, mutual understanding, and the ability to brainstorm and collaborate to solve real problems."

In "Stop the Lies," the poet and essayist Luis J. Rodríguez offers another suggestion for productive conversation. Do "you want to talk about race in America?" he asks. "Then stop the lies." Rodríguez goes on to cite a litany of lies that he believes perpetuate the nation's racial division. The conflicts surrounding Clinton's Initiative on Race, argues Wayne State University student Jason Michael in "Reflections on Black History Month," themselves prove how much hard work remains ahead of us. For Michael the real question is not only a matter of productive dialogue; it is how to achieve a level of historical education and understanding among both blacks and whites that will someday make Black History Month unnecessary.

ALEX KOTLOWITZ

Colorblind

[THE NEW YORK TIMES MAGAZINE / January 11, 1998]

Before You Read

The author is often asked by whites how he can spend so much time in black communities without feeling "misunderstood or unwelcomed or threatened." Think about your own experiences with different racial groups. Are your experiences similar to Kotlowitz's?

Journalist ALEX KOTLOWITZ *(b. 1955) has written on urban affairs, social policy, poverty, and race for the* New York Times *and the* Wall Street Journal *and has appeared on National Public Radio and the* MacNeil/Lehrer NewsHour. *He is the author of* The Other Side of the River *(1998) and* There Are No Children Here *(1991) which earned him the Carl Sandburg Award and was one of the New York Public Library's 150 most notable books of the century. A native New Yorker, Kotlowitz now lives in Oak Park, Illinois.*

Words to Learn

eerily (para. 1): weirdly, mysteriously (adv.)

demilitarized (para. 1): deprived of military character, placed under civil control (adj.)

constrain (para. 3): compel by force, restrain (v.)

refute (para. 3): prove to be false (v.)

municipality (para. 6): district incorporated for local self-government (n.)

raze (para. 6): level to the ground, tear down (v.)

monolithic (para. 9): like a large block of stone, massive (adj.)

regale (para. 10): entertain agreeably, divert (v.)

stark (para. 11): bare, extreme (adj.)

animosity (para. 12): feeling of ill will (n.)

certitude (para. 14): freedom from doubt (n.)

disparity (para. 14): inequality, dissimilarity, (n.)

embed (para. 16): enclose firmly (v.)

squall (para. 16): brief, powerful storm (n.)

flail (para. 16): beat (v.)

ballast (para. 16): something that gives stability (n.)

One Christmas day seven years ago, I'd gone over to the Henry Horner Homes in Chicago to visit with Lafeyette and Pharoah, the subjects of my book *There Are No Children Here.* I had brought presents for the boys, as well as a gift for their friend Rickey, who lived on the other side of the housing complex, an area controlled by a rival gang. Lafeyette and Pharoah insisted on walking over with me. It was eerily quiet, since most everyone was inside, and so, bundled from the cold, we strolled toward the other end in silence. As we neared Damen Avenue, a kind of demilitarized zone, a uniformed police officer, a white woman, approached us. She looked first at the two boys, neither of whom reached my shoulder, and then directly at me. "Are you O.K.?" she asked. 1

> We — blacks and whites — need to examine and question our own perspectives. Only then can we grasp each other's myths and grapple with the truths.

About a year later, I was with Pharoah on the city's North Side, shopping for high-tops. We were walking down the busy street, my hand on Pharoah's shoulder, when a middle-aged black man approached. He looked at me, and then at Pharoah. "Son," he asked, "are you O.K.?" 2

Both this white police officer and middle-aged black man seemed certain of what they witnessed. The white woman saw a white man possibly in trouble; the black man saw a black boy possibly in 3 trouble. It's all about perspective — which has everything to do with our personal and collective experiences, which are consistently informed by race. From those experiences, from our histories, we build myths, legends that both guide us and constrain us, legends that include both fact and fiction. This is not to say the truth doesn't matter. It does, in a big way. It's just that getting there may not be easy, in part because everyone is so quick to choose sides, to refute the other's myths, and to pass on their own.

We'd do well to keep this in mind as we enter the yearlong dialogue on race convened by President Clinton. Yes, conversation is critical, but not without self-reflection, both individually and communally. While myths help us make sense of the incomprehensible, they can also confine us, confuse us, and leave us prey to historical laziness. Moreover, truth is not always easily discernible — and even when it is, the prism, depending on which side of the river you reside on, may create a wholly different illusion. Many whites were quick to believe Susan Smith, the South Carolina mother who claimed that a black man had killed her children. And with the reawakening of the Tawana Brawley case, we learn that, although a grand jury has determined otherwise, many blacks still believe she was brutally raped by a group of white men. We — blacks and whites — need to examine and question our own perspectives. Only then can we grasp each other's myths and grapple with the truths.

In 1992, I came across the story of a sixteen-year-old black boy, Eric McGinnis, whose body had been found a year earlier floating in the St. Joseph River in southwestern Michigan. The river flows between Benton Harbor and St. Joseph, two small towns whose only connections are two bridges and a powerful undertow of contrasts.

St. Joseph is a town of 9,000 and, with its quaint downtown and brick-paved streets, resembles a New England tourist haunt. But for those in Benton Harbor, St. Joseph's most defining characteristic is its racial makeup: It is 95 percent white. Benton Harbor, a town of 12,000 on the other side of the river, is 92 percent black and dirt poor. For years, the municipality so hurt for money that it could not afford to raze abandoned buildings.

Eric, a high-school sophomore whose passion was dancing, was last seen at the Club, a teen-age nightspot in St. Joseph, where weeks earlier he had met and started dating a white girl. The night Eric disappeared, a white man said he caught the boy trying to break into his car and chased him — away from the river, past an off-duty white deputy sheriff. That was the last known moment he was seen alive, and it was then that the myths began.

I became obsessed with Eric's death, and so for five years moved   8
in and out of these two communities, searching for answers to both Eric's disappearance and to matters of race. People would often ask which side of the river I was staying on, wanting to gauge my allegiance. And they would often ask about the secrets of those across the way or, looking for affirmation, repeat myths passed on from one generation to the next.

Once, during an unusually bitter effort by white school-board   9
members to fire Benton Harbor's black superintendent, one black woman asked me: "How do you know how to do this? Do you take lessons? How do you all stick together the way you do?" Of course, we don't. Neither community is as unified or monolithic as the other believes. Indeed, contrary to the impression of those in St. Joseph, the black community itself was deeply divided in its support for the superintendent, who was eventually fired.

On occasion, whites in St. Joseph would regale me with tales of   10
families migrating to Benton Harbor from nearby states for the high welfare benefits. It is, they would tell me, the reason for the town's economic decline. While some single mothers indeed moved to Benton Harbor and other Michigan cities in the early 1980s to receive public assistance, the truth is that in the 1930s and 1940s, factories recruited blacks from the South, and when those factories shut down, unemployment, particularly among blacks, skyrocketed.

But the question most often asked was: "Why us? Why write   11
about St. Joseph and Benton Harbor?" I would tell them that while the contrasts between the towns seem unusually stark, they are, I believe, typical of how most of us live: physically and spiritually isolated from one another.

It's not that I didn't find individuals who crossed the river to spend   12
time with their neighbors. One St. Joseph woman, Amy Johnson, devotes her waking hours to a Benton Harbor community center. And Eric McGinnis himself was among a handful of black teenagers who spent weekend nights at the Club in St. Joseph. Nor is it that I didn't find racial animosity. One St. Joseph resident informed me that Eric got what he deserved: "That nigger came on the wrong side of the bridge," he said. And Benton Harbor's former schools superintendent, Sherwin Allen, made no effort to hide his contempt for the white power structure.

What I found in the main, though, were people who would like   13
to do right but don't know where to begin. As was said of the South's

politicians during Jim Crow, race diminishes us. It incites us to act as we wouldn't in other arenas: clumsily, cowardly, and sometimes cruelly. We circle the wagons, watching out for our own.

That's what happened in the response to Eric's death. Most everyone in St. Joseph came to believe that Eric, knowing the police were looking for him, tried to swim the river to get home and drowned. Most everyone in Benton Harbor, with equal certitude, believes that Eric was killed — most likely by whites, most likely because he dated a white girl. I was struck by the disparity in perspective, the competing realities, but I was equally taken aback by the distance between the two towns — which, of course, accounts for the myths. Jim Reeves, the police lieutenant who headed the investigation into Eric's death, once confided that this teenager he'd never met had more impact on him than any other black person.   14

I'm often asked by whites, with some wonderment, how it is that I'm able to spend so much time in black communities without feeling misunderstood or unwelcomed or threatened. I find it much easier to talk with blacks about race than with fellow whites. While blacks often brave slights silently for fear that if they complain they won't be believed, when asked, they welcome the chance to relate their experiences. Among whites, there's a reluctance — or a lack of opportunity — to engage. Race for them poses no urgency; it does not impose on their daily routines. I once asked Ben Butzbaugh, a St. Joseph commissioner, how he felt the two towns got along. "I think we're pretty fair in this community," he said. "I don't know that I can say I know of any out-and-out racial-type things that occur. I just think people like their own better than others. I think that's pretty universal. Don't you? . . . We're not a bunch of racists. We're not anything America isn't." Butzbaugh proudly pointed to his friendship with Renée Williams, Benton Harbor's new school superintendent. "Renée was in our home three, four, five days a week," he noted. "Nice gal. Put herself through school. We'd talk all the time." Williams used to clean for Butzbaugh's family.   15

As I learned during the years in and out of these towns, the room for day-to-day dialogue doesn't present itself. We become buried in our myths, certain of our truths — and refuse to acknowledge what the historian Allan Nevins calls "the grains of stony reality" embedded in most legends. A quarter-century ago, race was part of everyday public discourse; today it haunts us quietly, though on occasion — the Rodney King beating or the Simpson trial or Eric McGinnis's death — it erupts with jarring urgency. At these moments of crisis, during these squalls, we flail about, try-   16 ing to find moral ballast. By then it is usually too late. The lines are drawn. Accusations are hurled across the river like cannon fire. And the cease-fires, when they occur, are just that, cease-fires, temporary and fragile. Even the best of people have already chosen sides.

Vocabulary/Using a Dictionary

1. In paragraph 3, the author states that "from our histories, we build myths, legends that both guide us and *constrain* us." What does the word *constrain* mean? How is it different from *restrain?*

2. From what root word is *animosity* derived (para. 12)? What are the origins of *animosity?*

3. "At these moments of crisis, during these squalls, we flail about trying to find moral *ballast*," Kotlowitz concludes in paragraph 16. What does the word *ballast* mean? What is another definition of the word? How do you think the two definitions are related?

Responding to Words in Context

1. What does the word *prism* mean in the following sentence: "Moreover, truth is not always easily discernible — and even when it is, the *prism*, depending on which side of the river you reside on, may create a wholly different illusion" (para. 4)?

2. "As was said of the South's politicians during Jim Crow, race diminishes us. It *incites* us to act as we wouldn't in other arenas: clumsily, cowardly, and sometimes cruelly," remarks the author in paragraph 13. What do you think the word *incite* means?

Discussing Main Point and Meaning

1. What does the author's title suggest to you? How would you interpret it?

2. What is the main point of Kotlowitz's first three paragraphs? How are they related to the topic of dialogue between races?

3. Why do you think the author writes about St. Joseph and Benton Harbor? According to Kotlowitz, what is the towns' only connection?

4. How does each town explain Eric McGinnis's death? What is the author's reaction to these explanations?

Examining Sentences, Paragraphs, and Organization

1. Kotlowitz repeats the pronouns *we* and *us* in many sentences through the essay: "*We'd* do well to keep this in mind" (para. 4); "*we* grasp each other's myths" (para. 4); "race diminishes *us*. It incites *us* to act as *we* wouldn't" (para. 13); "We circle the wagons" (para. 13). To whom is the author referring? How does his use of these first-person plural pronouns affect your understanding of the essay?

2. A paragraph is *unified* when all its sentences clarify or help support the main idea. Unity is lost if a paragraph strays from the topic by including sentences unrelated to the main idea. Keeping this definition of *unity* in mind, does paragraph 3 have unity? Paragraph 15? Explain your answers.

3. How does the author make use of *narration* (the act or process of telling a story) as a technique for presenting ideas in his essay?

Thinking Critically

1. Do you think the author tries to evoke more pity from the reader for the residents of Benton Harbor or for the residents of St. Joseph? Why?

2. Kotlowitz concludes the essay with these lines: "At these moments of crisis, during these squalls, we flail about, trying to find moral ballast. By then it is usually too late. The lines are drawn" (para. 16). Do you agree with the author that after moments of racial crisis, "it is usually too late" to "find moral ballast"?

In-Class Writing Activities

1. Do you think you have ever been the victim of what Kotlowitz's title refers to — being blinded by racial or color distinctions? If so, how did the experience make you feel? How did you deal with it?

2. Discuss the community you grew up in. What groups do you think would feel accepted there? What groups would feel unaccepted? Would you consider this community to be enlightened (free of ignorance, false beliefs, or prejudice)? Write a short essay discussing these issues.

From the Bookshelf

Stephen L. Carter, *Civility*

As President Clinton's year-long Initiative on Race drew to a close in the summer of 1998, it was widely reported to have been a disappointment. The lively and thoughtful national conversation on race issues that its planners hoped to stimulate never materialized. The conversations were either too muted, too specialized, or too rancorous, and by the end no group seemed satisfied that important ground was covered or serious matters confronted. Part of the reason for the Initiative's lack of success may have been its assumption that free and open discussion would naturally occur, without first establishing a basis for how it would occur. Honest and informed dialogue does not spontaneously happen, Stephen L. Carter reminds us in Civility: Manners, Morals, and the Etiquette of Democracy, his splendid study of the dynamics of dissension and disagreement. Such dialogue depends on our trained ability to respect each other and to listen to opposing points of view with patience and civility. The brief excerpt below, taken from a chapter appropriately called "The Varieties of (Not) Listening," should perhaps have been required reading for all of those who participated in the national conversation on race. One of the country's most prominent law professors, Carter teaches at the Yale Law School and is the author of several critically acclaimed books, among them Reflections of an Affirmative Action Baby (1991), The Culture of Disbelief (1993), Integrity (1996), and The Dissent of the Governed (1998).

Listening Respectfully

But what does it mean to be open to what others have to say? It means, quite simply, to acknowledge the possibility that they may be right. We must approach each other, even in disagreement, with openness, not cynicism. Cynicism is the enemy of reason, and thus of civility: It suggests a deep distrust of the motives of our fellow passengers, a distrust that ruins any project of treating others well because they deserve it. But if I expect you to listen respectfully to me and give me a genuine opportunity to convert you to my way of thinking, civility requires me to first listen respectfully to you and give you a genuine opportunity to convert me to your way of thinking. And there lies the risk. If I listen to you in a truly open way, not searching for the flaws in what you say but accepting as real the possibility that you are right, I place my ego, my very sense of myself, at

> hazard. In other words, instead of changing your mind, I might change
> mine.
> And so we can now see a rule taking shape:
>
> > Civility requires that we listen to others with knowledge of the possibil-
> > ity that they are right and we are wrong.
>
> Carter, Stephen L. *Civility: Manners, Morals, and the Etiquette of Democracy.*
> New York: Basic Books, 1998.

LANI GUINIER

Finding a Space for Real Conversations on Race

[THE RADCLIFFE QUARTERLY, RADCLIFFE COLLEGE / Fall–Winter 1997]

Before You Read

Are we a culture that defines individuals with brief, striking statements and neglects to engage people in a dialogue? Do we speak
about and *for* people and not *to* them? Are people afraid to speak in
modern culture?

---

*LANI GUINIER (b. 1950), former professor of law at the University of
Pennsylvania, is the first African American woman tenured professor at Harvard Law School. In 1993, President Clinton nominated her to be the first
black woman to head the Civil Rights Division of the Department of Justice
and then withdrew her name without a confirmation hearing. Guinier was
prompted by this experience to write* Lift Every Voice *(1998), in which she
places the events of 1993 in the context of the past, present, and future civil
rights movement. This essay was adapted from an interview conducted by
Lisa Funderburg and published in 1996 in the* African American Review.

Words to Learn

heterogeneous (para. 1): composed of parts of different kinds (adj.)

discourse (para. 2): conversation (n.)

stratum (para. 2): layer, category (n.)

jargon (para. 2): vocabulary peculiar to a particular profession or group (n.)

litigation (para. 3): legal contest carried on by judicial process (n.)

polarity (para. 3): possession of two contrasting principles (n.)

hierarchy (para. 3): system of persons or things ranked one above another (n.)

mediation (para. 4): resolution of differences by means of a third party (n.)

resolution (para. 4): act of resolving to do something (n.)

methodology (para. 4): set of methods (n.)

thesis (para. 6): proposition proved or maintained against objections (n.)

hypothesis (para. 6): tentative assumption made for the sake of argument (n.)

correlation (para. 7): bringing into mutual relation (n.)

quantitative (para. 7): involving quantity (adj.)

Even though the United States is today a more heterogeneous nation than it once was, in some ways, it is still very segregated. But we can no longer talk about race just in the context of black and white. We have to think about relationships between whites and people of color, about relationships among and within communities of color, and about color in a global sense as well.   1

> *Not everything has to be resolved so that "I win and you lose."*

Very few people are participating in a national conversation right now — white, black, Latino/a, middle-class, working-class, or underclass. The public discourse is taking place only within a very elite stratum of society and frequently among   2
repeat players who often went to similar schools, live in similar neighborhoods, and talk to one another all the time. It's a very small group of people participating in a conversation in which only they know all the rules. They use jargon and shorthand, focusing on who's winning and losing without discussing what's at stake or the implications of either outcome.

Political discourse today resembles, to a great degree, the worst   3
excess of the adversary model of litigation, the "winner takes all" model of sports, and the "only one of you is going to be left stand-

ing" model of war. When we use that structure to talk about an issue like race, it reinforces all the divisions and polarities we are already experiencing on so many levels. The language is too often a representation of a process that also reinforces argument as hierarchy, as combat. Oftentimes our words, our choice of words, are weapons.

I'm working with a number of people — from a colleague at the   4
University of Pennsylvania Law School, Susan Sturm, who is an expert on mediation and alternative dispute resolution models, to graduate students in Penn's psychology department, to Howard Stevenson, a professor of education — on a race-talks initiative to transform this public discourse. Our goal is to develop a methodology for structured dialogue, for multiracial deliberation, and for collective decision-making among people of diverse backgrounds and perspectives. Together, we're trying to rethink the nature of our national conversation on race so that the focus is not just on performance and on talking, but also on listening, mutual understanding, and the ability to brainstorm and collaborate to solve real problems. We think that, through genuine conversation and multiracial problem-solving, ongoing efforts at collaboration will emerge. Not everything has to be resolved so that "I win and you lose."

According to surveys, most ordinary Americans believe that the   5
least trustworthy people are journalists, politicians, and lawyers — the three groups most engaged in the conversation right now. And whom do most Americans trust? Other ordinary Americans — the only group not presumed to have an agenda. What we are trying to do is give ordinary people, across race and class lines, the opportunity and the vehicle for having a public voice.

We are exploring this challenge in democratic decision-making   6
by convening focus groups to study competing hypotheses about the barriers to candid or honest public communication — particularly on race. We tested two major theses: The first is that you have to get people together to talk about race by providing them a mutual task that doesn't have an explicit racial text; the second hypothesis is that you have to confront, magnify, and explode stereotypes before you can get people to a point of trust and intimacy.

Take an issue like affirmative action. For many Americans, the   7
term is a code for preferences primarily based on race, for unqualified minorities, so that race trumps qualifications. But is that what, in fact, people who are implementing affirmative action think they are doing? What does it mean to be qualified to do a particular job?

Is there a relationship between the so-called credentials that we use as gatekeepers and the job that needs to be done and the ability of people to do the job? Is there a correlation between incoming credentials and performance first year? It turns out, for example, that the LSAT, the major quantitative indicator on which many law schools rely, is a very weak predictor of first-year performance — and that's what it's best at! But we have in our performance-ritual discourse elevated the LSAT score to a status that's almost mystical.

Like the LSAT, terms like *affirmative action, merit,* and *qualification* all need to be interrogated. Moreover, you can't have just one conversation on such matters, because the process of multiracial problem-solving requires engagement: It requires an opportunity to think and reflect and come back and perhaps even change your mind, along with the opportunity to clarify yourself, if you've been misunderstood.   8

Because we are in a sound-bite culture, we often define individuals by no more than three or four words. Today many people are being spoken about and spoken for, but they're not being spoken to and they're not speaking. And that, in and of itself, is very disempowering and contributes to the sense of alienation and withdrawal that we see on so many different levels in our culture. I am hopeful, optimistic even, that we can change the future to create a culture that is more inclusive and more consistent with our basic fundamental values of mutual respect, cooperation, equal opportunity, and fairness.   9

Vocabulary/Using a Dictionary

1. What does the word *heterogeneous* mean (para. 1)? What does the prefix *hetero-* mean? What is the origin of the prefix?

2. Does *methodology* (para. 4) mean the same thing as *method?* How do the words differ?

3. In paragraph 7, Guinier states that "it turns out, for example, that the LSAT, the major *quantitative* indicator on which many law schools rely, is a very weak predictor of first-year performance — and that's what it's best at!" What does the author mean by her use of the word *quantitative?*

Responding to Words in Context

1. In describing the two theses the author created in order "to study competing hypotheses about the barriers to candid or honest public communication" (para. 6), Guinier explains that the first thesis "is that you have to get people together to talk about race by providing them a mutual task that doesn't have an *explicit* racial text." What do you think the author means by her use of the word *explicit?*

2. What does Guinier imply when she calls modern America "a sound-bite culture" (para. 9)?

Discussing Main Point and Meaning

1. Why does the author believe "we can no longer talk about race just in the context of black and white" (para. 1)?

2. What does Guinier mean when she says: "Political discourse today resembles, to a great degree, the worst excess of the adversary model of litigation, the 'winner takes all' model of sports, and the 'only one of you is going to be left standing' model of war" (para. 3)?

3. According to surveys, who do most Americans believe are the least trustworthy people (para. 5)? And whom do most Americans trust? What do you think is the reason for this?

4. What reasons does the author give for recommending that Americans not limit themselves to just one conversation on such matters as affirmative action, merit, and qualification?

Examining Sentences, Paragraphs, and Organization

1. What does a transitional expression do? Find two or three transitional expressions in Guinier's essay.

2. Are the paragraphs in Guinier's essay arranged according to time, according to location, from general to specific, from specific to general, from least to most important, or from problem to solution?

3. How would switching the first and last paragraphs change the effectiveness of the essay?

Thinking Critically

1. Does Guinier offer solutions for how to go about "Finding a Space for Real Conversations on Race"? What space does she seem to recommend?

2. Do you agree or disagree with Guinier's claim about affirmative action — that "for many Americans, the term is a code for preferences primarily based on race, for unqualified minorities, so that race trumps qualifications" (para. 7)? Why?

In-Class Writing Activities

1. Besides in the classroom, have you ever had a serious discussion with someone about race? In a short essay, describe the dialogue (exchange of ideas and opinions) that took place.

2. In the last paragraph of her essay, Guinier states: "Today many people are being spoken about and spoken for, but they're not being spoken to and they're not speaking. And that, in and of itself, is very disempowering and contributes to the sense of alienation and withdrawal that we see on so many different levels in our culture." Write about a group that you think fits this generalization, and explain why.

LUIS J. RODRÍGUEZ

Stop the Lies

[HUNGRY MIND REVIEW / Spring 1998]

Before You Read

"Treason to whiteness is loyalty to humanity," say Noel Ignatiev and John Garvey, editors of the book *Race Traitor* (1996). Try to put this thought into your own words. Do you agree with their statement? Are whites responsible for perpetrating lies about history?

Words to Learn

farcical (para. 1): ludicrous, absurd (adj.)

retribution (para. 1): punishment (n.)

adherence (para. 1): attachment (n.)

renaissance (para. 6): revival (n.)

incipient (para. 6): beginning to exist or appear (adj.)

delineate (para. 7): portray or describe in words (v.)

chattel (para. 8): moveable article of personal property (n.)

crystallization (para. 8): taking the form of a crystal, taking definite form (n.)

faculty (para. 9): inherent power (n.)

monolithic (para. 10): like a large block of stone, massive

indigenous (para. 10): characteristic of a particular region, native (adj.)

exploitable (para. 15): able to be used, especially selfishly (adj.)

Luis J. Rodríguez (b. 1954) is a poet and journalist born in El Paso, Texas, who grew up in Watts and East Los Angeles. He is the author of three books of poetry — Poems Across the Pavement *(1989),* The Concrete River *(1991), and* Trochemoche *(1998). His memoir,* Always Running: La Vida Loca, Gang Days in L.A. *(1993), won the Carl Sandburg Award in 1993. Rodríguez, the recipient of the Lannan grant for writing, lives in Chicago where he is editor of* Tía Chucha Press.

In 1997 President Bill Clinton dared to open up the race debate   1
with a number of so-called town hall meetings. In my view, many of
these meetings were farcical and insulting. The basic lies were not
challenged. I believe because of this the lies were thus perpetuated.
Apologies and meaningless gestures of retribution are even more insulting. They only give the lies more adherence in our conscience.

You want to talk about race in America? Then stop the lies.   2

Stop the lie that Aryans were white and superior. According to   3
J. M. Roberts in *A Short History of the World* (Oxford University
Press, 1993), they were central Asian warriors and nomads who
settled into India, Iran (which means "Land of the Aryans"), and eastern Europe some 2,000 years before Christ. And although they contributed much (including the horse-drawn chariot, the Indo-European
family of languages, and the *Vedas*), they also held back certain aspects of culture and development in the areas they conquered.

> *The real social division governing how we live and think is that of class.*

"The Aryans had no culture so   4
advanced as what they found," says
Roberts. "Writing disappears with their
arrival, not emerging again until the
middle of the first millennium B.C.; cities,
too, had to be reinvented, and when they
appear again lack the elaboration and
order of their Indus Valley[1] predecessors."

Stop the lie that Jesus Christ was white. He was an Aramaic-   5
speaking[2] brown man who never set foot in Europe. The first Chris-
tians were from the Semitic[3] regions of the Mediterranean, including
Northern Africa, where many of the original Christians, including the
Coptic[4] Church of Egypt and Ethiopia, still exist. The teachings of
Jesus Christ are no less profound. He doesn't have to be white!

Stop the lie that Europe civilized the world. A case can be made   6
that it was the other way around. For example, the shaping forces of

---

[1]*Indus Valley:* Valley formed by the Indus River, which flows from Tibet through
Pakistan into the Arabian Sea.
[2]*Aramaic:* Semitic language (see note 3) used extensively in southwest Asia in com-
merce after 300 B.C. and adopted as customary speech by various non-Aramaean
people, including the Jews after the Babylonian exile.
[3]*Semitic:* Of, relating to, or characteristic of the Semites, especially Jewish or Arabic.
[4]*Coptic:* Member of the Christian church of Egypt, traditionally holding the
Monophysite belief that Christ's nature remains altogether divine.

the European renaissance of the fourteenth to seventeenth centuries include the opening of trade with China, the Moors' 800-year rule of Spain, the first circumnavigation of the world by Ferdinand Magellan, the conquest of the Americas (including the looting of gold and silver that fueled the engines of Europe's incipient capitalist economy), and the slave trade in Africa. Gypsies, Huns, Arabs, Tartars, Jews, and others have all contributed to "civilization" in Europe.

Stop the lie that humans can be delineated by race. There are no anthropological, spiritual, or biological grounds for such a concept. The American notion of race is a relatively recent construct predicated on the oppression and exploitation of one people over others.

"The traffic grew with the profits — the shuttle service importing human chattel to America in overcrowed ships," writes Earl Conrad in his 1967 book *The Invention of the Negro* (Paul S. Eriksson Publishers). "It was on these ships that we find the beginnings — the first crystallizations — of the curious doctrine which was to be called 'white supremacy.' . . . Among the first men to develop attitudes of supremacy were the slaveship crew."

This doctrine was later supported by pseudo-scientific papers that declared Africans, Amerindians, and Asians as inferior to Europeans, including from the mighty pens of such scholars as Kant and freedom defenders as Thomas Jefferson! According to Emmanuel Chukwudi Eze in *Race and the Enlightenment* (Blackwell Press, 1997), Kant stated in his master work, *Physical Geography,* that "humanity is at its greatest perfection in the race of the whites." And Jefferson had this to say in "Laws," from *Notes on the State of Virginia:* "Unfortunate difference of color, and perhaps of faculty, is a powerful obstacle to the emancipation of [black] people."

Stop the lie that we live in a monolithic culture. What we call America was forged with the ideas, blood, sweat, labor, laws, and cultural contributions of the indigenous peoples of the land as well as Africans, Eastern Europeans, Italians, Spanish, French, British, Irish, Chinese, Japanese, mixed-bloods — and on and on. Things we take for granted, such as cowboys, jazz, karate, chocolate, corn, tobacco, paper, surfing, gunpowder, pasta, rock-n-roll, and our system of government, have roots in non-European cultures.

Once a white acquaintance came with me to catch a *Quebradita* dance in Chicago of mostly Mexican and Chicano youth. The young people sported cowboy hats, and leather belts and boots. He looked at me and said, "These kids have no originality — they are trying to be American cowboys!"

You can imagine my response, since those cowboy hats and leather styles originated with the Mexican *vaquero* (a combination of Moorish-Spanish and Mexican-U.S. Indian influences) and was later appropriated by Americans conquering the West. In fact, the first cowboys were Indians recruited by the Spanish landowners of California and the Southwest!   12

We also don't properly acknowledge how Native Americans influenced our system of government. In *Indian Givers: How the Indians of the Americas Transformed the World* (Fawcett Columbine Books, 1988), Jack Weatherford credits the Iroquois Confederacy with providing many of the ideas American revolutionists used to frame a new government. "The Americans followed the model of the Iroquois League not only in broad outline but also in many of the specific provisions," writes Weatherford.   13

James W. Loewen, author of *Lies My Teacher Told Me* (The New Press, 1995), points out that the symbol of the United States, the eagle clutching a bundle of arrows, was a symbol of the Iroquois League.   14

The problem is you can't get rid of racism just by attacking racism. Its strongest foundation as an ideology and practice has been a growing industrial economy. In such growth, industry maintains a brutal competition between the most exploitable workers for the least possible pay. Color privilege is key to this competition.   15

However, this foundation is eroding. We are entering an era characterized by the "end of work." The technological advances in production, downsizing, and globalization are changing racial politics as we know it. As the nature of work changes — there is simply no longer a need in this country for a large, unskilled, and labor-intensive workforce — so do the concepts, ideologies, and divisions that arose under the previous circumstances.   16

I have been to the coal country of the Appalachias,[5] the rust belt of the Great Lakes region, and in towns along rural acres of untended farmland, where unemployment has reached over 50 percent, youth are on the corners with nothing to do, and rates of alcoholism, homicide, gang violence, and broken families are at epidemic levels — among whites!   17

---

[5]*Appalachias:* Appalachian Mountains, which run from central New York to central Alabama.

The real social division governing how we live and think is that   18
of *class*. Today class interests are forcing us to look deeper at any so-
called unity based on race. But how often have we been told that
class issues do not really exist in America?

Stop the lies. Stop the lies. Stop the lies.   19

Then let's talk.   20

Vocabulary/Using a Dictionary

1. What does the word *incipient* mean (para. 6)? What is the word's
   origin?

2. Rodríguez quotes Thomas Jefferson from *Notes on the State of
   Virginia:* "Unfortunate difference of color, and perhaps of *faculty,* is a powerful obstacle to the emancipation of [black]
   people" (para. 9). What did Jefferson mean by his use of *faculty*?

3. "Stop the lie that we live in a *monolithic* culture," urges
   Rodríguez (para. 10). What does *monolithic* mean? What is the
   root of the word? What similar origin do the two words share?

Responding to Words in Context

1. In paragraph 1, Rodríguez criticizes President Clinton's town hall
   meetings, stating, "In my view, many of these meetings were farcical and insulting. The basic lies were not challenged. I believe
   because of this the lies were thus *perpetuated*." What do you
   think *perpetuated* means?

2. "This doctrine [of white supremacy] was later supported by
   pseudo-scientific papers that declared Africans, Amerindians, and
   Asians as inferior to Europeans," the author asserts in paragraph
   9. What do you think the prefix *pseudo-* signifies? Can you think
   of any other words that have this prefix?

Discussing Main Point and Meaning

1. List four or five of the many lies that Rodríguez tries to expose.

2. Who were among the first people to adopt "the curious doctrine
   which was to be called 'white supremacy'" (para. 8)?

3. Why was Rodríguez so surprised at his friend's response to a
   Quebradita dance (paras. 11–12)?

4. Where does Rodríguez find hope for the erosion of racism's strongest foundation, the industrial economy (paras. 15–16)?

Examining Sentences, Paragraphs, and Organization

1. What is the topic sentence of paragraph 7? Why do you think so? Paragraph 8? Why?

2. Why does Rodríguez repeat the phrase "Stop the lie" at the beginning of so many paragraphs (paras. 3, 5–7, 10, 19)?

3. Which of the following does the author employ the most in the organization of his essay — *narration, example,* or *comparison and contrast?*

Thinking Critically

1. Is Rodríguez justified in saying that President Clinton's town hall meetings were "farcical and insulting" because the president did not address what the author refers to as "the basic lies" of the race debate (para. 1)?

2. In his essay Rodríguez claims that the doctrine of "white supremacy" was "supported by pseudo-scientific papers . . . of such scholars as [Emmanuel] Kant and freedom defenders as Thomas Jefferson" (para. 9). Do you feel that the author's claim is justified?

In-Class Writing Activities

1. In "Stop the Lies," Rodríguez discusses and dispels some of the lies perpetuated by America in regard to race. In your own experience, have you ever encountered a lie about race? How was the lie dispelled?

2. Henry Ford (1863–1947), the American automaker, once said, "I don't know much about history, and I wouldn't give a nickel for all the history in the world. History is more or less bunk. It is tradition. We want to live in the present and the only history that is worth a tinker's damn is the history we make today." In a short essay, comment on whether you think Rodríguez would agree with Ford's statement, citing specific examples from "Stop the Lies" if you need to.

JASON MICHAEL

Reflections on Black History Month

[THE SOUTH END PRESS, WAYNE STATE UNIVERSITY / February 1998]

Before You Read

When you think of Black History Month, what comes to mind? How does American culture treat Black History Month? On television? In school? At home? Through the media? How do you celebrate Black History Month?

Words to Learn

transpire (para. 2): occur, happen (v.)

gallant (para. 2): brave, spirited, noble-minded (adj.)

bandwagon (para. 5): cause attracting more and more followers (n.)

salve (para. 9): medicinal ointment for treating wounds, burns, and sores (n.)

As another Black History Month comes to a close, I'm full of mixed emotions. The month was a spectacular success. The media were at their best, helping to promote the cause of black history. I heard powerful Allstate-sponsored ads on the radio, saw beautiful McDonald's commercials on television, and read informative pieces on the subject in the Detroit newspapers.   1

JASON MICHAEL (b. 1972) is a junior at Wayne State University in Michigan and contributor to the South End Press. "Growing up in suburban Detroit, I didn't understand the concept of African American History Month and didn't see the need for such," says Michael. "It was only as an adult, through college-level courses and my own personal research, that I began to learn about the other history of this country." Michael's interests include urban music and writing poetry and fiction. He is currently pursuing degrees in journalism and Africana studies.

Now comes the conflict. While I'm content with what transpired   2
in the past twenty-eight days, I can't help but think about the eleven
months ahead. Allstate ads will go back to talking about insurance
needs, and McDonald's commercials will once again feature corny
jingles instead of Harriet Tubman stories. The African American experience will once again take a back burner to the slick version of
white history being taught in classrooms across the country. Teachers
will go back to talking about the gallant efforts of President Lincoln,
who freed the slaves by waging the Civil War. Not much, however,
will be said about the war for civil rights and equal treatment that is
still being fought over a hundred years later.

So little is taught about the struggle for civil rights that many   3
falsely think the war has been won. It hasn't. The battles against racism and discrimination are being continually fought. We've made great strides. We've gained much ground. But it's too early to break into a victory dance just yet. There's a lot of work still to be done.

> *The battles against racism and discrimination are being continually fought. We've made great strides. We've gained much ground. But it's too early to break into a victory dance just yet.*

If you think I'm wrong, ask President   4
Clinton. The proof is not that he's made
improving race relations a priority of his
second term or that he's established a
Race Initiative Advisory Board. The
proof is that the two sides can't even
agree on the purpose of the board or
on the members selected. Jesse Jackson
praised the president's choice of the distinguished African American
historian Dr. John Hope Franklin as chair of the board, while Newt
Gingrich quickly attacked Franklin's methods.

Although the primary purpose of the board was to establish a na-   5
tional dialogue on race, it appeared that only a few were entitled to
speak. Ward Connerly, the African American who led the fight
to abolish affirmative action in California, was excluded from the
board's panel talks on that particular topic. In fact, no one opposed
to affirmative action was invited to participate. "I thought the original idea was for a dialogue, not a monologue," Gingrich criticized.
The *New York Post* jumped on the bandwagon, nicknaming the
chairman John "Hopeless" Franklin when he was quoted as saying
that "whites are poor losers."

Tensions within the committee have been publicly acknowledged,   6
and the Race Initiative Advisory Board seems to have only widened

the divide it was created to close. "The president would probably like to start this thing over again," stated one White House official.

Maybe he should. Maybe the emphasis and focus are all wrong.   7
Maybe Franklin is not the leader Clinton needs. It is no longer the responsibility of strong African American leaders to declare what their people are entitled to. The burden is now on white America to prove it understands. The issue isn't about some apology for slavery from Clinton, who wasn't in office during the over two hundred years of American slavery.

The real issue is simple. "One America," the title of Clinton's initia-   8
tive, is not a new concept. We are supposed to be "one nation under God," right? The real issue is about making this nation live up to its creed. It's about pulling out the Declaration of Independence and rereading the line about "we hold these truths to be self-evident that all men are created equal." It's about confessing that Thomas Jefferson and the forefathers of this country never meant to include blacks when they wrote "all men." It's about admitting they were wrong.

The real issue is about putting salve on old wounds and not   9
pouring salt into them. It's about average people, black and white alike, declaring that Medgar Evers, Martin Luther King Jr., and Malcolm X did not die in vain. It's about students of all ethnic backgrounds learning daily, year-round, about the complete role of African Americans in this country and their ensuing struggle. It's about producing graduates who possess an accurate history of the United States. This is what will create better understanding. This is how a positive dialogue on race relations can begin.

The issue is not about leaders so much as about everyday heroes.   10
It's about people willing to show up at the polls and proclaim that affirmative action has not outlived its usefulness and will not until race no longer prohibits anyone from obtaining a job or attending college.

Finally, the issue is about people willing to stand up and say,   11
"OK, we get it now." Only then shall we have overcome our fears, our prejudice, and our ignorance. Only then will Black History Month no longer be necessary.

Vocabulary/Using a Dictionary

1. What does it mean when something (perhaps an event) has *transpired* (para. 2)?

2. Is *gallant* (para. 2) behavior regarded as desirable? What are some other words to describe *gallant*?

3. Have you ever used a *salve* (para. 9)? What would you use one for?

Responding to Words in Context

1. In paragraph 5, Michael quotes Newt Gingrich, who criticized President Clinton's Race Initiative Advisory Board by arguing that "I thought the original idea was for a *dialogue,* not a *monologue.*" What is the difference between the prefixes *dia-* and *mono-* of the two words? What does the root *-logue* mean?
2. The author states, "We are supposed to be 'one nation under God,' right? The real issue is about making this nation live up to its *creed*" (para. 8). What do you think the word *creed* means?

Discussing Main Point and Meaning

1. What conflict does Michael have with Black History Month (para. 2)?
2. Does Michael think that the United States has won the war for civil rights (paras. 2–3)?
3. The author states that "it is no longer the responsibility of strong African American leaders to declare what their people are entitled to" (para. 7). If this statement is true, then who does Michael claim should shoulder this burden?

Examining Sentences, Paragraphs, and Organization

1. How are sentences arranged in Michael's essay? From problem to solution? From least to most important? From general to specific?
2. What supporting evidence does the author give for his generalization that "there's a lot of work still to be done" (para. 3)? Do you think his support is feasible (suitable)?
3. Why does Michael continually repeat the phrase "It's about" toward the end of his essay?

Thinking Critically

1. Do you agree with Michael when he says that "so little has been taught about the struggle for civil rights that many falsely think the war has been won" (para. 3)?

2. "It is no longer the responsibility of strong African American leaders to declare what their people are entitled to. The burden is now on white America to prove it understands," the author remarks in paragraph 7. How do you feel about this statement?

In-Class Writing Activities

1. At what age do you think people should be initiated into the ideas of civil rights? How old were you when you learned about the civil rights movement? Freewrite for five to ten minutes about this experience.

2. How did you participate in your last Black History Month? Did you write a paper for a class? Discuss the idea of black history with a friend? Think about it in passing? Is Black History Month important to you? Jot down a few answers you have to these questions.

Discussing the Unit

Suggested Topic for Discussion

How important is creating a national dialogue on race? Should one group be responsible for creating this dialogue? If so, who? To what extent should college administrators, American families, and other social institutions be held responsible for holding these dialogues? What do you see as the future for how racism is treated in the United States?

Preparing for Class Discussion

1. Are you familiar with any organizations or programs on your campus that encourage discussions about race? If so, how effective do you think they are? If you aren't familiar with any such programs, what kinds of racial issues do you *think* should be dealt with in discussion groups? Provide reasons to support your answers.

2. The United States is a country that appears to be growing more multicultural every day, but still racism persists: Americans can't seem to eliminate their prejudices. Do you foresee a day when racial differences no longer matter?

From Discussion to Writing

1. In the movie *Higher Learning,* Fudge (Ice Cube), hanging out with his friends, looks around at the different racial groups on campus and comments: "Let's take a trip around the world. Look there . . . under the statue. You see them people [who are white]. That's Disneyland. And there's Chinatown. And over there, that's South of the Border. And this right here [looking around at his friends] is the Black Hole . . . 'cause we black folks." Write an essay explicating (explaining) the point you think Fudge is trying to make. Can you think of anyone you know who shares this opinion?

2. Lani Guinier's concern is about "Finding a Space for Real Conversations on Race," and Luis J. Rodríguez wants us to "Stop the Lies." Write an essay making a suggestion for a "Space" where we can hold a real conversation discussing how we can "Stop the Lies" about race.

3. In Jason Michael's "Reflections on Black History Month," he states that "so little has been taught about the struggle for civil rights that many falsely think the war has been won" (para. 3). Write an essay comparing and contrasting how you think the other writers in the chapter would respond to Michael's assertion.

Topics for Cross-Cultural Discussion

1. Do people from many different racial groups reside in your native country? Do people of different races freely intermingle with each other in your native country? Explain.

2. How, if at all, are young people in your native country educated about race or racial relations? Is one group held more accountable for educating the young in these matters? Why?

12

The Flag: What Does It Symbolize?

From time to time, American politicians propose laws that would make it a criminal offense to burn, mutilate, or otherwise show disrespect for the American flag. Since opponents of such legislation believe that these laws would violate First Amendment rights to freedom of expression, the latest legislative efforts have proposed an amendment to the U.S. Constitution that would explicitly prohibit attacks on the flag. Yet what does the American flag mean? How do we define it? And what sort of behavior toward it amounts to actual desecration? These questions are raised by the prominent historian Horace Freeland Judson in "Some Questions for My Senator about the Flag." "Suppose," he asks, "a couple with a small baby gets trapped in their car in one of those North Dakota blizzards, and they happen to have a flag, which they use to wrap around the baby for a little more warmth, and the baby spits up. Have they desecrated the flag?"

For many Americans, the flag's symbolic value is undoubtedly enhanced by its central presence in our national anthem, which, unlike the anthems of most other countries, is specifically about the flag — the enormous flag (originally thirty feet high by forty-two feet wide) that flew above Fort McHenry in 1814. If a flag amendment is ever passed, one might wonder whether it would also become a criminal offense to sing "The Star-Spangled Banner" disrespectfully. Some might argue, however, that given its musical difficulties, the national anthem often does sound mutilated. In "Star-Spangled Banter," polit-

ical commentator Hendrik Hertzberg says that perhaps it's time to re-
tire an immortal song that has been called "too martial, too irritating, too hard to sing." He suggests another, more stirring song, that
could take its place.

But the familiar stars and stripes — Old Glory — is not the only
flag Americans fly. Many Southerners still display and respect the
Confederate flag, which they argue is not a racist emblem but a
cherished symbol of a special heritage and way of life. "Could you
imagine saying the pledge of allegiance to a Confederate flag?" asks
Harvard University student Galit Sarfaty in "A Forgotten Past." For
Sarfaty, the dangerous influence the Confederate flag bears outweighs
its deep connection to Southern history. All traditions can come to an
end, suggests cartoonist J. Barrios, who satirically depicts what the
American flag might look like in the year 2022.

HORACE FREELAND JUDSON

Some Questions for My Senator about the Flag

[THE NEW YORK TIMES / June 16, 1997]

Before You Read

Should state governments have the right to ban the burning of the
American flag? Reflect on how you feel about this issue.

*HORACE FREELAND JUDSON is director of the Center for History and Re-
cent Science at George Washington University. He is the author of a history
of molecular biology entitled* The Eighth Day of Creation *(1979) and is currently completing a book on fraud and other misconduct in science. Judson's
articles have appeared in such journals as* The Atlantic Monthly, The New
Yorker, The New Republic, Nature, *and the* Journal of the American Medical Association. *He has been a fellow of the John Simon Guggenheim Foundation and the John D. and Catherine T. MacArthur Foundation.*

Words to Learn

desecration (para. 1): showing of contempt for something sacred (n.)
abstraction (para. 8): general idea of a concrete reality (n.)

Senator, we're sitting here drinking coffee and having a peaceable political discussion about the draft amendment to the Constitution, just passed by the House, that would allow the federal government or the legislature of any state to pass laws banning and punishing the burning or other desecration of the American flag. Hmm? I'd like to show you that such an amendment is not just mistaken — all those familiar arguments, counter to the sense and spirit of the First Amendment, of the Bill of Rights, of the Constitution, and so on. I'd like to show you that the amendment is meaningless.   1

> *The American flag is beyond desecration by physical means — any more than I could desecrate the Constitution by using a copy of it to light the barbecue.*

Here I have an envelope with a U.S. postage stamp on it, a first-class stamp, thirty two cents. It shows an American flag — part of a flag, anyway. And look: it's been cancelled. A big, old-fashioned thump of a cancellation, smearing black ink all over that flag. Is that desecrating the flag?   2

Here's an uncancelled stamp, same issue, same flag. To make this political point, I place the stamp in my saucer and set a match to it. It burns up. Is this desecrating the flag?   3

Senator, suppose two weeks from now my neighbor's child of seven draws a childish picture of the Fourth of July parade, with an American flag being carried down the street, and later that afternoon — the kid says she doesn't mind, she drew better ones — I twist up that piece of paper and use it to help light the charcoal in the barbecue. Have we desecrated the flag?   4

But artists, for instance Jasper Johns, have painted careful, detailed American flags, and some of these paintings go for a lot of money. I wouldn't want to burn a Johns — that's another kind of desecration, the money and all — but suppose I paint as best I can, ruling all the lines first, using the right colors, a picture of an American flag. And then, the paint dry, I unpin it from the drawing board and take it along to a political protest meeting and burn it publicly there. This political statement may make some people angry, but is it desecrating the flag?   5

Take it further. Maybe I had painted both sides of that piece of   6
paper? But wait: suppose I take pieces of cloth — red, white, and
blue — cut them correctly, and sew them together (à la Betsy Ross)
into an American flag — except that I put in only twelve stripes. And
take that along to the protest demonstration and try to start it burning. Cloth doesn't burn all that well, but I get arrested for desecrating
the flag. What can happen at the trial when I lay out the remains of
what I actually tried to set alight?

Well, none of those was a "real" flag. So take another tack. Sup-   7
pose I'm cleaning out the basement and find an old flag there, tat-
tered, stained, maybe the one I knew as a lad with forty-eight stars. I
throw it in the trash or toss it on the bonfire. Have I desecrated the
flag? Suppose a couple with a small baby gets trapped in their car in
one of those North Dakota blizzards, and they happen to have a flag,
which they use to wrap around the baby for a little more warmth,
and the baby spits up. Have they desecrated the flag?

Seems to me, Senator, that the American flag is an abstraction,   8
and all material versions of it, even with fifty stars and thirteen
stripes, are copies, mere representations — among which the law cannot clearly draw a line. The American flag is beyond desecration by
physical means — any more than I could desecrate the Constitution
by using a copy of it to light the barbecue. In sum, the draft amendment cannot define the flag, and it conceals the question of intent. If
it is not meaningless, it's far less simple than it appears — and sinister. Its aim is not defense but attack — to open an attack on freedom
of political argument.

Now there's a desecration for you.   9

As I could demonstrate were I fool enough to take these ques-   10
tions to a bar downtown tonight. Wouldn't even have to light the
postage stamp.

Vocabulary/Using a Dictionary

1. What does Judson mean in paragraph 1 when he says that the
   draft amendment to the Constitution "would allow the federal
   government or the legislature of any state to pass laws banning
   and punishing the burning or other *desecration* of the American
   flag"?

2. What are several synonyms for the word *abstraction* (para. 8)?
   Why does Judson use this word to describe the American flag?

Responding to Words in Context

1. What do you think the word *sinister* means in paragraph 8?
2. Often we use the word *amendment* while referring to the Constitution of the United States (para. 1). What do you think the word means?

Discussing Main Point and Meaning

1. What is the purpose of this essay, according to Judson (para. 1)?
2. What does Judson refer to when he says, "Well, none of those was a 'real' flag" (para. 7).
3. Toward the end of his essay, Judson proclaims, "Now there's a desecration for you" (para. 9). What is the author referring to?

Examining Sentences, Paragraphs, and Organization

1. Why does the author use questions at the end of paragraphs 2 through 7?
2. Do the paragraphs supporting Judson's idea that "the amendment is meaningless" (para. 1) provide enough evidence to make you believe the author's point?
3. Who do you think is the audience for this essay? Why does the author address it to a "Senator"?

Thinking Critically

1. Does Judson's essay help convince you that the draft amendment is meaningless, even sinister? Even if you disagree with the essay, which of his examples do you find most convincing?
2. What tone does Judson take in the essay? What was your reaction to this tone?

In-Class Writing Activities

1. In a brief essay reflect on your own childhood. In U.S. schools, students are asked to stand to recite the "Pledge of Allegiance" to the flag. Why do you think you were asked to pledge allegiance to the flag? On reflection, would you pledge allegiance *now*? Why or why not?

2. Does the author ignore any positive reasons why we should prevent the desecration of the American flag? Write an essay about
   some time in which the American flag had a positive impact on
   your life.

HENDRIK HERTZBERG

Star-Spangled Banter

[THE NEW YORKER / July 21, 1997]

Before You Read

Have you ever sung the American national anthem, "The Star-
Spangled Banner," by Francis Scott Key? Did you ever reflect on what
the words to the song mean? How does hearing the song make you feel?

Words to Learn

capital (para. 1): excellent or first-
rate (adj.)
bellicose (para. 2): inclined or eager
to fight or quarrel (adj.)
rampart (para. 2): mound raised as
a fortification (n.)

potboiler (para. 2): mediocre work
of literature or art produced
merely for financial gain (n.)
martial (para. 3): inclined to war
(adj.)

JOURNALIST HENDRIK HERTZBERG *(b. 1943) began his career as a corre-
spondent for* Newsweek *magazine and later became the editor of* The New
Republic, *where he also has been contributing editor, national political corre-
spondent, senior editor, and columnist. In 1992, Hertzberg was named the
executive editor of* The New Yorker *magazine and has recently become its
editorial director. He served on the White House staff throughout the Carter
administration and worked as Carter's chief speechwriter. Hertzberg currently lives in New York City.*

incumbent (para. 4): current holder of an indicated office (n.)
populist (para. 4): suggesting representation of the common people (adj.)
secularist (para. 5): person believing

that nonreligious issues should be the concern of government (n.)
twinned (para. 5): brought together in close association (v.)
medley (para. 5): mixture (n.)

Ted Turner set off a firecracker of his own this Fourth of July [1997]. Speaking in front of Independence Hall, in Philadelphia, he argued that it's time to dump "The Star-Spangled Banner." Over the years, Mr. Turner has had many capital ideas — CNN, Turner Classic Movies, and interrupting Jane Fonda's career as a serial monogamist, to name three. Now he has come up with another, and one cannot but agree with him. By all means, let us ease the old chestnut into well-deserved retirement. But not for the reason he offers and not to make way for the alternative he recommends.   1

> *Congress designated "The Star-Spangled Banner" our national anthem during the Hoover administration, when the country's judgment was impaired by clinical depression.*

Mr. T notes that the national anthem is warlike, whereas the age we live in is (relatively) peaceful. He is right on both counts, but his second point makes his first less compelling. Just as gun control is more urgent in Detroit than in Lausanne, bellicose songs are more worrying in bellicose times than in times of tranquillity.   2

"The Star-Spangled Banner" is warlike, yes. But so are a lot of first-rate national anthems. ("The Marseillaise,"[1] with its ghoulish call to "drench our fields" in "impure blood," makes its American counterpart sound like a Joni Mitchell ditty.) In any case, there are plenty of better reasons for getting rid of "The Star-Spangled Banner." Its tonal range corresponds to that of the electric guitar, as Jimi Hendrix proved, but not to that of the human voice. The lyrics include some fine phrases — "the twilight's last gleaming," "the ramparts we watched" — that are a reliable source of titles for the type of potboiler novel that goes in for raised lettering on the jacket, but on the whole the words don't convey what politicians call core American values. Francis Scott Key's poem was written to immortalize the siege of Fort McHenry, Maryland, during the War of 1812 — a silly war, a minor war, a war that ended in

---

[1] *"The Marseillaise"*: French national anthem.

what was at best a tie. (The British torched the White House and smashed our hopes of gobbling up Canada. We got to keep our independence.) The poem lends itself to mishearing, from the traditional "José, can you see" opening, through "O, sadists that stars spank," to the closing "Orlando D. Free and Homer D. Brave."

Congress designated "The Star-Spangled Banner" our national   3
anthem during the Hoover administration, when the country's judgment was impaired by clinical depression. The relevant bill — whose sponsor hoped to promote the tourist trade in his district, which included Fort McHenry — was rejected three times by the House before it finally passed, on a slow day. It was supported by the "Americanism" busybodies of the Daughters of the American Revolution and the American Legion but opposed by music teachers — an important group at a time when pianos were more common than phonographs. The complaints then were identical to the complaints now: too martial, too irritating, too hard to sing.

What's the alternative? Mr. T suggests "America the Beautiful" —   4
the music teachers' choice back in 1930, by the way. It's nice, but, like so many nice things, it's also wimpy. The best that can be said for it is that it's more singable than the incumbent. A third contender — "America (My Country, 'Tis of Thee)" — has O.K. words, but the tune is the same as that of "God Save the Queen." This would make for an unusually severe "Is there an echo in here?" problem during joint appearances by Bill Clinton and Tony Blair.[2] How about "This Land Is Your Land"? Plenty of progressive-school pupils already think Woody Guthrie's populist jingle is the national anthem, but the tune is a little too Barney the Dinosaurish, and the lyrics have a musty, Popular Front[3] feeling about them.

Our country has at hand what is perhaps the greatest patriotic   5
hymn ever written: "The Battle Hymn of the Republic." But secularists would object that it is too God-filled, and Southerners — white Southerners, at least — would complain that the vineyards it advocates trampling were their vineyards. ("The Star-Spangled Banner" was also popular with the Union Army, but never mind.) Perhaps "The Battle Hymn of the Republic" could be twinned with "Dixie," as in the Elvis Presley version, but "Dixie" has its own problems. Anyhow, serious countries do not have national medleys.

---

[2]*Tony Blair:* Prime minister of Great Britain.
[3]*Popular Front:* European union of 1930s leftist political parties that worked against fascism.

This space would like to offer a recommendation of its own: "Lift   6
Ev'ry Voice and Sing." James Weldon Johnson, a poet of the Harlem
Renaissance,[4] wrote it, in 1900, for a Lincoln's Birthday celebration.
It is already a national anthem of sorts; its alternative title, in fact, is
"The Negro National Anthem." Its tune (by J. Rosamond Johnson,
the poet's brother) is stirring, and so are its words. The opening
verse,[5] the one that would be sung at ballgames, goes, in part:

> Lift ev'ry voice and sing,
> Till earth and heaven ring.
> Ring with the harmonies of liberty . . .
> Sing a song full of the faith that the dark past has taught us,
> Sing a song full of the hope that the present has brought us;
> Facing the rising sun of our new day begun,
> Let us march on till victory is won.

No bombast, no boasting, no wimpishness — just good, solid   7
values that are both American and universal. How about it, Ted?

Vocabulary/Using a Dictionary

1. In paragraph 1, Hertzberg states, "Over the years. Mr. [Ted]
    Turner has had many *capital* ideas — CNN, Turner Classic
    Movies, and interrupting Jane Fonda's career as a serial mo-
    nogamist, to name three." What does the author mean by his use
    of the word *capital*?

2. What is a *rampart* (para. 2)? Can you think of two or three syn-
    onyms for the word?

3. "The complaints [about the 'Star-Spangled Banner'] then were
    identical to the complaints now: too *martial*, too irritating, too
    hard to sing," remarks Hertzberg in paragraph 3. What does
    martial mean? What is its origin?

Responding to Words in Context

1. Hertzberg titles his essay "Star-Spangled *Banter*." What do you
    think the word *banter* means? Who is the author speaking ban-
    teringly to?

---

[4]*Harlem Renaissance:* Period of outstanding African American literary creativity that
was based in the Harlem neighborhood of Manhattan during the 1920s.
[5]The full text of Johnson's poem follows this selection on page 243. — Ed.

2. We use the term *national anthem* to describe "The Star-Spangled Banner" and "The Marseillaise." How do you think an *anthem* differs from a song?

Discussing Main Point and Meaning

1. What was the "firecracker" Ted Turner set off on the Fourth of July (para. 1)?
2. What are the "plenty of better reasons" (para. 2) Hertzberg gives for getting rid of the national anthem?
3. What are some of the alternative choices suggested for the national anthem?
4. Why does the author suggest that "Lift Ev'ry Voice and Sing" by James Weldon Johnson should replace the traditional national anthem (para. 6)?

Examining Sentences, Paragraphs, and Organization

1. In a couple of sentences of his essay, Hertzberg calls Ted Turner "Mr. T" (paras. 2 and 4). How does this affect the tone of the essay?
2. According to *Merriam Webster's Encyclopedia of Literature,* an *allusion* is an implied or indirect reference to a person, event, thing, or part of another text. In his paragraphs, Hertzberg makes many allusions. For example, in paragraph 2, the author *alludes* (makes indirect reference) to the French national anthem "The Marseillaise." Can you spot any other allusions in "Star-Spangled Banter"?
3. The essay is organized in the rhetorical strategy of *problem to solution.* What is the problem that is introduced in the essay? What does Hertzberg offer as the solution?

Thinking Critically

1. What are Hertzberg's reasons for why we should get rid of "The Star-Spangled Banner" as our national anthem? Do you agree with him? Do you think it is too difficult to sing?
2. Consider Johnson's "Lift Ev'ry Voice and Sing" (see p. 243). Do you like the song? Do you think it could be used to replace "The

Star-Spangled Banner"? If the decision were yours to make, would you replace the national anthem? What would you replace it with?

In-Class Writing Activities

1. American Senator J. William Fulbright once said, "To criticize one's country is to do it a service. . . . Criticism, in short, is more than a right; it is an act of patriotism — a higher form of patriotism, I believe, than the familiar rituals and national adulation." Freewrite for a few minutes explaining what you think Fulbright meant by this statement, bringing in Hertzberg's essay if you need to.

2. Is there something within American culture that you would like to change? Something at home? In the media? In school? At work? In a brief essay, describe any aspect of American culture you'd like to change, and, like Hertzberg, offer an alternative.

Editor's Note

Following is the full text of James Weldon Johnson's poem, "Lift Ev'ry Voice and Sing," which was quoted in Hendrik Hertzberg's article, "Star-Spangled Banter."

Lift Ev'ry Voice and Sing

Lift ev'ry voice and sing,
Till earth and heaven ring,
Ring with the harmonies of Liberty;
Let our rejoicing rise
High as the list'ning skies,   5
Let it resound loud as the rolling sea.
Sing a song full of the faith that the dark past has taught us,
Sing a song full of the hope that the present has brought us;
Facing the rising sun of our new day begun,
Let us march on till victory is won.   10

Stony the road we trod,
Bitter the chast'ning rod,
Felt in the days when hope unborn had died;
Yet with a steady beat,

Have not our weary feet   15
Come to the place for which our fathers sighed?
We have come over a way that with tears has been watered,
We have come, treading our path through the blood of the
    slaughtered,
Out from the gloomy past,
Till now we stand at last   20
Where the white gleam of our bright star is cast.

God of our weary years,
God of our silent tears,
Thou who hast brought us thus far on the way;
Thou who hast by Thy might,   25
Led us into the light,
Keep us forever in the path, we pray.
Lest our feet stray from the places, our God, where we met Thee,
Lest our hearts, drunk with the wine of the world, we forget Thee;
Shadowed beneath Thy hand,   30
May we forever stand,
True to our God,
True to our native land.

        — James Weldon Johnson (1900)

GALIT SARFATY

A Forgotten Past

[PERSPECTIVE, HARVARD-RADCLIFFE / March 1997]

Before You Read

How would you feel if the Confederate flag replaced the U.S. stars and stripes? How do you think others might react? Which groups do you think would support the replacement? Which would be opposed?

Words to Learn

relegate (para. 1): classify (v.)

blatant (para. 3): conspicuous (adj.)

centennial (para. 4): relating to a hundred years (adj.)

impetus (para. 4): driving force; impulse (n.)

chattel (para. 5): article of personal property (adj.)

tariff (para. 5): tax imposed by a government on imports or exports (n.)

agrarian (para. 5): related to agricultural interests (adj.)

ante-bellum (para. 5): period before a war, in this case the American Civil War (adj.)

placate (para. 6): appease or pacify (v.)

referendum (para. 6): practice of referring legislative measures to the vote of the electorate (n.)

Could you imagine saying the pledge of allegiance to a Con-   1
federate flag? A relic of the past that one would usually expect to find relegated to textbooks, the Confederate flag is actually alive and still flourishing in the South today. A haunting symbol of those days of slavery that many Americans would rather forget, the flag is con-

GALIT SARFATY (b. 1978) was born in Israel and grew up in Los Angeles, California. She studies social anthropology at Harvard University and was a sophomore when she wrote this essay. Sarfaty is the recipient of a Mellon Undergraduate Minority Research Fellowship and plans to graduate in 2000.

tinuing to stir up emotions in groups with opposing interpretations of history: "A nation which does not remember what it was yesterday does not know where it is today," said General Robert E. Lee before leading the Confederacy's unsuccessful fight against the North during the American Civil War. The Confederate flag that his army proudly waved in combat has since become an object of much controversy. Tensions have arisen between Southern heritage groups who associate it with the honor and tradition of the Old South and blacks who view it as a symbol of racial hatred. Not only was the flag used in the 1800s to represent a union of states that promoted the institution of slavery, but it is also presently embraced by many hate groups to further their causes. These groups include the Ku Klux Klan, which waves the flag to encourage the readoption of racist attitudes toward blacks and other minorities. Yet supporters of the Confederate flag are not limited to these openly racist organizations. Statewide debates over the waving of the flag have uncovered a large number of Southerners who oppose the flag's removal since they do not associate it with racism.

Could you imagine saying the pledge of allegiance to a Confederate flag?

Avoiding the Root of the Problem

The most recent confrontation occurred in South Carolina late last year [1996], when Governor David Beasley proposed to remove the Confederate flag from the State House dome and relocate it at the Confederate Soldier's Monument on the north side of the State House. This has revived the debate over how the Old South's history should be interpreted.

Many blacks claim that those who see the flag as a representation of regional pride and identity in the South are refusing to remember the entire past, including the years of slavery endured by the ancestors of black Southerners. By selectively choosing which events to include in a region's history, supporters of the Confederate flag are only presenting the past from the perspective of the powerful white majority. Instead, all interpretations must be taken into account and every person's heritage must be respected when deciding whether the flag should fly above a state government building that is supposed to reflect the entire state, not just the majority group. To know where a nation is today, as General Robert E. Lee pointed out, requires one to remember the past. However, those who support the flying of the

Confederate flag over the State House dome are not recalling all the events of their history, especially the most blatant example of oppression by the U.S. government — slavery. Unless they are further educated in the horrors of this practice and its continued effects on the position of blacks today, they will, unfortunately, remain in ignorance.

The proposal to move the Confederate flag from the State House dome in South Carolina has been a heated issue for years. First raised at the centennial anniversary of the Civil War during the racial tumult of the 1960s, the Confederate flag has been viewed by many as a symbol of the heritage of the South. While the dome in South Carolina is the last statehouse where the flag flies, Mississippi and Georgia's state flags still incorporate the Confederate flag design. Georgia Governor Zell Miller failed to convince the state legislature in 1993 to pass a proposal to redesign the flag. In 1994, South Carolina also attempted to pass a resolution to relocate the flag, but the measure was not approved. The fight against the flying of the Confederate flag seemed to be over when David Beasley, one of the state's more conservative Republicans, was elected governor in 1994; prior to his election, he promised voters that he would never take the Southern banner down. Nevertheless, he proposed to move the flag late in 1996 due to rising racial tensions in the state. Pointing to the recent church burnings and a drive-by shooting of black teens by two men with ties to the Ku Klux Klan, Beasley claims that the changing times have led to this change in policy and admits he was wrong. Yet the main impetus behind this sudden political move may not be a concern for race relations but a desire to placate business leaders who can bring more industries into South Carolina. His proposal was eventually rejected by the GOP[1]-controlled state House of Representatives, which plans to let the issue be decided by the voters in a special 1997 referendum election. Since this is an odd year when there will be few important offices to vote for, the voter turnout will probably be very low, making it difficult to predict the outcome of this proposal.[2]

A Battle of Interpretation

The controversy over the Confederate flag stems from a debate over the interpretation of the Confederacy and the war. Groups such as the Dixie Defenders, the Sons of Confederate Veterans, and the South-

[1]*GOP:* Grand Old Party, a term for the Republican Party.
[2]The referendum was never held. As of publication of this book, the flag still flies above the State House.

ern Heritage Association claim that states of the Confederacy were not solely dedicated to preserving the institution of chattel slavery but primarily joined together in opposition to the centralization of power in the hands of the federal government, federally funded internal improvements, and high protective tariffs. The civil war, they believe, was a war between opposing visions of civilization, between the agrarian South and the industrial North, and not a war of black against white. Yet while slavery was not the only reason behind the division between North and South, its importance as a major aspect of the Southern way of life, a practice that the South refused to eliminate, must be recognized. If the South had won the war, it would have formed an independent nation and continued the practice of slavery within its borders. The flag's supporters, instead, accuse all who approve of Beasley's proposal of saying that there is nothing redeeming or honorable in the traditions of the Old South and the Confederacy. In their support of the Confederate flag, they are choosing to remember certain Southern traditions while purposefully failing to mention the institution of slavery, a key component in the lives of ante-bellum Southerners.

Instead of the proposal that is currently being debated, what is really needed is a measure that will completely remove the Confederate flag or any image of the flag from all state buildings and monuments that are meant to represent the entire population of the state, black and white. Simply relocating the flag strives only to placate everyone involved and does not provide an adequate solution to the problem. If Beasley's referendum is passed by voters in November, it will simply create the delusion that blacks no longer have the right to complain about the Confederate banner and will prevent the flag from being contested in the future. By eliminating all Confederate images from state grounds, the South Carolinian government would send a message to its residents and the entire country that it does not promote or tolerate racism or any other form of oppression. The danger of lingering symbols of hatred, which can instill racist beliefs into the minds of even more people, cannot be trivialized. While the past of the Confederate South must not be forgotten, it must also not be repeated.

6

Vocabulary/Using a Dictionary

1. What is an *impetus* (para. 4)? Can you think of a few synonyms for the word? Use the word *impetus* in a sentence.

2. "The civil war, they believe, was a war between opposing visions of civilization, between the agrarian South and the industrial North," Sarfaty states in paragraph 5. What does *agrarian* mean? What is its origin?

3. "Simply relocating the flag only strives to *placate* everyone involved and does not provide an adequate solution to the problem," says Sarfaty in paragraph 6. What does it mean to *placate* someone?

Responding to Words in Context

1. Throughout Sarfaty's essay she discusses the *Confederate* flag. What does the word *confederate* mean? Why do you think the states that seceded from the union called their new nation "The Confederate States of America"?

2. What does it mean when we *trivialize* something (para. 6)?

Discussing Main Point and Meaning

1. Why does Sarfaty consider the Confederate flag to be "a haunting symbol" (para. 1)?

2. How does Sarfaty interpret General Robert E. Lee's statement, "A nation which does not remember what it was yesterday does not know where it is today" (para. 1)?

3. What is the argument of groups such as "the Dixie Defenders, the Sons of Confederate Veterans, and the Southern Heritage Association" (para. 5) for accepting the Confederate flag?

4. Why is the attempt to relocate the flag not addressing the root of the problem?

Examining Sentences, Paragraphs, and Organization

1. What is the topic sentence of paragraph 2? Paragraph 4? Why do you consider these to be topic sentences?

2. The paragraphs of the essay are organized from *problem* to *solution*. The problem that is introduced is that "the flag is continuing to stir up emotions in groups with opposing interpretations of history" (para. 1). What is the solution offered by Sarfaty?

3. Make a short list of the organization of this essay, jotting down the function or main point of each paragraph and transitions between paragraphs.

Thinking Critically

1. Do you think the author is making too big of a deal about the issue of the Confederate flag?
2. Do you agree with Sarfaty's final suggestion, or is it too extreme (para. 6)? Would you agree to her terms?

In-Class Writing Activities

1. Write a brief essay providing your own solution to the problems created by the displaying of the Confederate flag. Try to discuss a few of the following issues: Could anyone display the flag? Where would you have the flag displayed? What population of the American people would support your decision? What population of people would be against your decision?
2. Sarfaty quotes Robert E. Lee to support her argument. Yet below is another more complex quote uttered by the general that might bear on the problem of the Confederate flag as discussed in the essay. In a five- or ten-minute freewrite, see if you can link this quote to the essay.

> In this enlightened age there are few, I believe, that will acknowledge that slavery as an institution is a moral and political evil in any country. . . . I think it, however, a greater evil to the white man than to the black race, and while my feelings are strongly on behalf of the latter, my sympathies are more strong for the former (Robert E. Lee to Mrs. Lee, December 6, 1856).

J. BARRIOS

America: 2022

[THE DAILY CALIFORNIAN, UNIVERSITY OF CALIFORNIA, BERKELEY / October 1, 1997]

Before You Read

When you think of the words *corporate America,* what images come to mind? How do you think corporate America affects the way we live? Do corporations make America a better place?

Responding to Words in Context

1. The Nike symbol is one of the most prominent logos (graphic designs) in popular American culture. What is the origin of the word *Nike*?

Discussing Main Point and Meaning

1. State briefly what comment you think the artist is trying to make about American culture.
2. What do you think the picture of the bird holding a sign that reads "Just do it" is supposed to represent? How might knowing the species of the bird affect your understanding of the cartoon's message?

Thinking Critically

1. Do you agree with the artist's conception of the McDonald's and Nike corporations and how they relate to America?
2. Do you think that the United States would ever put corporate logos on its national flag?

In-Class Writing Activities

1. Think of other symbols the artist could have placed on the American flag besides Nike swishes and McDonald's golden arches. In a quick freewrite explain why you picked your symbols.
2. Picture our flag not twenty but 200 years in the future. Do you think that the flag will have changed? In a brief essay, explain whether you think the flag will have changed, and give reasons to support your answer. If you think that the flag will have changed, then explain how you think the new flag would look.

From the Bookshelf

Alan Wolfe, *One Nation, After All*

For the past several years the distinguished Boston University sociologist Alan Wolfe has been monitoring the opinions of the American middle class. His findings, which are based on in-depth interviews with families representing a diversity of religious and ethnic backgrounds from eight suburban communi-

ties around the country, were recently released in the best-selling book One Nation, After All. *The book's subtitle indicates the enormous range of issues Wolfe covers —* What Middle-Class Americans Really Think About: God, Country, Family, Racism, Welfare, Immigration, Homosexuality, Work, the Right, the Left, and Each Other. *In the short excerpt below, Wolfe summarizes the "mature patriotism" that has replaced the flag-waving, old-fashioned patriotism of earlier generations. One of the nation's best-known sociologists, Wolfe writes regularly for a number of prominent periodicals and is the author of eleven books, including most recently* Marginalized in the Middle *(1996) and* America at Century's End *(1991).*

The New Patriotism

It was not just Vietnam that changed the country, but the assassinations of Kennedy and King, Watergate, periodic lesser scandals, and the failure of Great Society programs to fulfill, often at great expense, the promises made on their behalf. Tempered by so many disappointments, Americans have lost faith in many of their institutions, most especially government. Since government is supposed to embody the common values of society, suspicion and cynicism are difficult to reconcile with unabashed patriotism. The result, especially for the most patriotic of Americans, is a loss of innocence. They know that governments can lie, that promises can be broken, that ideals cannot always be followed. The reaction of the overwhelming majority of deeply patriotic Americans to the disappointments of the past two decades is to continue to love their country, but in an older-but-wiser fashion. "I think that there was a naïveté that was abounding in those years," said Denise Lott of Rancho Bernardo [California] of the period before Watergate. But there is a bright side as well: "I think there was a coming of age for an awful lot of people." Middle-class Americans are now more demanding before they give their unthinking loyalty to anyone.

Wolfe, Alan. *One Nation, After All: What Middle-Class Americans Really Think About: God, Country, Family, Racism, Welfare, Immigration, Homosexuality, Work, the Right, the Left, and Each Other.* New York: Viking Press, 1998.

Discussing the Unit

Suggested Topic for Discussion

The four pieces (three articles and a political cartoon) in this unit deal with how Americans regard the flag. Whether it is as the stars and stripes

("Some Questions for My Senator about the Flag"), "The Star-Spangled Banner" ("Star-Spangled Banter"), the stars and bars ("A Forgotten Past"), or the stars and arches ("America: 2022"), each author's or artist's representation of the American flag is drastically different. If you could redesign your own American flag, what would it look like?

Preparing for Class Discussion

1. How do you think Horace Freeland Judson might respond to Hendrik Hertzberg's idea of replacing "The Star-Spangled Banner" with "Lift Ev'ry Voice and Sing"? On what points would the authors agree? On what points would they differ?

2. What do you think all three authors' reactions would be to cartoonist J. Barrios's depiction of "America: 2022"? Explain your answers.

From Discussion to Writing

1. To what extent do you think the American flag is linked to other aspects of American culture such as television, movies, and literature? Write an essay in which you discuss how the symbol of the American flag is portrayed in American culture.

2. It has been commented that the youth of America lack patriotism (the love or devotion to one's country). How do you feel about this accusation? Write an essay discussing your views about patriotism, responding to the accusation. Do you agree with Alan Wolfe (pp. 252–253)?

3. In a well-organized essay describe what the flag symbolizes to you, good or bad. You may bring in examples from American history or your own life to support your opinion.

Topics for Cross-Cultural Discussion

1. What does the American flag mean to you? What does the American flag represent to your native culture?

2. Describe the flag of your native culture to the rest of the class. Does it have a specific name? Is that flag considered a symbol in your native culture? If so, what is it a symbol of? Do you have laws that protect the desecration of your flag?

13

Cloning: Is It Inevitable?

When news of a successfully cloned sheep reached the media in February 1997, the world was suddenly confronted with a moral dilemma: Will human clones be next? Cloning immediately became the media's top story, as scientists and philosophers throughout the world offered opinions on the issue. In "Fear and Loathing," Marc Zabludoff, the editor of the science magazine *Discovery,* reports on a conference he attended in which the featured speaker, the Scottish scientist who cloned the now-famous sheep, Dolly, expressed his disapproval over the rush to now clone a human being: "Why, he asked, would we *want* to clone ourselves?"

One of the most publicized reasons, which the philosopher Jean Bethke Elshtain examines in "Our Bodies, Our Clones," is to assist human reproduction. The cloning of human beings, if it can be technologically achieved, would permit infertile couples to bear children. Elshtain questions this response and wonders why there is such pressure on women today to replicate themselves biologically: "How does one account for the fact," she asks, "that the resurgence of feminism over the past thirty years emerged in tandem with the enhanced pressures on women to reproduce biologically?"

"Cloning human beings simply to allow families to have children may not be a good idea," agrees the editorial board of the *Daily Egyptian,* the school paper at Southern Illinois University at Carbondale. Yet unfounded fears about human cloning may be blinding us from seeing what benefits could come out of the process. "Cloning: A Cautious Defense" advises that "allowing such research to occur under close scrutiny is far better than secret experiments."

From the Bookshelf

Gina Kolata, *Clone*

How the little lamb Dolly — the world's first clone — came to be born is a fascinating and complex story that covers many intersecting themes — science, technology, ethics, business, medicine, and human psychology. Gina Kolata's Clone *weaves all of these themes together while providing the first full account of what may be the most significant scientific event since the discovery of DNA. Her book will appeal to anyone who wants to know more about the details and implications of cloning. A trained scientist, Kolata is the award-winning* New York Times *science reporter who broke the cloning story nationally.* Clone *opens with the birth of Dolly.*

A Clone Is Born

On a soft summer night, July 5, 1996, at 5:00 P.M., the most famous lamb in history entered the world, head and forelegs first. She was born in a shed, just down the road from the Roslin Institute in Roslin, Scotland, where she was created. And yet her creator, Ian Wilmut, a quiet, balding fifty-two-year-old embryologist, does not remember where he was when he heard that the lamb, named Dolly, was born. He does not even recall getting a telephone call from John Bracken, a scientist who had monitored the pregnancy of the sheep that gave birth to Dolly, saying that Dolly was alive and healthy and weighed 6.6 kilograms, or 14.5 pounds.

It was a moment of remarkable insouciance. No one broke open champagne. No one took pictures. Only a few staff members from the institute and a local veterinarian who attended the birth were present. Yet Dolly, a fluffy creature with grayish-white fleece and a snow-white face, who looked for all the world like hundreds of other lambs that dot the rolling hills of Scotland, was soon to change the world.

Kolata, Gina. *Clone*. New York: William Morrow, 1998.

MARC ZABLUDOFF

Fear and Longing

[DISCOVER / May 1998]

Before You Read

Do you closely resemble one of your parents, represent an even mixture of the two, or look nothing like either of them? Is there a striking similarity between you and your siblings? Physically or in personality? How much do you think you have been shaped by your genetic background, and how much by your environment?

Words to Learn

mammalian (para. 1): related to animals that are warm-blooded, milk-producing, and vertebrate (adj.)

confer (para. 1): bestow, meet to compare views (v.)

bespectacled (para. 1): wearing eyeglasses (adj.)

languorous (para. 1): have a lazy or dreamy quality (adj.)

colleague (para. 1): fellow member of a profession (n.)

appall (para. 1): fill with horror (v.)

tousle (para. 3): make messy, dishevel (v.)

divvy up (para. 4): divide, separate (slang) (adj.)

aria (para. 4): vocal musical solo (n.)

garner (para. 5): acquire (v.)

imperative (para. 5): requirement (n.)

enterprise (para. 5): complicated undertaking (n.)

disquieting (para. 6): troubling (adj.)

MARC ZABLUDOFF *is editor in chief at* Discover *magazine and was director of* Discover's Science of Race *issue, which won a 1995 National Magazine Award. Zabludoff has also worked at* Science Digest *and* Esquire, *has studied philosophy, and has taught sculpture at Hunter College in New York City. Zabludoff's wood and plaster sculptures and his interest in science, he says, reflect his profound respect for the law of gravity.*

In February [1998], at the annual meeting of the American Asso-   1
ciation for the Advancement of Science, in Philadelphia, I attended a
session entitled "The Rights and Wrongs of Cloning Humans."
Among the speakers was Ian Wilmut, of the Roslin Institute in Edin-
burgh. Now, Ian Wilmut, as the leader of the research team that
cloned the famous lamb Dolly, is rightly the "father" of mammalian
cloning, if such a title can be conferred. That is to say, Dr. Wilmut is
a man who has unblinkingly beheld the concrete future, has seen it
take shape under his own guidance. He is a balding, bespectacled,
soft-spoken scientist, with a Scottish accent characteristically clipped
but languorous. For all his world-shattering achievement, he is an
undramatic and unemotional speaker. Yet there was no mistaking
the passion of his sentiments on this subject. When faced with the
prospect of colleagues racing to bring forth a cloned human infant,
he was appalled.

First of all, he noted, the limits of current technology simply do   2
not allow the attempt: To get one successful birth, many babies
would have to die in failed procedures —
an absolutely unacceptable price. But even
assuming we solve the technical problems,
why, he asked, would we *want* to clone
ourselves? Even if we truly desire an exact
duplicate of someone — ourselves, a lost
loved one, a scientific or artistic genius — the plain truth is that we
won't get it.

> *That cloning won't fully work should be evident to all of us.*

We are more than our genes. We are our genes in a particular   3
place and time, whole people interacting with others in an infinitely
variable world. Only through that experience do we become who we
are. A cloned Einstein reared in twenty-first-century Los Angeles will
not become a tousled professor of new physics. A cloned Mozart will
not reelevate our souls or drive a cloned Salieri to distraction. A clone
of a child tragically and prematurely dead will not replace wholly and
without distinction the child who once was. All the clone will be for
certain is the bearer of unmet expectation.

That cloning won't fully work should be evident to all of us. We   4
are each a half-clone, after all, with respect to either parent. And
though we may at some time have heard that we got, say, our singing
voice from our mother or our temper from our father, we know it's
not strictly true. Talents and temperament aren't really divvied up,
trait by trait, and served intact down the genetic line. Not one of us is
identical to a parent, not even in the middle of an aria or rage. And

we would not be so even if we were the inheritor of all a parent's genes rather than half.

To be fair, cloning is not the focus of most biotech research. It has simply garnered the most publicity. But it does most dramatically illustrate what some have called the technological imperative — which means that if we *can* do something, we *will*, whether there is wisdom in the enterprise or not. 5

And cloning is not the only application of biotechnology that even the science-supporting public finds disquieting. Yes, we're eager to have the entire human genome laid out before us. Yes, we're eager to see the day when the genes that cause truly terrible diseases can be repaired. But are we ready for casual tinkering with the genes of plants that feed us? Are we ready for the genetic manipulation of cows and pigs for the sole purpose of human convenience? Are we ready to turn loose all the forces of technology to further — surely unnecessarily — the pace of human reproduction, no matter what the material, societal, and psychological costs? 6

We are preparing for our children a new world, and we don't yet know its borders. 7

Vocabulary/Using a Dictionary

1. Dr. Ian Wilmut is described as *bespectacled* (para. 1). Spectacles are glasses, but what does *spectacle* in the singular mean? How are the two meanings connected?

2. Both *languorous* (para. 1) and *languishing* come from the same Latin root, but they have somewhat different meanings. Look up *languish* in the dictionary. How is it different from *languor*? Use each word in an original sentence to illustrate that difference.

3. How many synonyms can you think of for *garner* (para. 5)? Try to come up with at least four.

Responding to Words in Context

1. Why is *tousled* (para. 3) the word Zabludoff uses to describe Einstein? How does the word choice hint at a common stereotype?

2. By using the slang expression *divvied up* (para. 4) instead of the more formal *divided up,* what effect does Zabludoff create? How

does slang change the tone of a sentence, particularly when the sentence refers to a serious issue?

Discussing Main Point and Meaning

1. Why is Zabludoff surprised by Dr. Ian Wilmut's appearance?
2. When Zabludoff writes that "we are more than our genes" (para. 3), what does he mean?
3. What is the main point of this article? Is Zabludoff against all biotechnological research? If not, where does he draw the line? What problem does he find with cloning?
4. What is the unacceptable price of human cloning research, according to Zabludoff?

Examining Sentences, Paragraphs, and Organization

1. Zabludoff defines the "technological imperative" as the knowledge "that if we *can* do something, we *will*, whether there is wisdom in the enterprise or not" (para. 5). What meaning do the italics add to the sentence that would otherwise not be there? In what context are italics appropriate?
2. Why does the author devote almost a third of his article to the description of Dr. Ian Wilmut, the head of the Dolly research team? Is Wilmut the subject of this piece?
3. Several rhetorical questions are raised in the penultimate (second-to-last) paragraph. How does the final paragraph fulfill or not fulfill the substance of those questions?

Thinking Critically

1. For many critics of human cloning research, the main problem with cloning humans is that it would diminish the unique character of individuals. This article suggests that environment is significant enough in human development that a clone would actually be quite different from its genetic predecessor. Is Zabludoff's logic sound? Or does he unknowingly make an argument in favor of human cloning?
2. Examine the following question: "Are we ready to turn loose all the forces of technology to further — surely unnecessarily — the

pace of human reproduction, no matter what the material, societal, and psychological costs?" (para. 6). Analyze the assumptions that Zabludoff makes about the opposing viewpoint in this question. Is he being fair to those who support further biotechnological research, or is he misrepresenting their point of view as uniformly reckless?

In-Class Writing Activities

1. Household pets rarely outlive their owners. Most children, in particular, have suffered the loss of a favorite pet. Would you clone a favorite childhood pet if you could? Do you think an adult experience of this pet would be the same? Would your relationship with the pet gain or lose any significance if you could repeat it? Write your answer in a few paragraphs.

2. Think of a famous person from a past era whose contributions to society were significant and whose talents could be well used today. Write a short essay taking one of two perspectives — either that it would be beneficial to society if we could clone this person because his or her talents and traits are in short supply today or that this person could never have developed into the same significant individual in today's society so cloning him or her would be futile. Explain why you took the perspective you did.

JEAN BETHKE ELSHTAIN

Our Bodies, Our Clones

[THE NEW REPUBLIC / August 4, 1997]

Before You Read

Why are genetic offspring thought to be preferable to adopted children? Do you think that being biologically related to one's children makes one feel closer to them or have greater control over them? What does it mean to be a parent, exactly? And why do some infertile couples go to such great lengths to conceive a child rather than adopt one?

Words to Learn

fail-safe (para. 3): built-in backup or safeguard (n.)

obscenity (para. 4): something offensively indecent

proponent (para. 4): supporter (n.)

heartrending (para. 5): causing great sorrow (adj.)

generative (para. 6): able to create (adj.)

trump (para. 7): outrank (v.)

dubious (para. 7): doubtful, questionable (adj.)

tumult (para. 8): noise and commotion of a crowd, mental or emotional agitation (n.)

rail (para. 9): complain bitterly or abusively (v.)

bedrock (para. 9): solid rock underlying loose sand or gravel, foundation (n.)

redoubt (para. 9): small or temporary refuge, defense (n.)

chimerical (para. 9): imaginary, fantastic (adj.)

JEAN BETHKE ELSHTAIN (b. 1941), Laura Spelman Rockefeller Professor of Ethics at the University of Chicago, is a political philosopher whose goal has been to show the connections between political and ethical convictions. She is the author of numerous books, including Women and War *(1987);* Public Man, Private Woman *(1981);* Meditations on Modern Political Thought *(1986);* Power Trips and Other Journeys *(1990); and* Democracy on Trial *(1995). Her many essays and reviews have appeared in scholarly journals and journals of civic opinion. Elshtain has won a number of academic awards for her teaching and writing and has been a National Endowment for the Humanities Fellow and a Guggenheim Fellow.*

When last we left Dolly, the cunning cloned ewe, she was standing alone, or beside herself, as the case may be. But cloned company is bustin' out all over, even as the presidential commission ponders its implications. There are now cloned calves in Wisconsin, and cloned rodents are running around various labs worldwide.

The even more frightening story, however, may lie in the fertile field of infertility science — that is, the world of human reproductive technology. Many procedures once considered radical are now routine. These include in vitro fertilization, embryo flushing, surrogate embryo transfer, and sex preselection. Now comes Dr. Mark Sauer, described by the *New York Times* as an infertility expert at Columbia Presbyterian Medical Center, who "dreams of offering his patients a type of cloning some day."

According to the *Times*, it would work like this. You take a two- or three-day-old human embryo and use its cells — there are only about eight at this stage — to grow identical embryos. The next step is to implant some of these embryos in a woman's uterus in the hopes that one or more may grow into babies and to freeze the extras. Because initial attempts at impregnation may fail, you would have spare embryos in cold storage as a kind of fail-safe for future attempts. Even if the woman successfully carries the initial implants to term, she might want more babies. The upshot, of course, is that a woman could wind up with "identical twins, triplets, or even quadruplets, possibly born years apart." And why would anyone want this? Sauer has a pragmatic answer: otherwise there "might be no babies at all" for the infertile women who have come to him for expensive, high-tech treatment.

Many procedures once considered radical are now routine.

To be sure, the premise of this procedure isn't as obviously morally repugnant as a scenario that emerged in the immediate aftermath of Dolly: cloning a dying child so that parents might replace him and forestall their grief. This image borders on an obscenity, which is why cloning enthusiasts are so enthralled with this latest embryo cloning scenario. By contrast, the new debate will rage on more sanitized territory, around whether this is cloning at all. Sauer and other proponents say that, because cloning is a "politically dirty word," they hope that their proposed method of crypto-cloning may slip off the radar screen. Besides, they argue, it's much better for the women involved: You don't have to give women lots of drugs, Sauer notes, to "force their ovaries to pump out multiple eggs so that they could fertilize them and create as many embryos as possible."

You can be sure that this "attractive" method of replicating embryos will generate unattractive political demands. A group will spring up proclaiming "embryo duplication rights," just as an outfit emerged instantly after Dolly was announced arguing that to clone oneself was a fundamental right. Several of the infertility specialists cited in the *Times* piece — all male doctors, interestingly enough — spoke of the desperate pleading of women, of "the misery my patients are living through." But surely a good bit of that misery comes from raising expectations (with procedures like in vitro), only to find, time and again, that the miracle of modern medicine has turned into an invasive, expensive, heartrending dud.

Whatever happened to accepting embodied limits with grace? There are many ways to enact what the late Erik Erikson called "generative" projects and lives. Biological parenthood is one but not the only one. Many of the women we consider great from history — I think here of one of my own heroes, Jane Addams of Hull House — were not mothers, although they did an extraordinary amount of mothering. Either through necessity or choice, they devoted their lives to civic or religious projects that located them over the years in a world of relationships with children who were not their own. These relationships involved loving concern, care, friendship, nurture, protection, discipline, pride, disappointment — all the complex virtues, habits, and emotions called forth by biological parenting.

And there is adoption, notwithstanding the frustrations many encounter and the recent fear instilled by such outrageous cases in which children were wrenched from the only family they ever knew in order to be returned to a biological parent who has discovered belatedly the overwhelming need to be a father or a mother. How odd that biology now trumps nearly all other claims and desires. In several popular books such as Kristin Luker's *Dubious Conceptions: The Politics of Teenage Pregnancy,* adoption is surrounded with a faintly sinister odor and treated as an activity not all that different from baby selling.

These trends are undoubtedly linked, and they raise a host of questions. For instance, how does one account for the fact that the resurgence of feminism over the past thirty years emerged in tandem with the enhanced pressures on women to reproduce biologically (pressures women frequently helped place upon themselves)? And why are these developments surrounded by such a desperate aura and a sense of failure — including the failure of many marriages that cannot survive the tumult of infertility and high-tech medicine's intrusion into a couple's intimate lives? One possible explanation is our obsession, at the end of the twentieth century, with identity: who we are. Sometimes this takes the form of identity politics in which one's own identity gets submerged into that of a group, likely a group defined in biological or quasi-biological terms on grounds of sex, race, or ethnicity. That's problematic enough as a basis for politics, to say the least. But we've further compounded the biological urgencies, upping the ante to bear one's "own" child as a measure of the success or failure of the self.

I do not want to downplay how heartbreaking it is for many couples who want to have a baby and cannot. But, again, there are many ways to parent and many babies desperate for loving families. Rather than expand our sense of gracious acceptance of those who may not be our direct biological offspring, which means accepting our own limits but realizing that these open up other possibilities, we rail against cruel fate and reckon ourselves worthless persons if we fail biologically. Perhaps with so much up for grabs, in light of the incessant drumbeat to be all we can be, to achieve, to produce, to succeed, to define our own projects, to be the sole creators of our own destinies, we have fallen back on the bedrock of biology. When all that is solid is melting into air, maybe biology seems the last redoubt of solidity, of identity. But, of course, this is chimerical. In demanding of our bodies what they sometimes cannot give, our world grows smaller, our focus more singular if not obsessive, and identity itself is called into question: our own and that of our future, identical offspring.

9

Vocabulary/Using a Dictionary

1. The words *proponent* (para. 4), *propose*, and *purpose* share the same origin. What kind of purpose does a proponent have? How are purposes related to proposals?

2. Based on the definition given above for *generative* (para. 6), can you guess what the linguistics term *generative grammar* refers to?

3. How is an identity based on biology *chimerical* (para. 9), according to Elshtain?

Responding to Words in Context

1. What does Elshtain mean when she refers to "the fertile field of infertility" (para. 2)?

2. Without a definition, one might interpret the literal meaning of *fail-safe* (para. 3) as either "failure to make safe" or "safe from failure." Which is closer to the actual definition?

Discussing Main Point and Meaning

1. Is Elshtain's critique limited to human cloning as an optional fertility treatment? Or do her criticisms address a broader issue in human reproduction?

2. What is the scenario that Elshtain says is "morally repugnant" and "borders on an obscenity" (para. 4)?

3. What is the primary rationale, according to Elshtain, for infertility experts who want to use cloning techniques?

4. When Elshtain suggests that we should see that our biological limits "open up other possibilities" (para. 9), what does she mean?

Examining Sentences, Paragraphs, and Organization

1. Elshtain interrupts herself in the third sentence of paragraph 5 to remark that the fertility specialists cited in a procloning article in the *New York Times* were "all male doctors." Why does she find this point "interesting"? And why does she make it such an incidental point by placing it between dashes?

2. Compare and contrast the tone of the opening and closing paragraphs. Consider the length and complexity of sentences, word choice, and the subject matter of each paragraph.

3. Why doesn't Elshtain mention the word *adoption* until paragraph 7? Why doesn't the title allude to the option of having nonbiological children?

Thinking Critically

1. Should Elshtain's real focus be on our cultural obsession with raising biological children rather than on the issue of human cloning? Is she using the biotechnology industry as a scapegoat

for the public relations problems of the adoption industry? Would more infertile couples adopt children if it were an easier, cheaper, and faster process?

2. The article seems to represent the proponents of cloning exclusively as people connected to infertility treatment — whether patients or doctors. What other people do you think might have a stake (political, financial, social) in the cloning issue? Is it fair to pin most of the blame on couples struggling to have children and the physicians trying to help them?

In-Class Writing Activities

1. Imagine that you are part of a couple struggling with infertility. You have tried every treatment available to you, and you are still unable to conceive a biological child. Write a letter of response to Elshtain, explaining why it is important for you to have cloning as a reproductive option.

2. The field of medical ethics is filled with issues of life and death and of the role of doctors and technology with respect to life and death. For example, euthanasia, abortion, religious prohibition against particular medical treatments, use of experimental drugs, and the role of insurance coverage in emergency room admissions all call into question whether medicine's main purpose is to preserve or promote life whenever possible. Choose one of these topics, and write a short essay that reveals your opinion on the subject.

EDITORIAL BOARD
OF THE DAILY EGYPTIAN

Cloning: A Cautious Defense

[DAILY EGYPTIAN, SOUTHERN ILLINOIS UNIVERSITY AT CARBONDALE / January 15, 1998]

Before You Read

Technology is often feared to be a tool of an immoral (or at least amoral) society. Birth control, television, the Internet, and biotechnology, for example, have all been called unnatural and thus immoral at times. But if technology is produced by human beings, who are natural, isn't technology a product of nature in a way? Isn't the manner in which a technology is used, morally or not, more important than the fact of the technology itself?

Words to Learn

revelation (para. 1): disclosure, manifestation of divine will (n.)
ethical (para. 5): related to principles of right conduct, moral (adj.)

encroach (para. 5): gradually take another's space or rights (v.)
turf (para. 5): layer of grass and sod, range of area of one's authority or ownership (n.)

Since "Dolly" was introduced last spring [1997], the world has been up in arms about the idea of cloning humans. The revelation that cloning animals was possible prompted President Bill Clinton to impose a temporary ban on the use of federal funds for research on human cloning in the United States, and he has urged other nations to

1

As is often the case with professional newspapers, the editorial board at the Daily Egyptian, *the student publication of Southern Illinois University at Carbondale, contributes a periodic and unsigned column on current issues. This piece represents the consensus of the students on the* Daily Egyptian *editorial board.*

do the same. So far, nineteen other nations have signed an agreement to prohibit human cloning.

The issue again was thrust into the spotlight when independent   2
Chicago scientist Richard Seed vowed to clone a human within two years. A bill to ban cloning in Illinois has been introduced into the state Senate, and there is a similar bill in the state House of Representatives. With all the arguments and fear, it may have been overlooked that some good could possibly arise from human cloning in the future.

Opponents argue the issue of morality: People are born unique   3
and should be allowed to continue to do so. Some experts say clones will be like twins, with similar physical features but not with the same mentality.

Human cloning should not be conducted simply to create more   4
people. The earth already has a population problem. But some researchers say it will be possible to clone headless bodies. These could be utilized for the many people awaiting organ transplants throughout the world. If such an idea is possible, then it is possible to imagine the ability of cloning organs, limbs, and blood to help those in need. Such bodies also could be used to further the research of cancer, AIDS, cystic fibrosis, and the many other diseases that plague the world. Some argue the right-to-life issue. If the cloning of organs is made possible, no lives will be taken, only saved.

> *Human cloning should not be conducted simply to create more people.*

Some argue the ethical issue: Humans should not encroach on   5
mother nature's turf. Yet if we believe that, then the McCaugheys' septuplets in Iowa and all other babies born using fertility drugs or in vitro fertilization are immoral. Scientists celebrated the birth of the first test-tube baby almost twenty years ago.

Others argue the inaccuracy of cloning. It took scientists 277   6
failed attempts before Dolly was born. Opponents fear deformed or retarded babies will be born after failed cloning experiments. According to the March of Dimes, every three minutes a baby is born with a birth defect in the United States. In time, animal cloning will be perfected, and that information could be used to prevent birth defects in the future. The world has embraced vast technological advances to date, including chemotherapy, radiology, transplants using animal organs, and laser technologies.

Although the moral debate may never cease, much like that of   7
abortion or capital punishment, the world should take the opportu-

nity to further research such a topic before burying it under legislation brought about by fear. Human cloning should not be left to run free, however. There is a need to closely monitor and regulate the actions of those conducting the research to prevent abuse of the technology. But allowing such research to occur under close scrutiny is far better than secret experiments by those not accountable for abusing the technology.

Cloning human beings simply to allow families to have children   8 may not be a good idea, but the research and advancement that could be achieved through such a process might help the world.

Vocabulary/Using a Dictionary

1. How is an *ethical* (para. 5) person or practice different from a moral one?

2. Why do you think the word *revelation* (para. 1) is often used in a religious context?

3. Have your rights or your space ever been "encroach[ed] on" (para. 5)? Write a sentence or two describing how. Be sure to use the word *encroach* properly in your description.

Responding to Words in Context

1. This article calls Richard Seed an "independent Chicago scientist" (para. 2). What does the word *independent* mean in this context?

2. President Clinton imposed a ban on "federal funds for research on human cloning in the United States" (para. 1). What possible sources of funding does that ban leave open to use?

Discussing Main Point and Meaning

1 Why do the authors invoke the example of the McCaughey septuplets in paragraph 5?

2. How do the authors counter the argument that there will be many failed attempts at cloning humans, which will result in birth defects and retardation?

3. What good, according to this article, could human cloning do for society?

4. What do these authors think will happen with this technology if it is legally banned?

Examining Sentences, Paragraphs, and Organization

1. "Some experts say clones will be like twins, with similar physical features, but not with the same mentality" (para. 3). This sentence is meant to answer what argument?
2. What is the thesis of this article? Why is it located where it is?
3. Does the overall structure of this article resemble an outline, a list, or a chronology? Is the structure effective, in your opinion?

Thinking Critically

1. The authors of this article refer to "some experts" in paragraph 3 and "some researchers" in paragraph 4 in arguing for the moral and ethical values of their position. Would their points be more effectively made if these experts and researchers were identified? Should readers be expected to place automatic trust in the authors of an argumentative editorial — that is, that there *are* specific experts and researchers making these points?
2. A statistic on birth defects from the March of Dimes is used to excuse the rate of inaccuracy in cloning procedures. Is it fair to compare undetected birth defects that result from traditional pregnancies with those that would come as a result of scientific experimentation? Deaths also would surely result from such experiments. Why do the authors neglect the issue of that kind of failure?

In-Class Writing Activities

1. This essay briefly lists many of the possible objections to cloning and then as briefly counters those objections. The authors address the moral necessity of human individuality, the fear of overpopulation, the right-to-life issue, the ethics of intervening in the natural process of reproduction, the ramifications of a trial-and-error process, and the potential for abuse of this technology. Choose one of these issues about which to write a fuller treatment. Begin with a summary of the authors' point(s) about the issue and then add to their logic — with related issues, hypotheti-

cal situations, and so on — until you feel you have exhausted all of that issue's ramifications.

2. Write a counterargument from the point of view of someone who supports the research ban, addressing each of the editorial board's points in succession.

Discussing the Unit

Suggested Topic for Discussion

The selections in this unit illustrate three basic stances about cloning: that it is (1) a positive scientific development with great potential; (2) dangerous and should be banned; and (3) neither inherently good nor bad and should be approached with caution. How do you feel about cloning? If you chose to be cloned, what would be your most important concerns? Would your ability to have children affect your opinion?

Preparing for Class Discussion

1. Are ethics more significant in the medical sciences than any other? Should they be? What other sciences have significant ethical dilemmas? List as many as you can.

2. How do you think Jean Bethke Elshtain and Marc Zabludoff would respond to the editorial board of the *Daily Egyptian*? Would either of them disagree with the students' argument for the potential benefits of human cloning? Are the main points of all of these three pieces reconcilable into one general point, or are they hopelessly incompatible?

From Discussion to Writing

1. To what extent is this issue guided by money? For example, biotechnology companies may be motivated to win the first copyright for a cloning procedure by the potential windfall for the copyright holder. Cloning technology, moreover, like most fertility treatments, would likely be so expensive that only the wealthy would be able to afford it. Write an essay that discusses the monetary issues involved. Is money the bottom line?

2. Imagine that your parents had cloned you as an embryo — in the manner that Jean Bethke Elshtain's article describes — and have decided to produce another "you" now that you have grown up and begun the process of starting a life of your own, separate from them. Describe what it would be like watching your clone develop. What misgivings would you have about it? What advice would you have for the new "you"?

Topics for Cross-Cultural Discussion

1. Americans can take credit for the invention of television, airplanes, and the Internet, and the United States was the first country to put a person on the moon and develop a useable atomic bomb. Do you think Americans are obsessed with being first when it comes to technology, at the expense of other, more pressing problems? Is technology as highly valued in your native country?

2. What is the relationship between the government and scientific research in your native country? Does government there have more or less control over scientific research than the U.S. government has?

14

Is Affirmative Action Still Needed?

Affirmative action — selecting members of groups that traditionally have faced discrimination and providing them with educational and employment opportunities — has been a hotly contested policy since 1978, when the U.S. Supreme Court ruled in a landmark case that universities are entitled to consider race as a factor in admissions. Proponents of affirmative action argue that the program, though it may be imperfect, remains the only way to ensure that minorities are fairly represented in business, government, and education. Opponents, however, say that using race as a factor in deciding who receives educational and job opportunities can lead to "reverse discrimination" and other problems. Nowhere is the controversy more heated than on campuses where students — perhaps affected by affirmative action policies while applying to college — prepare for a job market where such policies may have a hand in determining their career opportunities. The student debate over affirmative action has intensified since California's passage of Proposition 209, which bans the use of race or ethnicity in the state's public colleges. The controversial referendum was passed in November 1996 and went into effect in 1998.

Although the issue is complex and has sparked numerous book-length studies, this unit introduces a few of the most commonly argued positions. In "Affirmative Action: Another Name for Discrimination," Andy Miller, a University of Wisconsin at Madison freshman, calls for an end to all affirmative action programs and a return to decisions based exclusively on merit. But "college admission officers know merit is an amorphous concept," argues Emory University sophomore, Benson Cohen, in "Pursuing King's Dream." Cohen believes that only affirmative action policies can correct the current racial and gender imbalance in education caused by decades of culturally sanctioned discriminatory practices. Finally, in "Affirming Affirmative Action," columnist Bernice Powell Jackson examines the policy through the lens of American history: "By ending affirmative action," she warns, "we once more repeat the mistakes of the past and endanger our future."

ANDY MILLER

Affirmative Action:
Another Name for Discrimination

[THE BADGER HERALD, UNIVERSITY OF WISCONSIN AT MADISON / January 29, 1998]

Before You Read

In the following selection, you will read about one person's experience with what he feels are the negative aspects of affirmative action. Before reading the article, answer the following two questions: Why do you think affirmative action was created? Do you think affirmative action has been effective in accomplishing its goals?

ANDY MILLER *(b. 1979) was a sophomore at the University of Wisconsin at Madison when he wrote this piece for the* Badger Herald. *Miller's interest in affirmative action was sparked during a sociology course that he took during his freshman year, and this essay was inspired by classroom discussions on racial and ethnic minority issues.*

Words to Learn

quota (para. 2): allotment, number of persons admitted to a country or an institution (n.)

implement (para. 2): put into effect according to a plan or procedure (v.)

advent (para. 2): arrival (n.)

bias (para. 3): particular tendency or inclination, prejudice (n.)

beneficiary (para. 7): one that receives benefits (n.)

defer (para. 7): postpone, delay (v.)

Do you think that when President Kennedy said Americans should "take affirmative action to ensure that applicants are employed, and that employees are treated during employment without regard to their race, creed, color, or national origin," he meant to deny qualified students entrance into our fine institutions of higher education?

1

Maybe you should ask the University of Wisconsin Admissions Office that same question. Many students who have high enough GPAs and excellent SAT and ACT scores are turned down every year due to the quota system implemented by the advent of affirmative action.

2

> *Wasn't the point of affirmative action to eliminate the judging of people on the basis of race?*

The debate is continuous. But should I be denied a job just because I check a certain box on an application form? Affirmative action was originally put into effect in order to curb discrimination and bias based on certain characteristics attributed to minorities. However, it can get to a point where I could begin to think that I am being discriminated against. Say that I went into a local State Street bar to apply for a job. In the "previous experience" section of the application, I put down the following: I have gone to bartending school, have worked in a bar for four years, and have worked a cash register before. To any employer, this would seem to be a well-qualified resume.

3

What if the bar needed to fill a quota, however, and hired a less qualified, less experienced person from a minority group to occupy the position. Is this fair? Can it possibly be the case that in America, "the land of opportunity," a more qualified, better-skilled majority male could be turned down just to appease pro-affirmative actionists?

4

This seems like discrimination to me. Wasn't the point of affir-   5
mative action to eliminate the judging of people on the basis of their
race? What is happening now, all around the country, is that women
and minority men are bypassing better-qualified white males for positions. We are now back where we started. The problem of discrimination has not gone away but has simply been shifted over to another
group.

I have personally been witness to an act of "fake affirmative ac-   6
tion," as I call it. By this I mean a person who uses minority status as
an "excuse" to be accepted by a university. One of my good friends is
of Panamanian descent. We have spent countless hours together,
doing what friends do. The fact that he was a minority never once
came up throughout our relationship. My friend grew up in a
wealthy suburb, went to a nationally ranked high school, and had a
close-knit family his whole life. Also, he did not celebrate Panamanian holidays, did not speak Spanish in the home, and did not even entertain a thought about his heritage in any way. His last name is not
even of Hispanic origin but of European origin.

My friend clearly should not be a beneficiary of affirmative ac-   7
tion. However, by making a simple check in a box next to the word
"Hispanic" on the application form, his application was automatically placed in a different pile. Although he had not had as good ACT
scores as I had, did not participate in as many school activities as I
had, and did not have as high a GPA as I did, he got a response back
from the admissions officers within a few weeks, congratulating him
on his acceptance into the University of Wisconsin at Madison, and I
got deferred admission until June of that year. Is this fair?

Just a simple check in a box caused a world of difference in   8
someone's life. I say that if a person is qualified to enter a university,
that person should be granted admission regardless of race, creed,
color, sex, or national origin.

To curb this problem of reverse discrimination, I propose to ban   9
affirmative action as a whole, just as the state of California did in
1996.

Why should we care about race, religion, sex, or national origin   10
in the first place when talking about applications? If we are all American, united under one country, one ideal, and one flag, then why
should we even discuss the superfluous issues attached to affirmative
action? Is having more whites or more minorities at one university
that big of a deal?

If there is only one woman working in an executive position at a   11
Fortune 500 company, why should this matter? We can assume the
other women who applied for the position were not as qualified as
the men who are there now were. Why can't we all just accept that
some of us are better qualified for some positions than others are? If
that person is an African American woman, then who cares? If it is a
white homosexual male, then who cares?

Having blind applications is another solution to the problem. If   12
applications just forgot about the sections regarding race, sex, and
national origin and concentrated more on the section about work experience, then that would solve a lot of problems.

Vocabulary/Using a Dictionary

1. In paragraph 2, Miller says, "Many students who have high
   enough GPAs and excellent SAT and ACT scores are turned
   down every year due to the *quota* system *implemented* by the *advent* of affirmative action." What does the author mean by this
   statement?

2. What is a *beneficiary* (para. 7)? What is the word's origin?

3. Miller states that his admission to the University of Wisconsin at
   Madison was *deferred* (para. 7). What does he mean? What are
   some synonyms for *deferred*?

Responding to Words in Context

1. What is a *resume* (para. 3)? What word is it similar to? What do
   these two words have in common?

2. In paragraph 10, Miller declares that "if we are all American,
   united under one country, one ideal, and one flag, then why
   should we even discuss the *superfluous* issues attached to affirmative action?" What do you think the author means by his use
   of the word *superfluous?*

Discussing Main Point and Meaning

1. Why does the author think affirmative action was put into effect?
   What objection does he make to this reason?

2. What disturbed Miller about the admissions policy at the University of Wisconsin at Madison?

3. How does the author propose "to curb this problem of reverse discrimination" (para. 9)?

Examining Sentences, Paragraphs, and Organization

1. What would happen to the essay if the first sentence were switched with the last?

2. What is the claim Miller establishes in paragraph 1? What examples does Miller use to support the claim he established in paragraph 1?

3. Does Miller organize the examples in his essay from *least to most* important or from *most to least* important?

Thinking Critically

1. Do you think that because the author had a bad personal experience with affirmative action he is devaluating the entire policy of affirmative action?

2. Do you agree with the author when he says, "If we are all American, united under one country, one ideal, and one flag, then why should we even discuss the superfluous issues attached to affirmative action? Is having more whites or more minorities at one university that big of a deal?" (para. 10)? Why do so many university administrators continue to see such imbalances as a "big deal"?

In-Class Writing Activities

1. Miller assumes that SAT and ACT scores are important factors that contribute to a student's success at college (para. 2). How true do you think this is? In a brief essay, agree or disagree with Miller's assumption, supporting your position with specific reasons and examples.

2. Have you ever been in a situation similar to Miller's, where, even though you did as much (or more) work as anyone else, another person was chosen instead of you? How did you feel? Did you make the person or people doing the choosing aware of your displeasure? Write a brief essay regarding this situation.

From the Bookshelf

Stephen Steinberg, *Turning Back*

Affirmative action policies didn't spring up overnight but evolved over decades of African American activism. Turning Back: The Retreat from Racial Justice in American Thought and Policy *closely examines the historical quest for civil rights and notes how that struggle was often undermined by the liberal intellectuals who appeared to be supporting it. A highly readable and informative history, the book (in the words of its publishers) "is a challenge to liberals as well as conservatives, blacks as well as whites, who have fueled the current backlash by providing spurious intellectual cover for gutting affirmative action and other policies designed to advance the cause of racial justice." Although Steinberg is an ardent supporter of affirmative action policies,* Turning Back *effectively covers so many arguments and so much historical ground in so little space that it will inform and interest a wide spectrum of readers, regardless of their opinions on the issue. Stephen Steinberg is a professor in the Department of Urban Studies at Queens College and in the Graduate Center at the City University of New York. He has also written* The Ethnic Myth *(1981).*

What Exactly Do We Mean by "Affirmative Action"?

Affirmative action is the single policy of the post–civil rights era that sought equality, not just as a right and a theory, but as a fact and a result. However, affirmative action was never formulated as a coherent policy but evolved through a series of presidential executive orders, administrative policies, and court decisions. Partly for this reason, the term itself is so fraught with ambiguity that it is not always clear what advocates and opponents are squabbling about.

To begin with, affirmative action must be distinguished from policies of nondiscrimination. Although both seek racial justice in the workplace, policies of nondiscrimination merely enjoin employers from practicing discrimination in the recruitment, hiring, and promotion of workers. It is essentially a passive injunction: *not* to discriminate. Affirmative action, on the other hand, commits employers to go a step beyond nondiscrimination and to *actively* seek out protected groups in employment. In this form — essentially "outreach" programs reliant on the good-faith efforts of employers — affirmative action arouses little or no opposition.

Another version of affirmative action, however, goes a step beyond outreach and involves granting "preference" to minority applicants in order to guarantee the desired result. This is where controversy begins. For example, in his confirmation hearings to the Supreme Court, Clarence Thomas spoke passionately of his support for outreach programs to extend opportunity to women and minorities, but he was equally adamant in his opposition to affirmative action programs that involve preference. What Justice Thomas and most opponents of affirmative action forget is that good-faith efforts to increase minority representation were generally ineffective until they were backed up by specific "goals and timetables" that, in effect, gave preference to minority applicants who met basic qualifications but might not have been hired or promoted without affirmative action mandates.

Steinberg, Stephen. *Turning Back: The Retreat from Racial Justice in American Thought and Policy.* Boston: Beacon Press, 1995.

BENSON COHEN

Pursuing King's Dream

[THE EMORY WHEEL, EMORY UNIVERSITY / February 20, 1998]

Before You Read

Do you think discrimination against women and people of color in education, and throughout American society, continues to limit your generation's educational opportunities? Have you even been the target or the victim of affirmative action? Explain your answers.

Words to Learn

affirmative (para. 1): favoring, optimistic (adj.)

institutionalize (para. 1): treat or confine at an institution (v.)

blanket (para. 1): cover, apply without exception (adj.)

monolithic (para. 3): like a large block of stone (adj.)

quota (para. 3): allotment, number of persons admitted to a country or an institution (n.)

lag (para. 5): fail to maintain a desired pace (v.)

amorphous (para. 8): lacking definite form (adj.)

tailor (para. 8): fashion or adapt to a particular taste or need (v.)

legacy (para. 8): something handed down from the past, as from an ancestor (n.)

BENSON COHEN *(b. 1978) grew up in Atlanta, Georgia. He is a student at Emory University and cochair of Emory Students for Affirmative Action. He wrote this article in response to a campus visit made by Ward Connerly (proponent of the California Civil Rights Initiative that effectively ended affirmative action in California) and Earl Ehrhart (Georgia State Representative and opponent of affirmative action). Cohen wrote this piece to counter these views. He plans to continue to speak out on this and other issues.*

Affirmative efforts to extend equal educational opportunities to [1] qualified individuals regardless of race or gender have been underway for over twenty-five years. These efforts have significantly increased the participation of underrepresented groups in the mainstream of our society. However, the extensive history of discrimination against women and people of color in education and its current manifestations in American society continue to limit the current generation's educational opportunities. Despite this continued institutionalized racism and sexism, many conservatives in both political parties are calling for an end to affirmative action, a blanket term used to describe a host of interrelated and unrelated programs. This is poor judgment.

Education is so fundamental to virtually every aspect of social and economic opportunity in America that we must take affirmative steps to equalize people's access to the best education possible.

Until the 1960s, many doors of the [2] nation's finest educational institutions were firmly closed to women and people of color. Racial and ethnic discrimination in federally funded activities was outlawed with passage of Title VI of the 1964 Civil Rights Act, and gender discrimination was prohibited with passage of Title IX of the Education Amendments of 1972. Nevertheless, educational opportunities for women and people of color are still limited by discrimination and stereotyping. Affirmative action, by taking an active role in reversing these historical trends, helps level what remains a very tilted playing field.

Affirmative action is not a monolithic program. It does not include [3] admittedly discriminatory practices such as quotas, preferences, or lowered standards. These practices are not continued anymore due to Supreme Court and lower court decisions. Instead, affirmative action in education spans a broad range of activities intended to expand educational opportunities to all Americans. Such activities include targeted scholarships and other targeted financial aid, additional review of applications by admissions committees looking at other merit factors in addition to grades and test scores, targeted recruitment efforts for undergraduate and graduate admissions, special educational programs, and mentoring, counseling, and other support programs.

Affirmative action does not allow unqualified individuals to enter [4] educational institutions. In fact, affirmative action was established to ensure admissions were decided on an equal basis from a more varied pool of applicants than the traditionally limited pool of white males. Ironically, considering the right-winged passionate hatred of quotas, in the old system, quotas were the norm, limiting the number of blacks, women, Jewish-Americans, and Asians admitted into universities.

Although these discriminatory practices have been ended, it is 5 not time to turn our backs on Martin Luther King Jr.'s goal of an equal society. Although affirmative action programs have made a crucial difference for countless qualified individuals, inequalities continue to exist. Women and people of color continue to lag behind, according to many educational measures. The gap in college participation for students of color is cause for concern. People of color, including blacks, Native Americans, and Hispanics, make up nearly a third of the population, yet college attendance by these groups is unnaturally limited to less than 18 percent of the population.

Among women, the rate of college attendance is high, but, be- 6 cause of societal stereotypes, women continue to be discouraged from pursuing nontraditional fields of study. Although women make up more than 53 percent of current college attendees, they receive only 11 percent of undergraduate engineering degrees and fewer than 22 percent of math and physical science doctoral degrees. Furthermore, women are constantly pushed into positions of lesser power. Despite graduation rates far in excess of men, women still receive only 41 percent of all first professional degrees. Until these numbers equalize, affirmative steps will be needed to counteract societal stereotypes.

What would happen if affirmative action programs were all 7 ended today? Well, the evidence is not positive. The devastating effects of eliminating affirmative action are already being felt in two of the nation's largest public universities. After California's Board of Regents voted to drop affirmative action in admission beginning with the 1996 class, the Boalt Law School in Berkeley admitted, out of a class of 270, only one black student, the same number of blacks the University of Mississippi admitted in 1962. This is not a positive role model for our increasingly multicultural society.

Although opponents of affirmative action claim everyone can be 8 ranked according to some abstract ideal of merit, college admissions officers know merit is an amorphous concept. Numbers are important, and everyone admitted to universities like Emory has numbers, but there is more to a human than that. Tailoring admissions only to those with the highest numbers can leave out talented singers, artists, athletes, and other able students. Interestingly, race is the only factor most affirmative action opponents want to take out of the equation.

Few argue for the elimination of the "legacy boost," an important qualification in over one-third of all Ivy League admissions.

Education is so fundamental to virtually every aspect of social and economic opportunity in America that we must take affirmative steps to equalize people's access to the best education possible. More than ever, educational achievement is linked to economic security and advancement for individuals as well as for the nation. Schools bear the unique responsibility of preparing the leaders of the country to effectively live and lead in a multicultural society.

As we approach the new millennium, our commitment to affirmative action — the pursuit of King's dream of a more just and equal society — is more important and necessary than ever.

9

10

Vocabulary/Using a Dictionary

1. In paragraph 3, Cohen states that "Affirmative action is not a *monolithic* program." What does he mean?

2. What does the word *tailoring* mean (para. 8)? How do you think the word *tailoring* came into being?

3. "Few argue for the elimination of the 'legacy boost,' an important qualification in over one-third of all Ivy League admissions," Cohen remarks in paragraph 8. What is a *legacy*? What do you think a *legacy boost* is?

Responding to Words in Context

1. "The extensive history of discrimination against women and people of color in education and its current *manifestations* in American society continue to limit the current generation's educational opportunities," Cohen states in paragraph 1. What is a *manifestation*? How does it relate to the word *manifest*?

2. Cohen mentions *mentoring* as a social program (para. 3). What do you think the word means? What is a *mentor*?

Discussing Main Point and Meaning

1. According to Cohen, what continues to limit the current generation's educational opportunities?

2. Affirmative action "spans a broad range of activities intended to expand educational opportunities to all Americans," declares the author in paragraph 3. What are some of these activities?

3. Describe what happened at the Boalt Law School in Berkeley after the California Board of Regents voted to drop its affirmative action program in admissions beginning with the 1996 class (para. 7).

4. What does the author think happens when colleges tailor admissions "only to those with the highest numbers" (para. 8)?

Examining Sentences, Paragraphs, and Organization

1. What does a *transition sentence* do? Find two transition sentences in this essay.

2. This essay could arguably be an essay of *definition* — an essay that states the meaning of something. If this is true, then what do you think Cohen is trying to define? In what paragraphs do you find support for the selection being called an essay of *definition*?

3. What is Cohen arguing for?

Thinking Critically

1. Do you agree with the author that racism and sexism are "institutionalized" (para. 1)? If so, *how* do you think these forms of discrimination are institutionalized?

2. Cohen concludes, "More than ever, educational achievement is linked to economic security and advancement for individuals as well as for the nation. Schools bear the unique responsibility of preparing the leaders of the country to effectively live and lead in a multicultural society" (para. 9). Do you agree with the author's judgment?

In-Class Writing Activities

1. Cohen assumes that "merit is an amorphous concept" and that "numbers are important, and everyone admitted to universities like Emory has numbers, but there is more to a human than that" (para. 8). In a brief essay, defend or oppose this assumption. Make sure to support your position with specific reasons and examples.

2. Pretend that you work in the admissions office of a college. Draft a list of qualities, abilities, and standards you would use for admitting students. On another sheet of paper, describe why you think these criteria are important.

BERNICE POWELL JACKSON

Affirming Affirmative Action

[THE BLACK WORLD TODAY / September 9, 1997]

Before You Read

How do you feel about "the now infamous" Proposition 209, which ended affirmative action in the state of California? What effect do you think this will have on the United States as a nation?

Words to Learn

ostensibly (para. 1): outwardly, apparently (adv.)
disenfranchisement (para. 1): act of depriving a legal right (n.)
déjà vu (para. 1): French, literally "already seen." The feeling that one has already experienced something that is actually happening for the first time (n.)
precipitous (para. 2): extremely steep (adj.)
laud (para. 2): praise (v.)

BERNICE POWELL JACKSON *(b. 1949) is the executive director of the United Church of Christ Commission for Racial Justice, a national civil rights agency based in Cleveland. She has served as Desmond Tutu's U.S. representative and has worked on the staff of New York Governor Carey and the National Urban League. She holds master's degrees from the Columbia University Graduate School of Journalism and Union Theological Seminary. Jackson writes a weekly syndicated newspaper column, "Civil Rights Journal," which reaches 200 newspapers, including the online publication* The Black World Today *(www.tbwt.com).*

epidemic (para. 2): prevalent or
   widespread disease (n.)

inclusive (para. 3): including much or
   everything, comprehensive (adj.)

I was reading an essay the other day that traced our nation's history as it relates to racial justice issues. It reminded me that after fighting the Civil War, ostensibly to end slavery, legislation was passed and efforts were made by government, churches, and others to ensure that former slaves could be equal members of society. But right after that brief period known as Reconstruction, there followed a time when political, economic, and social disenfranchisement took hold. There were Jim Crow[1] laws passed, poll taxes[2] were exacted, and much of the progress gained was then lost. It strikes me that we're living in déjà vu all over again, as Yogi Berra[3] put it.

The news is already grim for some of us. Stories of precipitous drops in applications and acceptances in law and medical schools in Texas and California, which are feeling the first fruits of the attacks on affirmative action. And while some are lauding that, saying those attending now are those who should be because they have the credentials and qualifications, I wonder who is going to provide legal services and medical services for poor African American and Hispanic people in the twenty-first century. In communities that already have health care epidemics that translate to higher mortality and disease rates, where will the people go for medical treatment? In communities where much larger percentages of their population are involved in the criminal justice system, where will the people go for legal assistance?

> *Because we as a nation seldom look honestly at our history, we cannot learn from it.*

Nearly 10,000 people recently marched across the Golden Gate Bridge to protest the now infamous Proposition 209, which ended affirmative action in the state of California. There were people of all ages — from school children to the elderly — and people of all races who could see clearly the damage this legislation can do. Jesse Jackson, mindful of the irony that it was on the thirty-fourth anniversary of Dr. Martin Luther King Jr.'s "I Have a Dream" speech that Propo-

---

[1]*Jim Crow:* Systematic discrimination against blacks by legal enforcement or traditional sanctions.
[2]*poll tax:* Tax that must be paid before voting.
[3]*Yogi Berra:* Lawrence Peter Berra, Hall of Fame baseball catcher for the New York Yankees, known for his memorable sayings.

sition 209 went into effect, told the crowd, "In this country there are those who are dreamers and those who are dream-busters," adding, "The dreamers need to outlast the dream-busters. We must pursue the dream of an inclusive society."

Affirmative action alone could not solve the problems of racial and   4
economic injustice that undergird our nation's entire history. But it must be acknowledged to be part of the reason for the increase in the African American middle class over the past generation. It must be acknowledged to be part of the reason for the professional success of many women (including European American women) as well. And it was beginning to make a difference in the Hispanic community as well.

The sad part is that because we as a nation seldom look honestly   5
at our history, we cannot learn from it. We cannot then see the cycles of racism and the impact they have had on my people's development and our nation's character. The sad part is that by ending affirmative action, we once more repeat the mistakes of the past and endanger our future.

Vocabulary/Using a Dictionary

1. What does the word *ostensibly* mean (para. 1)? What is the origin of the word?

2. In "Affirming Affirmative Action," the author uses the word *epidemic* as a noun (para. 2). What is its definition? Can you use the word *epidemic* as an adjective? What are some synonyms for *epidemic* as an adjective?

3. In paragraph 3, the author quotes Jesse Jackson: "We must pursue the dream of an *inclusive* society." What does Jackson mean by *inclusive society*?

Responding to Words in Context

1. The author uses the word *irony* in paragraph 3. What do you think the word means? What does it mean when something is ironic?

2. "Affirmative action alone could not solve the problems of racial and economic justice that *undergird* our nation's entire history," Jackson remarks in paragraph 4. Is there a word that looks similar to *undergird*? What do you think she means by the word *undergird*?

Discussing Main Point and Meaning

1. After the Civil War, the government passed legislation and made efforts toward what purpose, according to Jackson?

2. In paragraph 2, the author states that regarding social disenfranchisement "the news is already grim for some of us." To what is she referring?

3. In your own words, explain what happened at the Golden Gate Bridge (para. 3).

4. What does Jackson conclude to be "the sad part" of the attacks on affirmative action (para. 5)?

Examining Sentences, Paragraphs, and Organization

1. What is the purpose of the questions asked at the end of paragraph 2? Why does the author use this method?

2. *Comparison and contrast* is an effective rhetorical strategy that can be used in a paragraph. What two things are being compared in paragraph 1?

3. If the organization of the entire essay revolves around the strategy of *problem to solution,* what is the problem as stated by Jackson? The solution?

Thinking Critically

1. Do you think Jackson offers an alternative to the demise (death or decease) of affirmative action? If so, what is it?

2. Do you agree with the author's suggestion that because there have been "precipitous drops in applications and acceptances in law and medical schools in Texas and California," there won't be anyone to "provide legal services and medical services for poor African American and Hispanic people in the twenty-first century" (para. 2)?

In-Class Writing Activities

1. In paragraph 3, Jackson quotes Jesse Jackson: "In this country there are those who are dreamers, and those who are dream-busters. . . . The dreamers need to outlast the dream-busters. We must pursue the dream of an inclusive society." In an essay,

compare Jesse Jackson's lines to the following excerpt from Dr. Martin Luther King Jr.'s "I Have a Dream" speech. "I have a dream that some day every valley shall be exalted, every hill and mountain shall be made low, and rough places will be made plains, and the crooked places will be made straight. . . . I have a dream that my four little children will one day live in a nation where they will not be judged by the color of their skin, but by the content of their character."

2. Discuss whether you support affirmative action. Do you think the policy is necessary, or do you think it should be totally abolished, or do you think it should be improved? Give the reasons for your opinion.

Discussing the Unit

Suggested Topic for Discussion

Who should be responsible for reinforcing affirmative action policy in America? The state government? The local government? The federal government? Do you think racism still affects the jobs people get and the schools students attend in the United States? Are there better alternatives to affirmative action, or is the current policy effective?

Preparing for Class Discussion

1. What do you think society would be like if affirmative action didn't exist? Think of the institution you attend and the place you work. Would the world be better or worse off? Discuss these issues aloud in class.

2. For one of the authors, affirmative action has "significantly increased the participation of underrepresented groups in the mainstream of our society," yet for another, the policy instead denies "qualified students entrance into our fine institutions of higher education." Consider how these different opinions reflect different attitudes toward the policy. Try coming up with a policy of your own.

3. After reading Stephen Steinberg's brief description of affirmative action (see "From the Bookshelf," p. 280), formulate a clear definition of what you think the policy means.

From Discussion to Writing

1. Andy Miller and Bernice Powell Jackson take opposite positions in the affirmative action debate. Miller argues that affirmative action should concentrate more on "the section about work experience" on college applications, while Jackson (in the words of Jesse Jackson) wants us to push "to pursue the dream of an inclusive society." Create a dialogue between the two writers in which they discuss the policy of affirmative action. Perhaps discussing main points of each person's philosophy is the best place to start.

2. Write an essay entitled "Affirmative Action Helps _____." Choose the people that you think are most likely to be helped by affirmative action, and state your reasons for choosing that group.

3. In his essay, "Pursuing King's Dream," Benson Cohen reviews some common misconceptions about affirmative action. Research the topic of affirmative action, and write about a common misconception that exists on either side of the argument.

Topics for Cross-Cultural Discussion

1. How is a person deemed to be "underprivileged" in your native culture? Are the qualities that determine this different from those you've encountered in the United States?

2. Does your native country have anything similar to the policy of affirmative action in America? What is the name of this policy? What exactly does the policy do? Who is it for? If your country does not have a policy similar to affirmative action, do you think it would benefit by having one?

15

Is the Death
Penalty Necessary?

The death penalty has for decades been one of the nation's most controversial issues. Lately, however, with a rapid increase of executions (seventy-four prisoners were put to death in 1997), the debate has become more urgent, as opponents of capital punishment seek to halt what some regard as state-sanctioned murder. This unit begins with the voices of two condemned murderers, a Connecticut man and a Florida woman.

What forces drove an intelligent human being, a Cornell University graduate, to rape and murder eight women in three different states? In "My Name Is Michael Ross," a condemned serial killer deals with his guilt and offers society constructive advice on how to avoid "future tragic murders."

Although women comprise a very small percentage of death row inmates, the Texas execution of Karla Faye Tucker in February 1998 drew national attention to the situation of women sentenced to die. In "A Voice from Death Row," Teresa Allen, a professor of journalism, records the sentiments of Andrea Hicks Jackson, a Florida woman condemned to die for murdering a police officer in 1983. "There's nothing I can do to bring him back," says Jackson. "But I have given him thirteen years of my life now. What is the sense of keeping me here?"

The unit next presents the different thoughts and emotions of three students as they confront the death penalty issue. In "Witnessing Execution," Abbie Gibbs of Oklahoma State University reports on something few college students have ever experienced — seeing the death penalty carried out. Acknowledging the growing number of executions, the editorial board of the *Collegiate Times* at Virginia Polytechnic Institute suggests in "Death Penalty Alternatives" that "there are ways to make criminals pay, without soiling the nation's hands with their blood." In the final selection a Northern Illinois University freshman argues that the death penalty is not only an evil thing to enact but that it makes us all guilty of murder. "Whatever evil the criminal has perpetrated," says John Lloyd in "The Death Penalty Makes Murderers of Us All," "is multiplied exponentially."

Two Voices from Death Row

MICHAEL ROSS

My Name Is Michael Ross

[NOTRE DAME MAGAZINE, THE UNIVERSITY OF NOTRE DAME / Winter 1997–1998]

Before You Read

Should mental illness be considered a factor in deciding punishment for the worst of crimes? Can any rape, murder, or mutilation be considered the act of a sane individual?

MICHAEL ROSS *(b. 1959) is a prisoner at the Northern Correctional Institution in Summers, Connecticut. In 1994, Ross's death sentence was overturned on the grounds that during the sentencing phase of his trial, evidence of his mental illness had been improperly excluded. Ross has offered to waive his right to a resentencing hearing and allow the execution to take place. As of June 1998, his request is still awaiting court approval.*

Words to Learn

tedious (para. 2): boring (adj.)

sadism (para. 3): practice of getting pleasure through inflicting pain on others (n.)

compulsion (para. 3): irresistible, irrational impulse to perform an act (n.)

perpetrate (para. 3): commit (v.)

degradation (para. 4): decline to a lower position (n.)

insatiable (para. 4): unable to be satisfied or appeased (adj.)

abhorrence (para. 4): repugnance, hatred (n.)

noxious (para. 5): poisonous, unhealthy (adj.)

ludicrous (para. 6): laughably absurd (adj.)

malevolent (para. 11): wishing harm to others (adj.)

cursory (para. 12): hasty and without attention to detail (adj.)

anguish (para. 14): grief, great suffering (n.)

reconciliation (para. 16): harmony, state of having settled differences (n.)

I am a condemned man on Connecticut's death row. When most people think of death-row inmates, I'm the type they think of. I'm the worst of the worst, a serial killer who raped and murdered eight women in three different states, assaulted several other women, and stalked and frightened many more. I have never denied what I did and have fully confessed to my crimes. The only issue in my case was, and still is, my mental condition. For years I have been trying to prove that I am suffering from a mental illness that drove me to rape and kill and that this mental illness made me physically unable to control my actions. I have met with little success. 1

> When most people think of death-row inmates, I'm the type they think of. I'm the worst of the worst.

So here I sit on death row, waiting for the judicial system to complete the tedious process that will in all likelihood result in my eventual execution. When I am finally executed, many people will celebrate my death. Sometimes, when I close my eyes, I can envision the hundreds of people who will likely gather outside the prison gates on the night of my execution. I can see them waving placards, drinking, and rejoicing, and I can hear their cheers as my death is officially announced. 2

Who is Michael Ross? And what could possibly motivate a clearly intelligent individual, a Cornell University graduate, to commit such horrendous crimes? As you might expect, I have been exam- 3 ined by a multitude of psychiatric experts over the past twelve years since my arrest in June 1984. All of them, including the state's own expert psychiatric witness, diagnosed me as suffering from a paraphilic mental disorder called *sexual sadism* — a mental illness that in the experts' words resulted in my compulsion "to perpetrate violent sexual activity in a repetitive way." These experts also agreed that my criminal conduct was the direct result of uncontrollable sexual impulses that were caused by my mental illness. The state's only hope of obtaining a conviction and death sentence was to inflame the jury's passions and emotions so that they would ignore any evidence of psychological impairment. In my particular case that was quite easy to do, and the state succeeded in obtaining convictions and multiple death sentences.

I'm not sure that I fully understand paraphilic mental disorder, and I have been trying to understand what has been going on in my head for a very long time now. Basically, I was plagued by repetitive thoughts, urges, and fantasies of the degradation, rape, and murder of women. I couldn't get it out of my mind. These unwanted thoughts and urges filled my mind when I was awake. They were in my dreams when I slept. They were insatiable. Imagine trying to control such urges, day by day, hour by hour. And try to imagine the self-hatred, loathing, and abhorrence that I developed toward myself when I ultimately failed.

The best way for someone who is not plagued with this problem to understand the obsessive and repetitive nature of these thoughts, urges, and fantasies is to remember a time when you had a song or some catchy tune stuck in your mind, playing over and over and over again, driving you crazy. Even if you like the melody, its constant repetition, over and over and over again, becomes more than merely annoying. When this happens, the harder you try to push that melody out of your mind, the louder and more persistent it becomes, driving you almost to the point of madness. Now replace that sweet little melody with noxious thoughts of physically and mentally degrading women. Now you can begin to understand what I had running wild in my head — and that is not something that I wanted in my head.

The urge to hurt women could come over me at any time, any place: powerful and sometimes irresistible urges that welled up for no apparent reason and with no warning. Even after my arrest — while facing capital charges — the urges continued. I remember one day being transported back to the county jail from a court appearance just prior to my trial. I was in the back of the sheriff's van in full restraints, handcuffs, leg-irons, and a belly-chain, when we passed a young woman walking along a wooded stretch of road. I cannot begin to adequately describe the intensity of the urges that enveloped me that day. I wanted . . . no, I *had* to get out of that van and go after her. The situation was ludicrous. There I was, in the back of the sheriff's van on my way back to jail, and all I could think about was how badly I wanted to get hold of her. Later, back in my cell, I fantasized about what would have happened had I gotten hold of her.

That ignorance, and its resulting guilt, is a very heavy burden on   7 my mind, and a burden that I will carry with me for the rest of what remains of my life.

Even after I was sentenced to death and living on death row the   8 urges persisted. One day I was being escorted from the mental health unit back to my cell after seeing my psychiatrist. I was being escorted, without restraints, by a young, petite, female correctional officer. When I got to a secluded stairwell that leads from the unit back to the main corridor, I suddenly felt an overwhelming desire to hurt her. I knew that I had to get out of that stairwell, and I ran up the stairs and out into the hallway. I'll never forget how she shouted at me and threatened to write me a disciplinary report — she didn't have a clue as to what was going on. She never knew how badly I wanted to hurt her that day. She never knew how close I came to attacking her.

You would think that being sentenced to death and living in a   9 maximum security prison would curb such thoughts and urges. But this illness defies rationality. I am fortunate to have eventually found some relief, however. Almost three years after I came to death row, I started to receive weekly injections of an antiandrogen medication called Depo-Provera. Three years later, after some trouble with elevated liver function levels, my treatment was switched to monthly Depo-Lupron injections, which I receive to this date. What these drugs did was significantly reduce my body's natural production of testosterone, the male sex hormone. For some reason, be it because of some abnormal biological hook-up in my brain or some sort of chemical imbalance, testosterone affects my mind differently than it affects an average male. A few months after I started to receive treatment, my blood serum testosterone levels dropped below prepubescent levels. As this happened, nothing less than a miracle occurred. My obsessive thoughts, urges, and fantasies began to diminish.

Having those urges and fantasies is a lot like living with an obnox-   10 ious roommate. You can't get away from them because they are always there. What the Depo-Lupron does for me is to move that roommate down the hall to his own apartment. The problem is still there, but is easier to deal with because it isn't always in the foreground intruding on my everyday life. The "monster within" is still present, but the medication has rendered him impotent and has banished him to the back of my mind. And while he can still mock me — he kicks me in the side of the head from time to time so that I don't forget him — he no longer controls me. I control him. I am human once again.

What a milestone this was in my life. A whole new world opened   11
up to me. I had my mind back — a clear mind free of the malevolent thoughts and urges. It was an unbelievable, incredible sense of freedom. It sounds strange for a condemned man to speak of being free on death row, but that is the only word that I can think of that adequately describes the transformation that I have undergone. And there are no words to express the gratitude that I feel toward the man who made this all possible — Dr. Fred Berlin, founder of the Johns Hopkins Sexual Disorder Clinic and director of the National Institute for the Study, Prevention, and Treatment of Sexual Trauma, both in Baltimore. He testified on my behalf at my capital trial, but, more important, *after* the trial was over and I was sentenced to death, he continued to help me and was essential in my fight to get the department of corrections to acknowledge and treat my paraphilic disorder. Without his letters and phone calls, I never would have received treatment for my disorder and to this day would still be captive to the monster that resides in my mind.

That's not to say all is well. I am now forced to look at myself.   12
I'm not talking about the cursory, superficial manner in which most people look at themselves but rather a quite painful, unrelenting search into the depths of my very soul.

Many inmates in prison are able to lie convincingly to them-   13
selves, to see themselves as basically good people who are the innocent victims of a corrupt judicial system or of an unfair and uncaring society. Sometimes it is difficult to honestly see ourselves as we truly are and much easier to blame others as justification for our actions. For years that is exactly what I did. During this period I was so very angry at everyone and everything except for the one person that I should have been angry with — myself. It took years for that anger to subside and for me to begin to accept who I was and what I had become, and even longer before I was ready and willing to accept responsibility for my actions.

Now I had a whole new set of problems. Not only did the Depo-   14
Lupron free my mind; it allowed my moral judgment to awaken. It

gave me back something that I thought I had lost forever — my humanity. Now that my mind was clear, for the first time in years, I began to see — *really see*. It was like a spotlight shining down on me, burning away the fog, exposing every shadow of my being. I began to be aware of things as they really were, as opposed to seeing things through the colored glasses of my mental illness. I began to be aware of things that I didn't like about myself. And many of the things that I now understand brought me great anguish.

I realized how weak and afraid I really was. I had always thought 15 that I was strong and confident; I now understood how I had allowed the monster in my mind to take control of me. I saw what I had become. Worst of all, for the first time, I became truly aware of the pain that I had brought so many — such great and unceasing pain.

After my mind was finally clear and I saw the truth of what I had 16 become and what I had done, I began to feel unpleasant, disturbing things. I began to feel the terrible agony and distress that I had brought so many — my victims, the families and friends of my victims, my own family. I also began to feel the awesome weight of my responsibility for my actions and of my responsibility to the people that I have harmed. Finally, I felt a profound sense of guilt. An intense, overwhelming, and pervasive guilt that surrounds my very soul with dark, tormenting clouds filled with a mixture of self-hatred, remorse, regrets, and sorrow. All of which leaves me with a deep desire to make amends and achieve reconciliation, something that under the present circumstances seems all but impossible.

Yet it is the sense of reconciliation that I yearn for the most. Rec- 17 onciliation with the spirit of my victims. Reconciliation with the families and friends of my victims. And, finally, reconciliation with myself and my God. If this happens, it will be the final part of my transformation — and undoubtedly the most difficult part. If only science could create a drug to help me with this problem.

So what can be learned from my story? I'm not really sure be- 18 cause it seems pretty tragic all the way around. However, one thing that is surely true is that there are other "Michael Rosses" out there in various stages of development. They need places where they can go for help. One of the most difficult and painful things for me to deal with today is knowing that had I begun receiving just one little 1 cc injection of Depo-Lupron once a month fifteen years ago, that eight women would be alive today. That ignorance, and its resulting guilt, is a very heavy burden on my mind and a burden that I will carry with me for the rest of what remains of my life.

Society needs to act now to make the necessary changes to pre- 19
vent a failure of diagnoses and lack of early treatment, such as mine,
from recurring in the future. Learn from my case and others like
mine. It's easy for society to point its finger at me, to call me "evil"
and condemn me to death. But if that is all that happens, society
also will be condemning itself — to future "Michael Rosses." Future
tragic murders such as I committed can be avoided, but only if society
begins to squarely acknowledge and treat the problem. Only then will
something constructive come out of the events that took the lives of
eight women, destroyed the quality of life of their families and
friends, resulted in my incarceration and probable execution, and
caused untold shame and anguish to my own family. The past has
already happened; it's up to you to change the future.

Vocabulary/Using a Dictionary

1. *Degradation* (para. 4) is also a geological term that relates to a
   specific process that affects land surfaces. Can you guess what
   happens in that process?

2. *Malevolent* (para. 11) comes from the Old French words *mal* and
   volens. If *mal* means "evil," what do you think that *volens*
   means?

3. What is the cursor on a computer screen? How is what it does
   cursory (para. 12)?

Responding to Words in Context

1. Given its meaning as "laughably absurd," what do you think of
   Ross's choice of *ludicrous* (para. 6) to describe the urge he had to
   hurt a woman he saw walking along the road?

2. What does Ross mean when he says that he began to *"really see"*
   (para. 14)?

Discussing Main Point and Meaning

1. How does the medication Ross takes affect his criminal urges?

2. Does Ross argue that because of his condition he should not be
   sentenced to death?

3. What analogies does Ross develop to describe to healthy people what his urges and fantasies are like? How convincing do you find them?

Examining Sentences, Paragraphs, and Organization

1. "I'm the worst of the worst," Ross writes in his first paragraph. Having read the entire article, do you think he believes this statement himself? Or is it meant to represent another point of view?

2. What is the effect of Ross's two anecdotes in paragraphs 6 and 8, where he takes the time to tell specific stories in detail? Why doesn't he tell the stories of his actual crimes in detail?

3. How does Ross shift the focus from himself to society in his final paragraph? Why does he do this?

Thinking Critically

1. Does Ross express enough remorse for his victims, in your opinion? Or is he more concerned with how his illness ruined his own life?

2. Does it surprise you to learn that Ross offered to waive his right to a resentencing hearing in order to spare the victims' families any more pain? Why or why not?

In-Class Writing Activities

1. In paragraph 19, Ross writes, "It's easy for society to point its finger at me, to call me 'evil' and condemn me to death. But if that is all that happens, society also will be condemning itself — to future 'Michael Rosses.'" Write a brief response to this statement of Ross's, agreeing or disagreeing with his assessment of society's role in preventing crimes committed by people with mental illness.

2. Compare and contrast Michael Ross's story with another death-penalty case or capital-murder case — such as the Oklahoma City bombing case, the Unabomber case, or the Menendez brothers case — that you have read or heard about. Point out the similarities shared by the defendants and their crimes, as well as their differences. Are different punishments warranted in each case? Or is murder always equally heinous?

TERESA ALLEN AND
ANDREA HICKS JACKSON

A Voice from Death Row

[GRAND STREET 62 / 1998]

Before You Read

Do women receive easier sentences for committing the same crimes as men? Should they? Should the law treat victims of sexual abuse with less severity than other criminals? Why or why not?

Words to Learn

felon (para. 3): person guilty of a major crime (n.)

makeshift (para. 5): temporary substitute (adj.)

stay (para. 5): postponement of a legal action (n.)

misdemeanor (para. 6): minor offense of law, small crime (n.)

commandeer (para. 10): seize for military or government purposes (v.)

audacity (para. 11): boldness, insolence (n.)

institutionalize (para. 13): make into an institution, put a person in the care of an institution (v.)

TERESA ALLEN *is a journalist who has held staff and reporting positions at the* Seattle Times, *the* Marin Independent Journal, *and the* San Jose Mercury News. *She is currently an associate professor of journalism at Boston University. Her specialized focus on crime reporting, prison culture, and death-row issues sprang from her assignment in 1985 to cover California's San Quentin Prison. This interview with Andrea Hicks Jackson, published in* Grand Street 62, *will appear in a different form in Allen's upcoming book* Honey, This Ain't No Country Club: Women Doing Hard Time.

ANDREA HICKS JACKSON (b. 1958) *was sentenced to death in 1984 for her conviction for the murder of a police officer. Since 1989, her sentence has been reversed and reinstated twice. She is an inmate at Broward Correctional Institute in Southern Florida.*

There are currently forty-seven women condemned to die in the 1
United States. Working with a partner or alone, they have been convicted of killing their husbands, children, boyfriends, and strangers. A
large percentage have documented histories of physical or sexual
abuse, as well as drug and alcohol addictions. More than half are
white. Many are mothers with school-age children. Few have murdered for monetary gain. The majority live in specially designed cell-
blocks, away from the mainline population, where movement is
greatly curtailed, lifestyle is bleak, and days and years pass indistin-
guishably and uneventfully inside their locked prison cells.

Compared to their male counterparts, who number in the hundreds 2
in many states, women comprise only about 2 percent of the nation's
condemned. California, Florida, and Oklahoma have the largest numbers of women on death row. A handful of other states, such as Idaho,
have only one condemned woman and must grapple with a unique problem. Most states are mandated by law to segregate condemned inmates
from the regular prison population. Because

I don't like saying this, of this, Idaho must require that its only female death-row inmate, who was sentenced
but I've gotten used to to death in 1993, eat alone, exercise alone,
being locked inside after and, until another woman joins her on
all these years. death row, pass the years with virtually no
human interaction.

A debate continues over why death sentences for women began 3
to rise in the mid-1980s in many states, especially when the number
of murders committed by women did not increase. There are those
who speculate that women have rightfully lost a "privileged" status
in the criminal justice system that has, until now, kept death-row
numbers down and often allowed women inmates to serve shorter
sentences — or even probation — for serious offenses. It is unclear
whether this new apparent toughness toward female felons is in any
way a feminist backlash, as some suggest, or simply society's new
willingness to prosecute aggressively and punish all criminals, regardless of gender.

No woman has been put to death in the United States since 1984 4
[until the executions of Karla Fay Tucker in Texas in February 1998
and Judy Buenoano in Florida in March 1998].

When Andrea Hicks Jackson arrived at Broward Correctional In- 5
stitute in southern Florida in 1984, she was the state's only condemned woman and lived alone on a makeshift death row in a cell

fortified with a steel door. Almost two years later she was joined by another condemned woman, nicknamed the "Black Widow," who was sentenced to death for poisoning her husband with arsenic. Today, the state's five condemned women live on a new death-row wing with cells that look like drum-tight submarine hatches, a shower room down the hall, a caged outdoor exercise yard with a basketball hoop, and additional cell space for future residents. Also located on the "row" is a room designed as the "death-watch" cell where the women are housed twenty-four hours prior to their execution date. No woman has been put to death in Florida since 1848, when a slave was reportedly hanged for murdering her white master. Twice, however, Jackson has had her death warrant signed and once was en route to be executed at Florida State Prison in Starke (where serial killer Ted Bundy was electrocuted in the late 1980s), when word came that she had been granted a stay. The "death caravan," as she calls it, was forced to turn around.

It was in 1983 that Jackson, then a twenty-five-year-old mother   6
of two young boys with a history of drug and alcohol abuse, was convicted of shooting and killing a police officer in her hometown, Jacksonville, Florida. The officer had been called to the scene to investigate a vandalized car — which belonged to Jackson. According to Jackson's current attorney, the officer arrested her on a misdemeanor charge for making a false statement about the car in order to file a fraudulent insurance claim. (Jackson denies this.) When the officer placed her in his squad car, a struggle erupted, and Jackson reportedly shot him four times in the head and twice in the chest with a .22-caliber handgun she had in her possession. He died instantly. Jackson, who says she was high at the time, claims not to remember shooting him. She also says that she was sexually assaulted as a child and repeatedly beaten by her husband, and she believes that, in her intoxicated state, she confused the officer with someone who had abused her in the past. Other than misdemeanor violations, Jackson did not have a criminal record prior to the shooting.

Strung out and a lean hundred nineteen pounds when she entered   7
the system, Jackson, now thirty-eight, weighs close to two hundred pounds — a condition she blames on little exercise and starchy prison foods. She has kicked her drug habit and was born again as a Christian several years ago. She spends her days reading the Bible, praying, weaving baskets out of old newspapers, and watching sporting events on the prison-regulation nine-inch, black-and-white television that is lashed to the wall above the toilet in her cell. Occasionally she re-

ceives a visit from her sons, but they live with their father, hundreds of miles away in Jacksonville, and seldom make the trip. Jackson, who continues to appeal her death sentence, has served the majority of her thirteen years at Broward, with occasional stints at the Jacksonville County Jail while awaiting resentencing.

The following text is taken from an interview with Jackson conducted in the prison interview room at Broward Correctional Institute and through the barred window of Jackson's cell door on February 20, 1997, and from earlier telephone conversations in 1994 and 1995, when Jackson was at the Jacksonville County Jail.

— Teresa Allen

Even when I heard that they had signed my warrant, I wasn't scared. Christ has told me that I won't die here, and I have faith in Him. They let me call my mother, and that was . . . hard. Then they took all my property and guarded me twenty-four hours a day. They stripped me down and put me by myself in the death-watch room. They took me to Starke five days early for security reasons. I had this motorcade with two armed officers inside with me, and two cars in front of me. It was like I was the president. I tell you, they were really mad when they had to turn around that death caravan and bring me all the way back. Coming down, they were laughing and joking. They said I'd fit just right in the chair. . . . I was riding with an officer, and she was angry. She said to me, "It might not be today, and it might not be tomorrow. But we're going to fry your black ass." As soon as I saw the superintendent standing in the road, waving his arms around at us like a crazy man, I knew I was stayed. They looked so disappointed. I put my feet up. "Home, James," I said. Boy, that made them mad.

On the way back we commandeered a rest stop, a gas station, because I had to use the toilet. People were sitting around, you know, pumping gas, and in we all come. They had shotguns and stuff. They made people inside the minimart stand up against the wall. It was like a television movie or something. Then I walked in, shackled, handcuffed, and chained. I mean, I was chained up. The only place I didn't have a chain was around my neck. All this just so I could take a pee. I'm sure everyone was wondering, "God, what did she do?"

Mostly my lawyers didn't have a defense for me.[1] For a while, they thought they would say I had PMS. They were constantly doing

8

9

10

11

---

[1]Jackson went to trial with a public defender.

tests, drawing enough blood out of me to make another person. My lawyer, he thought they was going to charge me with second-degree murder. When he found out it was murder in the first, well, he only had two months to prepare the case. He told the judge that I was competent to stand trial, that I understood the facts in my case. But I didn't. I admit that what I did was wrong. I don't think that anybody has the right to take another person's life. But it still remains that I did not have any control over the situation and I shouldn't be on death row. Do you think I would go out and kill somebody now? For what reason? I mean, I look like a sane person, right? I don't even know this man. And the state had the audacity to say that the reason I killed this man was because I didn't want to go to jail. If there's one sure way of going to jail, it's to kill a police officer.

It's a funny thing. The whole time I was in the county jail [awaiting trial], I had no idea what was going on around me. It was like I was in a play or watching a play. Later I got saved and I sobered up too. Want to hear my story about being saved? Because I love to tell it. All of a sudden I just felt a load of guilt and I started crying, and I was feeling so bad and vomiting at the same time. I remember I was wearing a green dress, and I pulled it up under my chin to catch the vomit, and I was vomiting my guts out and [the prison chaplain] is praying over me. I wish I had brought some pictures to show you because from then on, in every picture, there's a glow right here on the top of my head. It looks like a cross. And he was praying and speaking in tongues over me, and the vomit was just coming out. I believe I am saved, and I trust the Lord explicitly. If He says to me some day, "Andrea, it's time for you to come home," I expect I will wake up in His presence. . . . I remember when my death sentence was reinstated the last time. I came back to my cell and I wept. I said, "Lord, you know I didn't mean to do this." I was crying and crying. You know what He said to me: "Daughter, it is forgotten." He has told me that He has the last word on everything. And I trust that. If they take me to be executed, that's okay, too. I have that assurance that I am saved. I have a clean slate.

When I first got here in 1984 they didn't have a place for death-row women 'cause there weren't none. So they made a special room and locked me in there. There was this screen in front of my door, and one day, one of the girls helped me dig out a corner, helped me pull it out, so that she could sneak me cigarettes and matches. I was a smoker then. And sometimes the other girls would come over and talk. Later they built us a place of our own, and I was moved there.

Now I spend a lot of time just standing in my cell, looking out of the peephole. But there's not a lot to see. I tell you, and I don't like saying this, but I've gotten used to being locked inside after all these years. I can talk to the other girls when they take us out into the yard, but mostly I like to keep to myself. Sometimes I don't come out of my cell, and I don't talk to people for days. You see, this has been my life for thirteen years now. I guess I've become institutionalized. I get along with me. I guess what I'm saying is, over the years, you adjust. But one thing you never adjust to is the lack of privacy. This is one of the hardest things. They check through the peephole every hour, or any time they want. You think you're sitting in there alone and in private, but, you see, this isn't always the case. And we're talking about men guards, too. I'm not supposed to, but when I use the bathroom I put a piece of paper over the window of my cell.

The way it is today in society with everybody screaming that   14
prisons are not tough enough . . . people have no idea. Hell, I've had to fight for everything here, walk hours, ice cubes, even to shower more than three times a week. Over time I've learned to bathe in my sink, but can you imagine how hard it is to fit this big old body in the sink? They take you out in the yard for one hour a day, but not on Friday, Saturday, or Sunday. What if you are out in the yard on a Thursday on a hot summer day? You come back and you're sweaty, you're hot. And you can't take a shower until Monday. When I complained that there was nothing to do out there, they got us a jump rope. Once they bought us a basketball, but it busted almost immediately. We beg and beg and beg to be given a cooler to take outside with ice in it and to be able to bring just one little cup of ice back into our rooms in summer.

At first I tried to get things changed. I'd talk to the women. But   15
I've gotten tired of writing stuff up, writing the ACLU. What's the point really? Anyway, I expect to be out of here soon. Why not just sit here in my cell and relax. . . . The thing is, we may be sentenced to death, but we are still human beings. We still need to have outlets, like educational programs, even jobs. But as far as they're concerned, you're already dead if you're on death row. Try getting an operation you need or proper medical help. Why bother, they say. You're dead anyway.

Life on death row is all about the hardest punishment. You can   16
see for yourself. There's a bunk, a foot locker, a chair, a TV over the toilet. We can't keep nothing on the walls. It's a pretty monotonous life. I wake up around 5:30, and they come around at about 6:30

with breakfast that they serve through the slot. Lunch is at 11:30, dinner between 4:00 and 5:00. There are no programs. And we're not allowed to work. So I'm in my cell all of the time except for showers and when they let us out into the yard. One thing that I am is a basketball fan. I mean, passionate. I look forward to watching the games on TV. I read my Bible and I subscribe to *USA Today* for the sports section. And I do a lot of correspondence. I have sixty-five pen pals in the free world. The highlight of my day is getting my mail. When there's nothing, well, I just hate that.

You could give me a stereo, a color TV, a refrigerator, but the   17
truth of it all is, I just want to go home. Nothing else matters. I want to be with my boys and family. They live with their father in Jacksonville, and it's a long way to come. Last time? About a year ago. I don't let them come over the holidays because it's too dangerous on the roads. And on Christmas they have their own things going. . . . My boys are seventeen and eighteen now but when I came in they were just little 'uns. And I know this sounds like a small thing, but I can't even tell you what size shoe my oldest wears. You know what I'm saying? I don't know what size shirts they wear or their favorite foods. And these are the kinds of things a mother wants to know. I just want to go home. Please understand what I'm saying. I could never do enough time to replace a human life. There's nothing I can do to bring him back. But I have given him thirteen years of my life now. What is the sense of keeping me here?

Vocabulary/Using a Dictionary

1. A person's demeanor is his or her outward behavior or conduct. How would you relate this meaning to the meaning of *misdemeanor* (para. 6)?

2. What synonyms can you think of for *audacity* (para. 11)?

3. In what other environments do you think people can become *institutionalized* (para. 13)?

Responding to Words in Context

1. When Jackson says she got "saved" (para. 12), what does she mean? Saved from what? From whom?

2. Why do you think Jackson calls the motorcade that was to take her to her execution the "death caravan" (para. 9)? Isn't the purpose of a caravan usually to protect its passengers? Is Jackson being ironic? If so, why?

Discussing Main Point and Meaning

1. Why does Jackson think that she "did not have any control over the situation" (para. 11) in which she killed a police officer? What did she think should happen to her at the time she gave this interview?

2. What makes Jackson think she has "a clean slate" (para. 12)?

3. There are few "outlets" and there is poor medical attention for death-row inmates, Jackson claims (para. 15). What is her explanation for this?

4. What is "the highlight of [Jackson's] day" (para. 16)?

Examining Sentences, Paragraphs, and Organization

1. How does the introductory material affect or inform your reading of Jackson's statement?

2. Jackson says that she has "given [her victim] thirteen years of [her] life" and that there is little sense in keeping her in jail now (para. 17). Do you think this is a fair statement? What is the logic that underlies this statement? Is it sound?

3. Is the structure of Jackson's statement chronological? If not, how is it structured?

Thinking Critically

1. Should Jackson say more about the incident that resulted in her death sentence? Does it seem that she is more interested in her transformation since her crime than the actual crime itself? What effect does this have on the reader?

2. Do you agree with Jackson that inmates on death row deserve to have "outlets" (para. 15) and other privileges, like daily showers, educational programs, jobs, or more privacy? Why or why not?

In-Class Writing Activities

1. Pretend that you are the widow or child of the police officer who was killed by Jackson. Respond to her argument in a letter — point by point — that attempts to persuade her to accept responsibility for the murder and better understand the severity of her crime.

2. If you were to design a prison facility strictly for murderers, what would it be like? Describe what you think is an appropriate environment for convicted murderers. If you think that there should be different environments according to the type, number, or reasons behind murder, point out those distinctions.

Students Debate the Death Penalty

ABBIE GIBBS

Witnessing Execution

[THE DAILY O'COLLEGIAN, OKLAHOMA STATE UNIVERSITY / February 24, 1998]

Before You Read

Some have argued that if executions were accessible to the public, in person or via television, that the death penalty would be deemed unconstitutional and thus would be banned indefinitely at the federal level. At the same time, many family members of victims report expe-

Abbie Gibbs (b. 1975) was born and raised in Siloam Springs, Arkansas. She is a communications major at Oklahoma State University and plans to graduate in December 1998. She is the recipient of an Associated Collegiate Press Scholarship and a Hearst Journalism award for news writing for reporting on the death penalty. Gibbs wrote this piece for the Daily O'Collegian *at Oklahoma State University. Gibbs will be an editor at the paper when she returns to school in Fall 1998.*

riencing a kind of closure or catharsis at the executions of their loved ones' murderers. What do you think? Could you watch an execution if you were given the opportunity? Would it make a difference if you were related to the victim?

Words to Learn

morbid (para. 1): caused by disease, gruesome, pathological (adj.)
apprehension (para. 1): dread, anxious anticipation (n.)
remorse (para. 6): regret for past misdeeds (n.)

Watching a man prepare to die and gasp for his last breath is 1 something I never thought I would volunteer to witness. But Friday I put my name in a box, in some perhaps morbid hope of being chosen to witness an execution. My name was the last one drawn. I was told I was going to be the second college student in Oklahoma to witness an execution. My apprehension increased every time an official from the prison asked me if I was sure I wanted to do this. Was I ready? They wanted to know.

I and eleven other media witnesses were loaded into a van 2 and driven to the prison. It was dark and silent, and there was a heavy low-lying fog surrounding the prison. I couldn't change my mind, but at this point I wished that I could. We were escorted into the prison, searched, and frisked. All around us were cement walls, iron bars, and mechanical doors. It was silent. Prison guards led us to a small library and told us to wait until they were ready. Some of the reporters talked and joked. For some, this was their fourth or fifth execution.

> He never said he was sorry or asked the victims' families for forgiveness.

I knew that somewhere in the building where I waited there was 3 a man preparing for his last minutes on earth. I can't comprehend what it must feel like to be able to count the minutes until you will be dead. I couldn't comprehend what he must be feeling. However, I also can't imagine what it must feel like to lose my sister or mother to a senseless murder.

I've always been in favor of the death penalty, and witnessing an ex- 4 ecution did not change my mind. I thought it might, but it didn't. Perhaps because Michael Edward Long wanted to die: He seemed almost eager. After guards escorted us through the prison to the small witnessing room, we sat down shoulder to shoulder, about seven feet from the window looking into the execution room. The blinds on the window were closed. We waited and watched as Long's sister and other acquaintances filed into the room and sat in the front row. The blinds were opened, and Long lay in front of us strapped to a table with intravenous lines in both arms. He had a peaceful expression on his face. He was almost smiling. He told a happy religious parable as his last statement and told us all to accept Jesus into our lives. He never said he was sorry or asked the victims' families for forgiveness. Long gasped and moaned and shook as life left his body. I just sat and stared. I felt no emotions of sadness or fear. It didn't seem real to me. I didn't think about the fact that Long would not wake up in the morning.

I left the execution viewing room. I left the prison. I waited   5
for the overwhelming emotions I imagined I would feel after watching a man lose his life, but they never came. I was focused on doing my job — writing a news story — and thought the emotions would come after that, but they didn't. I was exhausted. I thought they would come after sleep, but they didn't. I wondered why the emotions didn't come.

Then I realized, behind me in the execution viewing room, be-   6
hind a darkly tinted glass, sat a group of people. Maybe the mother of the murdered woman was there, maybe the father of the murdered child was watching, maybe someone who lost a sister or a best friend. That's why the emotions hadn't hit me: There were none. I felt no emotion for this man who took two innocent lives. The victims did not get to request a last meal. They did not get to say their goodbyes. They did not get to make their peace. Long deserved to lose his life, and as he did not express any remorse for his victims, I express no remorse for him.

Vocabulary/Using a Dictionary

1. *Morbidity* is a medical term of measure. Based on the way *morbid* is used in paragraph 1, what do you think morbidity measures?

2. An older meaning of *apprehension* (para. 1) is a grasping or catching of an idea or fugitive. How do you think the meaning used here — "dread" — developed from this older meaning?

Responding to Words in Context

1. How can someone hope for something *morbid* (para. 1)? Explain in your own words what feeling Gibbs is experiencing when she says this.

2. Why does Gibbs repeat the word *remorse* in her final statement?

Discussing Main Point and Meaning

1. What did Gibbs think might happen after she witnessed the execution of Michael Edward Long?

2. What does Gibbs describe waiting for in the last third of her article? As a reader, were you waiting for it, too? Does it ultimately happen?

3. Do you think Gibbs would have had a different response if Long hadn't "seemed almost eager" to die (para. 4)?

Examining Sentences, Paragraphs, and Organization

1. Gibbs describes the prison as being "dark and silent," surrounded by a "low-lying fog," and having "cement walls, iron bars, and mechanical doors" (para. 2). Do you think these details would have a different effect if they were coming from a prisoner on her way to jail, rather than a young reporter who would soon be leaving?

2. Discuss the effectiveness of the transition between the beginning and ending of paragraph 3, where Gibbs wonders about the feelings of different people.

3. Why doesn't Gibbs allude to her lack of emotion in the introduction to her article?

Thinking Critically

1. Do you think Gibbs could have felt emotion at Michael Long's execution and still been in favor of the death penalty? What do you make of her unemotional response to this gruesome event?

2. Does Gibbs give any sense that she might have changed her mind about the death penalty after watching this execution? Why do

you think she wanted to watch it? What good reasons can you think of for wanting to watch someone die?

In-Class Writing Activities

1. Write a short essay arguing whether you think executions should be open to the public or available via television. Who would benefit from such accessibility? Who or what would be harmed? Do you think it would have any effect on the national homicide rate?

2. Try to describe the feelings that Gibbs cannot — those of Long and those of his victims' family members.

EDITORIAL BOARD OF THE
COLLEGIATE TIMES

Death Penalty Alternatives

[COLLEGIATE TIMES, VIRGINIA POLYTECHNIC INSTITUTE
AND STATE UNIVERSITY / February 6, 1998]

Before You Read

Is the role of the criminal justice system to protect and serve as many people as possible or to provide punishment, retribution, and rehabilitation for individuals? Where does the death penalty fit into that role? Does it fit at all?

This article was written by consensus by the editorial board of the COL-LEGIATE TIMES, Virginia Polytechnic Institute and State University's online student publication.

Words to Learn

volatile (para. 2): vary widely (adj.)

grisly (para. 4): horrifying, ghastly (adj.)

parameter (para. 4): guideline, limit (n.)

mandate (para. 4): command (v.)

equitable (para. 5): fair (adj.)

discrepancy (para. 5): inconsistency (n.)

incompetent (para. 6): unskillful, incapable (adj.)

rehabilitation (para. 7): restoration to health or suitability for society (n.)

Karla Faye Tucker, thirty-eight years old, was put to death via   1
lethal injection on Tuesday [February 3, 1998] at 6:45 P.M. Eastern
standard time. Her last moments were spent on her back in a Texas
death house, and her last words to her husband were, "Baby, I love
you" before sodium thiopental, pancuronium bromide, and potassium chloride entered her veins.

When news of her death reached the crowd outside, the response   2
was varied. Many cheered, triumphant smiles plastered on their faces.
Others sank their heads low in depression. Their reactions mirror the
division of opinion within the United States over capital punishment,
which, along with abortion and affirmative action, is an extremely
volatile subject. Many believe that death is deserved by those who
commit horrendous acts of murder and that capital punishment saves
the nation money and relieves society of an unwanted presence. Others feel that the nation has no right to sentence people to death and
that other options should be considered. Regardless of these differing
opinions, people are sentenced to death every year in this country. In
1997, seventy-four people were executed, bringing the grand total,
since the death penalty was restored in 1976, to 432. As many as
3,200 convicts are on death row.

On average, a convicted murderer is put to death every five days,   3
but rarely do they receive as much press or sympathy as Tucker did.
Tucker was the first woman executed in Texas since the Civil War
and the second since the death penalty became common practice
again. Tucker was also a born-again Christian. Because of her gender
and seemingly new life philosophy, Texans, 61 to 75 percent of
whom supported the death penalty, were more sympathetic to her
cause.

In Tucker's situation, only 45 to 48 percent of Texans believed   4
she should die. Everyone from Jerry Falwell to Pope John Paul II
begged the state board, governor, and even the president to grant
her a reprieve. Tucker's crime was every bit as grisly as any other
on death row. She hacked into a man with a pickaxe. A jury sentenced her to death in 1983. And if this justice system is to oper-
ate fairly under established parameters, she must die. Just because
she is a woman and a born-again Christian does not exempt her.
While it may seem she is a changed woman, there is no real way
to tell for sure, so she must face the penalty given to her. Fairness
mandates that she die. But it is not that simple. The Texas government is doing the right thing by carrying out the sentence given
by a jury of Tucker's peers. But it is not that simple. The question
remains and surfaces to some degree after every man and woman
is put to death: Should a penalty of death be imposed for *any*
crimes?

Some say the death penalty is an effective way to deal with crimi-   5
nals. On the surface, it seems an equitable
way to make murderers pay for their
crimes. It saves the country money: That's
one less person taxpayers must pay
$20,000 a year to support. But are the ad-
vantages of the death penalty worth its
disadvantages? There is a gray area caus-
ing much trouble in the hearts of Americans and for good reason.
Thousands of murders are committed every year in the United States,
but only a fraction of them are considered awful enough to merit
death. Why should there be a discrepancy? Murder is murder.

There are ways to make criminals pay, without soiling the nation's hands with their blood.

Jurors decided Tucker's case in 1983. Tucker had to wait fif-   6
teen years for the justice engine to get rolling — fifteen years of
waiting, waiting to die. Many believe that the delay in itself is cruel
and unusual punishment and shows the incompetence of the justice system. They are right. The justice system is incompetent. Ever
since its conception, it hasn't been able to deal fairly or efficiently
with crime in this nation.

One reason this is so is that the justice system is based on pun-   7
ishment rather than a rehabilitation mentality. The justice system
would rather impose what it deems to be a proper punishment instead of going the full nine yards to see if the criminal can be rehabilitated. In today's society, where actions and attitudes are reaching a point where they can be understood, there has been more

sympathy for the criminal. It has been proven many times that criminals can be rehabilitated and can learn to live a life different from the one they were living.

But the U.S. Justice Department would rather dole out punishments than therapy sessions. Punishment should not be put on the back burner. Criminals should pay for their deeds. But there are better ways to make them pay. There are alternatives to the death penalty. People who murder others should not be returned to society. Even if they learn their lesson, they need punishment. Instead of death, they should get life in prison without parole. Instead of living in a cell, using up precious taxpayer money, the system should be modified so that these criminals are working to offset their living costs or to create some benefit for society. At a maximum security factory or farm, criminals could make products whose profits will pay for their room and board.   8

There are alternatives to death. There are ways to make criminals pay, without soiling the nation's hands with their blood. There are ways to encourage change in an individual's heart and spirit. So far, there hasn't been much encouragement in that direction. There should be. This issue is dividing a nation. It shouldn't have to.   9

Vocabulary/Using a Dictionary

1. Why does the editorial board refer to the death penalty, abortion, and affirmative action as *volatile* subjects (para. 2)? What "varies widely" in discussions about these subjects?

2. What does it mean when a criminal defendant is found competent or *incompetent* (para. 6) to stand trial?

3. How does *equitable* (para. 5) relate to *equal*?

Responding to Words in Context

1. "Murder is murder," the authors write (para. 5). What is the meaning of this sentence? Isn't it redundant? Does it make sense?

2. In paragraph 4, the authors write that Tucker "hacked into a man with a pickaxe." Why don't the authors just say that Tucker "killed a man with a pickaxe"? What is the point of using such graphic language?

Discussing Main Point and Meaning

1. What is the position of these authors on the death penalty? Do they feel sorry for convicted murderers? Or do they provide another reason for their position?

2. The authors suggest that murderers be put to work in factories or on farms. Why?

3. Why do the authors use Karla Faye Tucker's case as an example? What problems does the Tucker case illustrate?

Examining Sentences, Paragraphs, and Organization

1. What is the "gray area" referred to in paragraph 5?

2. Why, in the first paragraph, do the authors list the contents of the lethal injection Tucker received? How would the effect be different if the chemicals were not named?

3. At what point do the authors reveal their opinion about capital punishment? Why is this revelation placed where it is? Is the placement effective?

Thinking Critically

1. Do these authors underestimate the value of punishment in a democratic society where individuals deserve to be protected by law? Isn't it possible that some criminals cannot be rehabilitated?

2. The authors seem to make a claim that all murderers should be treated equally. Do you agree? Why or why not?

In-Class Writing Activities

1. Write a definition of the word *punishment* without referring to a dictionary or other sources. What is the purpose of punishment? How does one know what a just punishment is? Who reaps the benefit of a punishment?

2. Write a response to the editorial board from one of the other authors in this unit, addressing each of the board's main points from the point of view of the writer you've chosen.

JOHN LLOYD

The Death Penalty Makes Murderers of Us All

[THE NORTHERN STAR, NORTHERN ILLINOIS UNIVERSITY / February 9, 1998]

Before You Read

Does the legal system have an obligation to set an example with respect to killing? Does the concept of a state-sanctioned killing seem contradictory? Should all degrees of murder be punished with execution? If not, where should the line be drawn, and who should draw it?

Words to Learn

desert (para. 2): punishment that is deserved (n.)
gratuitous (para. 2): uncalled for, without justification (adj.)

efficacy (para. 4): power to produce intended results (n.)
liable (para. 4): likely, legally bound (adj.)

Whenever a jury must decide whether to sentence someone to   1
death, the case of the prosecution inevitably is the extent to which the accused *deserves* to die. Whenever death penalty apologists defend capital punishment, they inevitably cite the extent to which the accused *deserved* to die. Again and again, this argument is used to defend the practice of capital punishment. Often, opponents of the death penalty have attacked this argument and have argued that the accused do not *deserve* to die. I will not.

JOHN LLOYD *(b. 1977) grew up in suburban Chicago, graduated from high school in 1995, and is currently a student at Northern Illinois University. His score on the National Latin Exam won him the honor of* maximus cum laude. *He wrote this essay for the* Northern Star, *the university's online student newspaper, in the spring of 1998.*

There is a famous line by Hamlet, Prince of Denmark. He said, 2 "Use every man after his desert, and who should scape whipping?"[1] I agree with Hamlet's assessment. That is, all humans are more or less evil and deserve severe punishment. I'm sure all Christians will agree with me on this. It is explicitly stated in the Bible. Moreover, very rarely do humans receive anywhere near the punishment they deserve. Clearly, the very notion of *desert* is gratuitous in criminal justice. Making an exception of giving only a few people what they deserve is neither just nor ethical. The law should be unconcerned with desert, unconcerned with retribution. Of course, the enforcement of law is necessary, but it is not necessary that the enforcement of that law be cruel and murderous.

The problem with capital punishment is not that it is not deserved. 3 The problem is not that the innocent are occasionally executed; imprisoning the innocent is only less cruel by degree. Instead, the problem is that it is an evil thing to do, in all circumstances, to anyone.

The enforcement of law is necessary, but it is not necessary that the enforcement of that law be cruel and murderous.

The efficacy of capital punishment in 4 preventing crime is likely nonexistent. Even if it were effective, it would be too horrible of a compromise with what is right to consider. I am not unaware that some will say, "The criminal might escape prison and hurt someone or might hurt someone in prison." Do we really want a society in which citizens are executed for what they might do? In that case, anyone, however blameless, is liable to be executed.

When someone is executed, the jurors become murderers. The 5 prosecutors become murderers. The technicians who ultimately do the deed become murderers, and society is guilty for standing by while it happens. Whatever evil the criminal has perpetrated is multiplied exponentially.

Even though the jurors and everyone else involved are guilty of 6 murder, in fairness, I expect them to follow their own consciences, not mine. If their consciences tell them that for some people, some of the time, murder is permissible, then I can forgive them. I will even give them the benefit of the doubt and assume they indeed followed their consciences. If only they were as forgiving as I am.

---

[1]Hamlet to Polonius in act II, scene ii of Shakespeare's *Hamlet*. He means: "If you treat everyone as he or she deserves, no one will escape punishment."

Vocabulary/Using a Dictionary

1. What is a gratuity? Is a gratuity always *gratuitous* (para. 2)?
2. Can you think of any antonyms for *efficacy* (para. 4)?
3. Does Lloyd's use of the word *liable* (para. 4) imply a double meaning? To what other situations can *liability* be applied?

Responding to Words in Context

1. Why does Lloyd focus on the concept of *desert* (para. 2)?
2. Is it fair for Lloyd to label those involved in the carrying out of an execution as *murderers* (para. 5)?

Discussing Main Point and Meaning

1. By Lloyd's logic, do those who carry out death sentences deserve themselves to be put to death?
2. Why does Lloyd end his argument with a discussion of conscience?
3. With whose assessment of punishment does Lloyd agree?

Examining Sentences, Paragraphs, and Organization

1. What do you make of Lloyd's last line? What is the tone of the sentence? How might it hurt the reader's overall assessment of Lloyd's argument ?
2. In paragraph 4, Lloyd writes that "even if . . . [capital punishment] were effective, it would be too horrible of a compromise with what is right to consider." What does he mean by "what is right to consider"?
3. Do you think that Lloyd's claim that he can forgive those who truly favor the death penalty (para. 6) is sincere? Why or why not?

Thinking Critically

1. How can Lloyd use the words of a fictional character from the English Renaissance (Shakespeare's Hamlet) as evidence of a twentieth-century American's point of view? Is this issue timeless? Or is murder in contemporary America a special case?

2. Is it fair to say that since capital punishment (indeed, any punishment) can never be meted out in a perfectly equitable fashion, that such imperfection is evidence against that kind of punishment? Should we not punish any rapist because some are falsely accused? Should we not punish anyone in possession of drugs because sometimes people hold things for friends? How, exactly, can Lloyd argue that capital punishment is wrong because not everyone who deserves to be executed will be executed?

In-Class Writing Activities

1. Choose a fictional character (from a novel or play) whom you admire. Discuss the morals or values of that character that appeal to you or a particular action or statement that you think is relevant to a contemporary issue.

2. Write a response to Lloyd from the point of view of a juror who was seated for a death penalty case. Explain the juror's rationale for the jury's decision to assign the death penalty as a punishment.

From the Bookshelf

Helen Prejean, *Dead Man Walking*

The most frequently cited book on capital punishment is Helen Prejean's Dead Man Walking: An Eyewitness Account of the Death Penalty in the United States, *which appeared in 1993 and two years later was made into a major film starring Sean Penn and Susan Sarandon (who received the Academy Award for best actress). Although the book is an impassioned indictment against the death penalty, Prejean never loses sight of the horrible criminal behavior of the accused and the awful loss experienced by the family and friends of the victims. A Catholic nun, Helen Prejean is a member of the Sisters of St. Joseph of Medaille and a community organizer in her home state of Louisiana. She has written and lectured extensively on the subject of capital punishment. She became closely involved with the issue when in 1982 she was asked to become a pen pal to a death-row inmate, Patrick Sonnier, who was convicted of the brutal murder of two teenagers. In the following passage from the book's opening chapter Sister Prejean sorts out her feelings and beliefs about the morality of execution and the desire for retribution.*

The Morality of Retribution

I cannot accept that the state now plans to kill Patrick Sonnier in cold blood. But the thought of the young victims haunts me. Why do I feel guilty when I think of them? Why do I feel as if I have murdered someone myself?

In prayer I sort it out.

I know that if I had been at the scene when the young people were abducted, I would have done all in my power to save them.

I know I feel compassion for their suffering parents and family and would do anything to ease their pain if I knew how. I also know that nothing can ease some pain.

I know I am trying to help people who are desperately poor, and I hope I can prevent some of them from exploding into violence. Here my conscience is clean and light. No heaviness, no guilt.

Then it comes to me. The victims are dead and the killer is alive and I am befriending the killer.

Have I betrayed his victims? Do I have to take sides? I am acutely aware that my beliefs about the death penalty have never been tested by personal loss. Let Mama or my sister, Mary Ann, or my brother, Louie, be brutally murdered and then see how much compassion I have. My magnanimity is gratuitous. No one has shot my loved ones in the back of the head.

If someone I love should be killed, I know I would feel rage, loss, grief, helplessness, perhaps for the rest of my life. It would be arrogant to think I can predict how I would respond to such a disaster. But Jesus Christ, whose way of life I try to follow, refused to meet hate with hate and violence with violence. I pray for the strength to be like him. I cannot believe in a God who metes out hurt for hurt, pain for pain, torture for torture. Nor do I believe that God invests human representatives with such power to torture and kill. The paths of history are stained with the blood of those who have fallen victim to "God's Avengers." Kings and Popes and military generals and heads of state have killed, claiming God's authority and God's blessing. I do not believe in such a God.

In sorting out my feelings and beliefs, there is, however, one piece of moral ground of which I am absolutely certain: if I were to

continued on next page

continued from previous page

be murdered I would not want my murderer executed. I would not want my death avenged. *Especially by government* — which can't be trusted to control its own bureaucrats or collect taxes equitably or fill a pothole, much less decide which of its citizens to kill.

Prejean, Helen, C.S.J. *Dead Man Walking: An Eyewitness Account of the Death Penalty in the United States.* New York: Random House, 1993.

Discussing the Unit

Suggested Topic for Discussion

The five essays in this unit deal with the death penalty from two perspectives: the viewpoint of death-row inmates and the viewpoint of students debating the death penalty. How do the selections by the death-row inmates inform your understanding of the arguments presented by the students? How do the voices from death row affect your own opinions about the death penalty?

Preparing for Class Discussion

1. Has your opinion of capital punishment been altered or fortified by any of the selections in this unit? Describe what concepts or points surrounding this issue were new to you and affected your thinking on this issue.

2. In small groups, discuss each of the articles in this unit, and locate what you think to be the strongest point of each author. Discuss whether any of the points you've selected are compatible with each other or could be used together to make an even stronger argument.

From Discussion to Writing

1. Write a letter to one of the prisoners in this unit who is on death row. Using the other material in this unit, describe why you support or oppose the prisoner's arguments.

2. Write an essay comparing and contrasting the benefits of life in prison versus capital punishment for society as a whole. Try to avoid favoring your personal preference, and instead give each option equal weight — as if you are asking the reader to assess the value of each and to express his or her preference.

3. Compose a dialogue among the three student authors in this unit about the merits and weaknesses of the case of one of the death-row inmates whose story is featured in this unit. When using a dialogue format, be sure to identify the speaker of each line and to use the language and tone of voice appropriate to each of the student authors.

Topics for Cross-Cultural Discussion

1. Is the death penalty a sentencing option in your native culture? How do the citizens of that culture feel about the issue? Are they as divided as people are in the United States? Or do they have a more unified national opinion?

2. Occasionally, criminals are tried in countries that are not their own. Which standards of justice should be applied to a criminal in such a situation — those of his native society or of the society in which he commits the crime? Explain your answer, making sure to address the possibility of capital punishment in the case of murderers.

Alternate Tables of Contents: Rhetorical Patterns, Integrating Information, and Motivations for Writing

I. Rhetorical Patterns

EXEMPLIFICATION

DEFINITION

CLASSIFICATION

COMPARISON AND CONTRAST

CAUSE AND EFFECT

PROCESS ANALYSIS

PERSUASION

ARGUMENT AND DEBATE

II. Integrating Information

FROM PERSONAL EXPERIENCE

III. Motivations for Writing

CLAIMING AN IDENTITY

PROPOSING SOLUTIONS TO PROBLEMS

OFFERING EXPLANATIONS

REPORTING INFORMATION

The Periodicals:
Information for Subscription

A. *Magazine: Inside Asian America:* bimonthly. $2.95/issue, $15/yr. A "national consumer magazine, by, for, and about Asian Americans, covering personalities, events, and experiences that shape the Asian-American community." Subscription address: *A. Magazine,* 131 W. 1st St., Duluth, MN 55802-2065; or call (800) 346-0085 ext. 4077; Web site, *@LIVE/A Magazine Online:* <http://www.amagazine.com>.

American Enterprise: bimonthly. $5/issue, $28/yr. Magazine of economics, domestic and foreign policy, politics, and public opinion. Subscription address: *American Enterprise,* 1150 17th St., NW, Washington, D. C., 20036; or call (800) 862-5801. Web site, *American Enterprise Magazine:* <http://www.theamericanenterprise .org>.

American Prospect: bi-monthly. $4.95/issue, $25/yr.; students $15/yr. "A national magazine of politics, business, and culture," with a liberal focus. Subscription address: *American Prospect,* P.O. Box 383080, Cambridge, MA 02238-9809; or call (800) 872-0162. Web site, *American Prospect:* <http://www.epn.org/prospect.html>.

The Atlantic Monthly: monthly. $2.95/issue, $17.94/yr. A magazine of public affairs and the arts, addressing contemporary issues through journalism, commentary, criticism, humor, fiction, and poetry. Subscription address: *The Atlantic Monthly,* Customer Service, Box 52638, Boulder, CO 80322; or call (800) 234-2411. Web site, *The Atlantic Unbound/The Atlantic Monthly:* <http:// www.theatlantic.com>.

The Badger Herald: daily. $40/yr./weekly, $160/yr./daily. An independent student newspaper of the University of Wisconsin. Web site, *The Badger Herald Online:* <http://www.badgerherald.com>.

The Black World Today: daily. A webzine concerned with the social, political, economic, and cultural experience of black communities in America and around the world; featuring national and world news, guest columnists, and links to African American newpapers, periodicals, and networks. Web site, *The Black World Today:* <http://www.tbwt.com>.

The Boston Globe: daily. Rates vary according to area; 50¢/issue, $35/mo. in New England; $45/mo. outside New England; student rates available. General newspaper covering local, national, and international news; sections include metro/region, business, living arts, sports, and editorial. Subscription address: *The Boston Globe,* Subscription Dept., P.O. Box 2378, Boston, MA 02107; or call (617) 929-2215 or (800) 622-6631. Web site, *The Boston Globe Online:* <http://www.boston.com/globe>.

Boston Herald: daily. Rates vary according to area; 50¢/issue, $4.25/wk. in Massachusetts; $28.20/mo. outside Massachusetts; students $18.80/mo. Focuses on regional and national news, with some international news; with entertainment, sports, and opinion sections. Subscription address: *Boston Herald,* P.O. Box 2096, Boston, MA 02106; or call (617) 426-3000, x 7714, or (800) 225-2334. Web site, *Boston Herald.com:* <http://www.bostonherald.com>.

The Chicago Reader: weekly. $50/yr.; free in Chicago area. Newspaper covering local news, arts, and entertainment events in and around Chicago. Subscription address: *The Chicago Reader Subscriptions,* 11 E. Illinois, Chicago, IL 60611. Web site, *The Chicago Reader Online:* <http://www.chicagoreader.com>.

The College Reporter: daily weekdays. $35/yr. A student newspaper of Franklin and Marshall College. Subscription address: *The College Reporter,* Franklin and Marshall College, Box C-70, P.O. Box 3003, Lancaster, PA 17604; or call (717) 291-4095. Web site (weekly), *The College Reporter:* <http://www.fandm.edu/CampusLife> (click on *The College Reporter*).

The Collegian: daily weekdays. $75/academic yr. The official student newspaper of Kansas State University. Subscription address: *The Kansas State Collegian,* Student Publications Inc., Kansas State University, Kedzie Hall 103, Manhattan, KN 66506; or call (785) 532-6555. Web site, *eCollegian/The Kansas State Collegian:* <http://collegian.ksu.edu>.

Collegiate Times: twice a week. $35/yr.; free to Virginia Tech students. An independent student newspaper of Virginia Polytechnic Institute. Subscription address: *Collegiate Times,* 363 Squires Student Center, Blacksburg, VA 24061; or call (540) 231-9860. Web site, *Collegiate Times:* <http://www.collegiatetimes.com>.

Commonweal: biweekly. $2/issue, $44/yr. An independent review of public affairs, religion, literature, and the arts, edited by Catholic lay people since 1924. Subscription address: *Commonweal,* 475 Riverside Dr., Rm. 405, New York, NY 10115; or call (212) 662-4200. Web site, *Commonweal:* <http://commonwealmagazine.org>.

The Daily Aztec: daily weekdays (except Fridays). $80/semester, $140/yr. A student newspaper of San Diego State University. Subscription address: *The Daily Aztec,* BA-2, SDSU, San Diego, CA 92182-4591; or call (619) 594-6975. Web site, *The Daily Aztec:* <http://www.dailyaztec.com>.

The Daily Beacon: daily weekdays. $165/yr. A student newspaper of the University of Tennessee-Knoxville. Subscription address: *The Daily Beacon,* 1340 Circle Park Drive, 5 Communications Bldg., Knoxville, TN 37996-0314; or call (423) 974-3226. Web site, *The Daily Beaconline:* <http://beacon-www.asa.utk.edu>.

The Daily Californian: daily weekdays. $65/yr. A student newspaper of the University of California, Berkeley. Subscription address: *The Daily Californian,* P.O. Box 1949, Berkeley, CA 94701-0949; or call (510) 548-8300. Web site, *Daily Cal/The Daily Californian:* <http://www.dailycal.org>.

Daily Egyptian: daily weekdays. $75/yr. A student newspaper of Southern Illinois University at Carbondale. Subscription address: *Daily Egyptian,* Southern Illinois University, Mail Code 6887, Carbondale, IL 62901; or call (618) 536-3311. Web site, *Daily Egyptian:* <http://www.dailyegyptian.com>.

The Daily Nebraskan: daily weekdays. $55/yr. A student newspaper of the University of Nebraska-Lincoln. Subscription address: *The Daily Nebraskan,* Nebraska Union 34, 1400 R St., Lincoln, NE 68588-0448; or call (402) 472-2588. Web site, *The Daily Nebraskan Online:* <http://www.unl.edu/Daily Neb>.

The Daily O'Collegian: daily. $60/semester (1st class mail), $38/semester (3rd class mail). A student newspaper of Oklahoma State University. Subscription address: *The Daily O'Collegian,* 109 Paul Miller Bldg., Oklahoma State University, Stillwater, OK 74078; or call (405) 744-8372. Web site, *The O'Colly Online:* <http://www.ocolly.okstate.edu>.

The Daily Vidette: daily weekdays. $100/yr. A student newspaper of Illinois State University. Subscription address: *The Daily Vidette,* Campus Box 0890, Corner of University and Locust Streets,

Normal, IL 61790-0890; or call (309) 438-5929. Web site, *The Daily Vidette Online Edition:* <http://www.ilstu.edu/depts/vidette>.

Discover: monthly. $3.99/issue, $29.95/yr. General interest science magazine focusing on innovations in science, medicine, and technology. Subscription address: *Discover,* P.O. Box 37283, Boone, IA 50037-0283; or call (800) 829-9132. Web site, *Discover:* <http://www.discover.com>.

The Emory Wheel: daily weekdays. $75/yr. A student newspaper of Emory University. Subscription address: *The Emory Wheel,* Emory University, Drawer W, Atlanta, GA 30322; or call (404) 727-6178. Web site, *The Emory Wheel Online:* <http://www.emory.edu/WHEEL>.

The Gateway: daily weekdays. The official student newspaper of the University of Nebraska-Omaha. Subscription address: *The Gateway,* University of Nebraska at Omaha, Omaha, NE 68182; or call (402) 554-2470. Web site, *The Gateway:* <http://www.gateway.unomaha.edu>.

Glamour: monthly. $2.50/issue, $15/yr. A magazine primarily for young women, with articles on fashion, health, and lifestyle. Subscription address: *Glamour,* P.O. Box 53716, Boulder, CO 80322; or call (800) 274-7410. Web site, *Glamour:* <http://www.glamour.com>.

Grand Street: quarterly. $12.95/issue, $40/yr. Journal of fiction, poetry, and journalism; visual arts and science. Subscription address: *Grand Street* Subscription Service, Dept. GRS, P.O. Box 3000, Denville, NJ 07834; or call (800) 807-6548.

Hungry Mind Review: quarterly. $3/issue, $10/yr. Journal of reviews of poetry, literary fiction, and literary nonfiction; essays and commentary on a wide range of topics. Subscription address: *Hungry Mind Review,* 1648 Grand Avenue, St. Paul, MN 55105; or call (612) 699-2610. Web site, the *Hungry Mind Review Online:* <http://www.bookwire.com/hmr>.

The Iowa State Daily: daily weekdays. $62/yr; students $40/yr. A student newspaper of Iowa State University. Subscription address: *The Iowa State Daily,* 108C Hamilton Hall, Ames, IA 50011; or call (515) 294-2609. Web site, *The Iowa State Daily Online Edition:* <http://www.daily.iastate.edu>.

Mademoiselle: monthly. $2.50/issue, $16/yr. A magazine primarily for young women, with articles on fashion, health, and lifestyle. Subscription address: *Mademoiselle,* Box 54348, Boulder, CO

80322; or call (800) 274-4750. Web site, *Mademoiselle:* <http://www.mademoiselle.com>.

Mainstream: 10 issues/yr. $4/issue, $24/yr. A magazine "produced by, for, and about people with disabilities," advocating for disability rights, and covering news and current affairs, lifestyle, products, and technology. Subscription address: *Mainstream,* 2973 Beech Street, Suite 1, San Diego, CA 92102; or call (619) 234-3138. Web site, *Mainstream Online:* <http://www .mainstream-mag.com>.

The Nation: weekly. $2.75/issue, $52/yr. "A liberal journal of critical opinion, committed to racial justice, anti-imperialism, civil liberties, and social equality," with commentary on politics, culture, books, and the arts. Subscription address: *The Nation,* P.O. Box 37072, Boone, IA 50037; or call (800) 333-8536. Web site, *The Nation Digital Edition:* <http://www.thenation.com>.

National Review: bi-weekly. $3.50/issue, $59/yr.; students $21.95/18 issues. A conservative journal of news and opinion with analyses on national and international trends in culture, economics, and politics. Subscription address: *National Review,* Circulation Dept., P.O. Box 668, Mount Morris, IL 61054-0668; or call (815) 734-1232. Web site, *National Review Online:* <http:// www.nationalreview.com>.

The New Republic: weekly. $2.95/issue, $69.97/yr.; students $28/yr. Opinion journal with a mix of liberal and conservative articles and commentary on American politics, foreign policy, literature, and the arts. Subscription address: *The New Republic,* Subscription Service Dept., P.O. Box 602, Mount Morris, IL 61054; or call (800) 827-1289. Web site, *The New Republic:* <http:// www.thenewrepublic.com>.

Newsweek: weekly. $2.95/issue, $41.43/yr. News and commentary on the week's events in national and international affairs. Subscription address: The Newsweek Building, Subscriptions Dept., Livingston, NJ 07039-1666; or call (800) 631-1040. Web site, *Newsweek.com:* <http://www.newsweek.com>.

The New Yorker: weekly. $2.95/issue, $39.95/yr.; students $20/yr. Magazine of commentaries and reviews, current events, cartoons, biographical profiles, short fiction, and poetry. Subscription address: *The New Yorker,* P.O. Box 52312, Boulder, CO 80323-2312; or call (800) 825-2510. Web site, *The New Yorker:* <http://magazines.enews.com/magazines/new_yorker>.

The New York Times: daily, with large Sunday edition that contains *The New York Times Magazine* and *The New York Times Book Review,* as well as other supplements. Rates vary according to location and frequency of delivery. Considered the definitive source for current events; daily, national, and international news; and business and arts reporting. Subscription address: *The New York Times,* 229 West 43rd St., New York, NY 10036; or call (800) 631-2500. Web site, *The New York Times On the Web:* <http://www.nytimes.com>.

The Northern Star: daily weekdays. $55/yr. A student newspaper of Northern Illinois University. Subscription address: *The Northern Star,* Campus Life Building, Suite 130, DeKalb, IL 60115; or call (815) 753-0101. Web site, *Northern Star Online Edition:* <http://www.star.niu.edu>.

Notre Dame Magazine: quarterly. $20/yr. A publication of the University of Notre Dame addressing "institutional and Catholic concerns," and examining cultural issues and covering the university's discussion of science and the arts, society, and spiritual matters. Subscription address: *Notre Dame Magazine,* 538 Grace Hall, Notre Dame, IL 46556-5602; or call (219) 631-5335. Web site, *Notre Dame Magazine:* <http://www.nd.edu/~ndmag>.

Perspective: Harvard-Radcliffe's Liberal Monthly: monthly. $15/yr. A "politically progressive, general-issues" student magazine at Harvard-Radcliffe. Subscription address: *Perspective,* P.O. Box 2439, Cambridge, MA 02238; or call (617) 495-4290. Web site, *Perspective:* <http://www.digitas.harvard.edu/~perspy>.

The Philadelphia Inquirer: daily. Rates vary according to location and frequency of delivery. General newspaper covering local, national, and international news. Subscription address: *The Philadelphia Inquirer,* P.O. Box 8263, Philadelphia, PA 19101; or call (215) 665-1234. Web site, *The Philadelphia Inquirer:* <http://www.phillynews.com> (and click to *The Inquirer*).

The Progressive: monthly. $3.50/issue, $32/yr., $52/2 yrs.; students $22/yr. "A journal of cultural and political opinion from a left/ progressive perspective." Subscription address: *The Progressive,* P.O. Box 421, Mount Morris, IL 61054-0421; or call (800) 827-0555. Web site, *The Progressive:* <http://www.progressive.org>.

The Radcliffe Quarterly: quarterly. Magazine published by the Radcliffe Alumni Association. Showcases articles written by notable women authors, with updates on alumni, and covering activities on campus. For subscription information call (617) 495-8608.

Web site, *The Radcliffe Quarterly Online:* <http://www .radcliffe.edu/quarterly>.

The South End Press: daily weekdays. The official student newspaper of Wayne State University. Subscription address: *The South End,* 5425 Woodward Ave, Bowen Complex, Wayne State University, Detroit, MI 48202; or call (313) 577-3494. Web site, *The South End:* <http://thesouthend.wayne.edu>.

The Tufts Daily: daily weekdays. $30/yr. A student newspaper of Tufts University. Subscription address: *Tufts Daily,* P.O. Box 18, Medford, MA 02153; or call (617) 627-3090. Web site, *The Tufts Daily Online:* <http://www.tufts.edu/as/stu-org/tuftsdaily>.

Acknowledgments (continued from p. iv)

American Civil Liberties Union (advertisement). "Let Me Ask You Something...If There's Prayer in School, Whose Prayer Should It Be?" American Civil Liberties Union op-ed ad, created by The PlowShare Group and published in the April 14, 1998, edition of *The New York Times*.

J. Barrios, cartoon: "America: 2022," *The Daily Californian*, October 1, 1997. Copyright © 1997, *The Daily Californian*. Reprinted with permission.

Campaign for Tobacco-Free Kids (advertisement). "Without National Tobacco Legislation...The Lives of Five Million Kids Could Go Up in Smoke." Reprinted with permission.

Kathleen Carlin, "You Become What You Wear," *Commonweal*, June 1, 1996. Copyright © 1996 *Commonweal*, reprinted with permission.

Nancy Carlsson-Paige and Diane Levin, "The Profiteering That Kills Kids," *The Boston Globe*, April 2, 1998. Reprinted with permission of the authors.

Steven L. Carter, "Listening Respectfully," from *Civility* by Steven L. Carter. Copyright © 1998 by Steven L. Carter. Reprinted by permission of the author.

Benson Cohen, "Educational Growth Requires Affirmative Action" ["Pursuing King's Dream"], *The Emory Wheel*, Emory University, February 20, 1998. This editorial first appeared in *The Emory Wheel*. Reprinted with permission of the author and *The Emory Wheel*.

Gail Collins. "A Sweet Moment of Teamwork," *The New York Times*, February 27, 1998. Copyright © 1998 by the New York Times Co. Reprinted by permission.

Bennie M. Currie, "The N-Word and How to Use It." Copyright © 1997 Bennie M. Currie. Reprinted with permission of the author.

"Death Penalty Alternatives," *Collegiate Times*, Educational Media Company at Virginia Tech, Inc., February 6, 1998. Reprinted by permission.

Richard Dooling, "The Growing List of Forbidden Words," from *Blue Streak: Swearing, Free Speech, and Sexual Harassment*. Copyright © 1996 by Richard Dooling. Reprinted by permission of the author.

Susan J. Douglas, "Girls 'n' Spice: All Things Nice?" Reprinted with permission from the August 25/September 1, 1997, issue of *The Nation* magazine.

M. P. Dunleavey, " 'Guy' Envy," *Glamour*, May 1996. Courtesy *Glamour*. Copyright © 1996 by Condé Nast Publications, Inc.

Jean Bethke Elshtain, "Our Bodies, Our Clones," *The New Republic*, August 4, 1997. Reprinted by permission of *The New Republic*, © 1997, The New Republic, Inc.

G. Stuart Englebert, "Stereotyping and Racism Are Not the Same," *The Collegian*, Kansas State University, March 20, 1996. Reprinted with permission of the author and *The Collegian*.

Karen Epstein, "I'm a Barbie Girl," *The Tufts Daily*, Tufts University, November 21, 1997. Reprinted with permission of the author and *The Tufts Daily*.

Susan Estrich, "High Heels: What a Pain!" *Boston Herald*, October 21, 1997. By permission of Susan Estrich and Creators Syndicate.

Bryan Garvey, "Superficial Labels Belie True Identities" ["We Are More Than Labels"], *The Daily Beacon*, University of Tennessee, October 28, 1997. Reprinted by permission of the author and *The Daily Beacon*.

Henry Louis Gates Jr., "A Conflict of Identity," from *Colored People: A Memoir* by Henry Louis Gates Jr. Copyright © 1991 by Henry Louis Gates Jr. Reprinted by permission of Alfred A. Knopf, Inc.

Abbie Gibbs, "Witnessing Execution Proves True Convictions" ["Witnessing Execution"], *The Daily O'Collegian,* Oklahoma State University, February 24, 1998.
Reprinted with permission of the author and *The Daily O'Collegian.*

Meg Greenfield, "Kicking Away Your Freedom," *Newsweek,* Mar. 23, 1998. Copyright © 1998 Newsweek, Inc. Reprinted by permission.

Lani Guinier, "Finding a Space for Real Conversations on Race," *The Radcliffe Quarterly,* Fall/Winter 1997. Reprinted by permission of the author.

Hendrik Hertzberg, "Star-Spangled Banter," *The New Yorker,* July 21, 1997.
Reprinted by permission. Copyright © 1997 The New Yorker Magazine, Inc. All
rights reserved.

Anne Hollander, "Uniform Fashions," from *Sex and Suits: The Evolution of Modern
Dress* by Anne Hollander. Copyright © 1994 by Anne Hollander. Reprinted by
permission of Alfred A. Knopf, Inc.

Bernice Powell Jackson, "Affirming Affirmative Action," *Black World Today,* September 8, 1997. Reprinted by permission of Bernice Powell Jackson, Executive Director, United Church of Christ Commission for Racial Justice.

Denise Sherer Jacobson, "David," *Mainstream,* March 1998. Excerpted from *The
Question of David: A Disabled Mother's Journey Through Adoption, Family,
and Life* by Denise Sherer Jacobson, to be published in 1999. Copyright © 1998,
Mainstream, Magazine of the Able-Disabled, 2973 Beech Street, San Diego, CA
92102.

Horace Freeland Judson, "Waiving Our Freedom ["Some Questions for My Senator
about the Flag"]," *The New York Times,* June 16, 1997. Copyright © 1997 by
the New York Times Co. Reprinted by permission.

Lini S. Kadaba, "What's In a Name?" *The Philadelphia Inquirer,* December 7, 1997.
Reprinted with permission from *The Philadelphia Inquirer,* December 7, 1997.

Wendy Kaminer, "A Civic Duty to Annoy," *The Atlantic Monthly,* September 1997.
Copyright © Wendy Kaminer, 1997, as first published in *The Atlantic Monthly.*
Reprinted by permission of the author.

Justin Kaplan and Anne Bernays, "New Names, New Identities," from *The Language
of Names.* Copyright © 1997 by Justin Kaplan and Anne Bernays. Reprinted by
permission of the authors.

Gina Kolata, "A Clone is Born," from *Clone* by Gina Kolata. Copyright © 1998 by
Gina Kolata. Used by permission of William and Morrow and Co., Inc.

Susan Brady Konig, "They've Got to Be Carefully Taught," *National Review,* September 15, 1997. Copyright © 1997 by National Review, Inc., 215 Lexington
Avenue, New York, NY 10016. Reprinted by permission.

Alex Kotlowitz, "Colorblind," *The New York Times Magazine,* January 11, 1998.
Copyright © 1998 by the New York Times Co. Reprinted by permission.

Henry Han Xi Lau, "I Was a Member of the Kung Fu Crew," *The New York Times
Magazine,* October 19, 1997. Copyright © 1997 by the New York Times Co.
Reprinted by permission.

Richard Lederer, "How Words Change." Reprinted with the permission of Simon &
Schuster from *Crazy English* by Richard Lederer. Copyright © 1989 by Richard
Lederer.

Edmund Lee and Kenneth Li, "The Myth of the Asian American Superstudent,"
A. Magazine, August/September 1997. Reprinted by permission of the authors.

John Lloyd, "Those Who Carry Out Death Sentences Are Murderers Themselves"
["The Death Penalty Makes Murderers of Us All"], *The Northern Star,* Northern

Illinois University, February 9, 1998. Reprinted by permission of the author and *The Northern Star.*

Jason Michael, "Race Issue Out of Focus" ["Reflections on Black History Month"], *The South End Press*, Wayne State University, March 2, 1998. Reprinted with permission of the author and *The South End Press.*

Andy Miller, "Affirmative Action No End to Discrimination" ["Affirmative Action: Another Name for Discrimination"], *The Badger Herald*, University of Wisconsin, January 29, 1998. Reprinted with permission of the author and *The Badger Herald.*

Tim Mills, "Where Have All Our Heroes Gone?" *The Gateway*, University of Nebraska at Omaha, January 27, 1998. Reprinted with permission of the author.

Negative Population Growth, Inc. (advertisement). "Why Does Our Government Allow . . .". Reprinted by permission of Negative Population Growth, Inc.

Mary Pipher, "What Happens to Adolescent Girls?" from *Reviving Ophelia* by Mary Pipher. Copyright © 1994 by Mary Pipher. Reprinted by permission of Putnam Publishing.

Planned Parenthood Federation of America (advertisement). "Twenty-Five Years After *Roe v. Wade*, Planned Parenthood® Gives New Meaning to 'Choice'," *American Prospect*, April 1998. Photo by permission of Planned Parenthood Federation of America.

Helen Prejean, "The Morality of Retribution," from *Dead Man Walking* by Helen Prejean. Copyright © 1993 by Helen Prejean. Reprinted by permission of Random House, Inc.

Arnold Rampersad, "Jackie Robinson's Finest Moment," from *Jackie Robinson: A Biography* by Arnold Rampersad. Copyright © 1997 by Arnold Rampersad and Rachel Robinson. Reprinted by permission of Alfred A. Knopf, Inc.

Hobi Reader, "Identity through Clothing," *The Daily Aztec*, San Diego State University, September 29, 1997. Reprinted with permission of the author and *The Daily Aztec.*

Adolph Reed Jr., "Black Athletes on Parade," *The Progressive*, July 1997. Reprinted by permission by *The Progressive*, 409 E. Main St., Madison, WI 53703.

Karlene J. Robinson, "In Pursuit of the Impossible Body Image," *The Daily Vidette*, Illinois State University, February 18, 1998. Reprinted with permission of the author and *The Daily Vidette.*

Luis J. Rodríguez, "Stop the Lies," first appeared in *Hungry Mind Review*, 47, Spring 1998. Reprinted by permission.

Michael Ross, "My Name is Michael Ross (a Condemned Man)." Reprinted by permission of the author.

Dorothy J. Samuels, "A Shot Against Women's Sports," *The New York Times*, February 27, 1998. Copyright © 1998 by the New York Times Co. Reprinted by permission.

Galit Sarfaty, "A Forgotten Past," *Perspective*, March 1997. Reprinted with permission of the author and *Perspective.*

"Seed May Not be Entirely Wrong" ["Cloning: A Cautious Defense"], *Daily Egyptian* Editorial Board, first printed January 15, 1998, *Daily Egyptian*, Southern Illinois University at Carbondale. Copyright © 1998 *Daily Egyptian*. Reprinted with permission.

Tom Shachtman, "Sound Reasoning or Sound Bites?" Reprinted with the permission of The Free Press, a Division of Simon & Schuster, from *The Inarticulate Society:*

Index of Authors and Titles

From Discussion to Writing
Instructional Resources for Teaching

Third Edition

America
NOW

Short
Readings
from Recent Periodicals

Robert Atwan

Prepared by **Mark Bellomo** *and* **Jennifer Ivers**

Preface

Using America Now in Developmental and Composition Classes

With its strong focus on current issues and its thought-provoking assignments, *America Now* is ideal for both developmental and composition classes. Many of the questions and writing assignments in the book will give students the practice they need to pass basic skills examination. At the same time, these questions allow students to work within a real context, and all levels of writing classes might use them to practice writing skills, promote discussion, and prepare for take-home essay assignments. Though some questions and writing assignments in the book ask students to focus on just one selection, others require them to synthesize varying opinions and to come to their own conclusions about an issue, drawing on readings and their own observations for support. These more complex assignments might be more appropriate for composition classes or the latter part of developmental classes.

Because developmental writers often enjoy challenges, we believe *America Now* is an excellent choice for them. Developmental students need to know more than just where to put a comma or how to handle verb tenses; they need to read critically, to make connections among an author's various points, and to juxtapose these points with those of other authors. Most students can meet these challenges, and instructors report that developmental students effectively analyze texts far more complex than those found in many readers. Their students often say that they can think, but they need advice on how to write in a way that is accepted in academia. Often such students write best when they are asked to discuss topics meaningful to them, and *America Now* and this manual provide contexts for such meaningful expression.

Using this Instructors' Manual

The comments and suggestions that follow invite you to use the third edition of *America Now* to expand your students' reading and writing abilities. Each writing class is unique, and labels often do not adequately characterize the abilities, interests, and perspectives of a particular group of students. Therefore, the questions and activities in *America Now* and the suggestions provided here include a variety of options that may be adapted for students with a wide range of reading and writing experiences. We invite you to choose those that best suit your classes, those that best fit your particular teaching style, and those that work best within the curriculum for the specific course you are teaching. We hope that these materials will encourage students to read and write more thoughtfully and critically, challenge them to think about reading and writing in increasingly sophisticated ways; and make planning and organizing classroom activities more manageable for instructors.

This manual is organized to parallel the structure of the student edition of *America Now*. Each unit begins with a brief introduction to the themes and selections offered in that unit. Following the introductory material are suggested answers to questions in the text. These suggested answers correspond to the question sets that follow each selection in the student edition—Vocabulary/Using a Dictionary; Responding to Words in Context; Discussing Main Point and Meaning; Examining Sentences, Paragraphs, and Organization; Thinking Critically; In-Class Writing Activities—and those that follow each unit: Preparing for Class Discussion; From Discussion to Writing; and Topics for Cross-Cultural Discussion. These suggested answers are meant to anticipate possible student responses, to raise further questions for discussion and writing, and to help you to better use *America Now* as a tool for classroom discussion and more effective student writing.

Obviously, few classes will be able to read and work with all of the selections in the text in one semester. You may want to focus on thematic groupings of units, or you may prefer to select units that are of particular interest to your students. Some instructors may allow students to choose selections; others will be more comfortable making these selections or taking turns with the class. As an alternative approach you might ask a group of students to select a unit for the class to read; then the group of students in charge would be responsible for the discussion and the activities in which the class participates.

However you use this manual, we hope that it will help you and your students to use the text fully and thoughtfully, to think critically about the issues and readings, and to consider how these readings fit within the larger context that is America now.

Contents

Introduction
Writing and the Art of Discussion
by Robert Atwan

I enter into discussion and argument with great freedom and ease, inasmuch as opinion finds in me a bad soil to penetrate and take deep roots in. No propositions astonish me, no belief offends me, whatever contrast it offers with my own. There is no fancy so frivolous and so extravagant that it does not seem to me quite suitable to the production of the human mind.

— Michel de Montaigne,
Of the Art of Discussion (1588)

However unwillingly a person who has a strong opinion may admit the possibility that his opinion may be false, he ought to be moved by the consideration that, however true it may be, if it is not fully, frequently, and fearlessly discussed, it will be held as a dead dogma, not a living truth.

— John Stuart Mill and Harriet Taylor,
Of the Liberty of Thought and Discussion

Students often begin their college writing courses with a popular misconception. They think that writing is an isolating activity demanding extraordinary inner resources. They picture writers as sitting alone at their desks or computers anxiously staring at a blank page or screen until inspiration strikes. Indeed, this romanticized image of anxious solitude followed by a burst of creativity has for centuries served as a powerful model of how literature is produced. But for the average student, who has little understanding of how real writers work and has perhaps never observed people writing professionally, this popular image can lead to a distorted view of writing and the role writing plays in a person's intellectual development.

Most writers work within a lively social context, one in which issues and ideas are routinely discussed and debated. They often begin writing on topics that derive directly from specific professional situations: a journalist covers a murder trial; a professor prepares a paper for a conference; a social worker writes up a case study; an executive reports on a business meeting. Usually, the writer consults with friends and coworkers about the task and solicits their opinions and support, sometimes even asking them to comment on a draft of the work. If the work is to be published, the writer almost always

1

receives additional advice and criticism in the form of editorial comment, copyediting, proofreading, and independent reviews. By the time the work appears, it has probably gone through numerous drafts (for some writers as many as ten or twelve) and has been subjected to a rigorous sequence of editorial support, from fact checking to stylistic fine tuning.

Nearly all the published work a student reads has gone through this process. Even the most ephemeral article in a magazine has probably been revised several times by several people before publication. But, of course, none of this is visible in the final product. Students have little knowledge of all the various levels of work and collaboration that went into a piece of writing — the author's often extensive reading and research, the time spent traveling, interviewing, and discussing, the organization of the information, the composing of several drafts, and the concerted effort of editors and publishers. Unlike a film, a piece of writing shows only the author's name and seldom everyone else who helped make the published work possible (though some books include an acknowledgments page).

The point about student writing should be clear: Students write in a much narrower professional environment than do experienced people whose writing is a significant part of their work. Too often, the student writes in an intellectual vacuum. He or she may feel only minimally engaged by an assigned topic — which may seem to have come out of nowhere — and may not know anyone with whom the topic may be seriously and intelligently discussed. Unlike the professional writer, the student usually sits down alone and tries to write with little intellectual provocation or encouragement. No wonder students find it so hard to begin a paper. Instead of knowing they are writing for a group of interested people, they often feel that the writing will be read by only one other person — the instructor, who will read it not for further discussion but for immediate evaluation.

America Now is designed to help writing students avoid the intellectual and emotional vacuum that confronts them when they begin to write. Two of the biggest problems in composition, finding something to say and getting started, are in large part due to the student's lack of a vital connection with what other people have to say about an issue or idea. The basis of many student writing problems, I believe, is not so much grammatical or rhetorical as social. At their worst, these problems are clearly reflected in the writing, in a disjunctive prose that sounds oddly cut off from most public discourse.

The art of writing and the art of discussion are closely linked. Experienced writers invariably write in a climate of discussion. Their writing is usually embedded in a context of others' ideas and opinions. Many writers, especially in the academic community, are directly responding to other writers — a scientist reexamining the experimental procedures of other scientists; a literary critic taking exception to a prevailing method of interpretation; a sociologist offering an alternative explanation of a colleague's data; a historian participating as a respondent at a conference. Such people are not writing in a vacuum. Their ideas often originate in discussion, their writing is a response to discussion, and their papers are designed to stimulate further discussion.

The Art of Discussion

"Discussion" is one of those commonly used words from speech and rhetoric — like "essay" or "style" — that remains difficult to define precisely. The word has a long and complex history. It derives from a Latin verb (*discutere*) meaning to dash, scatter, or shake out, and it gradually came to take on the legal and, later, the rhetorical sense of "breaking" a case or a topic down into its various parts for investigation. Though the word is ordinarily used today to mean "to talk over" or "to consider carefully," it still retains a rhetorical sense of sifting a topic into separate parts for close examination.

It is easier to say what discussion is not: It is neither conversation nor debate. Unlike conversation, discussion is purposefully conducted around a given topic. Unlike debate, it is not formally organized into two competing points of view. Think of discussion as a speech activity that falls between the informalities of conversation and the formalities of debate. For the purpose of this book, discussion is defined as the free and open exploration of a specified topic by a small group of prepared people. The goal of such discussion is not to arrive at a group decision or a consensus, but to investigate as many sides of a topic as possible.

To keep discussion from rigidifying into a debate between two competing sides or from drifting into aimless conversation, a discussion leader or moderator is usually required. The discussion leader may adopt an active role in the discussion or may choose to remain neutral. But regardless of the extent of the leader's role, he or she will ordinarily introduce the topic, encourage participation, maintain an orderly sequence of responses, and ensure that the group sticks to the topic. With its regularly scheduled sessions, its diversified members, and its academic purpose, the typical college composition class of fifteen to twenty-five students makes an ideal discussion group.

It should be noted that there are many different kinds of discussion groups and techniques. Instructors who would like to read more about various discussion groups and methods may want to consult such standard texts as Ernest G. Bormann's *Discussion and Group Methods* or Mary A. Bany and Lois V. Johnson's *Classroom Group Behavior: Group Dynamics in Education*. These and similar texts on discussion can usually be found in the education and psychology sections of most college libraries.

Like writing, discussion is a learned activity. To be adept at group discussion requires the development of a variety of skills — in speaking, listening, thinking, and reading. By encouraging students to participate in group discussion, you can help them become more intellectually mature and better prepared for professional careers. Since participation in group discussion is almost always voluntary, your students can improve their discussion abilities by observing a few ground rules. They should (1) be willing to speak in public; (2) be willing to listen; (3) be willing to examine all sides of a topic; (4) be willing to suspend judgment; and (5) be willing to prepare. These rules are explained further in the introduction for students on page xxv of *America Now.*

Generating Classroom Discussion

Many college teachers in the liberal arts feel that a particular class has gone well when they've been able to generate discussion. This is not surprising. Lively class discussion surely indicates a healthy level of student interest in the course; it also minimizes the burden and monotony of classroom lecturing. I find that even teachers who conduct large lecture courses are pleased when students ask questions and raise relevant points. Anyone who has ever given a public lecture knows how awkward it can be when the moderator invites questions and no hands are raised. Many people instinctively measure the success of a lecture or talk by the number of questions from the audience.

Yet my talks with college instructors in many disciplines indicate that, though they invite class discussion, they don't expect to generate much. "These kids have nothing to say. They just sit there," a professor complained of his introductory European history course. "I do get some students to discuss the reading," a literature teacher told me, "but it's always the same two or three talking every class. The rest are silent." "At the end of class," a writing teacher remarked, "I'll ask, 'Does anyone have any questions about the assignment?' No hands. As I dismiss class and prepare to leave, I notice five or six students gathered around my desk. Each one has a question about the assignment." These experiences, it appears, are quite typical.

Every year hundreds of thousands of college students walk into classrooms throughout America with little knowledge of how to participate in intelligent, informed discussion. One can only speculate about why this is so, but there are clearly several contributing factors: the average student's native shyness and lack of training in extemporaneous speech; an overreliance on lecturing in classrooms; the dismal models of discussion found in the media, especially on radio and television talk shows; and the decline of family conversation as people have less leisure time and as family life grows more fragmented.

One important obstacle to discussion has grown directly out of a seriously misguided educational trend. As schools concentrate more and more on the mastery of isolated and "testable" skills, they leave less and less room in the curriculum for the tentative and exploratory discussion of complex topics. This trend can easily be seen in the growing importance of college and graduate school entrance examinations, which reduce all educational achievement to the "question-answer" level. Such educational instruments not only eliminate discussion and exploration entirely, they foster a mental attitude that is directly opposed to the free and open discussion of ideas: Their rigid format implies that for every question there is always one correct answer.

All of these factors add up to silent college classrooms. In composition courses, lack of discussion can be especially counterproductive to education, since most writing instructors expect their classes to respond to reading assignments and participate in workshop sessions. Few college courses, in fact, are more dependent upon class discussion than freshman composition. This often puts a special strain upon the instructor who, in addition to handling a semester's worth of writing assignments, must normally engineer ways to stimulate the discussion of each class's reading material. In over twenty years of speaking with writing teachers about their teaching, I've noticed how frequently they define a "good class" as one in which the students talk.

The third edition of *America Now,* like its predecessors, is specifically designed to get students talking in class. The apparatus following each unit make it clear to students that the readings are *meant* to be discussed. More important, it gives them questions to consider and small preparatory writing tasks that will help you get class discussion started. The material in the manual is directly linked to the student exercises in the book. The possible "answers" provided here are intended to anticipate student responses to the questions following the selections, and to provide some suggestions for using *America Now* in your course. We hope they will also offer you several ideas for building on what students have prepared and for moving the class discussion of the topic toward the writing assignment.

The book and manual are so directed toward improving class discussion that I'd like to offer a few practical suggestions for generating it and using it as a basis for writing. These suggestions are based on the trial and error of my own experience and on observations of other instructors and their reports. But because class discussion is so often spontaneous and unpredictable — and is rarely the subject of systematic educational inquiry — I'd like to remind instructors that these suggestions are largely the result of impressions (mine and others') of what works and what doesn't in a classroom. I hope that this book and manual will stimulate the further study of discussion techniques in the field of composition.

Here are a few suggestions for generating class discussion and directing it toward the primary goal of the course — student writing:

1. *Emphasize the Importance of Discussion.* Inform students from the start of the course that class discussion is an essential ingredient of the program and that you will be counting on full participation. Remind students that both speaking well and writing well are important factors in anyone's career (it is difficult to think of any profession in which participating in discussion meetings is not essential). Remind students, too, that discussion is neither systematic debate nor aimless conversation, but is the free and open exploration of an agreed-upon topic. Since most students are naturally shy,

the exploratory nature of class discussion should be emphasized: Questions should be freely asked and points raised without anyone feeling stupid.

2. *Create a Climate of Discussion.* Free and open discussion cannot exist in a tense or anxious atmosphere. From the start, therefore, try to know who your students are (learn their names as quickly as possible) and help them become familiar with each other. You might ask your students to stand up and introduce themselves one by one to the entire class and to say something about themselves (where they're from; their major; what they want to be, etc.). This procedure helps break the ice and gets students talking in class. Remember: Productive classroom discussion is not a matter of students talking only to their instructor; they must also talk to each other.

You may have students suggest questions that they believe would make an interesting interview — what they would like to know about a person. Then divide the class into pairs and have students use those questions as a framework for interviews with each other. The students should write down each other's responses (if a class doesn't pair off evenly, a student can do two interviews or two students can handle one). This interview is then read by the interviewer as a way to introduce the student. Clearly, this method takes the burden off individuals who would feel shy about introducing themselves in front of the class; it also gets the students writing as they learn about each other.

To create a relaxed atmosphere for discussion, it is important to avoid an overbearing manner or a sarcastic tone. Many students are dreadfully afraid of appearing stupid in front of their peers, and an adversarial or sarcastic style of teaching — though it may appeal to a few "knowing" students — may easily lead diffident students to retreat into the safety of silence. A teacher who wants to maintain a lively atmosphere of discussion will also need at times to restrain the sarcasm of the other students toward irrelevant or "stupid" comments. This is easily done by reminding everyone of the exploratory nature of this discussion and the ground rule that no one need be afraid to say anything. I've found that many disarmingly blunt comments or "off-the-wall" questions that I tended to dismiss proved later to be quite good. Questions that sounded ill-informed were merely ill-formed. Many students have not yet learned the art of posing questions, and everything possible should be done to encourage them to do so.

3. *Beware of the Socratic Method.* So many instructors were themselves taught by this method that they often resort to it instinctively in their classrooms. If conducted in the proper dialogic spirit, the method is, of course, a superb tool for both instilling knowledge and creating intellectual drama. But too often it becomes a question-and-answer game in which instructors ask a series of questions for which they possess definite answers. Often, these questions are posed as though the instructor didn't know the answer, but it becomes evident as answer after answer is rejected that this is a pretense of inquiry, that the process is simply leading to the answer the instructor wants.

The apparent inquiry is merely a disguised lecture. Students see through this game quickly. Many are put off by it and refuse to play; a few others, adept at reading the instructor's mind, soon become the class's dominant participants. One of the dangers of this type of Socratic method is that it leads to classes in which discussion is limited to the instructor and several "star" pupils.

Quite clearly, some question-and-answer procedures are necessary to generate and direct discussion. But instructors are encouraged to expand class participation by asking more open-ended questions that invite a variety of "right" answers. The topics and instructional apparatus of *America Now* contain many questions designed to elicit more than one answer.

4. *Set Up Collaborative Tasks and Small-Group Activities.* People like to work together — consider how many composition texts are coauthored and coedited. A good way to broaden class participation is to get students working together in small groups. Most composition classes have from fifteen to twenty-five students. Though groups of this size can accommodate lively general discussion, it is sometimes useful to divide the class into several subgroups (preferably four to five per group) to work on specific tasks. These smaller groups can work together to brainstorm ideas, to consider subdivisions of a topic, or to prepare in-class reports.

Another way to expand participation and to organize discussion is the use of panel sessions or forums. These can take a variety of forms, ranging from the delivery of finished papers to brief statements of positions. One of the most practical ways to conduct panel sessions in the classroom is to divide the class into several groups of four to five students to discuss the various subdivisions of a topic. Either in or outside class, each group collaborates on a written response to the topic or takes a position on it. Each group then selects one of its members to participate on a panel in which papers from all of the groups are read for open discussion. Panels introduce students to more organized methods of discussion and expose the class to a wider range of viewpoints. Panel sessions — even very informal ones — take time, however. Instructors who use them should be sure to schedule assignments carefully; a well-constructed panel could take up as many as three class periods. (For more details on setting up panels or forums, see Liz deBeer's article on pp. 12–26 of this manual.)

Though setting up formal debates involves procedures that are outside the scope of this book (and of most composition courses), class discussion can also be enlivened by informal debates. Many topics in *America Now* suggest provocative issues for opposing points of view. If a class is not too large (fifteen students or fewer), it can be divided into two groups for debating purposes; larger classes may need to form smaller groups that come together as teams. As in the panel sessions, each group should select a member to represent its position. If the topic is one students are quite conversant with, impromptu informal debate can be arranged in class. With less familiar topics, outside preparation should be scheduled.

Panels and debates often involve the practical problem of seating arrangements. The most efficient way to set up small groups is to have students cluster their desks together in tight circles. For panel formation and informal debates, several students can bring their desks to the front of the classroom. The average composition classroom, with its instructor's desk set imposingly in front, is perhaps better designed for lecturing than for open discussion. Instructors who want to broaden student participation and interaction may want to experiment with different seating styles. Some instructors, for example, feel that sitting with students at one of their desks facilitates discussion. Others may ask the students to form a large circle of seats and then sit among them. If a class is relatively small and a seminar table is available, its use will generally enhance discussion.

5. *Keep Discussion Linked to Writing.* Though lively group discussion can be an end in itself, the agenda of *America Now* is to use class discussion as a basis for writing. This agenda works two ways: (1) it encourages students to get the composition started in the classroom, and (2) it encourages students to use class discussion as a stimulus and a context for writing.

As you direct class discussion, keep in mind how the discussion can bear directly on the writing assignment. You might want to point out ideas that contain the germ of interesting papers, a tactic that also helps student writers learn how to see ideas emerge. Another way is to periodically focus attention on specific writing strategies as the reading material is discussed. Students almost always want to discuss topics and subjects, rarely techniques and strategies. It is therefore a good idea to initiate discussion by focusing on topics and gradually turn to a consideration of how the writers handled these topics.

From Discussion to Writing

As they prepare to write for college courses, students often confront difficulties that have less to do with the routine tasks of composition — spelling, punctuation, correct grammar — than with the deeper problems of finding something to say and establishing a context in which to say it. It is not uncommon for beginning students to turn in papers that contain few serious errors, yet lack intellectual substance and a clear orientation. Using group discussion as a basis for composition can help remedy these problems. Group discussion can serve as a stimulus for an individual's ideas and provide a meaningful context in which to express them. Furthermore, as we will see, the art of discussion can function in many ways as an important model for the art of writing.

Finding something to say about a topic always ranks high on lists of student writing problems. It is the main reason that the blank sheet of paper or computer screen so often triggers a set of anxious questions: "What can I say?" "Where do I begin?" For many, intellectual panic sets in as the page or screen remains blank, the mind remains blank, and the entire writing process suddenly seems to exist in a total vacuum.

Exploratory discussion offers a solution to this dilemma. Years ago, an advertising executive, Alexander F. Osborn, developed a group method of generating ideas that became enormously popular in many fields. With typical advertising savvy, Osborn gave his technique a memorable name — *brainstorming*. Osborn's goal was to stimulate creativity by presenting a small group of people with a problem topic and then encouraging them to toss off as many ideas about it in as short a time as possible. Speed, spontaneity, and free association were essential to his method. But the most important part of his brainstorming procedure was a complete absence of criticism. No one in the group was allowed to criticize or disagree with any idea, no matter how silly or farfetched it seemed. This absence of criticism, Osborn found, kept ideas flowing, since people were not afraid to sound ill-informed or just plain stupid.

This brainstorming technique can clearly help students come up with ideas to write about. It could be done in the composition classroom for a brief period, or small groups of students could profitably conduct brainstorming sessions on their own. Moreover, most exploratory discussion — if it is free, open, and relaxed — will contain some degree of spontaneous brainstorming in which ideas can sprout and grow. Students who take note of these ideas will find that when they sit down to write they will not be starting out in a vacuum but will have a context of discussion out of which their composition can take shape.

An alternative type of brainstorming can also help students move from class discussion to writing. In this type of brainstorming (sometimes referred to by communication researchers as *nominal* brainstorming), each person, instead of vocalizing ideas in a group, works alone, silently jotting down a brief list of ideas. Afterward, all the lists are compared and, after some culling and combining, individual ideas are listed on a blackboard. This brainstorming method is very useful at the start of a class session in opening up various avenues of discussion. The written list also serves as a tangible source of ideas for individuals to pursue later in their papers.

If exploratory discussion can help reduce the anxiety students face in trying to develop ideas for papers, it can also alleviate another major writing problem — the student's alienation. Thinking and writing alone, with little awareness of an actual audience or of a practical situation, the beginning student often composes papers that sound hollow, disembodied, and disengaged. Ideas seem to come out of nowhere; transitions and connections are missing; conclusions that should grow out of the development of an idea are instead little more than blunt, unearned assertions. Though such papers are common, instructors find it difficult to pinpoint precisely what is wrong with them, since the problems are vague, not easily isolated, and therefore hard to identify by the usual marking symbols. The real problem with such papers is not in the writing but in the orientation of the writer. It is not one of style, structure, or content, but of overall *context*.

Experienced writers, as mentioned earlier, invariably work with a clear sense of audience and occasion. For example, a literature or composition teacher working on a critical article is writing within a clearly definable context: He or she has a sense of who the audience will be, where the article could be published, and — most important — why it is being written. No matter what its subject or point of view, the article will be intellectually oriented to a community of readers presumed to be aware of the topic and attuned to the various points of view involved in its discussion. That so many academic papers are first prepared for delivery at professional conferences underscores the vital importance of a concrete audience and situation.

As students discover the connections between discussion and composition, they will also find their bearings as writers. Their writing — no matter what the topic — will be oriented toward response. Their writing will be not only a response to an assigned topic, but more important, a response made in the context of a continuing discussion of that topic. The student, in other words, writes as an active participant, responding, as she or he would in group discussion, to the actual or anticipated responses of others. This texture of mutual response is what so often gives professionally written essays and articles their mature tone and clear orientation. Instructors might further encourage this climate of response by inviting students to cite comments by other class members in their papers.

Once your students see writing as a form of response, they will become more conscious of their social and intellectual attitudes as writers. Are they closed off to other opinions? Are they overbearing in their attitudes? Do they try to see all sides of an issue? Are they patient with complexity? Do they oversimplify difficult problems? Do they skirt issues? Do they base too much on personal experience? These are all values learned in group discussion that directly carry over into composition.

As your students work through this collection they will observe how participation in group discussion is relevant to all kinds of writing tasks. It is perhaps easy to see how an awareness of conflicting opinions can play an important part in critical, analytical, and argumentative writing. But personal essays can also profit from exploratory group discussion. By discussing their personal experiences, your students can begin to view them from a broader social perspective and to understand them within a context of divergent human experiences.

Composition that is closely linked to lively group discussion reminds students that they are not writing in a vacuum but as part of a group, part of a community. In a written work, as in discussion, someone is always speaking and someone (or some group) is always being addressed. *America Now* encourages your students to view their writing as an extension of group discussion, to see writing as public, not private, behavior, as a social act rather than a solitary one. To think of writing as an extension of discussion, however, students need to reimagine themselves as writers. When they sit down to write they should do so not as isolated individuals anxiously awaiting inspiration but as active participants in a process of communication with others. Students then will not expect ideas for writing to "come out of the blue." Rather, they will expect to find their ideas where they are most likely to originate — out of their considered responses to the ideas of others.

Forming Forums:
Student Presentations to Encourage Research, Discussion, and Better Writing
by Liz deBeer

"The forums give a chance for students to participate verbally and not just listen to the teacher."

"Forums enabled students to get to know each other as they worked in groups."

"Forums made people get up in front of class and talk who otherwise don't talk during class discussion."

"The forums presented lots of good information that I think I would not have learned anywhere else. They provided lots of discussion and I think that was the best part. The class got a chance to communicate about their cultures and share their experiences or anecdotes, which made the class a much better place to be at 8:30 in the morning."

"Forums: Keep doing this!"

As these evaluations reveal, students seem to enjoy my classes and learn the most when they are asked to work in groups and share their ideas with their peers. Panel presentations or forums help give students authority in the classroom and motivation to write in steps. Perhaps just as important, forums motivate teachers like me to listen more to their students. Even students who feared forums because they didn't like to talk in front of the class acknowledged that they benefited from them, as one student wrote: "I found the forums to be very informative and interesting, even though I hated speaking in front of the class."

Forums require students, working in small groups, to research a topic, make presentations, and lead classroom discussion. Forums motivate students to explore topics by interviewing experts, preparing surveys, and analyzing trends, just as the journalists did whose articles appear in *America Now*. This type of research allows students to observe the controversy implicit in most of the topics in the text and prepares them for writing papers that go beyond clichés. On the first day of class, I tell students that forums allow them to teach part of the class; this comment always gets their interest.

Why Bother? The Value of Forums

After my first few years of teaching composition, I realized that I was doing more research than my students to prepare for classes. Exhausted and overwhelmed, I decided to create a course in which the students were responsible for much of the research and, later, the presentation of it. Although several students balked at the idea of speaking in front of their peers, all followed through, which created the most successful classes I had ever taught. In fact, previous students accosted me in the hall demanding to know why we hadn't done forums when they took the course.

There is much research to support the use of collaborative work like forums. Lev Vygotsky's emphasis on collaboration has been well documented, he asserts that students learn from working with others: "With assistance, every child can do more than he can by himself. . . . What a child can do in cooperation today he can do alone tomorrow" (187–88). Douglas Barnes and Frankie Todd reflect on a thirteen-year-old who wonders why the teacher can't just write all the questions and answers on the board so that the students can memorize them. The authors comment that "Such students need opportunities and challenges that will enable them to see learning as constructing an understanding, not as reflecting and repeating ready-made formulae whose implications they have not grasped" (14). Talk is the antidote, according to Barnes and Todd, particularly talk that is student-centered, in which students can "try out new ways of thinking and reshape an idea midsentence, respond immediately to the hints and doubts of others, and collaborate in shaping meanings they could not hope to reach alone" (15). Forums provide students with time to talk about their projects, reconsider their ideas, and listen to new ideas; forums also hold students accountable for their talk, because forums eventually involve presentations and term papers, which are both graded.

In addition, talk in forums is genuine, unlike much classroom "discussion" in which the teacher is searching for someone who can "reproduce what the teacher has presented to them" (Barnes and Todd 15). Jeffrey Wilhelm, reflecting on his own practice and why so many students dislike reading, notes that "If we take the theoretical stance that reading is, in fact, producing meaning, then the way reading education is traditionally practiced in schools must be rethought. . . . [Teachers] must take responses beyond boilerplate questions and 'correct' answers" (10). Wilhelm uses drama and art to teach literature as an active enterprise between students and text; I suggest using forums as an active enterprise between students and *America Now*. Forums rarely disappoint me in my main goal, which is to learn something new —related to the curriculum — from each student, because forums require students to research areas that are often beyond the teacher's knowledge. For example, in past years students did forums on immigration and interviewed people whom I had never met, presenting information that opened my eyes. Other students shared their stories, such as one student who included an anecdote about how she traveled to the United States from Vietnam on a tiny fishing boat.

Forums also challenge teachers to look differently at the common complaint about lack of resources (Moll). Forums motivated me to embrace the community as a resource; forums became a way to reach beyond the classroom door and windows — which are usually shut — and connect student worlds to the text. Luis Moll calls this "mobilizing funds of knowledge" (231). Although he is referring to a program in which community members physically enter the classroom to teach their special skills, forums use students as facilitators of these "funds of knowledge" through their research, which often involves surveys and interviews. For example, in past years, forums on parenting resulted in students presenting research on parenting in other cultures, much of which was unfamiliar to me.

Research strongly suggests that group work can increase tolerance among diverse students, assuming the group work has "highly valued goals that could not be obtained without cooperation" (Schofield 13). However, research also suggests that if group work is not well planned and valued by the teacher, students may not take the tasks seriously (Weinstein). In fact, many teachers suggest that they do not use group work for fear of losing order (Weinstein). I have never experienced difficulty with classroom management when using forums, mainly, I believe, because so many students preferred forums to lectures. Moreover, since the group work led to graded work, students knew that if they were unproductive during group work, they might not have a successful forum or a strong paper.

Steps: Preparing Students

Because forums follow the philosophy behind process writing, there are several steps involved. Four major writing activities are involved during the semester. First, students brainstorm in small groups for ideas and strategies for researching and presenting information effectively, writing ideas on the sign-up sheet and in their notebooks. Then, they write a two-page paper that summarizes and analyzes the student's individual topic, which is handed in the day of the presentation and is summarized for the student's forum presentation. (Time limits may be necessary.) Each presenter should also prepare a discussion question on the subtopic being presented. Students who are not presenting must hand in a one-page critical response to each forum other than their own, to be turned in at the class following each forum. This paper should evaluate the effectiveness of each presentation — not summarize it. Finally, students in composition classes must write a research paper based on the data gathered for their forum presentation. (Basic skills instructors may choose to eliminate this step.) This paper should involve more sources, more analysis, more detail, and better editing than the two-page paper.

A typical syllabus for my 101 composition class, which meets for one semester, includes four or five forum topics, with five or six students as members of each group. I organize my syllabus by beginning with a few lectures in which I describe my goals and allow students time to research and prepare their projects. I spend several class periods preparing students for these forums at least two weeks before the first group's topic is due. We spend one class period working on interviewing skills, usually based on a topic from *America Now*. For example, I might begin the semester with "Our Clothing: Does It Matter What We Wear?" and ask students to interview somebody about his or her clothing choices. Then, students would be assigned to write an essay using a few quotes from the interviewee and possibly one essay from *America Now* as a supplement to the paper. Because many of the students interview an expert for their forum presentation, I like to assign one interviewing project well before the forum projects are due.

I schedule one week (or two class periods of 80 minutes each) for each forum topic. For the first class, students are asked to read the unit in *America Now* that covers the assigned topic, and we then analyze the articles and write on each topic in our notebooks. The second class is a student forum based on the same topic. The entire class period is devoted to presentations and discussion led by five students who are in charge of that topic. I organize my syllabus so that students are working on their projects at the same time. I usually reserve a class period in the middle of the projects for an in-class exam. We spend the rest of the semester concentrating on peer reviews, punctuation, writing, reading, and test-taking skills, and work on other small projects like the ones described in *America Now*. Usually I reorganize the table of contents to meet the needs of my syllabus.

I choose forum topics based on which issues I believe will most interest students and create the most compelling forum presentations. Because the material in *America Now* addresses current events, many students are already thinking about the issues they are asked to write about. Instructors should capitalize on students' interests and concerns when choosing broad topics for the forums. If students are concerned about body image, then this is a good topic for a forum. If issues about stereotypes have been debated regularly on the news or in the student paper, then this topic will have special appeal. Much of this evaluation of topics depends on a school's geography and demographics. I rely on past students' essays and discussion to gauge popular topics. Although all topics in *America Now* will interest most students, the ideal forum topic is one that students will be compelled to spend more than one class period discussing. The topic should be broad enough so that several students can explore different angles and should be covered by accessible research sources. The topics I picked from *America Now* are names, body image, gender differences, role models, and stereotypes. (Since gender differences is a separate topic, I might avoid addressing this issue in the stereotypes forum.)

At the beginning of the semester, I write on the board four or five forum topics chosen from issues addressed in *America Now* and ask that each student pick one. Through this process, the small groups are formed. For example, all students who pick the topic gender differences will work together on a forum for that topic. Because groups should be approximately the same size to allow for different angles to be addressed on each issue, instructors should limit the number of students allowed to pick each topic.

When groups have been formed, I hand each one a sign-up sheet with the chosen topic written on top. Then, each group member picks a subtopic or angle that relates to the general topic and lists some possible sources that will be used to research it. Students should be reminded that their research may require them to alter the proposed topic or sources.

Although I encourage students to create their own ideas for topics and sources, I provide each small group with some ideas to model how to create a specific topic from a broad one as well as some sources that might be applicable to the general topic. I usually give each group a separate handout along with the sign-up sheet. Examples of my ideas for approaching topics appear at the end of this essay.

At this point, I dedicate a whole class period to reviewing forums so students know what I expect. Although I define forums briefly before students pick their topics and subtopics, I define forums in more detail once students know what area they will be researching. After defining forums for at least the second time, I explain how students should prepare their research, presentations, and class discussion. I discuss the importance of asking questions that elicit thoughtful responses and of asking follow-up questions, both during their research and during presentations. I explain how I evaluate forums based on whether presentations — and written reports — are focused and informative, and I discuss the value of current sources. Since students have usually begun to work on their projects, they are encouraged to ask specific questions.

At the next class period, groups meet for the second time so that students can discuss their plans for research and their overall strategy. Instructors should visit each group to learn of individual concerns and should discuss wider concerns with the whole class. Often, group members discuss their fears of talking in front of others. I try to point out the value of speaking skills and sometimes encourage students to participate in later forums so that they can see other students do presentations before they take a turn.

After this meeting, students must conduct their research and prepare their presentations. I ask that they write a two-page (typed, double-spaced) report on their forum topic that includes at least one source other than *America Now*. Those sources may include books, magazines, interviews, or even personal experience. If students use personal experience as a source, they must also use one other source. To document their sources, I require a typed "works cited" page. Students may read from their papers, but they may not read the whole paper or they will go over their allotted time, and it is imperative to save time for class discussion. Remind them not to use names of people interviewed if the topic involves personal material, as might be the case in a presentation on stereotypes, for instance.

Letting Go: Letting Students Learn

Perhaps the greatest challenge for instructors working with forums is allowing students to research and explore topics on their own and working in groups during class time. This doesn't *feel* like teaching, but it is. If we want students to actually say something meaningful, as Berthoff suggests in *The Making of Meaning,* we must leave them alone to make their own discoveries. As Bartholomae and Petrosky write in *Facts, Artifacts, and Counterfacts,* "A course in reading and writing whose goal is to empower students must begin with a silence, a silence students must fill" (7). When students conduct interviews, research their forum topics, or lead class discussion, they are literally filling the silence. Forum projects allow students to think for themselves, to take risks. All this, of course, leads to better writing.

Usually, students ask for little help. Most of them are eager to interview people they know or to find their own sources. Occasionally, students panic and ask me to help with library research, particularly those with limited library experience. However, once I have given them enough pointers to get started, I try to leave them alone. Often, during such periods of silence, I observe students working together. Such collaboration confirms my belief that students learn not only from me and from sources, but from each other.

Other experiences have reinforced my belief in the value of forums and have helped me get through the waiting and worrying period. One student, who appeared to be half-asleep during much of the class time preceding the forums, became so involved and excited at interviewing his Vietnam-veteran uncle for a forum on the gun-control debate forum that he suddenly sparkled, waking up enough to complete and pass the course. Similarly, a student who lived in a local subsidized housing development ("projects") admitted to me later that he planned on dropping my class due to an overloaded schedule, but, instead, he stuck it out, comparing and contrasting attitudes about guns from ten males from the projects who did not attend college and ten males who did attend college, drawing conclusions about guns and lack of hope. He admitted that the reason he stayed in the course was because he felt impelled to work on his forum project and felt his dual background was valued in the class.

Teacher as Listener

I like to start with a forum on an accessible topic such as names or gender differences because these topics make students think critically about something with which they are already familiar. Although (or because) students' experiences vary, these topics should prompt a lot of class discussion. Students who are in these forum groups may interview campus counselors or social workers. One student might survey two generations' attitudes about gender and compare results or split the survey into two social or cultural groups. (Other ideas appear at the end of this essay.)

Some students may resent it if their group has to present first, but others actually like to "get it out of the way." Once, when a student in the first forum group was unable to finish his research, I moved him to a different topic that was due toward the end of the semester. However, I discourage such behavior by telling the class that I will give an "F" to students who do not perform on the due date, unless they can be excused because of an extreme circumstance. Only once did a student miss the deadline without an excuse, I allowed her to hand in her written paper and I averaged the "F" for the presentation with the written project.

On the day of the presentation, I take attendance and sit in the back of the class. The group presenting moves to the front of the room and presents its reports. At this point, the class asks questions only for clarification so that there is time for everyone to present. Students who are not presenting should be taking notes for their one-page critical response to the forum. This should not be a simple summary. (Students don't have to write a critical paper on their own forum topic or on the topics of those in their group. When all the students have presented, I average all of the critical responses to equal one paper grade.)

After the students have finished their presentations, the rest of the class may ask questions. Sometimes, presenters need to ask the class a question to prompt discussion. I prefer to keep quiet and let the presenters lead the discussion, but sometimes I'll intervene when I feel it's necessary. Often, I have to remind myself to let the students talk, to let them fill the silence. I usually learn from these discussions. In one class, a student from Nigeria responded to a parenting forum presentation about how divorced American men are fighting to get custody of their children. The Nigerian student commented that in his country it is the norm for divorced men to have custody of the children. This led to a discussion of cultural issues concerning gender roles.

Occasionally, students make poor presentations. In the weakest one I have seen, a bright woman simply chatted for a few minutes without presenting material from any source. Another student twisted data about rape so that it sounded like the violence was justified by the victim's flirtatious behavior. In both instances, the students learned from their peers' responses and my commentary on their papers, and their final research papers reflected their understanding. Much of this learning process occurs during the discussion following the presentations. Even a blunt comment, like "Why do you always call the rape victim 'she'?" can lead to a discussion about improving writing.

It is common for students to present too much general information without specific examples, to make rough transitions, or to analyze data inadequately. These problems can also be remedied with helpful commentary from fellow students and the instructor.

Because the forum project involves writing in steps, I rarely receive plagiarized or sloppy papers. Before I used the forums, students often had only one chance to write their final research papers and no time to learn from their mistakes. By presenting their ideas and research orally before writing a final research paper, students have time to think and rethink. They learn to value their audience by striving to be clear, concise, and original. Since the projects are staggered, I can spend more time on the two-page papers, offering advice about revising for the final research paper.

When students write critical responses to their peers' presentations, they learn to analyze. One student commented that "I tended to . . . learn more from the people who analyzed their information rather than the ones who dictated the information to the class." Another wrote that "when [presenters] read off a sheet of paper, they were boring. . . . I feel you must get the audience involved." These comments reveal that students were able to learn important writing lessons from the oral presentations.

Other student comments revealed that they enjoyed the forums. One wrote, "Forums are an excellent learning device. . . . Students taught students about what they had researched." Another reported that "the forums . . . forced the speakers to really know their topics. . . . I feel that a majority of the people got really involved in their subjects, enabling them to learn more about it than if they just read it out of a book. Also, the forums showed that how you say your information is important. You must try to catch the interest of your audience."

These remarks show how eager students are to fill the silence of the classroom, as long as we instructors are willing to give up some of our control. If we empower our students, they can provide the classroom with much more knowledge than any one person alone.

Works Cited

Barnes, Douglas, and Frankie Todd. *Communication and Learning Revisited: Making Meaning Through Talk.* Portsmouth, NH: Boynton/Cook, 1995.

Bartholomae, David, and Anthony Petrosky. *Facts, Artifacts, and Counterfacts: Theory and Method for a Reading and Writing Course.* Portsmouth, N.H.: Boynton/Cook, 1986.

Berthoff, Ann E. *The Making of Meaning.* Upper Montclair, N.J.: Boynton/Cook, 1981.

Moll, Luis. "Literacy Research in Community and Classrooms: A Sociological Approach." *Theoretical Models and the Process of Reading.* 4th ed. Eds. R. B. Ruddell, M. R. Ruddell, and H. Singer. Newark, DE: IRA, 1994. 211–44.

Schofield, Janet W. *Black & White in School: Trust, Tension or Tolerance?* New York: Teacher's College Press, 1989.

Vygotsky, Lev. *Thought and Language.* Cambridge, MA: MIT Press, 1987.

Weinstein, Carol. S. *Secondary Classroom Management: Lessons from Research and Practice.* New York: McGraw-Hill, 1987.

Wilhelm, Jeffrey D. *"You Gotta Be the Book": Teaching Engaged and Reflective Reading with Adolescents.* Urbana, IL: NCTE, 1995.

Overview of Ideas and Suggestions for Forum Topics

Names (Unit 1)

Sources for Forums

- Read Kaplan and Bernays's *The Language of Names* (excerpted in this unit).

- Review genealogy Web site: <www.inland.net> (cited in Kadaba's article).

- Read biographies or autobiographies of people who changed their names, such as Malcolm X, Marilyn Monroe, Prince, Muhammad Ali.

- Read Sheila Walker's "What's in a Name" *Ebony*, volume 32, June 1977, pp. 74–76.

- Read P. Robert Paustian's "The Evolution of Personal Naming Practices among American Blacks," *Names*, volume 26, 1978, pp. 177–91.

- Interview psychology professors, sociology professors, women's studies professors, or Black studies professors or other members of the Ethnic Studies Department, including Native Americans, Asians, and so on.

- Consult newspapers and magazines, past and present, that offer advice on naming (especially parenting magazines).

- Review naming books.

- Survey people to learn why they were given their first names or the meaning of their last names.

- Interview religious leaders.

Possible Forum Topics

- How do people pick names for their children?

- Discuss naming trends and compare at least two different time periods.

- What does the Bible say about naming? Who follows that advice?

- Compare two cultures to learn about the differences in naming customs and why those differences might exist.

- Discuss why people change their names, focusing on one person's story.

- Survey people about what they would change their name to if they could.
- Consider names of inanimate objects, such as cars, schools, companies, and so on. Research the background of one name.
- Consider how people name pets and research this topic.
- Interview an author or a researcher and ask how she develops names or pseudonyms.
- Survey new parents about how they picked their children's names.
- Analyze why some people are so fascinated by their ancestor's names, such as people who search the Web to find others who have the same (remote) ancestry.

Body Image (Unit 3)

Sources for Forums

- Read *The Beauty Myth* by Naomi Wolf (excerpted in this unit).
- Interview student-health personnel.
- Interview hotline workers about anorexia or bulimia.
- Interview body builders.
- Research people who have changed their bodies: read biographies or autobiographies of people like Oprah, Michael Jackson, or people who have had sex changes or cosmetic surgery.
- Research the history of dieting, cosmetic surgery, Barbie, or G.I. Joe.
- Interview professors in women's studies, history, economics, or nursing.
- Survey people about various topics discussed in this unit, including Barbie, cosmetic surgery, magazines like *Playboy,* and so on.
- Consult newspapers and magazines, past and current.
- Interview someone you know who has changed his or her body.
- Interview your high school nurse and ask about anorexia or bulimia.

Possible Forum Topics

- Why do people dislike their bodies?
- Who tends to change their bodies?
- What are the most common types of cosmetic surgeries? Why?
- Do current events affect the way people feel about their bodies? Have attitudes about bodies changed over time?

- Do different cultures have different attitudes about bodies? Do some cultures think obesity is attractive, for example?

- Research and analyze the "hottest" stars. Compare and contrast the reports noting what has changed over at least a twenty year time period.

- Report on someone who has changed his or her body significantly.

- Analyze the differences (or lack of them) between popular male and female magazines available at the supermarket or the public library. Are the articles more or less about body image?

Gender Differences (Unit 4)

Sources for Forums

- Read *Reviving Ophelia* by Mary Pipher (excerpted in this unit).

- Read *The Great Divide: How Females and Males Really Differ* by Daniel Evan Weiss (New York: Poseidon Press, 1991).

- Read *The Myth of Two Minds: What Gender Means and Doesn't Mean* by Beryl Lieff Benderly (New York: Doubleday, 1987).

- Read *Failing at Fairness: How America's Schools Cheat Girls* by Myra and David Sadker (New York: Charles Scribner, 1994).

- Read *Newsweek*'s "Boys Will Be Boys," May 11, 1998, pp. 54-60.

- Survey two specific groups about what feminism or gender roles mean to them.

- Interview a women's studies professor, anthropology professor, sociology professor, or biology professor.

- Read a book or article by bell hooks, Gloria Steinem, Urvashi Vaid, Naomi Wolf, Margaret Mead, Deborah Tannen, or John Gray.

- Observe play at a day-care center and apply theories.

- Consult newspapers or magazines, past and current.

Possible Forum Topics

- How do gender roles differ among cultures?

- How do observers' own cultural gender roles affect data collected?

- When does learning about gender roles begin? How does it begin?

- Do males and females really differ? How? Is this conclusion always true?

- How has history changed the way any one society views gender roles?

- How do toys differ for boys and girls? Books? Movies? Television? Clothes? How do these differences affect children? Do these differ among cultures and time periods?

- Is it possible to be androgynous? Think of a person who is. How is he/she received by society?

- How might people surveyed react to a controversial quote chosen from one of the articles? Analyze their reactions.

- How are characters received in movies when they are deviating from traditional gender roles, such as in *Thelma and Louise* or *Mrs. Doubtfire*? Read critics' reviews.

- How do divorce, work, religion, school, sports, and so on reflect gender roles?

- Analyze the gender roles in popular comic strips; relate the comics to the essays in this unit.

- Analyze who talks the most in various classes — boys or girls. To avoid missing notes ask an instructor's permission to sit in on a class, you normally do not attend. (Consult Sadker and Sadker's *Failing at Fairness*.)

Role Models (Unit 6)

Sources for Forums

- Read the chapters on folk heroes in Elizabeth R. Simons's *Student Worlds, Student Words* (1980).

- Read William Bennett's *The Children's Book of Heroes*.

- Read various versions of the same fairy or folk tale; also read an analysis of the tale, such as in *Tatterhood and Other Tales* edited by Ethel J. Phelps (1978).

- Interview sociology professors, psychology professors, women's studies professors, and political science professors.

- Consult newspapers or magazines, past and current.

- Read the chapter on history in Sadker and Sadker's *Failing at Fairness* (1994).

- Read Asante's discussion of Afrocentric education (1991), "The Afrocentric Idea of Education," *Journal of Negro Education,* pp. 170–80. Read critics of Asante's ideas, such as Diana Ravich (Summer, 1990) *The American Scholar.*

Possible Forum Topics

- Survey attitudes about heroes from two generations or two cultures.

- Anaylze books that list heroes (like William Bennett's) and evaluate the choice of heroes.

- Discuss the difference between folk heroes and media heroes (Simons).

- Discuss how a hero is made — consider Asante, Ravich, Sadker and Sadker, and Simons.

- Discuss how heroes alter over time; read the biography of a hero, including presidents, sports heroes, political heroes, pop heroes, and so on. Discuss one hero's rise and possibly his or her fall.

- Discuss how heroes are depicted in children's fiction, such as fairy tales (see Phelps and various children's books and movies).

- Interview someone on campus who may be considered a hero, like the class president, the football star, a survivor of cancer.

Stereotypes (Unit 7)

Sources for Forums

- Read *American Dreams: Lost and Found* by Studs Terkel (New York: Ballantine, 1980).

- Read autobiographies of new immigrants or minorities, like *The Autobiography of Malcolm X, The Woman Warrior* by Maxine Hong Kingston, *Farewell to Manzanar* by Jeanne Wakatsuki Houston, or anything by Elie Wiesel.

- Survey two groups of people, such as two generations, to determine what they feel are America's views about stereotypes.

- Interview people who experienced stereotyping, even a Holocaust survivor or other victim of racial intolerance.

- Interview a history professor, sociology professor, or psychology professor.

- Consult books, magazines, newspapers, or documentaries, including *Teaching Tolerance* or *Klan Watch,* magazines from the Southern Poverty Law Center.

- Review <www.splcenter.org.> (Web site of Southern Poverty Law Center).

- Visit museums like the Holocaust Museum in Washington, D.C. or a similar one that is local.

Possible Forum Topics

- What are the current laws involving stereotypes and hiring practices?

- What are past laws?

- Describe hate groups, either in the United States or other countries, past or present.

- How are various groups viewed by popular culture, such as movies and television. You may wish to focus on one group and analyze two time periods, such as how the Chinese are depicted in Susie Wong movies versus *The Joy Luck Club* (1993).

- How have people attacked negative stereotypes?

- Do stereotypes vary from country to country?

- Can stereotypes be positive?

- Analyze and discuss some of the stories in Studs Terkel's *American Dreams: Lost and Found,* perhaps comparing some of them to stories in *America Now* or to your own experiences.

- Report on someone who fought against stereotyping, such as Malcolm X, Rosa Parks, Mohandas Gandhi, or Gloria Steinem.

- Consider how stereotypes affected "objective" studies by reviewing selections from Stephen Jay Gould's *Mismeasure of Man.*

1
What's in a Name?

America Now begins with a unit on names because, of course, everybody has one. Surely all your students have made some sort of judgment about someone — a public figure or private individual — based on that person's name. (What would your students picture if they knew they were about to meet Charles Emerson Winchester III?) We buy (or don't buy) Nike sneakers based not only on the quality, but also on the name of the product. We go to see movies based not only on their titles, but also on the names of the stars in them. Consider, too, how many public figures have changed their names for effect.

One way into this unit is to consider the cliché "you can't judge a book by its cover" in conjunction with the quotation from Shakespeare's Juliet: "What's in a name? that which we call a rose/By any other name would smell as sweet." Both quotations question to what degree we can understand the essence of something from its surface appearance or by what we name it — likely a popular idea among students.

But the essays in this unit seem to suggest that names have considerable meaning. Indeed, each essay pays ample attention to the import of names and how those names affect that to which they refer. Lini S. Kadaba's "What's in a Name" discusses how our names — in particular our last names — affect our understanding of our heritage and, therefore, ourselves. And Denise Sherer Jacobson in "David" — though tending to pay more attention to pronunciation — does touch on how her inability to pronounce her own name altered her self-perception. More broadly, Robert Zeis examines the political and historical issues affected by naming public spaces and institutions.

So what is the power of names? You may want to start this unit with a general discussion of names. If you are using this unit at the beginning of your semester, it might be a fun, ice-breaking activity to have students write their first and last names on separate pieces of paper and then to distribute the first and last names randomly among the class. As students introduce themselves with the random composite names, the people to whom the names actually belong could stand up and claim them. This will give you and the class a chance to attach names with people, and students will have a chance to meet and talk to one another. Additionally, the activity opens the door for a discussion about what it was like to use a false name and, conversely, what it was like to have one's name used by another person.

For some perspective on names, this unit's "From the Bookshelf" selection, *The Language of Names*, will provide interesting information on names and celebrities, history, class, race, and ethnicity.

LINI S. KADABA, What's in a Name?

Vocabulary/Using a Dictionary

1. The root of each word is *genius*. Ingenuity is the noun form of the adjective *ingenious*, which means "clever and inventive."

2. Mecca, considered to be the holiest city of Islam, is the site of pilgrimage for Muslims. The name is used metaphorically as a noun to describe any other gathering place.

3. *Melange*, a mixture, is derived from the French word, *mesler*, which itself means "to mix," recalling, in this essay, the American myth of the melting pot.

Responding to Words in Context

1. *Anesthesia* literally means "without sensation" and is a combination of the Greek *aisthesis*, meaning "feeling" and the negative prefix *an*, meaning "without." Anesthesia in English generally refers to the effects of an anesthetic but can also be used generally to simply mean "loss of sensation."

2. Students will doubtless be able to come up with many English words that have been adopted from other languages and Anglicized — from names to words like *hors d'oeuvres*. It may be interesting to pick several words from the article such as *bureaucracy* (para. 15) and discuss the possible origins based on the word's sound and context.

Discussing Main Point and Meaning

1. According to the article, an increasing number of people are changing their "Anglicized" names to an ethnic version to get in touch with their roots, or to both acknowledge and pay homage to their heritage (before their ancestors — or they, themselves — immigrated to America).

2. Dr. Anastasiou, though interested in acknowledging his Greek heritage, recognizes the difficulties the extra syllable in his name would cause, namely in pronunciation and the placement of his name toward the back of the phone book.

3. The author doesn't editorialize much beyond stating that "the very notion of what it means to be American is changing." Kadaba, generally pointing to the shift toward what Henry Giroux calls "pluralism rather than . . . homogeneity" and "a dangerous time," lets her sources do the talking.

Examining Sentences, Paragraphs, and Organization

1. By repeating the word *names* as the first word of these three consecutive sentences, Kadaba not only emphasizes the import of the word toward her main point, but also shows the many functions of names beyond the obvious. Rhythmically, she creates a climax to her essay and signals a conclusion before discussing Kaplan and Bernays.

2. Kadaba's article appeared first as a newspaper column in the *Philadelphia Inquirer*, and it is generally written within the conventions of journalism, including a relatively objective narrative voice and many quotations. The quotations add credibility to the content, especially as compared with a number of the opinion pieces sprinkled through *America Now*, written without quotations and by clearly biased authors.

3. The "human interest" beginning of this essay will probably engage your students — if not in content, then in narrative style. It is an interesting story about a person who is doing an interesting thing. As an introduction, this narrative piece also sets the tone of the speaker as a *raconteur*, credibly relating whatever will follow.

Thinking Critically

1. Considering Giroux's quotation in paragraph 19 that "it is a dangerous time," many of your students may be on the lookout for parts of the "stew or goulash" that is unsavory. As a critical exercise, you may want to frame a discussion of this question by first defining what Kadaba means by "ethnic pride mov[ing] to the front burner" and then by discussing the larger social ramifications of such a move.

2. Kadaba's assertion that "none of us can escape our past" seems to imply that our past is something bad enough to require escape from, and then counters this assertion with "or, apparently, want to." Is Kadaba implying that we should want to escape our past? Certainly your students will have differing opinions on the extent to which memory of heritage affects America now — and differing opinions about how much is too much or too little.

In-Class Writing Activities

1. Many students will know the meanings, if any, of their names. The names Smith, McGowen, or Schmidt (as we know from the article) all mean "one who works with steel." Many names, however, will have no meaning — or will have meanings that are not readily apparent. You may want to discuss the impact (if any) of having a name that doesn't have a literal translation. What is the difference between names that mean something and names that don't?

2. Making a family tree may require resources that students do not have — or are not aware of. However, many students will have a fairly clear idea

of their own genealogy. Discussion of these students' heritages may prompt other students to go looking. There are many genealogy sites on the Internet where interested students can look up the origins of their names. Some require a fee, but a number of the sites are free. You can refer students to <http://www.connix.com/~ettinger/gen.htm> which is a list of genealogy resources on the Internet.

DENISE SHERER JACOBSON, David

Vocabulary/Using a Dictionary

1. *Sound* in *resound* has more stress than *re* and leaves the reader (listener) with the primary idea of the word. *Re,* though coming first, takes less stress and so alters, rather than overpowers *sound.*

2. From the Greek *ek,* meaning "out of" and *kentron* meaning "center," *eccentric* literally means "out of center." If your students tell of some eccentric characters they know, as surely they all do, it may be productive to talk about how the behavior of those people is "off center" and how that relates to our understanding of the word.

3. Jacobson's recollection of her doting Aunt Dinah is humorous and perhaps archetypal — everybody has an "Aunt Dinah" in the family. It may be interesting to note, then, that *dote* is from the Middle English word *doten,* meaning "to dote." What is the cultural significance of a word that has stayed almost exactly the same in meaning and spelling for many centuries?

Responding to Words in Context

1. The irony of Jacobson's and her husband's ability to only pronounce each other's names lies in the usually understood notion that we should be able to pronounce our own names — to pronounce our identities.

2. As a metaphor, *suffocating* describes Aunt Dinah's love quite appropriately. Not only was there too much love for Jacobson to breathe, figuratively, the love manifested itself in full-bosomed and fleshy-armed hugs that literally kept the air from Jacobson and her sister, suffocating them (to a certain degree).

Discussing Main Point and Meaning

1. The title of the essay — as do the first several paragraphs — gives little away in terms of the essay's theme. Is the essay "David" a song of praise for a lover or a tribute to a statue or a biblical figure? How does this withholding of information affect our reading of the essay? Perhaps by making us wonder for so long just what the essay is about, Jacobson forces us to rethink the word *David* in a different light.

2. Jacobson and her husband are nervous when introducing themselves because they aren't able to pronounce their own names. Chances are that your students will report that, if put in the same situation, they, too, would be nervous. Would they be embarrassed not being able to pronounce their own names (something most people take for granted)?

3. Though *David* is a boy's name, Jacobson and her husband chose it because, not only was it easy for them to say, but because it began with the letter *D*, as does *Dinah*. Naming their baby in a tribute to Jacobson's Aunt Dinah appeases Jacobson's guilt because she is finally returning the unrequited love of her aunt.

Examining Sentences, Paragraphs, and Organization

1. Jacobson may begin her essay with her own quotations so that the reader can experience her direct speech without needing to consider her pronunciation. From the outset, the reader knows that she can say her son's name easily.

2. By beginning each of the first three paragraphs with the word *David*, Jacobson lets us know her relationship to David and gives us a chance to see just how often she uses the word (each of the three uses is a direct quotation from her). Thus, she points out what may not be entirely obvious to all readers: just how important it is in everyday life to be able to pronounce a name.

3. If the last paragraph of this essay were switched with the first, the reader would have a better understanding of the issues related to the name *David* — though certainly not a full one. Jacobson's last paragraph is an excellent conclusion. It doesn't restate the thesis of the essay, but instead resolves, or concludes, a number of issues raised throughout the essay.

Thinking Critically

1. Although it is a surprise to find out in paragraph 5 that Jacobson and her husband have cerebral palsy, Jacobson does provide some hints. She cites, for example, that her "top priority . . . went to selecting a name that Neil and I could clearly pronounce," hinting that there are mitigating circumstances otherwise out of the ordinary in name selection. That she waits until relatively late to reveal the crucial fact of her article gives us a chance to approach her story without the bias that her voice, or the fact of her cerebral palsy, might invoke.

2. In choosing a "nice, *solid* name" (emphasis added), Jacobson calls attention to her cerebral palsy and gives a hint that, though she has obviously overcome difficulty in dealing with her condition, she hopes her son has the virtue of physical strength ("who even slew a giant") as well as mental strength. You may want to engage your students in a discussion at

this point of how imporant names can be in shaping identity. Will David be "nice" and "solid"? Are there examples to the contrary?

In-Class Writing Activities

1. So many names of people and places in America have ties to the Bible that this question will undoubtedly spark some discussion. Similarly, names from many other cultures also may carry religious weight. You may want to discuss with your class the effects of naming as a means of passing on religious belief. What connections, if any, are there among the names, the people the names represent, and the beliefs somehow inherent in the names?

2. Jacobson points out the difficulties in doing things that many people may take for granted. For example, recall how long it takes Jacobson to get dressed. Some difficulties Jacobson describes cause other difficulties that she points out in subtle ways. Note the seemingly trivial comment "I was hard on clothes" (para. 18). Ask your students to visualize a day in which they are Jacobson or her husband. What other words might cause them trouble?

ROBERT ZEIS, What's in a Name? Revisionist History Revisited

Vocabulary/Using a Dictionary

1. By calling up visions of sharpness and clarity, the word *crystal* in *crystallize*, coupled with the suffix *ize*, meaning "to cause to be or become," gives us a clear picture of the metaphorical meaning of the word — "to make clear, or exemplify."

2. The metaphor *short-sighted* literally means "not able to see far away." Many of your students may not recognize this at first glance as a metaphor because it has come to have only its metaphoric meaning: "not able to visualize and plan for the future or the larger picture of an issue." Discussing this word may give you a chance to point out other similar metaphors that we take as literal speech.

3. Many of your students will probably have performed a litmus test in a science class. Here, used in its common metaphoric sense, the *litmus test* is a descriptive term for what is happening. Discuss with your students the pink or blue relationship that suggests a thing is either acidic or basic (with minor variations within).

Responding to Words in Context

1. Students will surely be able to come up with several "norms" of American society, their campus, and classroom. It may be difficult to negotiate a discussion that could bring up strong feelings about the validity of certain norms. It may also be lively. Consider how the United States has

historically conceived of norms and what happens, if anything, to those who deviate. For some productive social perspective, you may want to also discuss non-American sets of norms — those from other nationalities, religious groups, and so on.

2. When discussing the word *shortcoming,* you may want to refer back to "Vocabulary/Using a Dictionary," question 2, about *short-sighted.* What does *shortcoming* mean literally? How can that be applied to its figurative use here and in everyday speech?

Discussing Main Point and Meaning

1. The title of this piece is straight-forward if the reader already has an understanding of "Revisionist History" and how it is generally received. Even without this understanding, however, readers may notice the apparent contradiction in the terms *revisionist* and *history.* In any case, the word *revisited* may reveal that the author will be providing arguments against Revisionist History.

2. Students may or may not agree with Zeis's assertion that it "was a foolish idea to name a school after an obviously evil person" considering some of the issues Zeis, himself, raises. Zeis is drawing an arbitrary line between those whose "accomplishments . . . outweigh their shortcomings" (para. 7). It has been argued, in fact, that owning slaves is such an egregious offense against humanity that no accomplishments could outweigh it. These arguments aside (or still in the air), you may want to ask your students who Zeis believes (and who they believe) should decide whose accomplishments outweigh their shortcomings.

3. As summed up in his conclusion, Zeis believes that judging past figures on current social standards is Revisionist History and is wrong. Furthermore, in order to understand history and historical figures, we should be willing to accept them as flawed human beings and weigh their accomplishments against their shortcomings.

Examining Sentences, Paragraphs, and Organization

1. Zeis's repetition of the word *clearly* in this paragraph adds rhetorical credence to his point — he states his opinions as facts. Furthermore, the word *clearly* signals an implicit understanding with the reader, as if to say, "this is a fact that we both understand." In a way, it's a trick (and a common one) to convince a reader of the "factual" validity of an opinion.

2. Zeis's last paragraph sums up his arguments particularly well, bringing the essay from the specific instances of naming schools to the broader issues of Revisionist History, patriotism, and understanding our past leaders within the context of their flaws and accomplishments.

3. By delaying his discussion of "the real issue at stake," Zeis has several paragraphs in which to discuss each specific instance — the Forrest school and the Washington school — in which to contrast them, and in which to interest readers. When he finally brings the issue into a larger context, his audience has already made an investment in resolving the issue.

Thinking Critically

1. It may be productive when discussing Zeis's notion of "Revisionist History" to find out how others have characterized it. Zeis seems to be saying that revising our understanding of history is wrong. Yet his essay is predicated on revising our understanding of past political figures as flawed human beings. How does this affect your students' understanding of the lines Zeis is drawing?

2. Zeis seems to put emphasis on honoring heroes of a certain type. If your students can define the various shades of judgment Zeis uses, they may find it easier to note how Zeis himself judges historically significant individuals. And they may find it easier to agree or disagree with either all or part of his system of judgment. It may be interesting to research George Washington and Nathan Bedford Forrest beyond what this essay provides and to weigh as a class their accomplishments versus their shortcomings.

In-Class Writing Activities

1. It might be interesting to assign the research for this activity as a homework assignment, dividing the class in groups to research the same figures. When it is time to discuss their faults versus their contributions, students will be able to see the differing assessments of such figures within their own class, and also from one historical account to the next.

2. In a brainstorming session, have students develop lists of people who would be eligible as the namesake for, say, the administration building of the college. As a class, it may be productive to stop after brainstorming and come to a classwide "agreement" on what the criteria are for eligibility alone. It may be instructive and fun to come to a class consensus on whom the building should be named after. In this scenario, draft a letter written collaboratively and discuss the process as well as the final draft.

Discussing the Unit

Preparing for Class Discussion

1. In discussing this question, you may wish first to focus the discussion on certain types of names and then move on to different groups. Try beginning with product names that your students are familiar with such as

Levi or Nike. This discussion could easily switch from brand names to the names of actors and actresses, political figures, etc. Do the sounds of the names affect your students, or does social context tend to carry more weight?

2. It's interesting that, for Jacobson, the pronunciation of her son's name *David* was primary in her selection of the name. Secondary (though important enough to warrant some space in her essay) is the name's significance — its allusion to the biblical King David and Jacobson's aunt, Dinah. Contrast Jacobson with Lini Kadaba's Dr. Anastasiou, who made his name more difficult to pronounce in order to give more weight to its cultural significance. Consider, too, that Dr. Anastasiou also considered the commercial aspects of choosing his name — something that Jacobson does not contemplate.

From Discussion to Writing

1. Of course, students' responses to this question will vary considerably. In discussing their answers, you might keep a running tally of what criteria in name selection are important to students. Discussing such a tally could provide an approach for summing up the unit by classifying the essays into one or more categories.

2. Students no doubt will have very different opinions about the historical significance of names. Ask students whether they think Washington, D.C., is an appropriate name for the United States capital. How would they feel if the name were changed? How would other countries react?

3. When preparing students for this question, be sure to refer them to this unit's introduction, if not to *Romeo and Juliet*, which may serve as a jumping-off point for discussion. Ask students to consider the damning effects of names for the young, star-crossed lovers and why Juliet asks her famous question. Have your students ever felt that way?

Topics for Cross-Cultural Discussion

1. Undoubtedly, answers to this question will vary. The possibilities are too diverse to enumerate, but certainly larger groups of responses will emerge, such as for religious reasons, familial reasons, and so on. Most interesting may be to locate the subtleties within each grouping that seem particularly alien or novel to your students and discuss the differences.

2. As with question 1 about personal names, answers to this question about public names will also vary. You may want to apply some of the standard rules for other cultures to American institutions, "renaming" American roads, schools, and so on.

2

Our Clothing:
Does It Matter What We Wear?

From Levis and Baby Gap to haute couture and the deification of supermodels, Americans express themselves (and their materialist individualism) through their clothing. They simultaneously conform and rebel, camouflage and reveal, and liberate and restrain themselves through the way they dress. Young adults are particularly affected by fashion options and obligations. They are perhaps the most ambivalent about clothing of all people: wanting both to begin taking control over their own identities and yet feeling unsure of how to do so while still "fitting in" to the general landscape of cultural imagery.

Ask your students to brainstorm a list of contemporary styles — grunge, preppy, hip-hop, Euro, retro — and talk about how certain styles are attached to certain social roles (e.g., rebel, conformist, materialist, cutting-edge, conservative, arty, etc.). Then have students brainstorm a list of clothes-specific situations — work that requires a uniform, job interviews, weddings, proms, gym class, church — and ask students to discuss the meaning and purpose of the clothing for each situation. Use their answers as a springboard for discussion about the readings in this unit.

To complement this unit's selections — and to offer a slightly different perspective — point students to the "From the Bookshelf" selection from Anne Hollander's book *Sex and Suits*.

SUSAN ESTRICH, High Heels: What a Pain!
Vocabulary/Using a Dictionary

1. Students should have no trouble seeing the physical similarity of *stiletto* heels and knives, but you may want to emphasize the severity of the heels for the students who have never seen them. You might also introduce the concept of irony — that a woman's shoe and a weapon have the same name and that some women's clothing articles are considered by feminists to be cultural "weapons" against women.

2. Death is the classical answer here, but people obviously *succumb* to sleep, chocolate cake, or the urge to smoke when trying to quit. A more complex answer would be that a woman might succumb to sexual intercourse with a man after resisting at first. Handle this kind of answer by

transitioning into the second question. A person *succumbing* has some volition and must make the decision to give in. A defeat does not involve the same kind of agency.

3. You should point out that a *podium* is itself "footed," and that one generally "stands" at a podium to speak.

Responding to Words in Context

1. The point here is to approach the strong cultural association between women and fecundity. To be *voluptuous* is to be "sexual" in a way that society insists is only "feminine"; thus, Estrich sandwiches voluptuous between the other two words. You might want to bring up the connection between female sexuality and fertility and nourishment, connecting curves and fullness with fertility and pregnancy.

2. A *bunion* is a painful swelling of the first joint of the big toe and comes from the Old French for bump; *hammertoes* result from the curling up of toes, often from constraining footwear (a largely female problem), and make the top of the foot appear hammered; *corns* are hard bumps on the toes, often caused by excessive friction (think corn kernels).

Discussing Main Point and Meaning

1. Shoe-shopping, according to Estrich, is less attached to self-esteem because one's feet are not one's "fault." According to this theory, then, not finding shoes that fit or look attractive on one's feet has little relationship to the cultural standards for women's bodies — which can trigger self-criticism when shopping for other articles of clothing.

2. Ultimately, the essay both praises and criticizes high heels — pointing out the negative physical and social consequences (paras. 5, 6, 7) of wearing them, while also praising the supposed emotional and sexual benefits (paras. 9, 10, 11).

3. Estrich means to suggest that if women find themselves sexier in high heels, they will walk with more confidence in their desirability. You might want to raise the question of internalized standards of attractiveness, suggesting that women might not *really* be thinking of the pleasure they get from their own appearances, but of the pleasure their appearance will provide for men.

4. The tone is suddenly shy and a little embarrassed. Raise the question of trade-offs. Estrich is a successful political strategist and journalist; she acknowledges her giddiness over shoes with a twinge of regret. Have students discuss whether this is a real or fabricated ambivalence on her part. Is Estrich making sure not to alienate either feminists or more traditional women?

Examining Sentences, Paragraphs, and Organization

1. The essay assumes a female audience by asking this rhetorical question. Ask students whether Estrich is doing a disservice to either men or women by excluding the former from the conversation. How does the author's assumption of audience affect her essay?

2. This question anticipates question 3. By turning from the salivation of men (over sexy women) to the salivation of women (over shoes that will ostensibly make them one of those sexy women), Estrich is making a very ambivalent point. She seems to make women the object of desire, but the subtext is that men are never "salivated over," never the object.

3. Estrich seems to want to guide the reader (and thus herself?) into the belief that the benefits outweigh the drawbacks of high heels. Discuss with students how important structure is to argument. If the article had ended with a discussion of the drawbacks, it would have de-emphasized the benefits. The impression the writer leaves the reader with is crucial to the persuasive power of an essay.

Thinking Critically

1. Bras, girdles, pantyhose, leotards, miniskirts, and tight jeans are some examples. Are there any comparable examples in men's fashion (spandex, for example)? This question might lead to a discussion of the expectations placed on women and those placed on men in regard to clothing and physical appearance.

2. Because Estrich openly acknowledges the contradiction, she can't really be labeled a hypocrite.

In-Class Writing Activities

1. You might want to look for a more objectively analytical approach than most students will generally take, even though Estrich's approach is highly subjective. Estrich's article is self-aware in a manner that could be difficult for students to imitate. You might even suggest that students avoid writing about an article of clothing to which they are particularly attached or of which they are particularly contemptuous.

2. Both essays should clearly have strong tones, given that the assignment in each case is to persuade. Look for pairs of essays that address similar points in each essay, but which are careful to really distinguish the points-of-view and tones-of-voice.

KATHLEEN CARLIN, You Become What You Wear

Vocabulary/Using a Dictionary

1. *Histrionics* try to endow something with importance, whereas something *historic* is automatically considered important. Discuss the role of *story* in both cases. *History* is given its narrative structure in a way somewhat like a person's *histrionics* are calculated for effect.

2. Both *stigmas* and *stigmatisms* get in the way of one's "vision."

3. *Civility* and *civilization* come from *citizen*, which means "to belong to," and "to owe something to, a particular nation or state." So there is an element of consideration in being a citizen; and being a good citizen is part of *civility* and being a part of *civilization*.

Responding to Words in Context

1. The author uses the word *become* to suggest that a change has taken place. By the end of the essay, the author and her companion have been affected by the negative reactions they have encountered while shopping in "street people" clothes. By "accepting and internalizing the biased judgments" of their appearances, they have stigmatized themselves and cannot bring themselves to enter a shop that was now "out of bounds."

2. *Histrionics* is arguably a poor choice, given that part of the stereotype of the homeless is mental illness. Since Carlin is critical of stereotyping, she should avoid engaging in it.

3. *Derision* and *distrust* can be purely internal actions; *mockery* and *rude stares* are more overt. All are different variations of condescension.

4. The repetition signifies the experience of being stigmatized. It calls greater attention to the author's feelings about being stigmatized, and weighs on the reader like a stigma might weigh on the stigmatized.

Discussing Main Point and Meaning

1. Carlin and her partner want to "walk in the shoes" of the homeless in a literal and figurative sense and to be perceived as homeless from the beginning of their experiment.

2. Carlin writes that the lattes and croissants they order in the coffee shop "blow their cover," presumably because homeless women would not be able to afford expensive coffees and pastries.

3. They are shocked by how quickly they internalize the stereotypes that are based on their appearances.

Examining Sentences, Paragraphs, and Organization

1. Carlin introduces a critique (stereotype) of sociologists in the first sentence and follows up on it in the last sentence. There seems to be a suggestion that the lesson she learned about the stereotypes of the homeless could be applied to the stereotypes of others, including the stereotypes by (and about) sociologists themselves.

2. The impact of the list is more significant than the specific details of any one experience of discrimination, especially since Carlin is trying to demonstrate the frequency and totality of the experiences, which are all sort of similar in effect.

3. The truism that "you become what you wear" (or "clothes make the man") is not fully illustrated until the end of the article because a reader would not fully appreciate Carlin's claim without seeing the entire process of her experiment.

Thinking Critically

1. The experiment did anticipate the reactions Carlin cites, so perhaps in some cases she saw what she wanted to see. Also, it is possible that the internalization Carlin and her partner experienced did cause a bit of paranoia.

2. According to Carlin, her experiment not only proves a commonplace assumption about attitudes toward clothing, but also gives her a fresh understanding of the complex relationship between clothing/appearance and identity. (Note: One definition of *truism* is a widely known truth whose utterance therefore seems superfluous. "Making a truism come alive," then, is to make it useful and relevant.)

In-Class Writing Activities

1. Look for answers that are introspective analyses rather than polemics.

2. These lists should be highly detailed — specific places, activities, and level of frequency, etc. Warn students to avoid generalizing.

HOBI READER, Identity through Clothing

Vocabulary/Using a Dictionary

1. An *adage* comes out of a long history of use (so that it is inherently familiar).

2. An *elitist* makes an unjustified demand for respect; an *elite* (athlete, for example) has earned respect or privilege.

3. "The implementation of" sounds more mechanized; it implies a dehumanization, which Reader is accusing the school administration of doing to the students.

Responding to Words in Context

1. A *sob story* is an often told tale of woe that has lost its emotional impact through overuse. The author sounds a bit bitter and unfeeling in tone as a result of this phrase.

2. School administrators would not say that they were trying to gain power over students, but that they were trying to provide security and equality. A *power play* characterizes them as bullies.

Discussing Main Point and Meaning

1. The author believes that uniforms stifle creativity and individuality. According to Reader, those in favor of uniforms are hypocritical (they don't wear uniforms), punitive (punishing before any wrong has been done), and impotent (they won't prevent gang behavior or classism).

2. Reader compares uniform schools to prisons and science fiction settings. The prison analogy is frequent among unhappy students, though education is meant to "liberate" more than it binds. The implication that science fiction predicts a more insidious uniformity in the future is founded, though much science fiction is more interested in how technology will make people more creative rather than more uniform.

3. This is a take-off of the "Just say no" antidrug campaign of the 1980s. Reader implicitly suggests that educators have misdirected their energy toward a less worthy issue.

4. The image of Einstein drowning is meant to evoke a feeling of loss or regret, and to give a concrete example of the general problem Reader sees with uniforms.

Examining Sentences, Paragraphs, and Organization

1. The concern is the author's. Discuss the use of the passive voice with your students.

2. The questions inspire fear, since there is no way of knowing what lies in the future. They are rhetorical — not meant to be analytical but emotional — and they directly implicate the readers, forcing them to be involved in the issue.

3. This is a psychologically informed argument because of its emphasis on creativity and individuality rather than social or economic issues.

Thinking Critically

1. Clothing is obviously a huge issue for adolescents and teens, though perhaps not for younger children. Sports, schoolwork, artistic expression, and friendships are a few examples of other outlets.

2. Class disparity might not disappear, but it would surely lessen with uniforms. Discuss the all-or-nothing fallacy here, to which Reader falls prey. The role of schools is to educate, so it might be argued that anything that enhances the ability of students to learn (even minimally) is within the scope of that rule.

In-Class Writing Activities

1. Advise students that fighting a vehement argument with calm analysis is usually preferable to an equally emotional response.

2. The thrust of a good analysis here should be the potential for technology to mechanize and to lessen the opportunity for creativity. An assembly-line mentality and the loss of human production are the feared outcomes of too much technology.

Discussing the Unit

Preparing for Class Discussion

1. Estrich seems to suggest that one makes one's own individual choices, though at times those choices might paradoxically be to conform rather than to differentiate. Students' discussion of the relationship between identity and clothing may touch on the impact of advertising, the effect of economics, and their sense of belonging to a particular group(s).

2. Ask students to be very specific, providing particular anecdotal or hypothetical examples.

From Discussion to Writing

1. Bring up the issue of gaining the sympathy of one's audience. Students need to encourage the reader to see the issue from the point of view of the population they write about, appealing to their open-mindedness and decency to gain that sympathetic reception.

2. Students want to avoid parody here and prove that they can identify with their audience rather than ridicule them.

3. Students want to avoid stereotyping and/or ad hominem attacks in this assignment, attempting to gain the trust and attention of a wide audience that may be defensive on the subject.

Topics for Cross-Cultural Discussion

1. As usual with highly subjective questions, you should look for specific examples and concrete details. Pressure students to avoid merely generalizing about the differences between other cultures and the United States.

2. This is a somewhat imitative assignment, and selections in the unit can serve as models for those struggling to produce an idea. Encourage students to analyze their own perspectives on the articles of clothing they choose to write about. Is the article one that they have worn themselves? Does it convey a kind of social status? A stigma? A sense of uniformity? If controversial, what groups find it so and why? For example, in some cultures, women wear veils for religious reasons. Some secular or less traditional members of a given community might object to this practice, arguing that the veil is a symbol of the oppression of women, whereas supporters of the veil may argue that it is a means of personal expression.

3

Body Image:
Why Is It a Serious Issue?

The female body is certainly the most defining subject for feminists: Society demands the impossible of the female body, while seeming to ignore the male body. The female body must be virginal yet sexual, adolescent yet childbearing, always accessible yet always defended, pleasing to others yet punishing to itself. But, of course, the most unforgiving paradoxical demand of the female body is that it be severely thin yet clearly voluptuous.

In American culture particularly, as the general population gets larger and larger, and older and older, the ideal female body grows thinner, more sickly and weak looking, and younger than ever. Some say that the "waif look," "heroin chic," and other vulnerable images of hurt women constitute a backlash against the social and economic progress women have made since the 1970s. Others struggle with the irony that while women (and their children) constitute the majority of the world's poor and malnourished, many females who have wealth are starving themselves voluntarily. Obviously the paradoxical social demands placed on the female body are playing themselves out in a frighteningly literal way.

The essays in this unit, though somewhat light in tone, address the cultural images and meanings of the female body in today's society. Jennifer Silver wants both to protect the freedom of expression (which ultimately protects the right of women to express their sexuality freely) of pornographers, and yet she is unsettled by her boyfriend's desire to be stimulated by bodies she can never hope to resemble. Karen Epstein sheepishly admits to supporting a body make-over for Barbie, despite having loved the glamorous fantasy her Barbies provided her with when she was a child. Finally, Karlene Robinson is disconcerted by the way women "disown" and abuse their bodies in pursuit of an unattainable ideal, one that looms all too large for college students just beginning to enter womanhood.

All students should have something to say about the issue of body image, as it is an often discussed topic, and the visual images that encapsulate these problems are ubiquitous. You might want to ask students to bring in pictures of what they consider to be the ideal female and male bodies. Once you have reflected on what all of the images have in common, ask students to explain, precisely, why the shared attributes are supposed to be ideal. Introduce ideals of the past — plumpness, pale skin, high foreheads, distorted waists, bound feet — and ask students whether they think today's standards make more or less sense.

To give students a larger sense of the issues involved with body image, point them to this unit's "From the Bookshelf" selection, from Naomi Wolf's important book, *The Beauty Myth*.

JENNIFER SILVER, Caught with a Centerfold

Vocabulary/Using a Dictionary

1. Death is traditionally the most sobering and serious of topics, so it makes sense that an adjective derived from a noun meaning "burial site" would carry an extremely serious tone.

2. One could certainly say that a person who is *gracious* "moves beautifully" in a social sense. Introduce the expression *social graces*, and discuss the way that etiquette and manners have both moral and aesthetic value. *Grace* in a religious sense is also related (to *say grace* is to pay a moral tribute to a creator) and a *saving grace* is a kind of moral or aesthetic force. In contrast, *disgrace* almost always comes from a moral failure. This is a good place to introduce the difficult connection between form (aesthetics) and content.

3. Extend the metaphor of the "nest" as home. Silver and her boyfriend are "nesting" for the first time and are thus "inexperienced." Silver's use emphasizes innocence; thus, there is an irony in her introduction of *Playboy* as the essay's subject. Try to get students to list related idioms ("nest egg," "leaving the nest" or "flying the coop," or "coming home to roost," for example).

Responding to Words in Context

1. PMS is a troubling issue for feminists. If one validates PMS as a pathology (e.g., Silver's use of "paranoid" in her description), then the sufferer loses some credibility; how can we take Silver's analysis seriously if she is "paranoid"? Ask students to consider the rationality/emotionality hierarchy. Point them to the end of her essay where she makes the case for emotion as a force that does not have to be subordinated to rationality, and discuss the traditionally reductive male/rational, female/emotional binary that often permeates sexist values.

2. This question would be a good springboard for a discussion about the tension between theory (or abstraction) and practice (concrete manifestations). Silver is not opposed to pornography in the abstract, but she does not have to approve of every manifestation of pornography to avoid hypocrisy. Her discomfort comes from a specific contextual application of pornography, not with the abstract notion that pornography is a legitimate (if exploitive) example of "free expression."

Discussing Main Point and Meaning

1. Silver's relationship with her body and with cultural ideals is what's at stake here. Her boyfriend's actions merely underscore or remind her of her insecurity in those more individual relationships.

2. Beware of the "sour grapes" critique here. Some might argue that Silver is jealous because she is insecure, or vice versa. This is a highly subjective question, and students should be pushed to provide a clear logic to support their answers. Perhaps you could ask them to list some of their own insecurities and to discuss whether they experience jealousy as a result.

3. Silver wants to know that she can be a middle-aged mother and still be sexy. Ask students to discuss the cultural ideal that excludes one of the most primary signifiers of sexuality (childbirth) as a source of sex appeal. Talk about what childbirth does physically to the female body, and ask students whether they can imagine those effects as sources of sex appeal. Silver might have done this in her essay to provide the reader with a competing image for the *Playboy* model.

Examining Sentences, Paragraphs, and Organization

1. Silver is obviously ironic in using a nineteenth-century convention to introduce such a racy twentieth-century issue. She also pokes fun at her own confessed "prudishness" by using this phrase.

2. Paragraph 12, with its invocations of Pat Robertson and sexist media, is the only overtly political paragraph. Silver deftly stays out of the morality debates about free speech and conservative values; thus, she can reach a broader audience by making such a strictly personal appeal.

3. While this is an obviously subjective question, students should consider the helpless and resigned tone of Silver's boyfriend (his insistence that "men are visually stimulated") as significant. In her mind, he actively subscribes to *Playboy*, as she would have to seek out actively the company of her classmates. Images and persons are hardly comparable in a physical sense, but Silver is comparing the emotional similarity of the two things.

Thinking Critically

1. The transition in paragraphs 13–15, from jealousy to insecurity, is key. There is no correct answer to this question, but it will provide good opportunities to teach "close reading." Return to paragraph 8, Silver's threat to have coffee with classmates. This is a clever attempt to get her boyfriend to experience jealousy, to worry that she fantasizes about another, which could be said to contradict her "have-your-cake-and-eat-it-too" philosophy laid out in paragraph 13.

2. *Playboy* is unabashedly meant to give sexual pleasure to men. That her boyfriend subscribes to it suggests that he is seeking out sexual pleasure from a source other than Silver. Still, she argues that her beef is with the standard of beauty and sexiness, so she should logically have the same criticisms of Victoria's Secret or even the *Sports Illustrated* swimsuit issues.

In-Class Writing Activities

1. You don't want students to oversimplify here: Sex, even graphically portrayed, does not necessarily equal pornography. A partial definition could be the presentation of sex without the context of a story and without an emotional or intellectual purpose; pornography may degrade or otherwise victimize the participants.

2. You should look for balance in these essays. Students will want to write polemics or ad hominem attacks rather than intellectual analyses. Suggest that they try to see this issue from the "other" point of view. Ask them to look at their own interests from outside themselves, or to play devil's advocate with themselves when they brainstorm for the essay. Students stuck for examples of female-directed media could be steered to soap operas, talk shows, or self-help/style magazines.

KAREN EPSTEIN, I'm a Barbie Girl

Vocabulary/Using a Dictionary

1. Start with the noun *play*, a "dramatic fiction," which can be compared to a *delusion* in a sense. Also, to *play* an instrument is to create a dramatic effect. The more obvious *playing games* is related in that a game is a type of escape from reality, as is a delusion. Also bring in the colloquial use of *play* as in *don't play me*, which means "don't lie to me or try to fool me."

2. This is a difficult question because it requires an understanding of the difference between the structure (parts) of a system and the functions (processes) of those parts in concert. Using an electronic metaphor — hardware versus software — might help. Or possibly a mechanical metaphor could be of use: One can't study the processes (velocity, durability, etc.) of a car unless all of its parts are working together simultaneously.

3. *Cannibal*, the Spanish variant for *Galibi*, only meant "eater of flesh" because Columbus directed it to. Clearly the Spanish explorers, out of fear, spun a negative meaning out of a positive attribute.

Responding to Words in Context

1. Barbie is the epitome of popular culture and superficial "cuteness." Epstein's "cutesy" language reflects this and is appropriate.

2. Epstein's use of fantasy is really restricted to children, which begs the question: Can children sufficiently distinguish between reality and fantasy? Student definitions may be vague and abstract. Urge them to illustrate and specify as much as possible. Talk about the need to define abstractions in expository writing so as not to confuse or mislead one's audience.

Discussing Main Point and Meaning

1. Perhaps Epstein is hedging her bets (i.e., "just in case fantasy creeps into reality subconsciously"). She wants to support Mattel but does not want to alienate readers who bristle at the thought of political correctness.

2. See paragraphs 1, 5, and 6. Here you want students to pick up on the fantasy of the all-service male — competent, dependable, able to juggle many women simultaneously. Epstein's use of Ken references takes some of the pressure off men, proving, in a sense, that they also are victimized by stereotypes.

3. The Barbies Epstein mentions in paragraph 5 (i.e., punk rocker Barbie, bride Barbie, permanently-puckered kissing Barbie) are so obviously reductive, one can really only be amused by them, which helps to further Epstein's case that the fantasy is all in fun. Still, if young girls learn through play, then it might be argued that they internalize these one-dimensional images to some degree.

4. Epstein says that her mother and sisters didn't look like Barbie, that no women did, and implies that she knew the difference between real female bodies and the bodies of female dolls.

Examining Sentences, Paragraphs, and Organization

1. Right away, Epstein expresses sympathy for Barbie, revealing that she will not blame or condemn her favorite childhood toy. The reader does not expect her to come out in support of Mattel as she later does. This balanced approach can give the reader a sense of the author as pensive and credible.

2. Epstein's support for Mattel's plan may surprise the reader since her argument begins by setting her own view apart from the idea that Barbie's unrealistic figure "gives girls a negative body ideal from a young age." "For me," Epstein writes, "Barbie was always, well, a doll . . . I knew she wasn't real." However, the author's stance by the end of the essay shows her ambivalence toward the effect Barbie may really have on young girls.

3. This is one of many attempts Epstein makes to "lighten up" the issue, in order to prevent alienation of skeptics.

Thinking Critically

1. This is a good opportunity to discuss with students the "either/or fallacy," where an argument about moral or political issues insists on absolute right/wrong dichotomies. Epstein is rhetorically clever in not oversimplifying or suggesting that one group is entirely wrong and one is entirely right. Perhaps her flippancy is a weakness in spots, and the essay certainly falls more heavily to one side (really only a few paragraphs address the possible harm Barbie's image could do).

2. The question must be asked: If Barbie resembles "NO women," yet she is the primary object of a young girl's fantasy life, then do all real women "fail" by comparison to be impressive, worthy, or attractive?

In-Class Writing Activities

1. G.I. Joe comes immediately to mind. There are also many "super heroes" that could provide ample material — especially Superman. The point is to engage those students who find the critiques of Barbie "whiny" or "ridiculous," particularly male students who may feel disconnected.

2. Parody and humor are certainly acceptable in this kind of assignment, although a student who wants to make a serious persuasive point in defense of Barbie may want to be more straightforward.

KARLENE J. ROBINSON, In Pursuit of the Impossible Body Image

Vocabulary/Using a Dictionary

1. A *code* is really a system, which is a unified whole of sorts — different parts or forces working together to perform a specific function. Looking at *racial integration* in light of these definitions is somewhat refreshing in that we so often think of integration as the forcing together of things that don't belong to the same "system."

2. Attaching the nervous system to anorexia and bulimia replaces the innocuous connotation with a more serious one. Nervous responses are involuntary physical responses also, so students should discuss the fact that these diseases ultimately are not voluntarily controlled by the sufferer. Ask students to compare them to other involuntary conditions: substance addiction, depression, or severe allergies, for example.

3. Create, develop, ratify, imagine, validate, value, promote, and acknowledge are just some examples of possible antonyms for *negate*. There is no one exact antonym for it. Something along the lines of *value* is probably the best opposite to Robinson's use.

Responding to Words in Context

1. In the last paragraph, Robinson slips in the word *myth* to modify the "ideal body," suggesting that this "ideal," in particular, will yield only a fruitless pursuit. There's no real evidence that Robinson eschews all ideals, but her repetition of the term seems to indict it somewhat.

2. By using the first-person plural pronoun, Robinson identifies with her audience, which is an effective strategy to use in relation to a topic that is emotionally delicate and deserving of sympathy.

Discussing Main Point and Meaning

1. Most students should be able to guess that eating disorders are rampant among college women. Many women are away from home for the first time, feel a bit out of control, and most importantly, often become sexually active for the first time.

2. The media connect superficial characteristics with internal strengths: "The implication in the media is that to have the ideal body is to be attractive, powerful, witty, and self-controlled." Point out the broader meaning of *attractive* here.

3. If one *disowns* one's body or refuses the responsibility of ownership, then clearly one has no concern for the welfare of that body. Thus, a person in pursuit of the ideal body will engage in that pursuit at any expense.

4. Robinson's suggestions come primarily in the last paragraph, and they are somewhat too general to be helpful. The final sentence about "a balanced diet" and making food a "normal part of life" seems particularly hollow, as these things are precisely the obstacle for those with eating disorders.

Examining Sentences, Paragraphs, and Organization

1. The quotes ring true to almost anyone and attach actual persons to the subject of Robinson's essays, pulling specific images out of generalities.

2. Behavioral suggestions are more concrete than psychological ones, which should make the essay as an argumentive piece more effective, but substantively, the logical leap from the psychological to the behavioral is a bit abrupt and insecure.

3. Resonant of the warnings on cigarette packages, the statement could lend some seriousness to the issue of dieting; however, many smokers obviously ignore the labels on cigarette packs.

Thinking Critically

1. You may want to engage students in a discussion about the difference between theory and practice. Robinson's remedies (i.e., that one eat a well-balanced diet) may not relate to her theory of what is wrong (i.e., the expectations set up "in the media via TV, in the movies, in magazines"), but she may be trying to be realistic about what can be done.

2. While many argue that eating disorders occur on a continuum, severe anorexia and bulimia require clinical attention rather than the self-help suggestions Robinson makes.

In-Class Writing Activities

1. In the college environment, meeting new friends and possible romantic partners, sharing a dorm room, being responsible for feeding oneself, becoming sexually active, and facing new academic stresses are just some possible triggers for self-esteem problems, and thus, in the case of women, for eating disorders. Once a student is struggling with an eating disorder, some helpful approaches might be the interventions by friends or dorm staff, required workshops in the dorms, healthier options in the dining halls, required yearly physical exams for all students, or group counseling sessions led by former sufferers of eating disorders. Students may have suggestions more specifically geared toward their own schools.

2. The key is specificity in this assignment. Students should be encouraged to produce feasible solutions that pertain to the specific resources of their colleges or universities.

Discussing the Unit

Preparing for Class Discussion

1. Most people would agree that men are buying into idealized body images that prize fitness and youth. Baldness and small physical frames have long been a source of shame for men. The cultural ideal for men emphasizes height, muscularity, athletic ability, strength, thick hair, and sexual prowess. More men are having hair transplants and cosmetic surgery (including liposuction and face lifts), coloring their hair, and worrying more about their wardrobes than ever before.

2. Our society is largely biased against the overweight, who unlike the underweight, are seen as the cause of their own problems. Epstein might come down on the thin-is-better side of this issue, but both Robinson and Silver seem to be arguing for more diverse images of the female body. You might poll students on their own opinions to expose our cultural

biases. Ask how many students would prefer to be fat and healthy as compared to thin and unhealthy.

From Discussion to Writing

1. Extreme wealth (a.k.a. the American Dream), Western European beauty, unchecked power over others, and elite-level athleticism are some other cultural "ideals" (or myths) that pervade our consciousness daily. Students will have different opinions as to which are the most insidious myths; let the discussion take its own course.

2. This would be a good question to work on as a class. Let students give suggestions while you write them on the chalkboard. When they have exhausted their examples, discuss whether or not the various characteristics are compatible with one another. Is the composite feasible? Or is it just another unattainable ideal?

3. Ask students for specifics from the texts. This should be an exercise in synthesis — of their own ideas and those of the authors in this unit.

Topics for Cross-Cultural Discussion

1. Ask students from other countries to talk about whether their perceptions of beauty have changed since they have been in the United States, or whether such perceptions are changing in their native cultures as a result of American influences in and on the media.

2. It's more than likely that women in most cultures are responsible for the production of beauty, and, therefore, for the adherence to body image ideals.

4

Who Has It Tougher — Boys or Girls?

Gender is one of the clearest dividing lines in our cultural debates, and there are many binary oppositions to prove it: feminist/misogynist, essentialism/constructivism, patriarchy/matriarchy, phallocentric/gynocentric, Mars/Venus. We commonly talk about gender as a barrier, despite the efforts of many activists, scholars, and others to talk about ways of bringing the sexes together.

In modern society we may be less likely to judge a woman for working, for controlling her own sex life, or for betraying or triumphing over a man. And we might applaud a man who stays at home with his kids, works as a nurse, or cries in public. But we would still be shocked at the sight of a woman spitting on the sidewalk or of a man applying lipstick at the dinner table. "Tomboys" and "momma's boys" are shunned, as we still believe that to know someone's gender is to understand something profound about him or her.

Gender, at least for the foreseeable future, is as fundamental as age and as nuanced as personality. Whether to preserve or meld gender differences and whether they are natural or conditioned (and is conditioning natural?) are among the most pressing questions in gender studies. From those questions spring additional quandaries about work, family, religion, politics, the media, and just about every other aspect of our lives.

The essays in this unit reflect that ubiquity. The Fortune 500, fraternities, primary school, and the basketball court all provide fruitful environments for the gender monster to rear its ugly head. What's fresh about these essays, however, is that they step slightly away from the general (and often abstract) notion of equality (though not too far away) to talk about some more practical applications.

Many students today feel that gender issues are passé, that the women's movement is over and that the "men's movement" was over before it started. They are cynical and wary, and you may want to shock them by getting them to see how profoundly gender affects their lives. As a prewriting experience, ask students to live for a day as the opposite gender. They could dress neutrally, but they should behave in a manner they feel projects a "masculine" or "feminine" image. They could "hang out" with friends of the opposite sex, explaining their purpose: to live one day as "one of the guys/girls." Their findings could be written in a journal entry or shared verbally with the class.

What was the hardest thing to remember to do? Did they feel liberated or confined? Did their friends respond differently to them? Ask them whether they were relieved to get back to normal or sad to leave the "other side." You may want to show film clips from *Some Like It Hot, Tootsie, Mrs. Doubtfire, The Bird Cage, National Velvet, Yentl, I Shot Andy Warhol,* or other gender-bending films before you send them out on this assignment to give them some ideas. You might also ask why men may cross-dress for comic effect whereas women do so for more serious purposes.

Because this unit's debate will be so immediate to many of your students, and has raged for so long, point them to this unit's "From the Bookshelf" selection from Mary Pipher's *Reviving Ophelia* for some perspective.

CHRISTINA HOFF SOMMERS, The "Fragile American Girl" Myth

Vocabulary/Using a Dictionary

1. Professionals in the fields of law or social work are sometimes referred to as *advocates.*

2. *Unduly* does not mean improper or not punctual, though one might be "unduly rude" or "unduly tardy."

3. *To fix* in the sense of "rig" or "set up" could connect them. Also, part of the Latin root is *injured;* so *mend* is to "fix an injury," whereas *mendacity* is a kind of "fixed" truth.

Responding to Words in Context

1. Because *logy* means "the study" of something, the study of victims is the best answer to this question.

2. *Underprivileged* means to have less than normal privilege, but *unprivileged* would be to have no privilege at all.

Discussing Main Point and Meaning

1. Sommers argues against treating girls as an "underserved population" or characterizing them as fragile. She attacks feminists and current ideas in education reform. She does not praise or advocate for any specific groups or theories, really. You might talk to students about the differences between a *negative critique* (a tearing down) and a *positive critique* (a building up).

2. She wants to expose the notion of girls as fragile as a false concept or myth. She wants readers to see beyond the "myth" to a truth.

3. The argument could be called feminist because it argues against thinking of girls as weak. However, it privileges the problems of boys over those of girls, so the answer could be *yes* or *no.*

4. Sommers suggests that feminists should be worrying more about boys and their frailties. Logically, what she really ought to do is make a call for boys' advocacy groups.

Examining Sentences, Paragraphs, and Organization

1. You could introduce the concept of red herrings here. What Sommers says in her last statement may be true, but it is not really substantiated or, more importantly, relevant to her argument.

2. This is a rhetorical question, which can be loosely translated to "there was no place for her to get this idea, therefore it is made up."

3. The repetition is meant to be cynical or sarcastic and illustrative of the few choices men apparently have. It is effective for those who see full-time work as oppressive, or for those who see men's roles as more restrictive than women's roles.

Thinking Critically

1. On one hand, Sommers is addressing a widespread assumption, so her examples are fair enough. On the other hand, she assumes that feminists are monolithic and are all of the same mind on this particular issue, which is unfair.

2. Perhaps both boys and girls are "underserved." If one is, that doesn't mean that the other isn't, as Sommers implicitly suggests.

In-Class Writing Activities

1. Ask students to read their responses to this question aloud. Have them compare and contrast their experiences with those of others to see if they can identify any trends.

2. Encourage a balance between the two genders here, even if their group members feel more strongly about the problems of one gender. Discuss the issue of credibility with students, instructing them that a balanced treatment is generally appealing to more readers than an absolute bias.

MARK ZMARZLY, Boys Don't Cry

Vocabulary/Using a Dictionary

1. A *complement* might fill the empty space in, or fulfill the needs of, someone or something; *compliment* might fulfill a kind of social obligation (politeness) or fill someone up with esteem.

2. What is *flowering* in Zmarzly's essay (i.e., the mistreatment of women) is neither beautiful nor delicate (like a flower). Also, flowers are generally associated with the feminine, sexually and aesthetically.

3. Capital punishment is the other connotation: where justice or retribution is carried out or *performed*.

Responding to Words in Context

1. *Ridicule* is a negative response to a personal trait or behavior since the narrator would not want to be exposed to it. Also, in Zmarzly's context, it could come as a result of public displays of emotion, thought to be shameful in men; therefore, it is most likely attached to shame.

2. *Male* and *female* as nouns are somewhat clinical as compared to *man* and *woman*, which are more human. Zmarzly makes the men in his article more like clinical objects while keeping the women human.

Discussing Main Point and Meaning

1. The creation myth (and the Adam and Eve story) is alluded to in Zmarzly's introduction to suggest that there was a different (more natural) definition of masculinity before the advent of modern culture.

2. Zmarzly argues that men hurt themselves and the women in their lives by suppressing emotion. He thinks that men should start allowing more emotion in themselves. They will then be healthier as individuals and in their relationships.

3. The guy with the girlfriend will always get made fun of the most because he is thought to be emotionally weak if he is in a steady relationship.

4. Zmarzly says that women are "the only real cure."

Examining Sentences, Paragraphs, and Organization

1. He seems to suggest that fraternities are not the cause of bad behavior in men but that they provide an environment with opportunities for bad behavior. The fault lies with the men, not the fraternities as institutions.

2. These rhetorical questions address male readers directly. This could alienate a man who feels attacked, but Zmarzly has a hunch that most men will recognize themselves in his scenarios.

3. Because Zmarzly firmly defends his fraternity, he may not want readers to get the idea that he thinks everything that goes on within a fraternity context is tolerable.

4. The structure is effective — moving from broad context, to the problems in a specific environment, to a solution. However, the solution/conclusion is a bit too vague and brief.

Thinking Critically

1. Zmarzly's statement here is thin and hasty. There is no real logical connection to the preceding argument and the role of women, and so the reader is expected to produce that logic to understand the point.

2. Emotional suppression causes bad behavior and relationships characterized by ridicule, according to this article. Zmarzly could have gone to greater lengths to describe the benefits of education.

In-Class Writing Activities

1. This assignment may inspire giggling and other silliness. Make sure to discuss *why* it is so funny to imagine emotionally healthy men. Curb any inability to take the assignment seriously.

2. Zmarzly explains and criticizes through identifying with his subject. Make sure students understand that they need to identify with their subject — to understand and accept the people they're writing about. They need to demonstrate how a woman's inability to express certain traits is hurting her and any men in her life, whether directly or indirectly, and the way to begin to demonstrate that is by trying to feel it.

Opposing Views: When Coaches Conspire to Set a Record

DOROTHY J. SAMUELS, A Shot Against Women's Sports
GAIL COLLINS, A Sweet Moment of Teamwork

Vocabulary/Using a Dictionary

1. A *patron* pays the patronized in some way out of a sense of obligation. A patronizing compliment does not have to be sincere; instead, it seems *paid* out of a sense of obligation.

2. A *paternal* parent is a father (note the Latin root *pater*, which means father). Traditionally, fathers are thought to bear little responsibility for children beyond providing for their most basic needs.

3. All relate to the act of believing or being believed.

Responding to Words in Context

1. *Paternalistic* suggests more of a pattern of behavior (or state of mind) than does *patronizing*, which seems to be attached to a single incident.

2. The second clause in the sentence describes a way for sports to teach lessons. Therefore, *endemic* must relate to the special relationship be-

tween sports and lessons (or disappointments). Additionally, the previous sentence previews this relationship.

Discussing Main Point and Meaning

1. Sales had an injured Achilles tendon.

2. The commissioner said he approved the "gift point" because "males are made differently from women . . . women break down . . . [and] get emotional" (Samuels, para. 3).

3. Collins argues that the point was to reward teamwork and a team player.

4. Collins gives the example of Denny McClain and Mickey Mantle to prove that the Nykesha Sales incident was not gender related. There are other examples, including two from the same year as the Sales incident (1997): Gordie Howe was allowed to play hockey for the Detroit Vipers for less than a minute on October 3, 1997, to become the first hockey player to have played professional hockey during six consecutive decades, and Donald Royal of the Orlando Magic was able to get a "triple double" (double digits in points, rebounds, and assists) during the last ten seconds of a game in which the Magic were obviously going to beat the Pistons, by calling a time-out to set up a play. The Pistons refused to contest the play in protest against Royal's and the Magic's poor sportsmanship.

Examining Sentences, Paragraphs, and Organization

1. Samuels calls Sales a "terrific" basketball player and person so as not to appear to be attacking Sales personally.

2. Samuels places more importance on Tranghese's remarks because she thinks they are emblematic of "harmful stereotypes." Collins dismisses Tranghese as unnecessarily "paternalistic" (not in touch with the purpose of the event).

3. Samuels is very serious in her concluding paragraph, whereas Collins seems to say "lighten up."

Thinking Critically

1. There is often an assumption about negative stereotypes — that the substance of the description is automatically bad. Sometimes the traits in a stereotypical description have been unfairly labeled as negative (in addition to being applied too broadly over a group).

2. This is a nice cushion for Collins, but it's not really the issue. What's at stake is whether exceptions to the rules should ever be made, not whether certain parties are offended by such exceptions.

In-Class Writing Activities

1. The paragraphs should be balanced evenly, as if written by different authors.

2. Good answers will address sportsmanship in general, this special case, the tradition at Villanova, and obligations to fans.

Discussing the Unit

Preparing for Class Discussion

1. Ask students to try to get beyond biology — or at least the idea that male and female differences are bigger than genetic differences, age differences, or environmental conditioning.

2. It's ironic that only the male author in this unit makes a case for emotionality. It may be a safer stance for Zmarzly precisely because he is a man (and heterosexual, and a fraternity member); he is less likely to be accused of being too emotional. Ask students to place a value on emotional "intelligence." Can it lead to success in the workplace, the family, and social life in general? A person who values emotion may inspire more trust in others, may have better intuition in the workplace, and may be better at arriving at compromise.

From Discussion to Writing

1. Ask students whether they are surprised by, or pleased, or disappointed with their lists, and why. Ask them if they might have formed their lists to adhere to traditional gender roles, and whether it would be more threatening for men or women to have traits associated with the opposite gender.

2. The better essays will analyze characters that are not extremely masculine or feminine, showing how stereotyping persists even on the most subtle levels (e.g., shows that are supposed to be progressive about gender).

3. This question asks students to explore one of the oldest (if not *the* oldest) and most confounding conundrums in human thought: nature versus nurture. Your students may or may not know the profundity of depth and the hundreds of years of intellectual history behind such a question and may find it an easy question to answer — or a difficult one. It would certainly be interesting to summarize various philosophers' answers to this question, either before or after students' essays are written, citing Locke, Descartes, their predecessors, and those who followed. You may also want to bring in and discuss articles relating to the current debate on the causes of homosexuality.

Topics for Cross-Cultural Discussion

1. Remind students that in some cultures emotional display is thought inappropriate for either gender. Also bring up certain stereotypes — Latin machismo, Italian emotionalism, or Asian stoicism — and ask students whether they can provide conflicting anecdotal or other evidence.

2. Answers will probably vary, although men may be more likely to favor race whereas women may favor gender. If so, ask them to examine why this is the case.

5
How Important Is Group Identity?

Forming an identity is a necessary product of living in the modern world. An identity, a sense of self, is by definition "the state or fact of remaining the same" — it is a stable aspect of our psyche that allows us to cope with a turbulently technological and rapidly evolving America.

Over time, Americans have embraced many different ethnic, racial, or religious affiliations, laying claim to multiple nationalities and possessing various roots and backgrounds. Of course, people who share the same ethnic background or religious heritage relate to these differing types of identity, befriend each other, and form *groups* to support one another. The concern that Meg Greenfield raises about this regards the insidiousness of group identity. As she states in "Kicking Away Your Freedom," "More and more people seem to be regarding themselves and behaving as embodiments of . . . groups, rather than as individual free agents."

Henry Han Xi Lau in "I Was a Member of the Kung Fu Crew" expresses the notion that having a group identity actually helped him acclimate to and learn about the "ghettoness" of New York City's Chinatown. This "ghettoness," Lau argues, is a facet of his identity which is needed when he returns home to Chinatown during semester break. Now that he and his crew attend college they live far apart, but they "always come back together in Chinatown" where their "home" and their "world" used to be.

Although group identity is also the subject of "They've Got to Be Carefully Taught" by Susan Brady Konig, she warns of the dangers of irresponsibly instituting cultural diversity curriculums in our schools. Because of her child's experience with the incompetent and incomparable Miss Laura, Konig's preschooler is confused about her group identity. As concluded by the author, "Sarah only knows what she has been taught: little Henry is white (he is), her daddy's from Iceland (untrue), and New York's in France (?)."

To add further perspective to the issue, point students to the excerpt of Henry Louis Gates's *Colored People*, this unit's "From the Bookshelf" selection.

MEG GREENFIELD, Kicking Away Your Freedom

Vocabulary/Using a Dictionary

1. *Manifesto* is similar to the word *manifest* which means "readily perceived; evident." Its original meaning comes from Italian meaning "denunciation, manifest" and is derivative of the word *maifestare*.

2. *Idiosyncratic*, the adjective form of *idiosyncrasy*, means "the quality of having a habit peculiar to an individual." *Idiosyncrasy* usually refers to a characteristic peculiarity of habit or structure — thus, an example would be a teacher arranging the classroom (desks, tables, chairs) a certain way before the start of every class. Another example would be a person who buys nothing but corduroy slacks because he feels that other pants aren't comfortable enough. Some other idiosyncrasies might be eating the cheese off a slice of pizza before eating the dough or always taking the crust off of a sandwich before you eat it.

3. While trying to rephrase Greenfield's statement, students may be tempted to simply replace the difficult words with their definitions — probably not a bad place to start. It may be more productive to replace the difficult words with synonyms to get a handle on the meaning before rephrasing altogether. If students have trouble with this question though, you may want to work together to summarize the sentence with a question as simple as "What does this mean?" moving on from there.

Responding to Words in Context

1. *Sillies* is a verb based on the adjective *silly* which means "lacking good sense; stupid or foolish, absurd; ridiculous." Thus, something that *sillies* up a relationship, makes the relationship absurd or foolish.

2. In the context of the essay, *mired* means "stuck." *Mired*, by definition, means "to sink or stick in" or as if in *mire* (an area of wet swampy ground).

Discussing Main Point and Meaning

1. The problem Greenfield describes as "kicking away your freedom" comes from letting yourself "be transformed into the emblem of some cause" from which you draw your identity (para. 6).

2. Greenfield uses the example of the Hippodrome to illustrate her point because it is an example that modern Americans can easily relate to. In a sports-crazed world where people are always taking sides in baseball, football, basketball, and hockey games, it is easy for us to understand an allusion to choosing "Blue" or "Green" at an ancient Roman sporting stadium.

3. The author "smile[d] in a pained sort of way" when the jogger said, "You know, people coming down the street on *this* side of your garage

are entitled to consideration, too" because, according to Greenfield, "People . . . claim to be one or the other and may not even have known the origin of the sides." People are constantly choosing sides (or groups) without considering what that choice represents. The author's smile said, "Who are these other people you claim to represent with your advocacy?"

4. Greenfield does not include herself with those people who let themselves be transformed. She does not say, for example, "To let *myself* be transformed into the emblem of some cause." She always refers to the *reader* as a person in jeopardy of losing individual identity to a cause or group.

Examining Sentences, Paragraphs, and Organization

1. The topic sentence in paragraph 5 is the first sentence. The words *them* and *they* refer to "your bosses and political leaders."

2. The writer's voice definitely changes between the first and last paragraphs. Greenfield's voice at the end of the essay seems more insistent in her urging the reader to action. Her tone is more serious, and she begins to address the reader directly. Her direct appeal at the end states, "There's nothing so dangerous for manipulators as people who think for themselves."

3. The author changes the style in which she relates the idea of an individual "behaving as (an) embodiment of (a) group" by changing her tone and address. Instead of relating her ideas and opinions through anecdotes (as in the beginning of the essay), she appeals to and directly addresses the sensibility of the reader. The movement in the essay on the part of the author/narrator is from that of an observer to an instigator.

Thinking Critically

1. Greenfield's opinion holds that in America, the individual is being recreated as the representative of a group. Students should use examples from their own experiences as representatives of a group to support or disprove Greenfield's theory. Some groups that they may name are musical groups, ethnic groups, social groups (jocks, gangstas), religious groups, and political groups.

2. After asking students whether they agree or disagree with Greenfield's motto ("There's nothing so dangerous for manipulators as people who think for themselves,") qualify the question by telling students to describe what Greenfield means by her use of the word "dangerous." Why would manipulators feel that individuality is "dangerous"? Ask the students if they ever felt they were misled by their bosses at work, or on a broader scale, by a government official.

In-Class Writing Activities

1. Students can list a number of groups of which they are representative. Probably the easiest way to elicit responses would be to ask students to question the slang they use that is exclusive to the group that they feel they represent, for example — a sports fan might talk to someone about a pitcher's E.R.A. or a hitter's "slugging percentage." Exclusive language, slang, and jargon help to identify what specific "group" someone belongs to and are key to discovering cultural identity.

2. The responses to this question may be varied: from a student exercising his or her right to assemble (attending a political rally or sit-in) to another who may have voted for the wrong candidate for president. In any case, students should explain in their essays whether they felt a loss of freedom because of the stand they took.

HENRY HAN XI LAU, I Was a Member of the Kung Fu Crew

Vocabulary/Using a Dictionary

1. The letter *a* in *asymmetrical* functions as a prefix, meaning "not" (as in *atypical*) or "without" (as in *amoral*). In the case of *asymmetrical*, the meaning is "not symmetrical."

2. *Karaoke* is the act of singing along to a music video, especially one from which the original vocals have been eliminated. *Karaoke* is a word of Japanese origin meaning "empty" (*kara-*) "orchestra" (*oke*).

3. *Kung fu* is a term of Chinese origin taken from the original *gongfu*, literally translated as "skill."

Responding to Words in Context

1. *Ghettoness* is best exemplified by Lau through a number of different examples, each relating to survival in the ghetto: grilling other punks, arguing about which meal provides you with the most meat, walking instead of taking the subway to save money, living with less brand-name items, and gorging on cheap hot dogs.

2. Two clues in the text suggest the definition of the word *assessing*. The sentence prior to the one that mentions *assessing* states: "Only a few years ago, *examination* of the hair was sufficient" (para. 6). Thus, *examination* is a synonym for *assessing*. Also, if you look closely at paragraph 6, Lau and his crew *scrutinize* and *evaluate* others' pants, both synonyms for *assessing*.

Discussing Main Point and Meaning

1. The title might suggest visions of a Bruce Lee or Jackie Chan kung fu movie, or a movie about an ex-martial artist. There will be a few different ways to interpret the title.

2. The answer to the question "What category does the author's K.F.C. belong to in Chinatown?" is best exemplified in paragraphs 3 and 4: "Most Chinatown kids fall into a few general categories . . . then there is the K.F.C. We work hard like the nerds, but we identify with the punks." In a discussion about other kinds of groups, there may be several answers: jocks, hippies, gangstas', straightedges, hardcores, intellectuals, musicians, and so on. This is an excellent way to begin a discussion.

3. Lau describes the conditions in Chinatown throughout the essay: "Chinatown is ghetto" (para. 1), "Most Chinatown kids fall into a few general categories" (para. 3) — almost every opening sentence of each paragraph hints at the ghetto identity of Chinatown, the basis of Lau's own identity and that of his friends: ". . . my friends are ghetto, I am ghetto."

4. In the last sentence of the final paragraph, Lau articulates his feelings about Chinatown: "For most of us, our home used to be here and our world was here." This statement suggests an attachment to the place that formed his identity. It also signifies regret over having moved, over losing his favorite "home" or "world." Note: Lau also compares Chinatown to an entire "world," perhaps giving the place a vastness which others may not appreciate as he does.

Examining Sentences, Paragraphs, and Organization

1. Lau may begin his essay with a story related by his *si-fu* Rocky, because interesting narratives often catch a reader's attention and make them want to read on. However, there may be a more personal reason for the use of the grand master story. Lau may be trying to show the reader the honored history behind the Kung Fu Crew. It is because of the latter reason that this narrative may affect our understanding of the author's experience. The Kung Fu Crew was modeling its lifestyle after a time-honored tradition.

2. The repetition of the word *we* in the phrases "we all met," "we practiced," "we work hard," "we are reunited," "we amble into," and "we stick out," identify Lau *not* as an individual but as a member of a close-knit group. (If Lau's thesis stresses the importance of having a group identity, then his repetitive insistence about himself being a member of a group is integral to reinforcing the main idea.)

3. Lau includes the trip to McDonald's because it shows the dialogue of the K.F.C. and the easy way the group gets along. The members of the K.F.C. speak in slang that is easily recognized by the other members: "But the Whopper gots more fat and meat. It's even got more bun." Nel agrees, "True that." This story and its use of exclusive slang reinforce Lau's main idea about the importance of group identity.

Thinking Critically

1. Students may note that Lau and his friends amongst themselves, "never exactly articulate what being ghetto entails, but [they] know the spirit of it" (para. 10). But in his essay, Lau does offer some aspects of "ghettoness," ranging from his discussion of Chinatown's inhabitants (the F.O.B.'s) (para. 10) to its economics: the alternative brand names in stores ("Dolo instead of Polo"), gorging on cheap hot dogs (para. 11), leaving good tips at Chinese restaurants "because our parents are waiters and waitresses too" (para. 11). Ask students to back up their opinions with three means of support from the story, citing paragraph and sentence numbers so the rest of the class can follow along.

2. This, again, is a matter of opinion, yet the answers to this question could be difficult to support by using evidence just from the story. Ask students to provide examples of support from their own experiences with group identity. This question is good preparation for In-Class Writing Activity 2.

In-Class Writing Activities

1. To get started, you may want to give students some examples from your own life on which they can model their answers or relate another illustration about a place where one can return and be reminded of their roots. If all else fails, read a few excerpts from Ernest Hemingway's short story "The Big Two-Hearted River." In this story Nick Adams returns to a river, a place where he can go to be reminded of the good days when he used to fish and camp before the trauma he suffered during World War I.

2. To get this discussion going, you might ask your students about the places where they grew up, whether it was elementary school, high school, community college, and so on. Ask them if they had a group of friends that they were close with at that time and if they get together anymore. This could be an opportunity for students to reflect on their group identities.

SUSAN BRADY KONIG, They've Got to Be Carefully Taught

Vocabulary/Using a Dictionary

1. *Interrogation* means "to ask questions of (a person) especially formally or thoroughly," like "to *interrogate* a suspect." Konig's word choice implies her perception that Miss Laura wished to grill the author about any cultural aspects Konig might possess. It possibly suggests a forceful act of questioning that the author is not comfortable with.

2. In paragraph 21, Konig describes the *culmination* of Cultural Diversity Month. *Culmination* means "to reach the highest point or climactic stage." Thus, the *culmination* of Cultural Diversity Month is when the parents join their children in the classroom.

3. At first glance, students may recognize the root *concert* in the word *concerted*. Discuss with them what *concert* implies, moving away from its particularly musical connotations, focusing more on the organization that needs to take place for a concert to happen. Surely Konig chose the word carefully, implying a sort of conspiracy — larger than one teacher — in the particular instruction given to the children.

Responding to Words in Context

1. In the context of this essay, *culture* means the ways of living built up by a group of people and transmitted to succeeding generations. If we apply this definition of *culture* to the term *cultural-awareness*, the definition is "being informed about the ways of living that have been built up by different groups of people and observing how these ways are transmitted to succeeding generations."

2. Konig uses the word *affiliation* to describe Sarah's relationship to the United States; Miss Laura "reluctantly changes Sarah's *affiliation* to USA." In this context, *affiliation* means "a close association or connection" (in Sarah's case, specifically to a country). Ask students to what country they share an *affiliation*.

Discussing Main Point and Meaning

1. The title of Konig's essay "They've Got to Be Carefully Taught" states her concern over the future of her daughter's education because of the irresponsibility of the instruction of certain teachers. As she concludes, "Sarah only knows what she has been taught: Little Henry is white, her daddy's from Iceland, and New York's in France" (para. 25).

2. Mainly, the author is concerned with the instruction of her daughter. Konig worries about Miss Laura teaching her class to talk "about things that separate rather than connect" (para. 24). Konig's concern is well founded because her daughter is confused as to where her father was born, where the location of New York State is, and what color she should be. Whether Miss Laura deliberately confused Sarah's cultural identity is a conclusion that students will have to support using examples from the text.

3. Konig does not explain Miss Laura's actions. Possibly she has been forced to teach a multicultural curriculum that she is not comfortable with, or she can't articulate her lesson plans to achieve her desired goals; possibly she means well but is not a good teacher. You may want to discuss whether multicultural curriculums should be taught to young children. Who should be responsible for deciding when and how such programs should be established?

4. A few examples of Konig's employing wit and sarcasm are as follows: "I could bring in potatoes and beer for the whole class" (para. 11); "Wrong

67

. . . but go on" (para. 16); and "Don't you want them to learn it?" in response to her singing "Take Me Out to the Ball Game." As a follow-up, ask your students if sarcasm is an effective method to accomplish something. How does it work in everyday life? Does the sarcastic abuse of Miss Laura persuade them to agree with Konig's thesis that "They've Got to Be Carefully Taught"? What is Konig's purpose for using sarcasm?

Examining Sentences, Paragraphs, and Organization

1. The topic sentence of the opening paragraph is sentence 3.

2. The criteria for judging where a new paragraph starts and where an old paragraph ends are as follows: A paragraph is formed when a group of sentences focuses on one point or idea; thus, when a new idea occurs, a new paragraph must be formed.

3. Narrative examples (including dialogue) usually make your argument more effective because you are providing examples based on experience and empirical evidence. Without the use of dialogue between Konig and Miss Laura, the reader would not be as convinced of the poor quality of the teacher's instruction. We would be left to deduce Miss Laura's incompetence from the author's conclusion alone.

4. By citing certain events, Konig creates a microcosm of the larger world into which she fears the children are being prematurely initiated. The two blond girls now notice their similarities and the dark-haired girl notices her difference and is excluded. Most sarcastic — and quite effective — is that Konig begins the last two paragraphs with what seems like an affirmation, that the children "are becoming culturally aware," but which turns out to be a biting commentary on cultural awareness.

Thinking Critically

1. There may be many varied definitions of what *politically correct* means. According to *Webster's School and Office Dictionary*, it describes things that are "marked by a typically progressive orthodoxy on issues involving gender, race, sexual affinity, etc." Whereas Konig is sensitive to issues involving gender, race, and sexual affinity, Miss Laura appears to be *oversensitive* to politically correct issues; and by presenting these issues to such young children who may not have the capacity to understand, she confuses the children about such things as race, ethnicity, and gender. Allow students to argue different points, asking them to refer to the essay to support their ideas.

2. It is a matter of opinion whether you believe Konig feels uncomfortable with the fact that her "culture isn't *diverse* enough," and whether she feels ashamed of being American and not Irish. Students will certainly respond differently to the author's views on cultural awareness. These

three questions can be refuted and supported by looking at the text, and also by deducing what the author's motives are by observing the tone of the essay. Ask students to discuss these questions and come up with conclusions that they can share with the rest of the class.

In-Class Writing Activities

1. The freewrite performed by students for this question could be used as part of a larger essay outlining the first time they had ever experienced learning about a different culture in school. This *literacy narrative* could grow into a much larger paper, focusing on the different subjects students have been interested in throughout their academic careers, along with good and bad learning experiences encountered along the way.

2. Before having students write about an "American identity," you should have a brainstorming session about what comprises the identity of the United States. You will probably get a list of things like: rock & roll music, McDonald's restaurants, talk shows, the Declaration of Independence, the Constitution, baseball, football, basketball, and so on. Ask students to pick one of these topics and research (or explain) why they think that topic is inherently American. What other topics can they think of that aren't immediately apparent to them? Political issues? Historical?

Discussing the Unit

Preparing for Class Discussion

1. As we change emotionally and physically, we have new experiences by which to formulate our identities. Perhaps we instinctually want new places to challenge our personal "Chinatowns" which we treasure. Conversely, we may need every day to be structured basically the same as the next (with one two-week tourist vacation a year), and may be perfectly healthy and happy.

2. Meg Greenfield might respond adversely to Henry Han Xi Lau's essay in this chapter because she believes that too many individuals are members of a group, where identity is "more determined by what they now see themselves as *representing* rather than by their individual instincts and tastes." Greenfield would not be likely to accept Lau's suggestion that forming a group identity helps you survive in modern America. She might be resistant to those who would let themselves "be transformed into the emblem of some cause, any cause, or demographic category . . . [because] to draw your identity and take your marching orders from it is to kick away your freedom." Would Greenfield make an exception for a member of the small "Kung Fu Crew"?

3. You may want to ask students to consider the classroom as an environment in which they are defined by each other (and in which they define themselves). Does their sense of their relationship to the group affect how they view themselves? If so, how? Does this awareness influence their behavior? Their participation in discussion? Their sense of conformity or individuality? It may be helpful for you to offer an example from your own experience as a student, perhaps in a particularly difficult or competitive course or a situation in which you were affected by a sense of belonging (or not belonging) to a group.

From Discussion to Writing

1. In order to prepare students for this assignment, it might be best to outline each of the three essays, making notes about introductions, major examples, conclusions, and major transitions. Ask students to formulate an idea first (or freewrite toward one) and then work on the structure of their own essays.

2. Students might find this to be an easy assignment to get started on, and even to write, but may find it difficult to share their answers in class. Most students will be too modest to tell their peers what they are very good at, but are not afraid to tell their instructors. Perhaps include a presentation component to this writing activity, where students could demonstrate their ability/talent/accomplishment, and make sure that students explain *why* they feel as proud as they do.

3. Some students, frustrated with cultural diversity, may attack those instructors who go too far to expand students' cultural awareness. Be prepared for some answers that are against too much cultural diversity, and ask students to support their views with examples.

Topics for Cross-Cultural Discussion

1. Two reasons for asking these questions might be: first, to make foreign students feel that their opinions are valuable by having them share facts about their native cultures, and, second, to educate American students about cultures different from theirs. This question could prompt a discussion about the value placed on group identity in *every* aspect of foreign cultures: gender, class, religion, race, ethnicity, and so on.

2. There are many different group identities in American culture that foreign students may be aware of: on campus, in towns, in cities, at every level of society. A follow-up question to this might be: "Did you have an idea of what groups might dominate American culture before you arrived in this country?" You'll be surprised how many people still think we are cowboys, surfers, gangsters, or members of the cast of *Melrose Place* or *Baywatch*. After discussing these aspects of American society, ask students to explain which of these identities they find most attractive and why.

6
What Good Are Role Models?

Before discussing this unit, it might be helpful to consider the definition of the term *role model* — "a person whose behavior is imitated by others." Keep in mind that the word does not automatically denote good behavior on the part of the model. By definition, a role model can be positive or negative, as the imitator could mimic either good or bad characteristics of the model.

A good way to start off the class may be to make the previous distinction, and then ask your students to give examples of people they consider positive role models (whether from family, friends, the entertainment industry, and so on). Make a list of these people on the board, checking examples for artists from the music industry that could possibly be one of the following musicians mentioned in Susan J. Douglas's article "Girls 'n' Spice: All Things Nice?": the Spice Girls, Mary Chapin Carpenter, Ani Difranco, Michael Jackson, the Beatles, the New Kids on the Block, Pearl Jam, Nirvana, Counting Crows, Rage Against the Machine, Chrissie Hynde, Tori Amos, Salt-N-Pepa, the Bay City Rollers, Madonna, Sleater-Kinney, Liz Phair, Melissa Etheridge, Laura Nyro, and Annie Lennox.

If students mention a modern sports star, perhaps you could discuss Adolph Reed Jr.'s "Black Athletes on Parade." In his article, Reed mentions the function of black athletes as role models and asks whether we should hold these figures to a higher standard. Some people that Reed includes are Tiger Woods, Michael Jordan, Bill Cosby, Oprah Winfrey, Jackie Robinson, Frank Thomas, Spike Lee, Charles Barkley, Alan Iverson, Larry Bird, Pete Sampras, Wayne Gretsky, Brady Anderson, J. R. Richard, Roberto Clemente, and Booker T. Washington.

In the student essay, "Where Have All Our Heroes Gone?" by Tim Mills, the author writes about his concern that the "concept of heroes is gone." This essay could help to further discussion about students' concerns regarding the lack of positive role models in the late twentieth century. Mills refers to many figures who dominate modern American pop culture, icons students can relate to such as: Luke Skywalker, Pee Wee Herman, Magic Johnson, Michael Irving, Barry Switzer, Kurt Cobain, Marilyn Manson, President Clinton, Bill Gates, the cast of *Friends*, the animated show *South Park*, Princess Diana, Christopher Reeve, and Colin Powell.

For a glimpse at a historically relevant role model and his reception, have students read this unit's "From the Bookshelf" selection, an excerpt from Arnold Rampersad's book, *Jackie Robinson*.

SUSAN J. DOUGLAS, Girls 'n' Spice: All Things Nice?

Vocabulary/Using a Dictionary

1. *Saccharine* can mean "overly or sickly sweet." It relates to the word *saccharin* — a synthetic powder used as a noncaloric sugar substitute.

2. Some ways to use the word *vacuous*: The storeroom was vacuous (empty); she has a personality that is vacuous (lacking); his brain is vacuous (empty; lacking contents). The definition of the word *vacuous* has a strong similarity to the word *vacuum*, which means "a void; a space entirely devoid of matter."

3. *Deferential* means "yielding respectfully to another's opinion." *Defer* is its root word, meaning "to put off, delay." Both come from the Latin *differre* — "to postpone, be different."

Responding to Words in Context

1. Douglas's use of the word *bustier* in the context of paragraph 1 seems to imply synonyms such as *gutsier, more forceful, robust,* or *daring,* but there is a hint of sarcasm present.

2. The dictionary definition of the verb *dis* is (1) to show disrespect; (2) to disparage; (3) disparagement or criticism. (*Disparagement* means "to speak of or treat slightly" — so is this the word that *dis* comes from?)

3. If someone were to say to you "Hey, your outfit looks antiquated!" they would mean that your outfit looks old-fashioned or out of style. *Antiquated* looks like the word *antique* which means "dated from a period long ago."

Discussing Main Point and Meaning

1. The controversy in paragraph 4 is whether the Spice Girls are: (1) "a group of no-talent flash-in-the-pan bimbos" or (2) "a refreshing fusion of politics and music."

2. British politicians wanted to win the Spice Girls' favor because "they were in the press on a near daily basis, and reporters hung on their every word" (para. 6). By allying with the Spice Girls, the politicians were getting their names into circulation.

3. Douglas quoted the *Guardian* because she wanted to show her audience how important the Spice Girls were to the British, not unlike the Beatles. After a record number of women were elected to Parliament in May, 1997, British reporters asked the Spice Girls if they felt their "girl power" message had contributed to this event. The quotation from the *Guardian* connects the popularity of the Spice Girls with that of the Beatles, who were considered by some to be cultural gurus.

4. Douglas concludes: "Despite all the huffing and puffing of adults, one way or the other, it doesn't matter much what we think of the Spice Girls. What matters is what they mean to their preteen fans."

Examining Sentences, Paragraphs, and Organization

1. By definition, a transition sentence connects one idea to another in discourse. Douglas's major transitions in the essay are effective for a number of reasons: They are not forced, her expressions ("Ever since the success . . ." [para. 9], "And male critics are not the only ones who have dissed . . ." [para. 11]) are unique, not trite, and each one makes signal connections between different ideas.

2. Some bands that the Spice Girls are favorably (if ironically) compared to are: Michael Jackson (see para. 3 and the reference to the production of their new Pepsi ad), the Beatles (their movie is characterized as "a girls' version of *A Hard Day's Night*," para. 3), and Madonna (a millionaire who was "originally dismissed as a flash in the pan," para. 13). They are unfavorably compared to the "inauthentic" New Kids on the Block (para. 8), and female groups of the early 1960s whose music is referred to as "overly commercialized trash" (para. 9). At the same time that the Spice Girls are contrasted against "genuine" male groups like Pearl Jam, Nirvana, Counting Crows, and Rage Against the Machine (para. 9), as well as against female artists such as Mary Chapin Carpenter and Ani Difranco (who, it is implied, are opposites of Barbie, in para. 1) as well as Chrissie Hynde, Tori Amos, and Salt-n-Pepa who have achieved both commercial success and critical respect — Douglas warns the reader against dismissing the Spice Girls "as nothing more than The Bay City Rollers in drag" (para. 12).

3. A concluding paragraph serves to bring a discussion to an end that logically follows from a thesis and its discussion. Therefore, Douglas's conclusion is present in the last paragraph because it logically follows her thesis about the "Spice Girls debate": that "while it's easy as pie to hold a group like the Spice Girls in contempt, we should be wary when music embraced by preteen girls is ridiculed. These girls are telling us they want a voice, that they want someone to take them seriously" (para. 18).

Thinking Critically

1. Answers will vary for this question, but many students may agree with Douglas's statement because of the number of popular female musicians that have come out of the late 1990s. Thus, popular music (an industry which is by no means "friendly") could be considered "girl-friendly." Other mediums that might be discussed in terms of their "friendliness" toward women could include film, television, advertising, and the Internet.

2. *Feminism* by definition is "a movement advocating social, political, and economic rights for women, equal to those of men." Students may discuss whether "girl power (a 'bustier feminism') is a nineties way of saying it (feminism)" (para. 2) or if it is the product of "a highly calculated and cynical marketing strategy that has fused bubble-gum music with a pseudofeminist message" (para. 4).

In-Class Writing Activities

1. To help students come up with good questions, you may want to steer them toward the more critical points raised by the essay. For example, do (or should) the Spice Girls have a voice in British politics? Do they represent a majority of women? What does it mean that the only woman of color in the group is called "Scary Spice"? You may want to write a list of the class's questions on the board, and then ask a panel of five students (representing the Spice Girls) to try to answer the questions.

2. Douglas emphasizes the wish of teenage girls to be taken seriously — to be loved and respected; desired, but not "messed with." Whether listening to the Spice Girls is an expression of this wish is a question that students may debate in class and discuss in their essays, backing up their opinions with examples from Douglas's text and from their own life experience. Students may also explore whether the Spice Girls' message is that "feminism is necessary and fun"; they may also discuss other messages that they feel the group conveys through their music, image, and commentary.

ADOLPH REED JR., Black Athletes on Parade
Vocabulary/Using a Dictionary

1. By stating this, the author means that if we argue "racial injustice has been defeated," our reasoning is founded on one of two different points: Our viewpoint is either a falsely conservative report or a willfully evaded judgment based on lack of experience.

2. The term *black political discourse* can represent the ways in which African Americans engage in discussions about politics or it may represent how Americans in general engage in a political discussion as it relates to blacks. Relating the line "nothing has changed since slavery" to black political discourse implies that there have not been *any* advances in equal rights "since slavery."

3. *Loutish* means "rude, or crudely clumsy." *Malingering* means "pretending illness especially to shirk duty or work." Both words are used to describe *negative attributes* of certain people, but they are not synonyms.

Responding to Words in Context

1. *Revalorize* comes from *valorize* meaning "to maintain (or fix) the value of." (Note that the root of *valorize* comes from the Latin *valere*, "to be of worth.") Attaching the prefix *re-* (denoting action done over) to *valorize* gives *revalorize* the following meaning: "to reestablish the value of." *The Nation* wishes blacks in South Carolina would "reestablish the value of" the Confederate battle flag.

2. *Invidious* looks similar to *invade*. Both share the similarities of "taking the offense" or being "offensive," but the adjective *invidious* means "offensively discriminating," whereas the verb *invade* means "to enter forcefully as an enemy."

Discussing Main Point and Meaning

1. The author explains his title in paragraph 3, saying "racialized expectations still prevail — especially in sports." The fact that black athletes have been scrutinized by (paraded in front of) Americans is in part an "ironic legacy" of Jackie Robinson because he solicited his views "on all manner of political and social issues that concerned black Americans." Other athletes following him were expected to do the same. Ask students to back up their interpretation of the essay's title with facts from the text.

2. Reed explains what is meant by "The myth of black athletic superiority," in paragraphs 16 and 17 stating: "On the average, blacks in pro baseball and football perform somewhat better statistically than their white counterparts. At first glance this may lend credence to the claim that blacks are more gifted. The reality, however, is quite the opposite: Marginal black players are more likely than comparably talented whites to get weeded out along the way. . . . The myth of black athletic superiority leads scouts and coaches to evaluate black athletes with *higher expectations* in mind. So the black player has to exhibit a higher level of skill or performance to impress." Reed indicates that the myth of black athletic superiority is perpetuated because the black player "has to exhibit a higher level of skill or performance" than the white player.

3. Before J. R. Richard's near death, he "had been complaining of weakness for some time, but the Astros' management and the Houston media . . . attacked Richard for dogging it." Because black players need "to exhibit a higher level of skill or performance to impress," Richard never complained. This specific example gives credence to Reed's argument. It supports the pervasiveness of the "myth of black athletic superiority" by indicating the attitudes held by the team's management and by the media.

4. According to Reed, it is unfair to expect an athlete to adopt any other role because "Jackie Robinson fought to bring into existence a world in

which he and others would be able to pursue their craft on an equal basis with everyone else . . . without unfair expectations and double standards. A world, that is, in which a ball player would be simply a ball player."

Examining Sentences, Paragraphs, and Organization

1. The topic sentence of paragraph 13 is sentence 2: "But the implication that they have some special obligation to do so because of their status as black — or in Woods's case, even Asian American — athletic icons is wrong." It is the topic sentence of the paragraph because it contains the paragraph's main idea.

2. If the first paragraph and the last were switched, the essay would not be as effective, and Reed's argument would not be as persuasive. In his first paragraph, Reed sets up an argument that he wishes to refute, "that racial justice has been defeated." The two paragraphs that follow this statement build directly from it; thus, the first paragraph is essential to the essay. The last paragraph contains the author's opinion, a concluding generalization that can only be made *after* Reed has provided us with evidence and support. It would weaken the essay to move this paragraph elsewhere.

3. Reed's essay begins by refuting the claim that "racial injustice has been defeated" and goes on to educate the reader, providing examples of Jackie Robinson's legacy and how inequality affects modern athletes. The essay's main function is to teach (and by teaching sets out to move the reader to action).

Thinking Critically

1. The answer to this question is a matter of opinion; however, you may want to point out that Reed provides evidence to support his claim. Perhaps students will agree that it is "unreasonable and unfair" to expect athletes "to adopt any public role other than simply that of athlete," but may not see athletes *choosing* to do so as a "waste of time." In any case, students *must* give reasons to support their opinions.

2. Students may or may not find Reed's informal approach to be persuasive. He probably used contemporary examples such as Alan Iverson and Charles Barkley to try to reach a broader, younger audience in *The Progressive*, the magazine for which he wrote the article. The question of whether to trust the author's authority is a matter of opinion (make sure students give support for their claims).

In-Class Writing Activities

1. Students may have varied impressions of Frick's character, and whether they see him as a role model (though it is likely that many will). To encourage discussion, have students read their freewriting ideas aloud.

2. To create writing topics, you could ask students to brainstorm about different examples of people whom they hold in high esteem and for whom they sometimes have unreasonable expectations: parents, friends, sports heroes, musicians, actors/actresses, government officials, and so on.

TIM MILLS, Where Have All Our Heroes Gone?

Vocabulary/Using a Dictionary

1. For Mills, the period of greatest success for the word *hero* was in the early 1980s when he learned about people like Christopher Columbus, Mother Theresa, Gandhi, and others. According to Mills, the early 1980s precede a later period in which "no one was talking about [heroes] any more" (para. 2).

2. Mills means that he eventually learned that George Washington was a ruler who exercised absolute power oppressively.

3. The word *pharmaceutical* is Greek in origin, from the word *pharmakeuein* meaning "to administer drugs," which came from *pharmakon*, "magic charm, poison, drug."

Responding to Words in Context

1. Mills's creation of the noun *virtuosity* relates to the word *virtuous*, meaning "conforming to moral or ethical principles." Therefore, the noun *virtuosity* could mean "possessing moral or ethical principles."

2. The meaning of the word *just* in paragraph 9 is "proper or right; morally right; righteous." *Just* can also mean: (as an adverb) (1) within a brief preceding time: *the sun just came out*; (2) precisely: *that's just what I mean*; (3) barely: *just in time*; (4) merely: *just a child*; (5) at this moment: *the movie is just ending*; (6) simply: *we'll just have to wait and see*; (or as an adjective) (7) guided by reason and fairness: *a just ruling*; (8) proper: *a just reply*; (9) lawful: *a just analysis*; (10) true; correct: *a just claim*; (11) deserved: *a just punishment*.

Discussing Main Point and Meaning

1. The author loses his faith in heroes because of the wrongdoings they committed in the arenas of politics, movies, sports, the music business, and even the office of the president.

2. In paragraph 7, Mills does not mean what he says when he states: "who needs heroes anyway?", rather, he is being ironic — using words to convey a meaning that is the opposite of their literal meaning. The author's ironic meaning is supported in the statements that follow the first sentence in paragraph 7: "Divorce rates are through the roof. Pharmaceutical companies are selling record numbers of antidepressants."

3. Mills explains this opinion in paragraph 10, stating: "Maybe, it gives us a chance to become heroes ourselves. We're no longer pressured to live up to someone else's deeds. We can accomplish our own goals." Again the author's observation is an ironic one — his real message is that the lack of heroes in some way reduces us to "a few . . . simpler acts of heroism." "We don't have to save the world," quips Mills. "We can feel good about just . . . saying 'please' and 'thank you.'"

Examining Sentences, Paragraphs, and Organization

1. The topic sentence in paragraph 9 is sentence 3: "But the concept of heroes is gone." It is the topic sentence because it expresses the main idea of the paragraph.

2. To support his idea that the "new crop of heroes" is "pretty bleak," the different groups that Mills makes use of are sports, music, movies and television, and politics. He sections these off in *groups* because this makes it easier to organize his essay, and his ideas are more clearly followed by the reader.

3. Some examples of irony in the essay:

   (a) "That was all right. I still had the movies and television to provide me with a new crop of heroes, people whose virtuosity we should aspire to attain and accomplishments we should strive to equal." (para. 3, sents. 1–2)
   (b) "There's still sports, right?" (para. 4, sent. 2)
   (c) "And, I guess if you're a football player who's into cocaine and prostitutes, it might be beneficial to have a coach in Dallas who carries a gun." (para. 4, sent. 5).
   (d) "But really, who needs heroes anyway? We're doing just fine without them, thank you very much." (para. 7, sents. 1–2)

Thinking Critically

1. A student might argue that the concept of heroes is gone perhaps because the 1990s have been a period in which America has been disappointed by its political leaders, athletes, and entertainers. As individuals and as a culture, we tend to view their scandals, crimes, and self-destruction as failings that have an impact on us all. Or, a student could argue that a move away from the concept of heroes (as witnessed perhaps by the lack of dialogue/media focus on heroes) is a healthy evolution away from idealization.

2. Answers to this question will possibly be followed by heated discussion. To manage the discussion, you may want to use the blackboard to make a list of your students' answers, the people whom the students chose to be "pillars of strength and icons of respectability." Remember that an icon is an object of critical devotion: an idol; a symbol.

In-Class Writing Activities

1. The answers to this question are a matter of opinion. If after reading the freewrites, you find the class to be divided, perhaps split the students into teams to debate the issue.

2. To answer this essay, students should understand the distinctions between *fame*, *hero*, and *positive role model*. *Fame* means "renowned; celebrated." *Hero* is a term used for "any person admired for noble qualities or special achievements." A *positive role model* is "a person whose positive behavior in a particular role is imitated by others." Answers based on this information may vary, and students should support their claims with detailed examples.

Discussing the Unit

Preparing for Class Discussion

1. Television, music, and other media constantly influence our opinions about people we consider role models. Michael Jackson (music industry), Bill Cosby (television), Johnny Carson (television), Roseanne Barr (television), Kelsey Grammer (television), Magic Johnson (sports), and Michael Irving (sports) are just a few people who have disappointed their fans at one time or another due to exposés by the media. Ask students to answer the most important part of the question: How did this make you feel? What was your emotional reaction to this incident with the media?

2. A list of traits or characteristics for a good role model could be: courage, patience, honor, calmness, fortitude, inner strength, creativity, intelligence, artistry, beauty, fearlessness, and so on. It should be easy for students to come up with a list of 5 to 10 characteristics. After they've done this, ask them to compare their lists with the person sitting next to them. If words are used twice, tell them to make a note. Then, keeping track on the board, make a class list of students' most common and desirable traits for a good role model. You may want to focus this discussion more specifically by asking: What characteristics make up a good teacher?

From Discussion to Writing

1. Regardless of who students choose to be on the show, the discussion of the program should focus on the value of role models. You may want to get the discussion started by offering your own examples. For instance, you might invite Magic Johnson to appear on your show. As a sports hero who is HIV positive (and public about it) does Johnson view himself as a particular type of role model for his audience? Does his view of himself affect his public life? You might explain that the goal of your

question is to get a role model's perspective on the issue of public responsibility — should Magic Johnson be expected (as Adolph Reed Jr. argues against) "to adopt any public role other than simply as athlete"? What does Johnson think?

2. To answer this question, students must be aware that there are four parts to it: (1) writing an essay describing some of the positive and negative role models they've encountered in their lives; (2) formulating their own definition of the term *role model*; (3) discussing how the people they've chosen fit their definition; and (4) explaining whether imitating the behavior of their chosen role models has made them better people. Remind students of the definition of a role model (positive or negative) — a person whose behavior is imitated by others.

3. In her essay, Susan Douglas believes that the Spice Girls are trying to help their teenage audience become aware of their strengths as young women. Whether this constructs the Spice Girls as heroes is another story. In her closing paragraph, Douglas claims that the Spice Girls are a decided improvement over "I Wanna Be Bobby's Girl," but it is unclear whether she would agree with the first part of Mills's statement that "the concept of heroes is gone." Students will have to make a decision about whether Douglas considers the Spice Girls to be heroes, based on their interpretation of the essay. Douglas doesn't deal with the final part of Mills's statement, his comment that because of a lack of heroes, "we can become heroes ourselves." But students could find tenuous support for this statement in Douglas's essay.

Topics for Cross-Cultural Discussion

1. Different cultures value different behaviors of their role models. Ask students to cite specific heroes and to reflect on their characteristics. Ask them to compare and contrast these examples with similar American heroes who may have been discussed previously in class.

2. It is entirely possible that the essays in this unit are students' first exposure to Jackie Robinson and the Spice Girls. It is nonetheless an interesting question to explore in the form of "*Would* Jackie Robinson and the Spice Girls be considered heroes or role models in your culture?" or, "in other cultures?" What is revealed about America by the fact that Jackie Robinson and the Spice Girls are generally considered heroes? What historical significance does it have, and what current cultural trends does it point to?

7

Can We Resist Stereotypes?

Stereotyping takes its name from an old printing process, in which a metal plate with a raised surface was used, and thus the meaning of *stereotyping* in the more modern sense has a lot to do with making many things the same (making copies). Ironically, *stereo* from the Greek means "solid, three-dimensional"; the printing process was named with this definition in mind, as it described the original plate from which copies were made. Contemporary stereotypes are anything but three-dimensional. A few very recent and specific examples are: the *welfare queen*, the *femi-nazi*, the rap *gangsta'*, the *deadbeat dad*, the Asian *model minority*, and the *gen-Xer*. Still, these modern images have not diminished the persistence of more traditional stereotypes too numerous to list. The most democratic nation in the world can also be the most reductive when it comes to perceptions and attitudes toward different ethnic and cultural groups.

As the United States becomes more diverse and complicated, its inhabitants become more confused about their identities and the identities of those around them. That confusion produces at least two major behavioral responses: the multicultural embracing of all identities as equally valuable and entitled, and the reactionary nostalgia for simpler times characterized by a strong desire for cultural homogeneity. Most of us hover somewhere in between these two poles, looking for ways to reconcile the various inconsistencies that plurality creates, and for ways to be culturally aware without relying on stereotypical information or imagery.

This balancing act is a theme in all of the essays in this unit. How can we differentiate between stereotypes and outright discrimination, G. Stuart Englebert asks. Or perhaps both tendencies are a part of the same fear of "the other," as Eric Waters suggests. Fear is also on Bryan Garvey's mind as he presents the idea that stereotypes are relied on mostly by those who are too afraid to look at themselves. In addition, Edmund Lee and Kenneth Li contribute to this analysis by examining how even the most "positive" of stereotypes can be harmful.

Ask students to write a description of themselves from their own perspective and then to follow up with a list of possible stereotypes that could be attached to that description by someone unlike them. After having students discuss their descriptions and lists, make a transition to the topics of the unit. Are the lists of stereotypes students came up with as hurtful as the ones that Waters faces? As misguided and dismissive as the one Lee and Li discuss? Or do students' lists have minimal significance and power, as Englebert and Garvey both suggest in different ways?

For another short narrative and a little perspective, encourage students to read this unit's "From the Bookshelf" selection from Brent Staples's book *Parallel Time* — a revision of his famous essay, "Just Walk on By."

EDMUND LEE AND KENNETH LI, The Myth of the Asian American Superstudent

Vocabulary/Using a Dictionary

1. A *chord* is "a harmonious combination of musical tones," so *discord* (para. 3) would be the opposite or absence of such harmony. *Concord* is "agreement of interests or feelings."

2. An *agenda* (para. 17) can be negative when it impedes compromise or conversation between two or more parties, or when the items on the list supersede common sense or the greater good. In this article, *agenda* is not used with an explicitly negative connotation, and yet it is clear that the authors and New York City school principals have different *agendas*.

3. *Laurels* (para. 20) are a wreath of greens bestowed upon the winners of various contests, particularly marathoning (n.b., *laurel* trees have a Mediterranean origin). To *rest on one's laurels* means "to believe that the honor one has received in one instance carries over into subsequent situations and/or contests."

Responding to Words in Context

1. The metaphoric *stellar* and *stratospheric* (para. 19) are used to demonstrate the *other-worldly*, starlike quality often ascribed to the academic performance of Asian American students. They are also meant to demonstrate the gap between Asian American success stories and failures.

2. A *pipeline* (para. 11) usually refers to "a conduit for essential needs like water, gas, or oil." The analogy between such life-sustaining substances and education is an effective one.

Discussing Main Point and Meaning

1. Kim's study looks at two starkly different statistical trends: the superior academic performance of some Asian Americans, and the serious difficulties some Asian Americans have completing even a basic education.

2. Weaker Asian American students often don't get the help and attention they need because they are assumed to be naturally capable academically.

3. Different immigration patterns and congressional relief acts have played a role in the varied performance levels of Asian Pacific Americans. Most notably, more recent immigrants like the Vietnamese and the Cambodians have largely been political and economic refugees, who generally have experienced a lower standard of living and come from uneducated backgrounds.

4. If there is a large number of Asian American students who are struggling as much or more than any other students, then not only is the stereotype unfair but it also contributes to the neglect of struggling Asian American students.

Examining Sentences, Paragraphs, and Organization

1. The two students provide real images (or evidence) so that the reader will be more easily convinced of the larger argument when the authors finally introduce it in the subsequent paragraphs. Given the popularity of the superstudent myth, real anecdotes are an effective way to introduce criticism of the myth.

2. Heather Kim's study (see para. 6) and Shirley Hune and Kenyon Chan's study (see para. 10) are the main sources, though there are several others. Kim's study is quoted in paragraph 7 and summarized in paragraph 8. Hune and Chan's study is briefly summarized in paragraph 10 and quoted in paragraph 11. Neither study is really paraphrased, which is a more detailed and comprehensive manner of use.

3. The strategy begins and ends with specific examples to counteract the dehumanizing effect of statistics. Concrete images will hopefully stay with the reader, though generalizations rarely do.

4. Tang recommends "qualitative" rather than "quantitative" research: looking at individual case studies rather than just statistical trends.

Thinking Critically

1. The authors' objective is to debunk what they perceive as the myth that all Asian Americans are excellent students, but a secondary point is that economics has a profound effect on academic performance. It could be argued that economics should be the factor that determines which students get the most attention. If Asian Americans, other racial minorities, and whites were all examined according to their economic status instead of their racial backgrounds, it is likely that the majority of students who need attention would be more visible.

2. Based on the findings of the studies discussed in the essay, it is possible that poor Asian Americans may have more in common with other poor Americans than with wealthy or middle-class Asian Americans. If asked to study the results of surveys conducted along ethnic and economic lines,

it is likely that economists and educators would consider the idea that class, more than any other factor, determines academic success.

In-Class Writing Activities

1. Ask students who are Asian American or who went to school with Asian Americans to explain whether they think they were affected by the kinds of stereotypes Lee and Li describe. If students report having attended a school with no Asian American students, ask them to talk about how that absence affected their impressions of Asian Americans.

2. Emphasize the specific details necessary to make a description like this convincing. Some students may have trouble writing from an Asian American point of view. The journal entries may show that students of all ethnicities can fall prey to stereotyping. If you have Asian American students or other nonwhite students in your class, you may want to compare their journal entries with those of the class as a whole. How do all of the entries (and the possible stereotypes within those entries) compare? What do the Asian American students think of their classmates' entries? This could be a good starting point for a discussion on how stereotyping affects our perceptions of ourselves and others.

BRYAN GARVEY, We Are More Than Labels

Vocabulary/Using a Dictionary

1. Animal life is *animate*. A blood cell and a grasshopper are *animate*; a tree is *inanimate* (para. 5).

2. *Fantasy, fantastic,* and *phantom* are the most obvious relatives. The connection is that they all relate to what is not real or what is better than real.

3. *Demos* means "people," so *demographic* (para. 6) literally means "to write (down) the people." The literal meaning of *autograph* is "to write the self"; *geography* is "to write the earth"; and *telegraph* is "to write to far away."

Responding to Words in Context

1. Since a label names the contents of a thing, it presumes that those contents are permanent, unchanging.

2. Hell is often characterized as having an unending cycle of punishment, similar to the one in the *Twilight Zone* episode Garvey talks about.

Discussing Main Point and Meaning

1. Garvey insinuates that stereotypes are at least usable joke material (para. 6), which he doesn't actually explain or describe in depth.

2. The story of Helen Keller, according to Garvey, is supposed to illustrate how dependent we are on labels to differentiate among things.

3. Garvey's professor said that "People are not statistics," which echoes Garvey's point that a person's identity cannot be pinned down according to superficial characteristics.

4. Identities change, labels are static (see para. 7).

Examining Sentences, Paragraphs, and Organization

1. Garvey is trying to suggest in this sentence that stereotypes have a kernel of truth, but he uses a light tone to do so in order not to seem too supportive of stereotyping.

2. *Doing with* and *doing* refer to material and behavioral concerns, respectively. *Being* is a more internal concern, the measure of one's self-worth. Thoreau's advice is to worry more about one's own self-worth than the material or behavioral characteristics of others.

3. Garvey asks the reader, jokingly, who he or she would be if not a character in his dream. The question is ironic, as Garvey has already suggested that being in that dream would be akin to being described only by a label, where one cannot get out of the label one is assigned and where all labels are ultimately meaningless. The purpose may be to keep the tone of the discussion a little lighter than most discussions on the same subject usually are.

Thinking Critically

1. Garvey's is an admirable position to take, though it may not be the most practical. Saying that one does not pay attention to the perceptions of others is easier than actually doing it. If students don't bring it up, you might introduce the question of Garvey's race, gender, and class. Who in our society would have the easiest time "just existing"?

2. The real problem is that Garvey glosses over the reference to comedians too quickly. He might have been able to make the point effectively if he addressed the origin, function, and effect of ethnic humor rather than use a cursory mention of it as evidence that stereotypes have some truth.

In-Class Writing Activities

1. You may wish to engage students in a discussion of how even the most harmless of stereotypes can be detrimental. For example, if a student has listed "football player" and the corresponding stereotype "dumb jock" or "Neanderthal," you might discuss how this student athlete could get taken less seriously by teachers, or perceived to be anti-intellectual and, therefore, less encouraged to pursue a career that requires academic rigor. Such stereotyping can affect the student's entire future.

2. This is a difficult assignment, in part because it asks students to think in grand terms. Allow parody or other creative interpretations of this assignment (for example, if a student wanted to divide people into bed makers and nonmakers, sugar-cone types and cake-cone types, dog people and cat people, or MTV watchers and VH1 watchers, and so on). Though they are eventually going to deconstruct their arguments, students should be encouraged to flesh out their initial analyses.

Opposing Views: Stereotyping and Racism

ERIC WATERS, Stop Stereotyping Young Black Males
G. STUART ENGLEBERT, Stereotyping and Racism Are Not the Same

Vocabulary/Using a Dictionary

1. The meanings of *conceive* both have to do with creation. A *misconception* (Waters, para. 2) is a bad or wrong idea about something; if referring to a pregnancy, it would most likely refer to a problematic pregnancy, or a pregnancy ending in miscarriage.

2. Englebert's *dogmatic* (para. 4) views may be arrogantly authoritative (and unfounded), but *absolutism* (para. 4) would build those views into a governmental authority that gave them singular power. In other words, the difference is between simply having controversial opinions and using those opinions to dictate legal policy.

3. Englebert uses *cower* (para. 1) to contrast with his ironic use of *brave writer* (para. 1) to describe Waters. Essentially calling Waters a *coward* in the first paragraph of this article, Englebert is setting up an almost polemical essay, the tone of which is quite angry and frustrated. You might introduce the term *polemical* to your students while discussing this article.

Responding to Words in Context

1. Waters introduces the word *racism* in paragraph 6, after — incidentally — introducing the popular term *eracism*. He does conflate the two terms rather easily. The question for students is whether racism and stereotyping are synonymous. Is one a less serious version of the other? Does one lead to the other? Can a person practice one and not practice the other? Ask students to consider these questions.

2. Englebert's use of "excuses" (Englebert, para. 8) is cryptic. Does Englebert mean Waters would no longer have excuses for the negative ways people view him? Or, more insidiously, does Englebert mean that Waters would

have excuses for any problems that may exist in the African American community?

Discussing Main Point and Meaning

1. The coverage of crime on Waters's college campus seems discriminatory to him, and he has had several experiences with students who assume that he is on an athletic scholarship because he is black or who are afraid to have him walk behind them late at night. (Note Waters's assumption that the female student feared him particularly because he is a black man. According to the article, two rapes were committed — one by a white man and one by a black man. The female student's actions, as described by Waters, may or may not have been a response to the heightened coverage of the black rapist.)

2. Waters thinks that stereotyping and racism are at least related, if not synonymous. Englebert believes that stereotyping and racism are not related at all. You might ask students to write their own definitions of the terms before deciding whether they think the terms are related.

3. Englebert says that his experiences lead him to stereotype. He suggests that people have come to dislike or distrust Waters based on their experiences of him. Ask students to think about whether it is possible to have the same expectations of any new acquaintance regardless of color, gender, class, or ethnicity.

Examining Sentences, Paragraphs, and Organization

1. Englebert himself doesn't really explain why misconceptions do exist, except to say that race is not a factor. Saying that Waters "cops out" of understanding creates an image of Waters as not looking beneath the surface of his interactions with others. Ironically this is how Waters suggests others respond to him on his college campus. Ask students whether they think Englebert should have addressed Waters's specific experiences more carefully.

2. Ask students whether people can develop stereotypical assessments based on only their own experiences. Once those stereotypes are formed, can one have an open mind to others? Englebert seems defiant in this statement and seems to believe that he has made a common-sensical statement with which others will identify. It's a risky strategy, unless Englebert expects his audience to identify with him. Discuss the fact that, as Waters suggests, the readership for this college newspaper is generally white. Perhaps Englebert is correct to assume a sympathetic reader.

3. Waters wants the reader to think about just how often we use race as an indicator. The imperative statement should inspire some clarity and optimism if indeed the reader takes Waters up on his challenge.

4. Englebert suggests that his prejudices are more valid because they are developed through personal experience, whereas Waters criticized the prejudices people learn from the media. Waters would disapprove of Englebert's assertion that stereotyping is a "necessary element of human survival," in large part because the two writers have different interpretations of stereotyping.

Thinking Critically

1. Englebert is a bit evasive about addressing the whole of Waters's argument. In paragraph 3, he says that he "agree[s] unfair stereotyping and discrimination are prevalent," but he then goes on only to discuss what he considers "fair" stereotyping and its disconnection with racism. If he had taken more time to differentiate between "unfair" and "fair" stereotyping, his argument would seem more comprehensive. Furthermore, Englebert bases that argument on a connection that is implied in Waters's article, though not fully explicated, which is perhaps why he doesn't quote Waters. Englebert infers and extrapolates a great deal from one paragraph in Waters's article rather than directly addressing Waters's argument.

2. Waters has clearly learned about stereotyping from his own experience, which is similar to Englebert's method, except that Waters is the object of the stereotyping rather than the subject. Both authors could attempt to reconcile the two kinds of experience if they could consider whether they have experienced the other position (Waters as the stereotyper, Englebert as the stereotyped).

In-Class Writing Activities

1. Specific examples are key here. You might introduce the concept of inductive reasoning (building a generalization from specific examples) to advanced students, especially if they produce very clear patterns in their lists.

2. Students should be encouraged to do close readings of the two articles, picking specific passages from each that could share some elements of possible compromise. Also ask whether there are any resources for dealing with intolerance at their own college that could be effective at other schools.

Discussing the Unit

Preparing for Class Discussion

1. This is a very subjective assignment. If students cannot think of ways that they label themselves, ask them to think about how they place themselves in specific peer groups: Can that be considered a kind of self-stereotyping?

2. Ask students to "rank" the descriptive characteristics that are most important. Is it best to "fully prepare" people to meet someone who is "different" in some way (for example, if a student is setting up two friends on a blind date who are of a different race, or one of whom has a physical disability), or does this preparation only reinforce stereotypical behavior?

From Discussion to Writing

1. Students will necessarily have to be specific here, so you will want to focus on the logic of students' arguments as to whether differences matter in modeling.

2. It might be useful to have a discussion about the continuum on which both the most "harmless" and the most "harmful" stereotypes exist. Should all stereotyping be avoided?

3. An episode of a popular television sitcom, for example, could provide students the opportunity for critical analysis. What stereotypes are apparent? What is the message of this stereotype? How might the episode be rewritten to offer a less reductive portrayal of characters?

Topics for Cross-Cultural Discussion

1. There is no correct answer to this question. Clearly, stereotyping is a human tendency and exists everywhere, though some argue that more pluralistic societies (the United States especially) are more prone to stereotyping.

2. This is a good opportunity for discussion between native and nonnative students. Students born and raised in the United States may be unaware of the stereotypes of Americans as rude, loud, gluttonous, lazy, and uncultured.

8
Can "Op-Ads" Change Your Mind?

Advertising appears just about everywhere: on television, on the radio, in print media, along the highways, on public transportation, in our mail, on the Internet, and even on our car windshields. We cannot avoid being subject to all kinds of sales pitches, including those that pitch opinions and ideas. In fact, American politics have drifted further into the realm of marketing than most of us would care to admit. Once political "photo ops" were as simple as the casual kiss of an infant, and political consciousness-raising was considered the art of grass-roots activists and campaign volunteers. Now it's sometimes difficult to tell the difference between a Nike ad and a charity appeal, between a Coca-Cola commercial and a stump speech, or between marketing gimmicks and election campaign strategies.

The ads in this unit represent just a small sampling of the opinions that are "for sale" in today's political "marketplace." In advance of class time that you set aside for this unit, ask students to be on the lookout for other examples, particularly in print media, on billboards, in their mail, and on public transportation. What differences can be observed between opinion and product advertising? Do "op-ads" work mainly by rhetorical argument? Are they more verbal and less visual? What cues do they pick up from commercial advertising? Begin class discussion by having students share their findings, and discuss whether they have ever been affected by opinion advertising.

Vocabulary/Using a Dictionary

1. [U.S. English] The reference to bureaucrats is somewhat vague and broad. U.S. English could be referring to government leaders or education executives who play some role in maintaining the status quo, but the reference is too vague to be certain.

2. [The National Center for Tobacco-Free Kids] *Legislation* really refers to the whole process of drafting, debating, and revising a law until it can be passed through Congress.

3. [Planned Parenthood Federation of America] There's no clear opposite for *genuine chance*, though a *conditional chance*, a *symbolic chance*, or a *slim chance* might be what the ad alludes to.

4. [The American Civil Liberties Union] An *official prayer session* would be one led by teachers or other school leaders, in which all students would

be compelled to participate (even if just by observing). It's possible that the ACLU would not oppose something like a *moment of silence*; however, any regularly scheduled spiritual activity could be interpreted as *official prayer* representing the religious majority at the school.

5. [Negative Population Growth, Inc.] Something that is *vitally important* is important to the life of something or someone. In this ad, the natural environment of the United States is considered to be of vital importance.

Responding to Words in Context

1. [U.S. English] U.S. English's definition of *a melting pot society* seems to be a society in which all types of people assimilate into one basic type, although they claim to allow for people who want to "hold on to" parts of their native cultures.

2. [The National Center for Tobacco-Free Kids] This is a plea for individuals to get involved in this issue, so using the second person pronoun, *you,* is a way of directly addressing the reader.

3. [Planned Parenthood Federation of America] Though they are indeed making a "political" claim themselves, Planned Parenthood is lobbying for the idea that the government should have no role in a woman's family planning choices, even if abortion is one of those choices. They would like those choices to be considered "moral" or "medical" only, and not political.

4. [The American Civil Liberties Union] The ad wants to appeal to as many different types of audiences as possible. By listing many kinds of prayers, the ACLU can be certain that many kinds of worshipers will identify with the scenario presented: one in which children of one denomination will have to recite prayers of another denomination.

5. [Negative Population Growth, Inc.] Though they modify different things (the economy and the environment), "sustainable" and "sound" could switch places with little effect, since both are referring to the general well-being of the things they modify. Still, the two words are not synonymous and would not be interchangeable in all contexts.

Discussing Main Point and Meaning

1. [U.S. English] U.S. English suggests that only English should be used in schools and at all levels of government, which really means that any documents, services, or information that the government provides would be available only in English.

2. [The National Center for Tobacco-Free Kids] The ad lists two other purposes: to "help adults quit smoking" and to "eliminate second-hand smoke in public places and worksites."

3. [Planned Parenthood Federation of America] Other issues addressed are access to and insurance coverage for contraception, and education for teenagers about birth control options.

4. [The American Civil Liberties Union] The intended audience is anyone who practices a religion. The tone is gentle and sympathetic, which reflects the inclusiveness of the intention.

5. [Negative Population Growth, Inc.] The most urgent concern stated is "population growth"; however, the "growth" referred to is restricted to that which comes as a result of immigration, not through reproduction. The term is somewhat of a misnomer as immigration represents a population increase nationally, but not internationally.

Examining Sentences, Paragraphs, and Organization

1. [U.S. English] The ad uses the past tense to suggest that there are no longer success stories like Mujica's, which would make the plea of U.S. English more urgent. The phrase is certainly still relevant. There may be more services for non-native speakers today, but it is still very difficult to "succeed" in this country without English fluency.

2. [The National Center for Tobacco-Free Kids] The idiom used is "going up in smoke," which usually refers to the destruction of a fire, but it's fairly effective in this context also.

3. [The Planned Parenthood Federation of America] The fragments form a list of qualifications for the last sentence in the previous paragraph, which ends with "the responsibility born out of our freedom to choose." The subsequent fragments represent a subset of "responsibilities," emphasizing the concept of responsibility to compensate for the frequent assumption that abortion comes as a result of "irresponsibility."

4. [The American Civil Liberties Union] "It" is the image of one's child being forced to say the prayer of another religious denomination. It is somewhat interesting that the ad features the face of an Asian girl. The assumed audience will be largely white, and the use of an Asian face is, therefore, provocative: Might this be a way of instilling a bit of fear into the Christian community, who are perhaps the biggest proponents of prayer in school?

5. [Negative Population Growth, Inc.] The numbers become a bit distracting, and they do not seem particularly organized. There is the chance that readers will tune out, or at least become suspicious of the numbers — as if the intention of the group is to overwhelm or distract the reader from the less admirable connotations of anti-immigration sentiments.

Thinking Critically

1. [U.S. English] It is odd that the ad features Mujica's picture and his story, but that the voice of the ad is not his. You may want to ask students whether they think that the U.S. English organization is afraid of the conservative backlash that might result from an ad that is completely dominated by an immigrant minority.

2. [The National Center for Tobacco-Free Kids] Parents may bear the ultimate responsibility for their children, but the government also has a responsibility to protect its citizens from the harmful behaviors of other citizens and from potentially harmful products. For example, alcohol consumption is limited to adults, as are driving and voting. And further, the findings on second-hand smoke have really crystallized the issue of government responsibility. Because second-hand smoke can hurt non-smokers — say, like driving drunk or dumping toxic waste — it becomes a civil rights issue, according to some.

3. [Planned Parenthood Federation of America] Planned Parenthood's platform really hasn't changed all that much since its inception, although the violence against women's health clinics in recent years has forced a renewed commitment. In that sense the organization may have to give new *protection* to the meaning of "choice," but its ultimate goals are the same.

4. [The American Civil Liberties Union] The ACLU is concerned with the rights of all students to receive equal educational opportunities. If the prayers of a particular religious denomination become "official" school policy, then there is some risk that the school environment could become hostile to children of other religions. Though it may seem unlikely, that kind of hostility could also turn into violence.

5. [Negative Population Growth, Inc.] Negative Population Growth might do better to focus on environmental issues, since it claims to be concerned with maintaining a healthy environment. Fifty-four percent is a small majority, indeed, and the organization admits to sponsoring the poll, which suggests that there could be some margin of error. One would want to see the actual poll questions and comprehensive results and also to hear about efforts to control other kinds of "population growth."

In-Class Writing Activities

1. [U.S. English] Non-native speakers may be reluctant to testify to the resources at their high schools (except in an ESL class), so this may not be an assignment that you want to ask students to read aloud.

2. [The National Center for Tobacco-Free Kids] Answers will vary but should refer to the specific offices and services of the students' college or university (as well as the weaknesses or lack of services). Clearly there should

probably also be some mention of the effectiveness of peer pressure with respect to an issue like this.

3. [Planned Parenthood Federation of America] For many students the key for this assignment will be to refrain from parody. Not all anti-abortion activists are extremists, and many choose logical tactics over emotional tactics. Students should be aiming to represent the former.

4. [The American Civil Liberties Union] It may be difficult for students who are religious to refrain from using their own denominational assumptions in this assignment. Before they begin, you might ask students to discuss whether they think a prayer or meditation necessarily has to make reference to the concept of "God" at all.

5. [Negative Population Growth, Inc.] The task here is to pinpoint the objective of this ad and to state it as directly and articulately as possible.

Discussing the Unit

Preparing for Class Discussion

1. Photos are meant to provide someone with whom the reader can identify or, at least, sympathize. Since the Negative Population Growth organization is essentially campaigning *against* a group of people (with whom it does not want its readers to identify), it does not use a photo. The other ads use images of people with whom readers may identify or sympathize. One caveat: The ACLU ad uses an Asian girl as both sympathetic and subtly threatening. She looks harmless, but the white reader may assume that she is not Christian (though she very well may be). The ACLU may suppose that the Christian reader will then more readily identify with the scenario laid out in the text in which one's child is forced to recite a prayer from a "foreign" denomination.

2. All of the ads basically summarize their points in the headlines, although the Campaign for Tobacco-Free Kids headline, because it is idiomatic, and the ACLU and Negative Population Growth ads, because they ask questions, have a bit more power as "hooks." Also, the featuring of children in the tobacco and prayer ads, in a largely adult-read publication (the *New York Times*), can help to hook the reader into the topics featured by the ads.

From Discussion to Writing

1. Advise students to consider the need to identify and "target" their audience. All aspects of the ad — language, layout, graphics, etc. — must be tailored to the target audience.

2. Advise students to credit any information they use from the ad as a source, but to produce an original piece of work that explores fully the subject, which may only be briefly summarized in the ad they choose.

Topics for Cross-Cultural Discussion

1. Encourage students to cite particular ad campaigns — whether for a product or a politician — that have been effective or controversial. What makes them so? How are these advertisements like/unlike comparable American ads?

2. You may want to bring up the issue of how American companies might use different ads for their products in different countries, and vice versa (e.g., many American candies have different names abroad, which may reflect that different sounds or words are more effective in one culture than another). Also, this may be a good opportunity to discuss the portrayal of other cultures in American advertisements (citing, for example, the controversial Taco Bell ads featuring a precocious Chihuahua).

9

Free Expression:
How Much Should We Tolerate?

"Congress shall make no law respecting an establishment of religion, or prohibiting the free exercise thereof; or abridging the freedom of speech, or of the press; or the right of the people peaceably to assemble, and to petition (ask) the government for a redress (correction) of grievances (wrongs)," declares the First Amendment to the Constitution. Why do we value this amendment, this declaration, so highly? Why do we feel so angry when people restrict the right of freedom of expression?

Every author in this unit deals with the issue of freedom of expression in great length. In "A Civic Duty to Annoy," Wendy Kaminer states that she sometimes feels guilt when she speaks freely and criticizes people, even though "we tend to forget that criticism sometimes expresses greater respect than praise." In her essay she fights against the "self-congratulatory air of consensus among people who consider themselves and one another right-thinking . . . [who share a] consistency of belief that devolves into mere conformity."

Nancy Carlsson-Paige and Diane Levin discuss their opinions about how big business uses the "violation-of-free-speech argument" to curtail the efforts to limit violence in children's media. The authors are concerned with the violence that is freely portrayed on the radio, in video games, and on television, and how it has aided to "more than double violent crimes among youth since the mid-1980s."

In the student essay, "How to Breed Intolerance," Sara Ziegler argues her opinion of how intolerance is bred: "Know as little as possible. Rely on rumor and speculation. Ignore facts. Utilize stereotypes. Spread your views to others in hopes that they, too, will learn to hate." The author discusses how people do not have to agree with one another, but they must try to tolerate another's opinion, even *if* the opinion seems poorly founded. She makes a final and romantic suggestion about how intolerance relates to freedom of expression: "All you need to do to avoid intolerance is to respect each person for who they are — something everyone should be doing anyway." And respect is the key to letting others express their ideas.

To get your students talking about free speech, refer them to this unit's "From the Bookshelf" selection by Richard Dooling, from his book *Blue Streak: Swearing, Free Speech, and Sexual Harassment.*

WENDY KAMINER, A Civic Duty to Annoy

Vocabulary/Using a Dictionary

1. By stating, "I'm not alone in my *irreverence*, but feminist *pieties* combined with feminist courtesy keep most of us in line," Kaminer means that she's "not alone in her *lack of respect* (for feminist gatherings or for the complaints of Harvard students), but feminist *acts of devoutness* . . . keep most of us in line."

2. Some synonyms for the word *puerile* might be: childish, foolish, idle, immature, youthful, juvenile, silly. These do not capture all the subtleties of the complex word *puerile*, which can also be used as a reference to a reversion to infantilism, a symptom of mental illness.

3. The root of the word *paradigmatic* is *paradigm*, which means "example; pattern." Both words originate from the Greek term *paradeiknynai*, "to show side by side," from *para* (side by side) + *deiknynai* ("to show").

Responding to Words in Context

1. In her use of the word *marginalized*, Kaminer uses the following definition of *margin*: "characterized by the incorporation of habits and values from the divergent cultures and by *incomplete assimilation in either.*" One who is "marginalized" is outside of or excluded from the mainstream.

2. The word *dysfunctional* is an adjective meaning "impaired or abnormal functioning." *Dys,* from the Middle English *dis-* ("bad, difficult"), means "abnormal; difficult, or impaired."

Discussing Main Point and Meaning

1. What Kaminer suggests by her title "A Civic Duty to Annoy" is supported throughout her essay. She writes, "Sometimes nurturing students means challenging their complaints instead of satisfying their demands for sympathy" (para. 6). "There would be no feminist movement if women never dared to give offense. . . . When nurturing gives way to pandering [catering], feminism gives way to femininity" (paras. 6 and 7). "We tend to forget that criticism sometimes expresses greater respect than praise. It is surely more of an honor than flattery. You challenge a student because you consider her capable of learning" (para. 9).

2. At Radcliffe College, where Kaminer teaches, "criticism and dissatisfaction are apt to be expressed in a feminine mode, covertly or indirectly. It's particularly hard for many of us not to react with great solicitude to a student who declares herself marginalized, demeaned, or "oppressed, even if we harbor doubts about her claim" (para. 8).

3. Kaminer's discussion about withholding sympathy is located in paragraph 10: "Sometimes withholding sympathy feels mean, insensitive, and

uncaring; you acquire all the adjectives that aren't supposed to attach to women. You take on the stereotypically masculine vices when the virtue of niceness is being revived."

Examining Sentences, Paragraphs, and Organization

1. The repetition of the word *scoff* definitely helps provide an understanding of Kaminer's tone. *Scoff* cues the reader to the tone, which is "sometimes mocking, derisive, and scornful."

2. Kaminer's audience for "A Civic Duty to Annoy" might be people who consider themselves and one another "right thinking" — people who use the word "empower" (para. 1). Other audiences could be "self-conscious feminists" (para. 2), average everyday people in nuclear families (para. 2), people who are white and middle-class (para. 2), and upper-class female college students (paras. 4–9). Her difficult vocabulary reinforces the fact that her audience is college-level people.

3. Kaminer's paragraphs are mainly organized around the rhetorical strategies of moving from general to specific (the essay starts with a generalization and moves to specific examples of Radcliffe and Harvard students), and from problem ("too many 'right-thinking' people") to solution (people should embrace disagreement).

Thinking Critically

1. This question should make students aware of Kaminer's point that "you challenge a student because you consider her capable of learning. You question her premises because you think she's game enough to reexamine them." Some students will disagree with the statement, so be prepared for statements expressing doubt and discouragement about the methods of some teachers.

2. This statement is easy to refute. Americans are sensitive to the plight of the "oppressed" because there have been many oppressed minorities throughout American history. This may raise the question of restitution. As a country, are we overcompensating for past transgressions? Or are we dealing with them adequately and responsibly? Could (should) we do better?

In-Class Writing Activities

1. For this activity make sure students address all three parts of the question in their freewrites. Have the students read their experiences aloud in class after they've finished writing. One thing you should be prepared to do: Provide your own example for students to model their writing on. (In my own undergraduate experience, I respected those teachers who discussed my papers with me and told me how I could improve my writing skills. They wanted to initiate a positive change with their criticism of my work.)

2. Most students at one time or another have exercised their "Civic Duty to Annoy," whether it's arguing with an elderly relative at a family gathering, inciting the class into volatile discussion, or debating the merits of different types of music with a group of friends. The point of this activity is to have students become aware that they are exercising their freedom.

NANCY CARLSSON-PAIGE and DIANE LEVIN, The Profiteering that Kills Kids

Vocabulary/Using a Dictionary

1. When the authors say that big business *perpetuates* entertainment violence, they mean that big business, because it profits from violence (see para. 4), preserves entertainment violence from "extinction into oblivion."

2. *Deregulated* means "removed restrictions or regulations from." *Desensitization* means "to make less sensitive." The prefix *de-* means "away or off" (deplane); "down or lower" (degrade); "completely" (despoil); "reverse" (deactivate); or "remove" (decaffeinate).

Responding to Words in Context

1. In the title of the essay, "The Profiteering that Kills Kids," the word *profiteering* means "making what is considered an unreasonable profit (especially on the sale of essential goods during times of emergency)." "Corporations control the airwaves and the public have little or no access" (para. 7). "Children . . . just want the toy they saw explode on an exciting TV show or ad" (para. 8).

2. The definition the authors give for *entertainment violence* is "a media-saturated popular culture that glorifies violence through images, actions, and models marketed to children via television, toys, and other products, videos, video games, and Hollywood films."

Discussing Main Point and Meaning

1. The authors are annoyed at the shock some people display in respect to these killings because "since the mid-1980s . . . children in the United States [have been] swimming in a culture of violence that has its effects from subtle to deadly on every child."

2. The lines "Violence is fun. No one gets hurt," sarcastically refer to how "violent video games and episodes of cartoons" portray a falsely violent conception of what the world is like.

3. The authors write, "Efforts to limit violence in children's media never get past the violation-of-free-speech argument. But whose free speech are we talking about? . . . You don't have free speech when corporations control the airwaves and the public has little or no access. Children can't speak for themselves" (paras. 7 and 8).

4. The final plea of the authors toward the end of the essay is that *adults* have to do something to protect children from entertainment violence. Their audience is not governments or corporations, but "the rest of us . . . [who] must demand an end to irresponsible marketing practices and profiteering" (para. 10).

Examining Sentences, Paragraphs, and Organization

1. Carlsson-Paige and Levin are concerned with the reaction of American children to the violent messages entertainment sends to them.

2. The main idea of Carlsson-Paige and Levin's essay is stated in paragraph four: "With deregulation it became possible to market toys and other products with TV programs. Quickly after deregulation, the kid culture from the earliest stages of play became saturated with violence, and teachers began reporting increases in violence. . . . From that time, the violent culture has grown in intensity with each new marketing ploy, media-product-linkup, and innovation."

3. The conclusion of the essay does logically follow the introduction. In the first paragraph, the authors introduce the idea that people have not been paying attention to "the more than doubling of violent crimes among youth since the mid-1980s." The authors then clarify and support their argument in the following paragraphs, ending (logically) with a plea to "demand an end to irresponsible marketing practices and profiteering that end up hurting all of us."

Thinking Critically

1. If students agree with the authors' statement, then they can use examples from the text as support for their claims. If students disagree with the statement that violence is the most important single factor contributing to "the more than doubling in violent crimes among the youth since the mid-1980s," then they should explain what caused the meteoric rise in violent crimes among the youth.

2. Since most of the cartoon programs that aired in the mid-1980s have been rerun on the Cartoon Network, students most likely will be aware of shows like *The Transformers, G.I.Joe, Thundercats, He-Man and the Masters of the Universe,* and others. These shows could be considered tame in comparison to today's television shows, movies, and ultra-violent video games. (For instance, in the entire series run of *G.I.Joe,* only one person was ever shot. Yes, planes and vehicles blew up, but pilots and drivers of these vehicles always managed to escape the wreckage.)

In-Class Writing Activities

1. The answer to this question is tricky: The government (the FCC) has decided that the media can portray violence, but they must be *respon-*

sible in their portrayal such as using advisories or warnings. Unfortunately, sometimes these warnings are not enough to protect children whose parents don't have the time or aren't concerned enough to monitor what their children watch.

2. This is an excellent activity to generate ideas about the nature of freedom of expression. Students can argue for either the view of the media or the view of the "oppressed" masses. In either case, make sure students support their claims. There is a generous amount of support for the parent in "The Profiteering that Kills Kids" (paras. 2–5). If you are defending the television station, remind students that the First Amendment to the Constitution states: "government cannot abridge freedom of expression."

SARA ZIEGLER, How to Breed Intolerance

Vocabulary/Using a Dictionary

1. The dictionary definition of the word *intolerance* is "the quality or state of being unwilling to grant equal freedom of expression to."

2. In paragraph 4, by stating "In fact, knowledgeable *dissenters* are important for any belief," Ziegler means that "people who differ in statements and opinions . . . are important for any belief" in that they raise questions that must be considered by the group of believers.

3. A *creed* is "a set of fundamental beliefs; also: a guiding principle." Some synonyms for the word *creed* are: belief, notion, tenet, thought, view, doctrine, idea, opinion. A *creed* is different from a *religion* because a religion could be considered "a personal set or institutionalized system of religious attitudes, beliefs, and practices (or creeds?)."

Responding to Words in Context

1. *Manifest* means "made evident or certain by showing or displaying." By stating that "intolerance *manifests* itself in hatred," Ziegler means that intolerance is "easily recognized, or readily perceived" in hatred.

2. *Ignorance* is a noun meaning "lacking in knowledge, education, or training, uninformed or unaware. Showing a lack of knowledge." Ignorance is *not* a "bad word." It doesn't mean someone is dull or stupid; it simply means that someone doesn't know about something.

Discussing Main Point and Meaning

1. According to Ziegler, you breed intolerance by "know[ing] as little as possible. Rely[ing] on rumor and speculation. Ignor[ing] facts. Utiliz[ing] stereotypes. Spread[ing] your views to others in hopes that they, too, will learn to hate" (para. 1).

2. The author uses the example about homosexuality to support her statement: "Intolerance does not stem from disagreement. It stems from fear. And fear stems from ignorance." Ziegler then gives her example: "When you are ignorant about homosexuality, you will distort the facts to fit your opinions."

3. According to Ziegler, to tolerate a belief or stance does not mean that you share these views: In fact, the *Webster's New World Dictionary* defines the verb *tolerate* as "to respect others' beliefs, practices, etc. without sharing them." You may wish to discuss the popular expression "teach/learn tolerance" — ask students what attitudes might be behind this slogan? What audience does this slogan try to reach?

4. Ziegler suggests that we need "to respect each person for who he or she is" to avoid intolerance.

Examining Sentences, Paragraphs, and Organization

1. If you read the first four lines of the essay and then stopped, without looking at the rest of the composition, you would most likely think the writer of the essay was a racist, or, at least, a hatemonger. She uses these first four sentences to capture the reader's attention and then refutes these four points in her essay.

2. Ziegler defines these words in the context of the essay because she wishes to extensively research and discuss what the word *intolerance* means. After defining intolerance, she has to compare and contrast its meaning to the meaning of several other related words.

3. Whether Ziegler's essay suffers from a lack of specific examples is a matter of opinion. Ziegler cleverly weaves support for her main idea about "how intolerance is bred" through comparing and contrasting other words with "intolerance." Whether these could be considered generalizations is, again, subjective, based on the reader's preference of style. If you like reading passionate writing, which may not be entirely grounded in statistical proof, then this essay will be satisfying.

Thinking Critically

1. Ziegler generalizes that "there are many explanations for intolerant attitudes." These explanations are: "Intolerant folks grew up imitating intolerant parents"; "Perhaps intolerant people are so set in their ways that they find it easier to ignore anything that might not conform to their limited view of life"; and finally, "Maybe intolerant students have simply never been exposed to anyone different than them." If students agree with any of Ziegler's explanations, make sure that they provide support to back up their arguments (possibly citing examples from real-life situations).

2. The assertion Ziegler makes in paragraph 5 — "When you are ignorant of homosexuality, you will distort the facts to fit your opinions" — is based on the author's definition of *ignorance*. The dictionary definition of the term does not say that people who are ignorant will "distort facts to fit opinions," the author created this qualifier for the word.

In-Class Writing Activities

1. To write an essay that accomplishes the same goal as Ziegler — to explain what breeds intolerance — students will have to analyze Ziegler's essay, reflect upon her methods (evaluating which methods have merit), and then synthesize their own approach to the topic of "breeding intolerance." Make sure to review the essay a number of times in class, to facilitate students' evaluation of Ziegler's work.

2. There should be many interesting answers to this question. Try to set up the various social groups on campus: jocks, intellectuals, hippies, gangstas', ravers, hip-hop, and so on. Regardless of their answers, make sure students explain which groups they think are tolerant of others, which groups they think are intolerant, and why they have those beliefs. Remind students not to generalize and to back up opinions with evidence.

Discussing the Unit

Preparing for Class Discussion

1. Wendy Kaminer might respond to Carlsson-Paige and Levin's complaint that "efforts to limit violence in the children's media never get past the violation-of-free-speech argument" with a comment about how important it is for us (and big business) to exercise the right of free speech. Kaminer has commented before, that disagreement is (almost) necessary in today's society, and only by presupposing disagreement can there ever be a compromise. Kaminer might suggest a compromise between the concerned parents of children exposed to violence and the companies who are making a fortune off "entertainment violence."

2. Ziegler's statement — "It is likely that intolerant folks grew up imitating intolerant parents, and the cycle of prejudice has simply continued for generations" — is linked with Carlsson-Paige and Levin's declaration — "What about the millions of parents who deplore the violent culture marketed to their children but can't find a vehicle (means of communicating) for expression?" — because the sentiments behind both statements point to a cycle of ignorance. This inherited ignorance stifles children's ability to thrive as productive, positive members of society.

From Discussion to Writing

1. In this essay about a panel on a talk show, make sure students reread and review all three essays a number of times before they provide answers to the authors' questions. It may also be helpful to get students started in class, creating questions as a class and writing them on the board for reinforcement. Modeling questions is very important for this essay.

2. When students try to interpret the statement "Your right to swing your fist ends where my nose begins," you may want to read the "Suggested Topic for Discussion" section aloud to them. This will provide a brief explanation that may help students to get started on this assignment. Perhaps ask them to give examples of support for the statement, and then ask them to write.

3. Asking students to write about a time when they were afraid to exercise their right to freedom of expression requires that they question the nature of freedom and how it applies to their own lives. Students may not realize that they exercise this right nearly every day, and you may want to remind them of such things as McCarthyism and the Red Scare. This could serve to contrast the authoritarian control of personal expression of the past with the broader individual freedom of contemporary society.

Topics for Cross-Cultural Discussion

1. This question serves two purposes: It may make foreign students aware of the particular freedoms that American students have, and it may cause American-born students to appreciate the liberties that they may otherwise take for granted. These are often ideas that students are not asked to consider unless they enroll in a social studies or American history course. You may also want to raise the question: What liberties do other cultures have that American culture does not?

2. The purpose of these two questions is to offer foreign students an opportunity to articulate their opinions about America and to encourage them to do so hereafter. It will be interesting to hear what foreign students have to say and whether they consider their opinions to be taken seriously in the United States. Hopefully this topic will also help to make American-born students more conscious of the opinions of foreign students and immigrants.

10

Do Words Matter?

Catherine Drinker Bowen, an American historical biographer, once wrote: "For your born writer, nothing is so healing as the realization that he [or she] has come upon the right word." Perhaps this statement is factual, but if it is, then couldn't the reverse be true? "Nothing is so destructive as the realization that he [or she] has come upon the wrong word"? Building upon this idea, various writers in this unit discuss the capacity of words, if used improperly, to mislead, hurt, frustrate, segregate, or terrify.

M. P. Dunleavey in "'Guy' Envy" discusses how women don't have a word comparable to the male word "guy" in their repertoire. She states that women need a word of their own "that captures our most laid-back, casual sense of ourselves — our 'guyness.'" She does not advocate giving up womanhood, she just wants better choices for women, so they can be totally "confident, centered, sympathetic, yet amusing human being[s]."

In "The N-Word and How to Use It," Bennie M. Currie discusses one of the most vile epithets in the English language: the word *nigger*. Currie begins the essay with a personal anecdote about his roommate, who was shocked to be affectionately referred to as a "brother" or a "nigger." To make his point, Currie quotes comedians who use the N-word in various ways in their performances, arguing for a halt to the use of the word altogether.

The student essay by Melissa Stein, "Radicals: Threats or Heroes?" tries to define what is meant by the word *radical* and discusses the disturbing fact that people in modern-day America can be afraid of a *word*. Her realization that "there would simply be no progress without radicals" leads her to defend and embrace the feared term, stating: "That being said, the next time someone calls me a radical, I for one will accept that label with pride."

For a humorous and insightful perspective on language, point your students toward this unit's "From the Bookshelf" selection by Richard Lederer, from *Crazy English*.

M. P. DUNLEAVEY, "Guy" Envy

Vocabulary/Using a Dictionary

1. *Dialectical* means "manner or means of expressing oneself." It originates from the Greek *dialektos* meaning "conversation," which is from *dialegesthai*, "to converse."

2. When Dunleavey says that women "are on borrowed terminology" and that "this is not just *semantics*," she means that the problem of women using borrowed terminology to describe themselves is not simply a complication regarding the *meaning* of the word *woman*, the issue is with the fact that "Until fairly recently, women could not be all that guys were and are" (para. 9).

3. When Dunleavey states, "After all, we successfully *co-opted* the original guy symbol: blue jeans," she means that women have successfully won over, or chosen blue jeans to be a symbol of their group. *Cooperate* means "to work or act together for a common purpose or benefit." *Coordinate* means "to place in the same order or rank." These words relate to one another because of the prefix *co-* meaning "together; joint or jointly; or equally."

Responding to Words in Context

1. In the context of paragraph 2 in which Dunleavey says "it's clear why we've fought so hard for [the] nonpejorative term [*woman*]," *nonpejorative* means "not having negative connotations, not tending to belittle."

2. In paragraph 3, "We just hired a woman to run the ad-sales division and she's a *dynamo*," the word *dynamo* means "an electric generator," or "an energetic, forceful person."

3. In the remark, "we'll always be women — no one is *advocating* giving that up," the word *advocating* means "supporting or urging by argument, especially publicly." *Advocacy* means "the act or process of advocating; support." *Advocate* means "one that pleads the cause of another."

Discussing Main Point and Meaning

1. Dunleavey believes that women have not "gained ground" when it comes to "calling ourselves something besides 'woman'," because the word "speaks of maturity, motherhood, and busting through barriers. And that's exactly why we need a term to give us a break from all that. A word that would let us kick back and not shave for a couple of days."

2. The problem Dunleavey has with Natalie Angier is that, in her opinion (and according to *The Oxford English Dictionary*) the word *gal* is nothing more than "a vulgar or dialectal pronunciation of *girl*." "Oh," says the author, "that's progress. . . . Gal has a warm heart, big hips, and a bad dye job."

3. The point Dunleavey is trying to make when she says "Whatta *girl*! . . . She's a great *babe*. . . . She's a *woman's woman*," is that women are defined by borrowed (male) terminology.

4. By concluding her essay with "we need choices, and unless something better comes along we may just have to stake our own claim to 'guy'," Dunleavey means that women should "co-opt" or claim the word *guy* just as they "successfully co-opted the original guy symbol: blue jeans."

Examining Sentences, Paragraphs, and Organization

1. The first sentence of paragraph 3 is not the topic sentence because it does not contain the main idea of the paragraph, nor does it shape or control the content of the rest of the paragraph. Therefore, the topic sentence is sentence 5: "We females . . . have no shorthand that unhooks us from the biological and political implications of our sex."

2. In the paragraph development of her essay, Dunleavey analyzes the idea that women "need a word of [their] own" (para. 1).

3. Dunleavey uses many examples to support her thesis that women lack a word for "something that captures our most laid-back casual sense of ourselves." She uses generalizations (like mentioning that the word *woman* is too honorable, "[it] speaks of maturity, motherhood") and specific details (exemplified by her use of *The Oxford English Dictionary* to define the word *gal*), remembering that what separates most good writing from bad is the writer's ability to move back and forth between generalizations and specific details.

Thinking Critically

1. In the statement "having a word for what you're being makes it easier" (para. 10), Dunleavey means that women do not have enough words (or as many words as men do) to describe their *state of being*. The answer to the question — "Do you agree with the author that it is harder for women to be 'guys' because there is no word for female guyness?" — is difficult. One possible answer is that if there isn't a word for a particular state of being, then maybe that state does not exist. Another answer may be that perhaps women feel comfortable being "guys" even without their own word to describe it.

2. According to Dunleavey, a *guy* is "laid back . . . casual" (para. 1), a man who "would . . . kick back and not shave for a couple of days" (para. 2), "a word that conveys snazziness and style, a casual term" (para. 4). "When men take off their uniforms; jackets and ties . . . in part, it's an attitude thing" (para. 7). Dunleavey does not make mention of whether certain men and boys are excluded from guyness. However, from sifting through the information she does provide, we may assume that a man who can't relax after work may exclude himself from guyness.

In-Class Writing Activities

1. A possible list of words which are similar in meaning to describe men and women could be:

Men	Women
male	female
fellow	lady
chap	damsel
guy	gal
gentleman	gentlewoman
beau	belle
swain	maid
husband	wife
boy	girl

Students should try to base their distinctions on dictionary definitions of the words. Encourage them to use the more unusual terms for *men* and *women* — it makes for more interesting essays.

2. In this essay, students can use examples from their own lives to support their main ideas. Perhaps talking about the way their mothers or fathers use different words than the students do to describe the same type of person (i.e., *fella* [past] and *dude* [present]: *dude* is the slang expression for a *fellow*).

BENNIE M. CURRIE, The N-Word and How to Use It

Vocabulary/Using a Dictionary

1. *Query* looks similar to the word *question*. The definition of *query* is "question; inquiry," and *inquiry* indicates *more* than one question: a barrage, a string, or process. The definition of *question* is "an interrogative expression used to test knowledge," or a *single* problem. Both these words have a similar origin, coming from the Latin *quaerere*, "to ask."

2. *Ubiquitous* means "existing everywhere at the same time." The origin of the word is from the Latin *ubique*, meaning "everywhere."

3. *Vociferous* means "loud or noisy." Some synonyms for *vociferous* would be: clamorous, blatant, strident, boisterous, obstreperous, and vehement.

Responding to Words in Context

1. *Synonymous* means "alike in meaning and significance." For instance, the city of Boston is largely *synonymous* with "marathon" (the Boston Marathon).

2. By definition, an *accidental utterance* is "the unexpected expression of something verbal." Examples from students may vary. For example, a

classroom of third-graders are going over their *Weekly Readers*. When the teacher asks the question "Who was the first black baseball player?" a student raises his hand and says, "Jackie Gleason" (the comedian, not Jackie Robinson, the first black baseball player). This is an incorrect and completely unexpected verbal expression.

3. *Epiphany* means "a sudden manifestation or perception of the essential nature or meaning of something." In the context of his essay, Currie implies that during his trip to Africa, Pryor experienced a "perception of the essential meaning" of the word *nigger* and didn't like it; thus, Pryor never used the word again.

Discussing Main Point and Meaning

1. The first time Currie accidentally used the word *nigger* in mixed company was when he attended the University of Missouri and casually called Kent, his white roommate, "nigger." Kent's "eyes widened and his body flinched." He said, pointing to Currie, "*I'm* not a nigger." His tone implied that the *author* was one. Currie finished the argument saying: "You can't call me that. Not ever."

2. By stating — "If my kids are destined to be introduced to a world born of racial hatred, then their parents should be the ones to do it" — Currie means that the responsibility of presenting the issue (reality) of racism to children should fall to their parents rather than the media.

3. Kathryn Williams was shocked by the definition of the word *nigger* in *Merriam-Webster's* dictionary because the definition read: "a black person — *usually* taken to be offensive." Williams wanted the definition to be changed so that the people who read it would realize that the word is offensive to everyone.

4. Richard Pryor's *Live on the Sunset Strip* inspired Currie and "lots of blacks" to make the vow not to use the word *nigger*. Pryor explained that on his voyage to the motherland he didn't see any "niggers."

Examining Sentences, Paragraphs, and Organization

1. Currie's introduction grabs your attention because of the use of a "loaded" word in his first sentence for shock value ("N-I-G-G-E-R" — all in capital letters), and because of his use of a personal example in the first paragraph. The purpose of an introduction is to set the stage, to prepare a reader for what lies ahead, as Currie's introduction does: We know he will discuss the "N-word" in his essay.

2. Currie makes a major transition at the beginning of paragraph 18, stating: "blacks took the loaded term *nigger* and disarmed it by making it a household word. In fact, we went on to embrace it by using it to spice up

poetry, rap lyrics, and many a stand-up routine." This transition is effective because it smoothly connects one idea to another in the author's discourse: the idea of *detesting* the word (Pryor), to the idea of *embracing* it (poetry, rap lyrics, stand-up comedy).

3.   Currie's audience is the American public at large. He wishes to reach blacks whom he addresses directly ("black people are hardly unified in their understanding or usage of this piece of slang [the word *nigger*]"). He also wishes to reach whites ("several whites have told me of their own struggles to understand the term [*nigger*]"). Most importantly, though, Currie wants his appeal to be universal, pleading to *all* parents to introduce their children to the horrors of racism.

Thinking Critically

1.   Some comedians can be regarded as social critics who satirize topics which are of immediate concern to the American public. They make us laugh at things we otherwise find serious. Because Currie uses comedians to support his ideas, the author adds readability to his essay and also reaches an audience who might be "turned off" by the language of academics or other formal language.

2.   In paragraph 11 Currie states: "If my kids are destined to be introduced to a world born of racial hatred, then their parents should be the ones to do it." Some students may disagree with this statement, possibly arguing that it is also the responsibility of the media (television, movies, the Internet, schools) to deal with these issues responsibly.

In-Class Writing Activities

1.   Responses to the statement — "*nigger* [is] one of the most complex, perplexing, and emotionally incendiary words in the American lexicon" — will vary. Students could agree with what the author states in the beginning of the essay, that "where calling a buddy *nigger* was synonymous with calling him *brother* or *man. . . .* It was just another way to talk cool" — like rap artists or hip-hop stars. It is doubtful that students will admit their use of the word as an insult they've spoken to a black person, but some may relate incidents in which they've witnessed someone using the word in a derogatory manner.

2.   The purpose of freewriting about the dictionary definition of the word *nigger* is to generate class discussion about the harm that can be created when publishers (among others) irresponsibly define terms. Here the point is to make students question the meaning behind words.

MELISSA STEIN, Radicals: Threats or Heroes?
Vocabulary/Using a Dictionary

1. With her use of the term *status quo*, Stein tries to explain that when certain groups are labeled radical, they will retreat into submission, maintaining "the existing state or condition."

2. A *stigma* is "a mark or reproach, blame, or disgrace." Stein is trying to explain that many women are afraid to call themselves "feminists" because the word has a "mark of reproach or disgrace" to it. She wants women to lose the stigma attached to feminism, and to reclaim the basic foundation of the word: "that women deserve equal rights in all facets of life."

3. In her use of the word *metamorphosis*, Stein means that the status quo is unstable and subject to relentless change.

Responding to Words in Context

1. Stein's definition for the word *radical* is given in paragraph 6: "Radicals are people who effect change; they are the people about whom history is written." The dictionary definition of the word *radical* is "a person who advocates drastic reforms."

2. An *editorial* is "a newspaper or magazine article (or Web page) that gives the opinions of the editors or publishers." It provides editors or publishers with a forum to relate their own opinions, apart from reporting the hard facts of news.

3. *Entity* is a noun meaning "being, existence; especially: independent, separate, or self-contained existence." When Stein says that the norm "is constantly evolving and therefore is not a constant entity," she means that the norm is always developing and therefore does not have a constant existence or being.

Discussing Main Point and Meaning

1. The author's title suggests the controversy that will be dealt with in the essay: Are radicals threats or heroes? An effective title sets a writer on course and tells the reader what to expect.

2. According to Stein "It has gotten to the point that many women are afraid to call themselves feminists . . . because of the *stigma* [mark of reproach or disgrace] attached to the word."

3. In her last paragraph, Stein remarks, "the next time someone calls me a radical, I for one will accept that label with pride." If students try to put Stein's thought into their own words, perhaps it would be helpful to refer them back to paragraph 4, which provides the strongest evidence for the basis of the author's final thought: "there would simply be no progress without radicals."

Examining Sentences, Paragraphs, and Organization

1. Stein does provide support for her claim that "It seems today that people are terrified of the term" *radical*. This support exists in paragraph 2, with her extended example of feminism.

2. A paragraph of *definition* develops a topic by explaining the meaning of a word or concept. A paragraph of definition (like Stein's entire essay) is an *extended definition* — it is more extensive than a dictionary definition. In paragraphs 1 and 2, Stein questions the definition of the term *radical* and explains how people fear the word. Then she offers her own extended definition of the word in paragraph 3: "To me, a radical is simply someone who rebels against the 'norm'." In paragraph 4, the author looks at the word *radical* again but this time in a historical context, refining her definition, which leads to her acceptance of the term in paragraph 5.

Thinking Critically

1. Stein may not adequately explain why "people are terrified of the term *radical*." She asserts that they do react adversely, as in her example of feminism, but she does not go into detail about *why* people are averse to the term. The reason could possibly be extrapolated from paragraph 1: People may be averse to the word *radical* because they do not want to anger or irritate the select minority who possess power.

2. Stein's declaration — "undeniably, there would simply be no progress without radicals" — is a loaded statement that could engender discussion. The fallacy in the statement could be questioned and followed with questions such as: "So, without radicals, there wouldn't be *any* progress?" Or: "Is *radical* change necessary for progress?"

In-Class Writing Activities

1. Students should understand that radicals are known by their actions, which favor drastic political, social, or economic reforms. Have students question their responses: Is Madonna really a radical? Are the Wu-Tang Clan members radicals? President Clinton? The Spice Girls? Chris Rock? Jerry Springer? If so, then what makes them radicals?

2. For this assignment students should question the nature of the word *radical* as it relates to their answers, keeping in mind that *radical* means (1) thoroughgoing or extreme [adj.]; (2) favoring drastic political, social, or economic reforms [adj.]; or (3) a person who advocates drastic reforms [n.]. *Radical* to one student could mean attending a sit-in or going to a million-man march. To another, the word might have a more personal meaning, like changing a mode of dress, style, or haircut.

Discussing the Unit

Preparing for Class Discussion

1. What is meant by "ownership of language" is best defined by a statement from "The N-Word and How to Use It," paragraph 17: "It's what blacks have always done since we hit America's shores: We take what's given us and we find a way to make it our *own*." Blacks have had to claim ownership only after they took the things which white people didn't care for. The ownership of language is secondary. (See paragraphs 11–13 for examples of support.) The same problem is encountered by Dunleavey and other women who do not have a word to describe their "most laid-back, casual sense of ourselves." They need a word of their own to express "guyness." Again, ownership is secondary. (Examples of support are in paragraphs 2–8.)

2. There is a strong case for Dunleavey agreeing with Stein, that "the women's movement has been plagued by stereotypes" (see Dunleavey, paras. 1–2). Dunleavey would absolutely agree with Stein's point that "the foundation of feminism is simply that women deserve equal rights in all facets of life" because she firmly believes that women "need choices" (para. 2). Dunleavey would probably go further than Stein, advocating that women "may just have to stake [their] own claim to 'guy'" (para. 11).

From Discussion to Writing

1. For essays about the power of words, students could use experiences with language at school, work, home, church, the mall, the basketball court, a trip, and so on. The essays are likely to be narratives, from the first-person point of view. It is important to stress that a lesson must be learned about the power of words. You may want to steer students away from writing short stories simply about how someone called them a "bad name." The incident in question must be a learning experience.

2. This question about who should be responsible for defining words in a dictionary should elicit vastly different responses. Some students will hold that teachers and professors should be responsible. Others might suggest that everyone should be involved in writing the dictionary so that the writers would be sure not to offend anyone. There will be few who claim that nothing is wrong with the dictionary as it is. In any case, the student's point of view should be supported with details.

3. You may find that this question prompts students to produce ambitious but interesting essays. When students start this assignment, ask that they address all three of Chesterton's questions in their essays: (1) Why shouldn't we quarrel about a word?; (2) What is the good of words if

they aren't important enough to quarrel over?; and (3) Why do we choose one word more than another if there isn't any difference between them? Each author deals specifically with certain questions: Currie — questions 1 and 3; Dunleavey — questions 1–3; Stein — questions 1 and 2.

Topics for Cross-Cultural Discussion

1. It may take a little time for students to warm up to this discussion, but they may feel more comfortable discussing stereotypes that their native cultures hold about Americans, rather than stereotypes Americans hold about their cultures.

2. The goal of this challenging question is to invite non-native English speakers to become involved in class discussion by speaking about particular words from their native tongues. Hopefully this discussion will help to illustrate how language changes and evolves based on the demands of contemporary society. (Note, for example, how American English dictionaries have more words than ever that deal with computer technology.)

11

Race Relations: Is Dialogue Possible?

Each of the essays in this unit deals with the question of whether a productive dialogue on race can be established in this country. The first selection "Colorblind" by Alex Kotlowitz asks: "How can you have a dialogue on race when blacks and whites can see no gray?" Kotlowitz's narrative about two small towns in southwestern Michigan, Benton Harbor (92% black) and St. Joseph (95% white), relates the story of how the people of the two towns react to the death of a sixteen-year-old black boy. The towns' opinions differ based on their racial make-up: a difficult starting point for a successful dialogue.

Lani Guinier, in "Finding a Space for Real Conversations on Race," encourages the reader to consider that "even though the United States is today a more heterogeneous nation than it once was, in some ways, it is still very segregated." Her concern lies with the observation that "very few people are participating in a national conversation right now. . . . Today many people are being spoken about and spoken for, but they're not being spoken to and they're not speaking." Her work to transform our public discourse has made Guinier optimistic that "through genuine conversation and multiracial problem-solving, ongoing efforts at collaboration will emerge."

"Stop the Lies" by Luis J. Rodríguez enumerates the many lies perpetrated in the United States that must cease before we can talk about race. According to Rodríguez, these lies include the beliefs: that Aryans were white and superior, that Jesus Christ was white, that human beings can be delineated by race, that whites are superior to others ("white supremacy"), that we live in a monolithic (undifferentiated) culture, and that class issues do not really exist. It is with this final point that Rodríguez concludes his thought-provoking essay, stating that "the real social division governing how we live and think is that of *class*. Today, class interests are forcing us to look deeper at any so-called unity based on race."

In the final essay "Reflections on Black History Month" student Jason Michael laments the ending of another Black History Month during which he "heard powerful Allstate sponsored ads . . . [and] saw beautiful McDonald's commercials on television." Michael can't help but think of the upcoming eleven months during which the experience of African Americans "will once again take a back burner to the slick version of white history." He states that "the battles against racism and discrimination are still being constantly fought . . . [but] there's still a lot of work to be done." He cites examples of failed attempts at repairing the damage of racism and creating a dialogue about race. For Michael, like Rodríguez, a dialogue on race depends on the uncovering of certain truths, as well as the real inclusion and awareness of African American history and experience in universities, politics, and the workplace.

To provide your students with another perspective on the American dialogue on race, refer your students to this unit's "From the Bookshelf" selection by Stephen L. Carter, from *Civility: Manners, Morals, and the Etiquette of Democracy.*

ALEX KOTLOWITZ, Colorblind

Vocabulary/Using a Dictionary

1. *Constrain* means "repress or restrain." *Constrain* is different from *restrain* ("to hold back; check or control") because the prefix *con-* means "with; together; jointly," whereas the prefix *re-* means "again; anew."

2. The word *animosity* derives from the root *animus* (meaning: disposition; intention; basic attitude or governing spirit"). *Animosity* originates from the Latin *animosus*, meaning "spirited."

3. *Ballast* means "something that gives stability, as in character or conduct." Another definition of the word is "a heavy substance used to improve the stability and control the draft of a ship or the ascent of a balloon." The first definition possibly derived from the second and was borrowed from nautical terminology (originally coined in 1530).

Responding to Words in Context

1. In sentence 4, paragraph 4, the word *prism* means "a medium that distorts or colors whatever is viewed through it." Kotlowitz refers to truth as a prism which depends on the side of the river you reside on.

2. In sentence 3, paragraph 13, the verb *incite* means "to move to action; stir up; spur on; urge on." It doesn't necessarily have a negative denotation.

Discussing Main Point and Meaning

1. The dictionary definition of the word *colorblind* means "not recognizing differences of race; free from racial prejudice." The author seems to imply the opposite meaning — that the members of the two towns are "blinded by color," specifically in terms of their responses to the death of Eric McGinnis.

2. The main point of Kotlowitz's first three paragraphs is shown in paragraph 3, that colorblindness is "all about perspective — which has everything to do with our personal and collective experiences, which are constantly informed by race."

3. The author writes about St. Joseph and Benton Harbor because "while the contrasts between the two towns were unusually stark, they are, I believe, typical of how most of us live: physically and spiritually isolated from one another" (para. 11). Kotlowitz explains that the towns' only connections "are two bridges and a powerful undertow of contrasts" (para. 5).

4. "Most everyone in St. Joseph came to believe that Eric, knowing the police were looking for him, tried to swim the river to get home and drowned. Most everyone in Benton Harbor, with equal certitude, believes that Eric was killed — most likely by whites, most likely because he dated a white girl" (para. 14). The author reacts to these explanations, declaring, "I was struck by the disparity in perspective, the competing realities, but I was equally taken aback by the distance between the two towns — which, of course, accounts for the myths."

Examining Sentences, Paragraphs, and Organization

1. The author uses first-person plural pronouns such as "we" and "us" in his essay because he wants to create sentences that directly address and implicate the reader (as he does with himself).

2. Paragraph 3 has unity because all its sentences help clarify or support its main idea that "everyone is so quick to choose sides, to refute the other's myths, and to pass on their own." Paragraph 14 has unity (possibly with the exception of sentence 1 which refers to paragraph 13) because all of its sentences help clarify or help support its main idea that the author "was struck by the disparity in perspective, the competing realities."

3. To better arrange his ideas of "colorblindness," the author makes use of narration (storytelling) twice in his essay: His first use is in the story of Christmas Day, 1991; his second narration is the story of the sixteen-year-old black boy Eric McGinnis.

Thinking Critically

1. It seems that the author may be trying to evoke more empathy for the residents of Benton Harbor than St. Joseph. There is support for this throughout the essay: "[Benton Harbor] is 92 percent black and dirt poor. For years, the municipality so hurt for money that it could not afford to raze abandoned buildings" (para. 6); ". . . in the 1930s and 1940s factories recruited blacks from the South, and when those factories shut down, unemployment, particularly among blacks, skyrocketed" (para. 10). There are also some examples of the residents of St. Joseph being portrayed as bigoted, racist people.

2. At moments of crisis (the Rodney King beating, the Simpson trial, or Eric McGinnis's death), Kotlowitz claims that "we flail about, trying to find moral ballast [stability]. By then it's usually too late" (para. 16).

Students could find support for this statement throughout the essay, or they could argue against the statement, claiming that *after* these moments of crisis Americans have a heightened awareness and sensitivity to racial issues.

In-Class Writing Activities

1. With so many different ways to create racial/color distinctions, students have many examples to choose from: MTV (Music Television) versus BET (Black Entertainment Television); popular music versus hip-hop; jocks versus gangstas'; hockey versus basketball; and so on. Some questions are: Who propagates these distinctions? Why do we accept these racial distinctions dictated, for instance, by the media?

2. The purpose of this essay is twofold: to have students reflect on what groups they are accepted in within their communities and, more importantly, to question how the place they grew up in affected their personalities. Does growing up in a town that is free from prejudice make *you* free from prejudice? Does growing up in a town that is racist affect whether a person could be a racist?

LANI GUINIER, Finding a Space for Real Conversations on Race

Vocabulary/Using a Dictionary

1. *Heterogeneous* means "composed of parts of different kinds." The prefix *hetero-* means "other than usual; other; different." *Hetero-* comes from the Greek *héteros* akin to *heis*, "one."

2. *Methodology* means "a *set* of methods," where *method* means "a procedure employed by a particular discipline or art."

3. In paragraph 7, through her use of the word *quantitative*, Guinier means that the LSAT is the major test which determines the *amount* of information you need to know about practicing law.

Responding to Words in Context

1. In paragraph 6, what the author means by her use of the word *explicit* is that "you have to get people together to talk about race by providing them a mutual task that doesn't have a *fully and clearly expressed* racial text." People need to express their ideas to each other, not by challenging the pre-existing ideas of some arbitrary text.

2. When Guinier calls America a "sound-bite" culture, she implies that American culture is characterized by "brief, striking statements excerpted from an audiotape or videotape for insertion in a broadcast news story": We are a culture built on instant gratification.

Discussing Main Point and Meaning

1. The author believes that "we can no longer talk about race in just the context of black and white," because "we have to think about relationships between whites and people of color, about relationships among and within communities of color, and about color in a global sense as well" (para. 1).

2. What Guinier means by this statement is that political conversation today resembles the worst excess of the enemy-like model of legal contest, the model of "winner take all" in sports, and the "last man alive wins" model of war, and these structures, when talking about race, reinforce divisions between people, not similarities (para. 3).

3. "According to surveys, most ordinary Americans believe that the least trustworthy people are journalists, politicians, and lawyers — the three groups most engaged in the conversation [about race] right now." Most Americans trust other ordinary Americans, possibly because other ordinary Americans are "the only group not pressured to have an agenda" (para. 5).

4. Guinier states, "You can't have just one conversation on such matters because the process of multiracial problem-solving requires engagement: It requires an opportunity to think and reflect and come back and perhaps even change your mind, along with the opportunity to clarify yourself if you've been misunderstood" (para. 8).

Examining Sentences, Paragraphs, and Organization

1. Transitional expressions are words and phrases that signal connections among ideas. In Guinier's essay some transitional expressions are: "oftentimes" (para. 3), "first" (para. 6), "second" (para. 6), "it turns out" (para. 7), "like" (para. 8), "moreover" (para. 8), and "today" (para. 9).

2. The paragraphs in Guinier's essay are arranged from general to specific, and from problem to solution (i.e., the essay begins with commentary about the problem with the United States (para. 1), the problem with the American public (para. 2), and the public's adversarial/political discourse (para. 3), and moves toward talking about the discourse of a few people (author included), and offering a solution (para. 4).

3. Switching the first and last paragraphs would affect the organization of the essay because the problem introduced and criticized in paragraph 1 (the United States is still very segregated), would be replaced with the solution offered in paragraph 4 (that, through dialogue, we can change to create a culture that is more inclusive). An essay should not offer a solution to an unstated problem.

Thinking Critically

1. Guinier concludes, "I am hopeful, optimistic even, that we can change the future to create a culture that is more inclusive and more consistent with our basic fundamental values of mutual respect, cooperation, equal opportunity, and fairness." But she does not offer a solution and actual "space" where dialogue would be possible; she is exploring this challenge.

2. Students could take one of two positions regarding Guinier's claim about affirmative action: first, that they agree with the claim that "the term is a code for preferences primarily based on race, for unqualified minorities so that race trumps qualifications." Students could hold that there is a problem with placing unqualified minorities into positions solely because of race. On the flip side, students could argue that affirmative action is necessary to compensate for historical inequities that most minorities have encountered.

In-Class Writing Activities

1. This writing activity encourages students to go beyond the classroom in their discussions about race. Make sure students try and find a moment in their lives in which they *seriously* engaged in a discussion about race. The point here is to try and figure out where people feel comfortable to have Guinier's suggested "conversations on race": in the dorm room, at town hall, at the mall, at the park, at a concert, at the dinner table, or sitting around the television?

2. Some groups that fit this generalization are *mostly* the people we consider to be minorities, based, for example, on gender, sexuality, race, or ethnicity. The key to answering this question is the explanation as to why these groups are not being spoken to, and why they're not speaking. Ask students to explain why they think the Americans most engaged in race dialogue are not speaking to these groups.

LUIS J. RODRÍGUEZ, Stop the Lies

Vocabulary/Using a Dictionary

1. *Incipient* means "beginning to exist or appear." The word comes from the Latin *incipere* meaning "to begin."

2. In his use of the word *faculty*, Jefferson suggested that perhaps an unfortunate difference between white and black people is that the ability of black peoples' minds is a powerful obstacle to their emancipation.

3. *Monolithic* means "constituting a massive undifferentiated and often rigid whole." The root of the word is *monolith*, which means "a single great stone often in the form of an obelisk or column." Both words originate from the Greek *monolithos* from *mon-* ("alone, single") + *lithos* ("stone").

Responding to Words in Context

1. In paragraph 1, *perpetuated* means "made to last indefinitely."

2. The prefix *pseudo-* means "false; spurious." Some other words that utilize the prefix *pseudo-* are *pseudonym* (a false name) and *pseudoscience* (a system of theories erroneously regarded as scientific).

Discussing Main Point and Meaning

1. A list of lies that Rodríguez tries to expose might include: (1) that Aryans were white and superior; (2) that Jesus Christ was white; (3) that Europe civilized the world; (4) that humans can be delineated by race; (5) that whites are superior to others ("white supremacy"); and (6) that we live in a monolithic culture.

2. "'It was on these [slave] ships that we find the beginnings . . . of the curious doctrine which was to be called "white supremacy" . . . among the first men to develop attitudes of supremacy were the slaveship crew,'" says Rodríguez quoting Earl Conrad (para. 8).

3. Rodríguez was surprised at his friend's ignorance; when the two attended a Quebradita dance, this friend exclaimed that "these kids have no originality — they are trying to be American cowboys!" Rodríguez knew that "cowboy hats and leather styles originated with the Mexican vaquero and was later appropriated by Americans conquering the West" (paras. 11 and 12).

4. Rodríguez sees the potential for the destruction of the industrial economy because "we are entering an era characterized by the 'end of work'. . . . As the nature of work changes — there is simply no longer a need in this country for a large, unskilled, and labor-intensive workforce" (para. 16).

Examining Sentences, Paragraphs, and Organization

1. The topic sentence of paragraph 7 is sentence 1: "Stop the lie that humans can be delineated by race." The topic sentence of paragraph 8 is sentence 2: "'It was on these ships that we find the beginnings . . . of the curious doctrine which was to be called "white supremacy". . . .'" These are both topic sentences because they shape and control the content of the rest of the paragraph — the function of a topic sentence.

2. Rodríguez repeats the phrase "stop the lie" at the beginning of so many paragraphs because he wants to emphasize the lies that students are taught to believe. The use of "stop the lie" also catches our attention and signals a transition to another topic Rodríguez will discuss.

3. The author does make use of narration in his essay (see paragraphs 11, 12, and 17), and tells us, in a story, what is happening, or what *has* happened, but this is not his major rhetorical strategy. Comparison and contrast is rarely employed as a strategy, if at all. The major rhetorical

strategy that Rodríguez employs is *example*: He uses many illustrations ("lies") to provide evidence in support of his main idea (to "stop the lies"). ·

Thinking Critically

1. Students who agree with Rodríguez's claim can use examples from his essay to support their opinions. There will be some students, however, who will support the president's less radical way of addressing the "race debate."

2. Both writers commented that whites seemed to be a superior race to blacks — Kant stating that "humility is at its greatest perfection in the race of the whites," and Jefferson saying that "unfortunate difference of color, and perhaps of faculty, is a powerful obstacle to the emancipation of [black] people." Though neither man ever directly claimed to be a white supremacist, their writings do support the basic attitudes held by white supremacists.

In-Class Writing Activities

1. Perhaps one way to dispel racial "lies" is to approach with an open mind those whose ethnicities and races are different from ours. When we leave behind assumptions about different racial/ethnic backgrounds, we are more likely to learn the truth about an individual, not a stereotype about a race: This is the way to make dialogue possible.

2. In this statement, Henry Ford says that history is "empty talk," that tradition is "bunk." (Note: *bunk* = "bunkum" or "empty talk.") He also claims that we Americans should want to live in the present, in the world we make *today*. Rodríguez might agree with Ford because, if the automaker's statement were widely believed, then perhaps people would ignore the lies about race perpetrated by American history. Or, more likely, Rodríguez would disagree because of his belief that it is the exposing of the lies of history (i.e., the lie that Europe civilized the world, the lie that cowboys are American) that can open up a real dialogue on race and class in America.

JASON MICHAEL, Reflections on Black History Month

Vocabulary/Using a Dictionary

1. When an event has *transpired*, it means that an event has "occurred or happened."

2. *Gallant* behavior, in other words, "brave, spirited, or noble-minded" behavior, is regarded as desirable. Some other words you could use to describe a *gallant* might be "suitor, a paramour, a ladies' man."

3. Most people have used a *salve*. *Salves* are medical ointments used for treating wounds, burns, and sores.

Responding to Words in Context

1. The prefix *dia-* means "through or across," whereas the prefix *mono-* means "one; single; alone." Thus *dialogue* means "conversation between (through, across) two or more persons," whereas *monologue* means "a prolonged talk or discourse by a single speaker." The root *logue* is from the Greek *legein*, "to speak."

2. In paragraph 8 the word *creed* means "a guiding principle, or a set of fundamental beliefs," as listed in the Declaration of Independence.

Discussing Main Point and Meaning

1. The conflict Michael has with Black History Month is that "he can't help but think about the eleven months ahead" (para. 2). Allstate ads, McDonald's commercials, newspaper articles, and teachers will all go back to business as usual, rather than focus on raising awareness about Black history.

2. Michael does not think that America has won the war for civil rights: "So little is taught about this war that many people falsely think it's been won. It hasn't. The battles against racism and discrimination are still being constantly fought. We've made great strides. We've gained much ground. Still, it's too early to break into a victory dance just yet. There's a lot of work still to be done" (para. 3).

3. Michael claims that "the burden is now on white America to prove they understand . . . [that] 'we hold these truths to be self-evident that all men are created equal'" (paras. 7 and 8).

Examining Sentences, Paragraphs, and Organization

1. In Michael's essay, sentences are arranged from problem ("The battles against racism and discrimination are still being fought" [para. 3]) to solution(s) (paras. 7–11).

2. The supporting evidence for the author's assertion that "there's a lot of work still to be done . . . in the battles against racism and discrimination" is located in paragraphs 4 through 6: "President Clinton can't even get the two differing sides of his Race Initiative Advisory Board to agree on the purpose of the board or the members selected" (para. 4). This example is feasible because it is an illustration used to provide evidence in support of the main idea.

3. Michael repeats the phrase "it's about" seven times toward the end of his essay because he is using a writing technique called *parallelism*. Using parallel, balanced structures serves to emphasize the meaning that sentences deliver and reinforces the impact of a message.

Thinking Critically

1. Most students would agree with Michael that we have *not* won the war for civil rights yet, but some may not agree with the author's point that "so little has been taught about the struggle." It is likely that many students learned about the war for civil rights in American history classes in elementary school. The question may be how was the history taught? Through what perspective? What information was included? Omitted?

2. This is perhaps a difficult statement to agree with because a successful initiation to change racial issues in America would need to fall on African American leaders *and* white America. Stating that "it is no longer the responsibility of strong African American leaders to declare what they are entitled to" seems to be a hasty expression.

In-Class Writing Activities

1. The purpose of this activity is to emphasize that no age is too early to learn about the civil rights movement. Get students to write down their initial impressions of the movement, how it was introduced to them, and why they think it was introduced to them (because it was part of a curriculum, because their parents felt it was necessary, and so on). Sharing these freewrites could open up a discussion about dialogue and race.

2. The purpose of this activity is to question the value of Black History Month. You might reinforce the author's idea: that we need to think more about civil rights — not just during one month of the year, but through all twelve. You may want to ask students how they think they would feel about Black History Month if they didn't learn about it in school. Would they have known about it anyhow?

Discussing the Unit

Preparing for Class Discussion

1. There are likely to be a number of programs on campus that could provide discussion groups about race and racial issues: sororities, fraternities, student government, minority organizations, language clubs (Latin club, French club), and so on. These groups are effective in that they preach a philosophy of tolerance to the converted — you have to be a member of the group to engage in the discussion of that group. A question that you could ask students would be: "How could people/groups encourage you to go to a discussion group?" Or ask another question of them: "What issues or questions would you like to have addressed at such discussions?"

2. This is an idealistic question which may provoke some interesting answers. Answers will likely be of two basic types: the glass is half-full ("Sure, I foresee a day when racial differences will no longer exist!") or the glass is half-empty ("There will never be a day when racial differences will no longer matter."). Be prepared for arguments from both of these groups and encourage students to listen to both sides of the discussion.

In-Class Writing Activities

1. There are two ways students may explicate Fudge's statement: They could say that it is your choice to hang out with the same "folks," a necessary choice to hang out with a group that is racially similar to you. Others might suggest that you hang out with a group of people as a matter of survival. Do you need to hang out with a certain group to survive? Ask students to support their opinions with examples from their own lives.

2. Students may suggest a number of things: that we could use our colleges as tools to repair the damage done by racism, that we may need to hold a world summit for all countries to discuss the issue of racism, or that state or local governments could hold discussion groups or town meetings.

3. Alex Kotlowitz might respond to this assertion by stating that any lack of teaching about the war for civil rights would necessarily have a profound effect on Americans whose "personal and collective experiences are constantly informed by race" (para. 3). It is likely that Luis J. Rodríguez would embrace Michael's argument, asserting that of the few "facts" taught about the war for civil rights, many could be considered "lies." Lani Guinier might react to Michael's assertion by taking the view that because "many [people] falsely think [the war for civil rights] has been won, very few people are participating in a national conversation [about race] right now" (para. 2).

Topics for Cross-Cultural Discussion

1. The purpose of this question is to encourage students from different cultures to discuss their native countries in terms of race. Possibly they have found a way to discuss or hold a dialogue about the problem of racism in their native countries. Another reason to engage students from other cultures is to show Americans that racial problems also exist in countries outside the United States.

2. This question to meant to prompt all students to reflect on where they first learned about race and racial relations. This discussion will perhaps lead into a conversation about how cultures different from that of the United States deal with issues of race, possibly offering suggestions about how (and how not) to establish a dialogue on race.

12
The Flag: What Does It Symbolize?

This unit deals with the topic of the American flag, a national symbol that many students may not, at first, give much thought to. But the flag has been the subject of debate among those who would praise and protect it, and those who reserve the right to use it as a means of protest.

In "Some Questions for My Senator about the Flag," Horace Freeland Judson addresses a senator about a draft amendment to the Constitution, which would allow states to ban the burning or other forms of desecration of the American flag. Judson states that the goal of his article is to show "that such an amendment is not only mistaken — counter to the sense and spirit of the Constitution, of the First Amendment" — but that "it is meaningless." By raising a number of hypothetical situations, Judson aims to illustrate the impracticality of trying to define desecration. He concludes that "if the amendment is not meaningless, it's sinister. Its aim is not defense but attack — an attack on freedom of political thought."

Hendrik Hertzberg's "Star-Spangled Banter" criticizes not the flag but "The Star-Spangled Banner" — the national anthem devoted to the flag. The author sides with media mogul Ted Turner, claiming that we should "ease the old chestnut into well-deserved retirement." Hertzberg argues that it's time to get rid of "The Star-Spangled Banner" and to replace it with any one of a number of options: "America the Beautiful," "America [My Country 'Tis of Thee]," "This Land Is Your Land," "The Battle Hymn of the Republic," or "Dixie." Hertzberg recommends James Weldon Johnson's "Lift Ev'ry Voice and Sing," because it is about "good, solid values that are both American and universal." [Note: This selection lends itself well to a comparison/contrast writing assignment based on listening to audio tapes of these alternative anthems.]

In "A Forgotten Past" student essayist Galit Sarfaty offers her opinion on the great debate: "Should we display the Confederate flag?" The author's analysis includes views that support the pro and con of the issue and concludes that "what is really needed is a measure that will completely remove the Confederate flag or any image of the flag from all state buildings and monuments which are meant to represent the entire population of the state, black and white."

The unit's final selection is a cartoon of the American flag drawn by student artist J. Barrios, which portrays the power of corporations (specifically Nike and McDonald's) over American culture. "America: 2022" is a political cartoon that could ignite great discussions in the classroom.

To add another point of view to the discussion of this topic, ask students to read this unit's "From the Bookshelf" selection by Alan Wolfe, from *One Nation, After All.*

HORACE FREELAND JUDSON, Some Questions for My Senator about the Flag

Vocabulary/Using a Dictionary

1. When Judson says that the draft amendment to the Constitution "would allow states to ban the burning or other desecration of the American flag," he means that the Amendment would allow states to ban *any* "instance of treating [the flag] with sacrilege: any profanity [against the flag]."

2. Several synonyms for the word *abstraction* are: notion, idea, theory, thought, concept, mock-up, generality, and hypothesis. Judson uses the word *abstraction* to describe the American flag because "all material versions of it . . . are copies, mere representations — among which the law cannot clearly draw a line."

Responding to Words in Context

1. Judson refers to the draft amendment as "sinister" because he believes that its real aim is to attack "freedom of political argument," which is currently protected by the Constitution. In this sense, *sinister* implies dishonesty — the amendment is overtly intended to protect the flag, but it could be argued that it (covertly) threatens an existing liberty.

2. The word *amendment* means "the alteration of or addition to a bill, law, etc."

Discussing Main Point and Meaning

1. Judson reveals the purpose of this essay when he declares "I'd like to show you that such an amendment [to ban the desecration of the American flag] is not just mistaken — . . . counter to the sense and spirit of the First Amendment . . . of the Constitution . . . I'd like to show you that the amendment is meaningless" (para. 1).

2. In saying "Well, none of those was a 'real' flag," Judson is making reference to his previous examples, which were not actual, physical, "real" flags: his neighbor's seven-year-old's hypothetical picture, artist Jasper Johns's paintings, and the hypothetically sewn twelve-striped flag.

3. When Judson proclaims "Now there's a desecration for you," he is making reference to his conclusion that "the draft amendment cannot define

the flag, and it conceals the question of intent. If it is not meaningless, it's
. . . sinister. Its aim is not defense but attack — to open an attack on
freedom of political argument" (para. 9).

Examining Sentences, Paragraphs, and Organization

1. The author makes use of so many interrogative sentences at the end of
    his paragraphs because occasional questions involve the reader more.
    Also, the use of interrogative sentences helps to emphasize an author's
    main idea: in Judson's essay, the idea that the draft amendment is mean-
    ingless.

2. The answer to this question is a matter of opinion, but it may be helpful
    to consider that Judson's supporting paragraphs (paras. 2–6) are fictional
    examples of specific instances that could pertain to the amendment. The
    author reinforces this by saying: "Well, none of those was a 'real' flag"
    (para. 7). Does Judson's use of hypothetical scenarios make his argu-
    ment any less compelling?

3. The essay is written to persuade constituents in the United States that the
    proposed amendment is wrong. Judson addresses his questions to a senator
    to personalize his criticism, and to hold a government official account-
    able for what Judson views as an attack on the freedom of expression.

Thinking Critically

1. Judson puts forth a strong opinion in his essay and a few students
    (R.O.T.C., Army Reserves, veterans) may be turned off by his essay. This
    might be a good introduction to a discussion on patriotism. You may
    want to ask students, Do you consider yourself to be patriotic? Does
    patriotism necessarily mean protecting the flag?

2. The tone that Judson takes in this essay may be viewed as a bit sarcastic
    and smug at times. You may also want to point out that the author seems
    to focus only on his side of the argument rather than choosing to employ
    the strategy of presenting the case against, and then refuting it.

In-Class Writing Activities

1. This is a good activity to get students to question the nature of govern-
    ment rules and regulations concerning the flag. Why did the government
    ask/force us to "pledge allegiance" to the flag first thing every morning?
    What was the purpose? Besides this issue, the question raises another
    interesting point: Why do we not question the nature of patriotism when
    we are children? Why might we question it now?

2. The author does not present any positive reasons why we should prevent
    the desecration of the American flag. It can be argued that the symbol-
    ism of the flag makes it "sacred" in a sense, and students may cite broad
    examples such as the first time the flag was planted on the moon, the

the flag's value as a symbol of America's independence from England, and as an international symbol of liberty and democracy. Students may have difficulty citing personal examples, so you may note that "positive" experience can take many different forms. It could refer to a time when a relative explained what the flag means, or a time when a student journeyed to another country and compared and contrasted the "Stars and Stripes" with the flag of a different country.

HENDRIK HERTZBERG, Star-Spangled Banter

Vocabulary/Using a Dictionary

1. In paragraph 1, Hertzberg uses the word *capital* to mean that Ted Turner has had many "excellent, first rate" ideas.

2. A *rampart* is "a mound raised as a fortification." Some synonyms for the word *rampart* are barrier, barricade, defense, fortification, bulwark, and stronghold.

3. *Martial* means "inclined to war." It originates from the Latin *martialis,* meaning "of Mars" (the Roman god of war).

Responding to Words in Context

1. *Banter* means "to speak or address in a witty or playful manner." The author is speaking *banteringly* to Ted Turner.

2. An *anthem* is "a hymn of praise, devotion, or patriotism," whereas a *song* is simply "an often short metrical composition for singing."

Discussing Main Point and Meaning

1. The "firecracker" Ted Turner set off on the Fourth of July was his argument that it is time to dump "The Star-Spangled Banner" as our national anthem.

2. The "better reasons" Hertzberg gives for dumping the "Star-Spangled Banner" are: "Its tonal range corresponds to that of the electric guitar . . . but not that of the human voice" (para. 2); "the words don't convey what politicians call core American values" (para. 2); the poem "was written to immortalize . . . a silly war, a minor war, a war that ended in what was at best a tie" (para. 2); and finally, "the poem lends itself to mishearing" (para. 2).

3. Some of the alternative choices suggested for the proposed new national anthem are: "America the Beautiful" (para. 4), "America (My Country, 'Tis of Thee)" (para. 4), "This Land Is Your Land" (para. 4), "The Battle Hymn of the Republic" (para. 5), "Dixie" (para. 5), and "Lift Ev'ry Voice and Sing" (para. 6).

4. The author suggests that "Lift Ev'ry Voice and Sing" should replace "The Star-Spangled Banner" because: "it is already a national anthem of sorts . . . 'The Negro National Anthem'" (para. 6); "Its tune . . . is stirring, and so are its words" (para. 6); in the anthem, there is "no bombast, no boasting, no wimpishness — just good, solid values that are both American and universal" (para. 7).

Examining Sentences, Paragraphs, and Organization

1. By Hertzberg calling Ted Turner "Mr. T" he creates a casual tone that is accessible and comfortable for the reader. Hertzberg may also be making a comical allusion to "Mr. T" of the television show *A-Team*.

2. Some other allusions (indirect references) in Hertzberg's article are: Joni Mitchell (pop singer), Jimi Hendrix (guitarist), the War of 1812 (event), Woodie Guthrie (singer), Popular Front (political party), Elvis Presley (singer), and Harlem Renaissance (artistic movement).

3. The problem that the essay introduces is: What should we replace the "Star-Spangled Banner" with? The recommended solution is in paragraph 6: "Lift Ev'ry Voice and Sing" by James Weldon Johnson.

Thinking Critically

1. Students may begin by trying to answer the question — Do you think we should get rid of "The Star-Spangled Banner"? You may need to steer them back to the question that is asked, and urge them to evaluate Hertzberg's reasons for dismissing the anthem: "Its tonal range corresponds to that of the electric guitar . . . but not to that of the human voice. . . . The words don't convey what politicians call core American values. . . . [The poem] was written to immortalize . . . a silly war, a minor war, a war that ended in what was at best a tie. . . . The poem lends itself to mishearing" (para. 2).

2. Whether students "like" the song is a matter of opinion. The critical questions here are the final two. Perhaps mention to students that before making a decision they might take into account the general public. Are there people who really believe in/love "The Star-Spangled Banner"? An excellent scenario to begin a discussion with might be: Pretending you are a senator, take a class vote to see if you would replace the anthem. Make your decision based on information from your classmates.

In-Class Writing Activities

1. Fullbright believes that "to criticize one's country is to do it a service because criticism is an act of loving, supporting, and defending the country — more important than obeying familiar rituals of acceptance and excessive flattery." He wants us to understand that criticizing one's country means wishing to make it a better place, just as Hertzberg wishes to do

by replacing "The Star-Spangled Banner" with "Lift Ev'ry Voice and Sing."

2. A possible example to provide your students with: A young boy's grandfather, along with the majority of the child's elementary school teachers, would make him take his hat off "as a form of respect," whether in the classroom or at the dinner table. If the boy meant no disrespect by this action, then why did his elders feel that he was being disrespectful? This might be something that the boy, when an adult, might like to change about American culture — offering an alternative to not taking one's hat off as a gesture of respect.

GALIT SARFATY, A Forgotten Past

Vocabulary/Using a Dictionary

1. An *impetus* is "a driving force; impulse." A few synonyms for the noun would be: motive, incentive, stimulus, purpose, catalyst, reason, or spark. An example of *impetus* being used in a sentence would be: Winning a baseball game is the impetus for trying to hit the baseball hard; winning a football game is the impetus for a quarterback trying to throw touchdown passes.

2. The word *agrarian* means "of farmers or agricultural interests." It originates from the Latin *agrarius*, which comes from *ager*, meaning "field."

3. To *placate* someone means "to appease or pacify" that person.

Responding to Words in Context

1. The word *confederate* means "united in a league: allied." The eleven states who seceded from the Union may have chosen this word to show their independence from and allegiance against the Union.

2. When something is *trivialized* it is "made commonplace, ordinary, of little worth or importance." In her essay, Sarfaty claims that "the danger of lingering symbols of hatred . . . cannot be trivialized [made ordinary, of little worth]" (para. 6).

Discussing Main Point and Meaning

1. Sarfaty considers the Confederate flag to be "a haunting symbol of those days of slavery which many Americans would rather forget, the flag is continuing to stir up emotions in groups with opposing interpretations of history" (para. 1).

2. Sarfaty interprets General Robert E. Lee's statement, "A nation which does not remember what it was yesterday does not know where it is today," in paragraph 3. "Many blacks claim that those who see the flag as a representation of regional pride and identity in the South are refus-

ing to remember the entire past, including the years of slavery endured by the ancestors of black Southerners."

3. The argument for the acceptance of the Confederate flag by such groups as the Dixie Defenders is located in paragraph 5. These groups claim that "states of the Confederacy were not solely dedicated to preserving the institution of chattel slavery but primarily joined together in opposition to the centralization of power in the hands of the federal government, federally funded internal improvements, and high protective tariffs" (para. 5).

4. "The attempt to relocate the flag from the State House dome to a prominent national Civil War monument does not address the root of the problem" because "supporters of this proposal . . . will create a new situation which is just as offensive to a large number of Southerners. The Confederate flag will still be flying proudly on state grounds, a celebration of a time in history which brings feelings of oppression to black residents of South Carolina" (para. 6).

Examining Sentences, Paragraphs, and Organization

1. The topic sentence of paragraph 2 is sentence 2: "This has revived the debate over how the Old South's history should be interpreted." The topic sentence of paragraph 5 is sentence 1: "The controversy over the Confederate flag stems from a debate over the interpretation of the Confederacy and the war." These sentences express the main idea of the paragraphs.

2. A solution to the problem — "The Confederate flag stirs up memories of prejudices past," — is offered in paragraph 6: "What is really needed is a measure that will completely remove the Confederate flag or any image of the flag from all state buildings and monuments which are meant to represent the entire population of the state, black and white."

3. The organization of "A Forgotten Past":

(Para. 1) Intro — presents the debate and (briefly) differing opinions about accepting/rejecting the Confederate flag; states the problem.

(Para. 2) Transitional paragraph — example of a confrontation, leads into the core of the "revived" debate.

(Para. 3) Example — presents one side of the debate, the rejection of the Confederate flag: "the years of slavery endured by ancestors."

(Para. 4) Development of the argument — briefly traces the history of the debate; makes predictions.

(Para. 5) Example — presents the other side of the debate, as interpreted by such groups as the Dixie Defenders: "against the federal government."

Criticizes the previous solutions; proves that the methods used by Beasley aren't working.

(Para. 6) Conclusion — states the author's solution.

Thinking Critically

1. This is a difficult question to answer because, as explained by Sarfaty, the issue is not only with the flag itself, but with what it symbolizes. To some it symbolizes oppression and chattel slavery: everything that was wrong with the Confederate South. To others (perhaps less initiated), it may only represent a piece of cloth.

2. Sarfaty's final suggestion is as follows: "what is really needed is a measure that will completely remove the Confederate flag or any image of the flag from all state buildings and monuments that are meant to represent the entire population of the state, black and white" (para. 6). Whether students find this an extreme decision will depend on their weighing the consequences that either a decision for or against will alienate and offend a segment of the Southern (and Northern) population. Which part of the population would you exclude? Do you have to make a decision at all?

In-Class Writing Activities

1. (Note: It might help students organize their essays if you share with them the organizational list from question 3, "Examining Sentences, Paragraphs, and Organization.") When students write this essay they should answer all four parts of the question. A brief sample essay might include four basic answers (noted here is an essay advocating that the flag to be displayed anywhere) : (1) anyone could display the flag; (2) people could display it in their front yard, in their homes, on state buildings, in public places, anywhere, because I believe that the flag is simply a piece of cloth; (3) the population that would be in support of this decision would be members of Southern Heritage groups (mostly traditional, conservative, white Southerners) and people who believe the reasons listed in paragraph 5 of Sarfaty's essay; and (4) the people who would be offended would be anyone who believes that the flag represents "chattel slavery" and all liberty that was restricted by the "Old South."

2. Students may find this to be a challenging activity but one which may prompt them to think about what the Confederate flag represents. The flag could represent not only a reminder of the brutality of slavery for all descendants of Southern slaves, but also a mark of shame for the descendants of Southern whites who helped to perpetuate slavery. (See Dr. Flint in Harriet Jacobs's *Incidents in the Life of a Slave Girl*.)

J. BARRIOS, America: 2022

Responding to Words in Context

1. The word *Nike* originates from the name of the Greek goddess of victory.

Discussing Main Point and Meaning

1. The author's comment about American culture may be that eventually big business will take over American government, permeating into the most basic foundations and symbols of our country (the flag).

2. The picture of the bird (possibly a condor, which is an endangered species) holding a sign that says "Just*e* Do It" may represent the callous attitude of American business toward the environment: Progress and finances should be put above ecological concerns. Also, the *e* added to Just*e* parallels the *e* in Nike (pronounced Nī-kēē).

Thinking Critically

1. In choosing to *satirize* (use irony, sarcasm, or ridicule in exposing vice or folly) the McDonald's and Nike corporations, the artist considers the trademarks of these two companies to be huge and ominous logos that pervade American culture. Try to go into a department store without seeing a Nike logo. Try to watch an hour of prime-time television without seeing a McDonald's commercial. Or ask a typical twelve- to fourteen-year-old how many shirts, hats, or pairs of sneakers he/she owns emblazoned with the Nike swish. Ask the same teenager how often he/she eats at McDonald's. The answers may shock you.

2. Many students may agree that it is a little drastic or rash to think that America would ever be so shallow as to put corporate logos on the flag, but the artist's purpose is to satirize the two logos — to use irony, sarcasm, or ridicule in exposing how pervasive the corporate logos have become.

In-Class Writing Activities

1. Other symbols that the artist could have placed on the flag are: Wu-Tang (for the Wu-Tang Clan), Fila (the Fila sportswear company), FUBU (sportswear), any logo of a sports team (the Dallas Cowboys' "star," the New York Yankees' "NY," the Chicago Bulls' "bull-head"). Ask students to explain why they chose a particular symbol(s).

2. The flag may well change 200 years into the future. One answer may be that Puerto Rico may become the fifty-first state, and this would change the configuration of the cluster of fifty stars. Signs point to individual countries joining together to form a world economy — the Euromark in Europe. Whether students agree or disagree with the idea that the flag

will change, ask them to explain in some detail the reasons for the way the flag will be 200 years from now.

Discussing the Unit

Preparing for Class Discussion

1. Horace Freeland Judson's response to Hertzberg's idea of replacing "The Star-Spangled Banner" with "Lift Ev'ry Voice and Sing" might be one of apathy or lack of interest. If Judson thinks that the "American flag is an abstraction, and all material versions of it . . . are mere representations, among which the law cannot clearly draw a line," a debate over a *song* about this mere "representation" might be of little interest.

2. Judson's response to "America: 2022" might be to agree with the cartoonist's point of view. (He would also likely approve of the cartoonist's use of satire.) If the flag is a representation of American ideals, then shouldn't it reflect the modern idea that corporations control America? Shouldn't the flag be constituted by the symbols which pervade American culture? Hertzberg's response to "America: 2022" could be more difficult to assess. If Hertzberg believes that the anthem honoring the flag should be without "bombast, boasting, [or] wimpishness — [one of] just good, solid values that are both American and universal," then he may not appreciate "America: 2022," a cartoon that uses the symbol of the flag to satirize America's consumer culture. Galit Sarfaty might respond to "America: 2022" by researching the ideas behind the political cartoon, citing examples of the effects of corporate advertising, and then formulating an educated compromise/suggestion based on her findings.

From Discussion to Writing

1. The American flag permeates all aspects of American culture. For instance, in the video for Nirvana's "Heart-Shaped Box," you'll notice that the background and colors are completely in red, white, and blue with ample use of stars and stripes. Did Kurt Cobain want to gain American respectability? In movies, especially American war movies like *Platoon, Born on the Fourth of July,* and *Full Metal Jacket,* the American flag is supposed to represent fighting for the honor and glory of America, which, when tarnished, becomes a sinister symbol all its own. For the symbolic flags in William Faulkner's *Flags in the Dust,* which represent the recklessness of the Sartoris clan "there is death in the sound of it [the music], and a glamorous fatality, *like silver pennons [flags] downrushing at sunset,* or a dying fall of horns along the road to Ronceveaux." And what about the living legend in Marvel comics, the Star-Spangled avenger Captain America, a man who, seemingly wrapped in a huge flag, fights for "liberty and justice for all"?

2. Because most students do not feel they have a voice in the government, in their workplace, in the classroom, they may not feel overly patriotic about America being "the land of the free and the home of the brave." Perhaps find out if any students have traveled to another country, and ask them how they felt when they returned to the United States. Students may say that they missed the country terribly: the food, the television, the security, the wide-open spaces. Regardless of their answers, ask students to give support for their ideas.

3. Because the flag can symbolize so many things to so many different people you will likely get a myriad of answers. This question is meant to prompt students to focus on what the flag means to each of them personally. Does it remind one student of a parent who fought in Vietnam or the Gulf War? Does the flag represent the opportunity to go on a "Right for Life" walk that made a difference in another student's life? Does the flag represent the fact that a student could not get citizenship in America for two years because of bureaucratic red tape? Does the flag represent election day when a student exercised the right to vote?

Topics for Cross-Cultural Discussion

1. There are many different views about the American flag that you may encounter depending on the culture(s) of the students asked. This discussion could easily shift into one focusing on the question: What does your native culture think about America? You may want to remind students that the question being asked is what does your native culture think about the American flag? And, more importantly, what do the students themselves, (particularly those from different cultures) think about the American flag?

2. This topic may intrigue American students and students from other cultures alike, opening up a potentially interesting discussion. You may want to steer students toward the more difficult aspect of the questions: "Is [the flag of your culture] considered a symbol?" The answers may be similar to answers about the American flag: It is a symbol of liberty, justice, and freedom. Keep in mind that some students' flags may represent a restrictive or oppressive government.

13
Cloning: Is It Inevitable?

Modern science has changed human reproduction in many fundamental ways; fertility treatments, surrogacy, in vitro fertilization, and some hospital birthing methods are just a few of the "intrusions" science has made into the realm of this "natural" process. Cloning, a remote but distinctly possible addition to the mechanization of human reproduction, is once again in the news as a result of the controversial cloning of "Dolly" the sheep.

Like euthanasia and abortion, the idea of human cloning offends many people who believe that humans should not control their own conception or mortality. And many others who feel that diversity is the most prized trait of humanity are equally offended at the prospect of parents "engineering" their children. Both positions assume that nature is a better arbiter than technology of reproduction and that human beings will necessarily make selfish and socially irresponsible choices whenever given the opportunity.

Proponents of human cloning include some couples with infertility problems, genetic disease specialists, scientists who believe in technological "progress" at all costs, and those who might be able to capitalize economically on the patents and sale of such technology and equipment. What these positions overlook is the probability of severe costs that this research will exact. Class discrimination, "made-to-order" human beings, errors that result in deformity or death, as well as the further alienation of people from their own reproductive capabilities are just some of the possible drawbacks of this technology.

An important question is how this technology can be used to treat genetic diseases and defects without being exploited for the purpose of tailor-making babies for desperate or selfish parents. None of the pieces in this unit openly advocates the unchecked use of cloning as a substitute for traditional methods of reproduction, but each attempts to crystallize the essence of the subject. Marc Zabludoff in "Fear and Longing" underscores society's underestimation of the role of environment in human development; Jean Bethke Elshtain in "Our Bodies, Our Clones" criticizes the human obsession with biological parenting; and the editorial board of the *Daily Egyptian* questions the fear-inspired objections of cloning opponents.

You should stress that students need clear and accurate information about the potential of this technology before they make judgments or form opinions about it. Advise students that to be undecided on the issue may be a perfectly mature and responsible position. Very few people are well-informed as to how cloning is already used in farming or as to what potential there is for cloning in human reproduction. This issue provides a good opportunity for students to learn that there is a difference between rhetoric and informed argument.

To introduce students to the world's first clone, have them read this unit's "From the Bookshelf" excerpt from *Clone*, by Gina Kolata.

MARC ZABLUDOFF, Fear and Longing

Vocabulary/Using a Dictionary

1. A *spectacle* (para. 1) is a remarkable or impressive sight. The two meanings of *spectacle(s)* are related through their emphasis on seeing.

2. To *languish* is to lose strength; *languorous* has more of an emphasis on a loss of speed. Students should be discouraged from writing sentences that do not demonstrate a contextual meaning of the words (for example, "John languished at the end of the race") and should write sentences that provide enough context for a reader who has no definition (for example, "John languished at the end of the race like a train running out of steam").

3. Collect, amass, acquire, gather, accumulate, draw in, accrue, aggregate, assemble, collect, and pile up are all reasonable synonyms for *garner* (para. 5).

Responding to Words in Context

1. The word *tousled* (para. 3) in this context refers to the typical image of Einstein as having hair that appears somewhat out-of-control — an image that is compatible with the stereotype of the eccentric scientist.

2. By using slang here, Zabludoff expresses some contempt for those who think that human traits are divisible gene by gene. The effect is to suggest that those who disagree with the author are not as serious as he is.

Discussing Main Point and Meaning

1. The doctor is unassuming in appearance, less "world-shattering" than his research.

2. Environment is as important as genetics.

3. Zabludoff's main point is that even with the ability to clone humans, it would be impossible to create an exact replica of any human being. Furthermore, there are high costs for developing that ability. He seems to draw the line at any use that falls outside of the realm of mapping human genes or developing gene therapies for "truly terrible diseases" (para. 6).

4. Many babies would have to die in the process of experimenting with human cloning, which Zabludoff calls "an unacceptable price."

Examining Sentences, Paragraphs, and Organization

1. The italics emphasize both the difference and the causal relationship between *can* and *will*. Italics are appropriate when they are used to emphasize words as words, or a subtle semantic difference between two or more words.

2. Wilmut's opposition to the cloning of humans is important because he is the foremost researcher in the field. Using Wilmut's position gives Zabludoff's criticism more credibility.

3. If the reader answers any of the rhetorical questions affirmatively, then the last sentence resonates strongly.

Thinking Critically

1. One could claim that Zabludoff's argument indirectly disarms one of the main criticisms of human cloning (that it would diminish individuality), but his criticism of the research costs would still stand.

2. His statement implies that those in favor of human cloning research are interested merely in increasing the "pace of human reproduction" at all costs, which is somewhat of a reductive characterization.

In-Class Writing Activities

1. In this activity you should look for comparison-and-contrast strategies in which students reflect on how they (and their lives) have changed and, therefore, how their relationships with their childhood pets would be different (or the same) now.

2. Because this is an either/or assignment, the stronger essays will address the position that they *do not* take, at least briefly, in addition to fleshing out the positions they do take. You may want to discuss the merits of "anticipating the opposition" with students.

JEAN BETHKE ELSHTAIN, Our Bodies, Our Clones

Vocabulary/Using a Dictionary

1. A *proponent's purpose* is to support or advocate for a cause, whereas *proposals* and *purposes* share a sense of someone's endeavoring to do something.

2. *Generative grammar* refers to the most fundamental grammatical principles of a language — where a language begins, in other words.

3. According to Elshtain, there are too many other factors that play into a person's identity, especially in the modern age, for biology to be that significant.

Responding to Words in Context

1. Elshtain is being playfully ironic in describing the very profitable and "productive" profession that feeds on the reproductive problems of some couples when she refers to the "fertile field of infertility."

2. The more accurate definition is something "safe from failure."

Discussing Main Point and Meaning

1. The broader issue that Elshtain raises is the obsession society has with biological parenting. She suggests that people spend their efforts and money on adoption and the public relations problems that plague the adoption industry.

2. The "repugnant" scenario would be one in which parents who lost a child would be able to instantly reproduce the child.

3. Their primary rationale is to ensure that women can have biological babies.

4. Elshtain is suggesting that perhaps we can develop our ability to form fulfilling relationships with children who are not biological.

Examining Sentences, Paragraphs, and Organization

1. That all of the experts cited are men is curious to Elshtain because they specialize in a strictly female experience of childbearing. She uses the dashes to make the remark provocative, like a whisper. It is amplified by its understatement.

2. The opening paragraph is irreverent and choppy, and the language is simple and direct. In the last paragraph, the writing is gravely serious and more fluid, with more complex word choice. The introduction needs to win the trust of the reader with an innocuous approach as Elshtain's position is somewhat radical (insofar as most people favor biological parenting and see other kinds of parenting as last resorts). The conclusion is meant to both give a nod to the object of Elshtain's criticism (those determined to overcome biological infertility) and to make a serious plea for her own position.

3. Because biological parenting is so ingrained in our society, people don't automatically think about adoption in infertility cases. The first thought is of fertility treatment, so Elshtain wants to coax the reader toward her perspective in a similar pattern: She discusses the downsides of infertility first and then the solution of adoption. Many may not have read the

entire article if the title or introductory paragraphs had alluded directly to her point.

Thinking Critically

1. On one hand, Elshtain's objection is not with cloning so much as the cultural values that make cloning an attractive option for infertile couples. At the same time, cloning enjoys a lot of attention and dialogue — which adoption, unfortunately, does not.

2. Pharmaceutical companies, ambitious scientists, and radical nationalists could all have a significant interest in cloning. And there are certainly some genetic traits that some would like to see engineered out of existence. Infertile couples and infertility experts are merely the most vocal and visible proponents of cloning because they have the most sympathetic cause.

In-Class Writing Activities

1. Encourage students to avoid emotional arguments and to respond directly to the points that Elshtain makes in a calm and logical manner. Their essays will naturally appeal to a reader's sense of emotion; they should not set out to do so in lieu of a sound argument.

2. Controversial issues should be addressed calmly and logically. Students should know that the nature of their topics will evoke emotional responses; they should not overdramatize the emotional aspects of those topics.

EDITORIAL BOARD OF THE DAILY EGYPTIAN, Cloning: A Cautious Defense

Vocabulary/Using a Dictionary

1. Something or someone *ethical* falls within the acceptable realm of behavior for a particular group or profession. Something or someone *moral* has a more universal relevance and is more related to judgment and conscience than to mere professional codes. Ethics are guidelines for primarily work-related behaviors; morals are guidelines for all behaviors and decisions and set standards of goodness regardless of context.

2. Many religious devotees report having divine *revelations* in which the god(s) whom they worship have disclosed important religious truths in a dramatic fashion. Also, religious awakenings and conversions are often referred to as *revelations*.

3. Encourage sentences that fully illustrate students' knowledge of the definition of *encroach*.

Responding to Words in Context

1. Richard Seed is *independent* in the sense that he is not affiliated with a hospital or a corporation. He works only for himself.

2. State, city, and private funds would theoretically still be accessible.

Discussing Main Point and Meaning

1. The authors use the example of the McCaughey septuplets because their birth was the result of fertility treatments, which, like cloning, are not an absolutely "natural" process.

2. The authors argue that the eventual prevention of birth defects and retardation will outweigh the certain failed attempts at human cloning.

3. According to this article, human cloning research will result in cures for many diseases, creation of organs for transplant, and the prevention of birth defects.

4. If this technology is legally banned, according to these authors, it will nonetheless be conducted without regulations and will, therefore, be abused.

Examining Sentences, Paragraphs, and Organization

1. The sentence is meant to counter the argument that cloning will diminish human individuality.

2. The thesis is located in the middle of paragraph 2, after the context of the issue is established. Because the authors have a controversial position, they do not present their thesis immediately so as not to alienate the reader.

3. The list structure is effective insofar as it demonstrates a methodological approach, though it is somewhat monotonous as a reading experience.

Thinking Critically

1. The credibility of the authors would be better established through the use of specific studies and experts. Readers should not be expected to assume automatically that there are indeed experts and studies that support the authors' argument.

2. It is not fair of the authors to compare expected and unexpected birth defects or to omit the likelihood of many deaths. Imagine someone trying to justify using nursing-home patients as human guinea pigs because they are close to the ends of their lives anyway. Imagine trying to argue in court that vehicular manslaughter by a speeding driver deserves the same punishment as a serial killer's crimes. The authors are trying to obscure the costs of human cloning research by suggesting that bad things happen all the time anyway, and the ends of the research (preventing birth defects) justify the means (causing birth defects).

In-Class Writing Activities

1. Be sure that students understand that their task is to supplement the authors' argument in this assignment, not to criticize it.

2. Students would do well to treat each point more thoroughly than these authors do; in this way, they stand to establish more credibility than the authors.

Discussing the Unit

Preparing for Class Discussion

1. A code of ethics is also fundamental to any research that uses animals as experimental subjects, to nuclear weapons research, to disease control studies, to space technology, and even to computer technology that calls legal standards into question. These are just some possible answers.

2. All three articles could be reconciled by the argument that human cloning should be used to help treat those already born, but not as a means of reproduction.

From Discussion to Writing

1. Students will most likely oppose cloning in the context of an economic argument, although some will extol the merits of free-market capitalism. Play devil's advocate for both sides.

2. The best essays will be explicitly self-reflective, exploring the possibility of seeing oneself from the outside.

Topics for Cross-Cultural Discussion

1. When discussing the first part of this question, you may want to cite a contemporary example, like the frequent (and expensive) launchings of the space shuttle. What purpose(s) (other than scientific) might the launches serve? What impact (if any) does the American push for technology have on students' native countries? Students should be encouraged to provide concrete descriptions of the differences between the United States and their native countries.

2. Answers will vary, and students should be as specific as possible in their descriptions. Perhaps ask students if they think there is a correlation between the government's control over scientific research and its control over other areas of society. Can they think of examples in which government control over research would be favorable (perhaps when it protects the public from harmful substances, like plutonium)? Unfavorable (when it limits the positive potential, say, of medical research)?

14

Is Affirmative Action Still Needed?

The policy of affirmative action is one that is hotly debated across the country, particularly since the creation of California's Proposition 209, the widely contested referendum which when signed into law in 1998, effectively ended affirmative action in that state. Is affirmative action, which has come under attack, still necessary? Effective? Fair? Each author in this unit offers the reader an opinion on these questions.

In the first of two student articles, Andy Miller discusses his negative experience with affirmative action, in which a friend of his, who is of Panamanian descent, was accepted more easily into college than he was, though the author had better grades, better ACT and SAT scores, and participated in more extracurricular activities. The author muses, "Just a simple check in a box caused a world of difference in someone's life." At the end of the essay, Miller suggests, as do many who favor the banning of affirmative action, that "if applications (for colleges) just forget about the sections regarding race, sex, and national origin, and concentrated more on the section about work experience, then that would solve a lot of problems."

Student writer Benson Cohen's "Pursuing King's Dream," reminds the reader that "these efforts [of affirmative action] have significantly increased the participation of under-represented groups in the mainstream of our society." In his insightful essay, Cohen defines affirmative action and outlines some common misconceptions dreamed up by the uninitiated. He points out that "although affirmative action programs have made a crucial difference for countless qualified individuals, inequalities continue to exist." After providing much support for this statement, Cohen concludes his essay: "As we approach the new millennium, our commitment to affirmative action, the pursuit of [Dr. Martin Luther] King's dream of a more just and equal society, is more important and necessary than ever."

In her essay "Affirming Affirmative Action," Bernice Powell Jackson warns readers that America is slipping back into a period in which we aren't reinforcing affirmative action policies, not unlike the time in history "right after that brief period known as the Reconstruction . . . a time when political, economic, and social disenfranchisement took hold." She provides examples to support her fears and warns of the problems the United States will encounter if all states were to create a law similar to Proposition 209. In her conclusion she reflects upon the demise of affirmative action, predicting that we will "once more repeat the mistakes of the past and endanger our future."

To add another voice to the debate on affirmative action, direct your students to this unit's "From the Bookshelf" selection by Stephen Steinberg, from *Turning Back: The Retreat from Racial Justice in American Thought and Policy.*

ANDY MILLER, Affirmative Action: Another Name for Discrimination

Vocabulary/Using a Dictionary

1. Miller means that many students with high GPAs who have scored well on standardized tests are turned down by colleges every year because of a system in which the number of persons of a specified group to be admitted is predetermined. This "quota" system, Miller claims, was put into effect with the arrival of affirmative action.

2. A *beneficiary* is "one who receives benefits." The word originates from *benefit* meaning "something that promotes well-being," which comes from the Latin *beneficium,* meaning "flavor, benefit."

3. When Miller says that his application for admission into the University of Wisconsin at Madison was *deferred,* he means that his application was "postponed, delayed." Some synonyms for *deferred* would be "postponed, delayed, adjourned, remanded, protracted, retarded, prolonged."

Responding to Words in Context

1. The noun *resume* is "a short account of one's career and qualifications prepared typically by an applicant for a position." It appears identical to *resume,* the verb, which means "to assume or take again, reoccupy." Both these words share the same origin (from the Latin *re- + -sumere,* "to take up, take") and share the similar denotation that you are *retaking/reviewing* something.

2. With his use of the word *superfluous* in paragraph 10, he means that all the issues attached to affirmative action are "marked by wastefulness; extravagant; exceeding what is sufficiently necessary."

Discussing Main Point and Meaning

1. Miller thinks affirmative action was put into effect "in order to curb discrimination and bias based on certain characteristics attributed to minorities" (para. 3). The issue he takes with affirmative action is that "it can get to a point where I could begin to think that I am being discriminated against" (para. 3).

2. What disturbed Miller about the admissions policy at the University of Wisconsin is that a good friend of his of Panamanian descent, who "grew up in a wealthy suburb, went to a nationally ranked high school, and

had a close-knit family . . . did not celebrate Panamanian holidays, did not speak Spanish in the home, and did not even entertain the thought of thinking about his heritage in any way" (para. 6), "got a response back from the admissions officers within a few weeks, congratulating him on his acceptance into the University of Wisconsin at Madison" (para. 7). Miller's ACT scores were higher, he participated in more school activities, and had a higher GPA, but his admission into the same college was deferred (para. 7).

3. "To curb this problem of reverse discrimination," Miller "propose[s] a ban on affirmative action as a whole, just like what occurred in the state of California in 1996" (para. 9).

Examining Sentences, Paragraphs, and Organization

1. If the first sentence were switched with the last, the essay would begin with the statement: "If applications just forget about the sections regarding race, sex, and national origin, and concentrated more on the section about work experience, then that would solve a lot of problems" (para. 12). The essay would then end with the question: "Do you think that when President Kennedy said Americans should 'take affirmative action to ensure that applicants are employed, and that employees are treated during employment without regard to their race, creed, color, or national origin,' he meant to deny qualified students entrance into our fine institutions of higher education?" (para. 1). The conclusion necessarily stems from the introduction, which, when developed through the use of supporting examples, makes sense. Without examples to support the opening question/concern, the essay would fall apart and would not lead to Miller's conclusion; thus, the essay would not make sense if the two sentences were reversed.

2. The examples that Miller uses to support his claim in paragraph 1 (that President Kennedy set up affirmative action to deny qualified students entrance into higher education) are as follows: a hypothetical example regarding "a local State Street bar" (para. 3), the personal example of the author being "witness to an act of 'fake affirmative action'" (paras. 6–7), and the hypothetical example of a woman working at a Fortune 500 company (para. 11).

3. It seems that the supporting examples in "Affirmative Action: Another Name for Discrimination" are not arranged in any particular order. The most important support for Miller's claim is the story about his Panamanian friend, which comes from his own experience. That story is presented in the middle of three examples. Thus, the examples of the essay do not seem organized in order of importance. (See question 2 for the other two examples.)

Thinking Critically

1. Because Miller had a bad personal experience with affirmative action (see paras. 6–7), he is ready to "propose a ban on affirmative action as a whole, just like what occurred in the state of California in 1996" (para. 9). He does not seem to be weighing the pros and cons of the issue, or considering that affirmative action may be necessary for the survival of some minority students in the twenty-first century.

2. The author's statement in paragraph 10 is one of the arguments at the heart of the discussion about affirmative action. Be prepared for students who will argue vehemently for one side or the other. "Is it that big of a deal?" the author asks us in regards to having more whites or more minorities at a university. Of course it is a big deal, but the issue to get students to address here is the effectiveness of affirmative action.

In-Class Writing Activities

1. In their essays, students should agree or disagree with Miller's assumption that ACT and SAT scores are important factors that determine a student's success in college. This is one of the most critical debates going on in colleges today. An example — a high school student did not apply himself in the classroom, but did very well on standardized tests (he got a 1300 on his SATs). When applying to colleges, he pointed out the potential that he could achieve (as indicated by his SATs) as compared to his actual and unimpressive GPA. If his college GPA is exponentially higher, does that suggest that the SAT is a good predictor?

2. The purpose of this question is to get students to think critically about affirmative action. If they can think of an experience similar to Miller's, then possibly they may feel sympathy for someone in his position.

BENSON COHEN, Pursuing King's Dream

Vocabulary/Using a Dictionary

1. In his statement, "Affirmative action is not a monolithic program," Cohen means that affirmative action is not a program having a uniform, massive, or inflexible quality or character. The author wants us to understand that affirmative action "does not include such admittedly discriminatory practices such as quotas, preferences, or lowered standards" (para. 3).

2. The word *tailoring* means "fashioning or adapting to a particular taste or need." It may have evolved from the word *tailor*, "one whose occupation is making or altering outer garments." It comes from the Latin *talea* meaning "twig, cutting."

3. A *legacy* is "anything handed down from the past, as from an ancestor." A *legacy boost* would then be "an aid in admission to college handed down from an ancestor."

Responding to Words in Context

1. *Manifestation* is a noun meaning "the act, process, or instance of manifesting: something that manifests or is manifest." The verb *manifest* means "readily perceived by the senses and especially by the sight; easily understood or recognized by the mind; obvious."

2. *Mentoring* as a social program means "tutoring or coaching." A *mentor* is "a trusted counselor or guide." The word originates from the character named "Mentor" whom Odysseus entrusted with the education of his son Telemachus.

Discussing Main Point and Meaning

1. According to Cohen, "the extensive history of discrimination against women and people of color in education, and its current manifestations in American society, continue to limit the current generation's educational opportunities" (para. 1).

2. Some of the activities that have been created by affirmative action in education are: "providing targeted scholarships and other targeted financial aid, additional review of applications by admissions committees looking at other merit factors in addition to grades and test scores, targeted recruitment efforts for undergraduate admissions, as well as for special educational programs, and mentoring, counseling, and other support programs."

3. "After the California Board of Regents voted to drop affirmative action in admission beginning with the 1996 class, the Boalt Law School in Berkeley admitted, out of a class of 270, only one black student, the same number of blacks the University of Mississippi admitted in 1962" (para. 7).

4. "Tailoring admissions only to those with the highest numbers can leave out talented singers, artists, athletes, and other able students" (para. 8).

Examining Sentences, Paragraphs, and Organization

1. A transition sentence connects one idea to another in discourse. Useful strategies for creating transitions include transitional expressions, parallelism, and planned repetition of key words and phrases. Two transition sentences are as follows: (1) "*However* [transitional expression], the extensive history of discrimination against women and people of color in education, and its current manifestations in American society, continue to limit the current generation's educational opportunities" (para. 1); (2)

"*Nevertheless*, [transitional expression] educational opportunities for women and people of color are still limited by discrimination and stereotyping" (para. 2).

2. This essay could arguably be an essay of definition, which states the meaning of something. Cohen is trying to define what affirmative action really is, not what uninitiated members of society think it is. You find support regarding this selection as a definition essay in paragraphs 3–6 and 8, where the author "clears up" what the term affirmative action means.

3. The main point that focuses the essay is found in paragraph 1 in which Cohen states, "These efforts (of affirmative action) have significantly increased the participation of underrepresented groups in the mainstream of our society."

Thinking Critically

1. Remind students that the definition of *institutionalized* is "treated or confined to an institution." So Cohen is saying that racism and sexism are continually pervading institutions, not that they are only confined to institutions. You should obtain examples from students' personal experiences. You could also use the affirmative action policy for your own institution as a primary source document. Discuss the policy in class and ask students if they agree with it; then lead the discussion back to Cohen's essay.

2. Ask students first to consider Cohen's definition of affirmative action: "[It] is not a monolithic program. It does not include such admittedly discriminatory practices such as quotas, preferences, or lowered standards. . . . Instead, affirmative action in education spans a broad range of activities intended to expand educational opportunities to all Americans" (para. 3). How does this definition affect students' responses to Cohen's argument? Do students generally agree with Cohen's ideas about the importance of education (para. 9)? How do they connect this with the role of affirmative action, and Cohen's assertion that affirmative action be used to "equalize people's access" to education (para. 9)? And if, as Cohen argues, schools are necessarily responsible for providing equal opportunities through affirmative action, what other institutions or individuals should be held responsible for using the policy of affirmative action?

In-Class Writing Activities

1. By assuming that "numbers are important, and everyone admitted to universities like Emory have numbers, but there is more to a human than that," Cohen opens the discussion about the really important qualities one obtains from college. Ask students to brainstorm or freewrite about these issues before they choose a topic for their essays. From the

freewriting, have students select three or four ideas they can use in their essays. Have students support their positions with specific reasons and examples.

2. Other criteria might be: academics (math level, English ability, reading comprehension level, grade point average, SAT scores, class ranking), or extracurricular activities (clubs, sports, honor society). More interesting answers would include: What is your greatest accomplishment? Favorite music? Likes? Dislikes? How strong are your interpersonal skills? How do you react to authority?

BERNICE POWELL JACKSON, Affirming Affirmative Action

Vocabulary/Using a Dictionary

1. The word *ostensibly* means "evidently; outwardly; apparently." It comes from the Latin *ostensus,* meaning "to show," from *ost-,* "in front of, akin."

2. Used as a noun, the word *epidemic* means "a prevalent or widespread disease." When used as an adjective, the word means "excessively prevalent; contagious": The comedian was so funny, the laughter from the audience was of epidemic proportions.

3. When Jackson refers to an "inclusive" society in paragraph 3, she means that "we must pursue the dream" of a society that includes everything, or more specifically, everyone, of all creeds and colors.

Responding to Words in Context

1. *Irony* is "the use of words to convey a meaning that is the opposite of its literal meaning." For something to be *ironic,* it has to be relating to, containing, or constituting irony; sarcastic."

2. The word *undergird* looks similar to *girder. Undergird* means "to make secure underneath; to form the basis of foundation of; strengthen; support."

Discussing Main Point and Meaning

1. According to Jackson, "after fighting the Civil War . . . legislation was passed and efforts were made by government, churches, and others to ensure that former slaves could be equal members of society" (para. 1).

2. When Jackson says "the news is already grim for some of us" (para. 2), she is referring to the types of social disenfranchisement that are occurring today — "Precipitous drops in the applications and acceptances in law and medical schools in Texas and California" — and her concerns over "who is going to provide legal services and medical services for poor African American and Hispanic people in the twenty-first century."

3. Students' explanations should follow the facts of the occurrence at the Golden Gate Bridge as related by Jackson in paragraph 3: "Nearly 10,000 people recently marched across the Golden Gate Bridge to protest the now infamous Proposition 209, which ended affirmative action in the state of California. There were people of all ages — from school children to the elderly — and people of all races who could see clearly the damage this legislation can do."

4. Jackson concludes that "the sad part" of these attacks on affirmative action "is that because we as a nation can seldom look honestly at our history, we cannot learn from it. We cannot see then the cycles of racism and the impact they have had on my people's development and our nation's character. The sad part is that by ending affirmative action, we once more repeat the mistakes of the past and endanger our future."

Examining Sentences, Paragraphs, and Organization

1. The author makes use of two interrogative sentences at the end of paragraph 2, because she knows that occasional questions in an essay help to involve the reader. These two questions also help to strike home the statements that come before: "The news is already grim for some of us. Stories of precipitous drops in applications and acceptances in law and medical schools in Texas and California . . . are feeling the first fruits of the attacks on affirmative action."

2. The two things that are being compared in paragraph 1 are: an essay that Jackson read "which traced our nation's history as it relates to racial justice issues," and the news that has been arriving in regard to the attacks on affirmative action.

3. Jackson indicates that the problem is that "we're living in déjà vu all over again" (para. 1). The time we live in now (the period just after the initiation of affirmative action) is like the period right after the Reconstruction, "a time when political, economic, and social disenfranchisement took place." The solution of "Affirming Affirmative Action" is more difficult to locate. Although Jackson states the problem, she does not truly offer an obvious solution. The author seems to mourn the death of affirmative action without suggesting alternatives or a strategy to reclaim it (see paras. 4 and 5).

Thinking Critically

1. Jackson does not offer an alternative to the demise of affirmative action. It seems that the author's concern lies in pointing out the necessity of affirmative action programs (paras. 4 and 5).

2. "Stories of precipitous drops in applications and acceptances in law and medical schools in Texas and California" don't necessarily mean that nobody is "going to provide legal services and medical services for poor

African American and Hispanic people in the twenty-first century." The first statement does not *cause* the second, though one could argue, perhaps using statistical evidence, that a shortage of these services could be a real outcome of a decline of people of color in the legal and medical professions.

In-Class Writing Activities

1. Both Jackson's and King's speeches are similar in their goal — to convince America that people should not be judged by the color of their skin. Everyone should be given equal opportunities. The key lines in interpreting the speeches are located in the last few words of each speech. In Jackson's case it is the line "We must pursue the dream of an inclusive society." With Martin Luther King Jr.'s speech, the thesis seems to be in the line "I have a dream that my four little children will one day live in a nation where they will not be judged by the color of their skin, but by the content of their character." An interesting approach could be to discuss how Martin Luther King Jr. might have felt about affirmative action.

2. Once students have supported/rejected affirmative action, ask them to write about what improvements (if any) might be beneficial to the policy, specifically, how it might be made more effective (1) on a local level (youth centers, high schools, town board meetings); (2) on a state level (the governor's office, state universities); and (3) on a national level (the Senate, House of Representatives, the president, the Constitution). This breakdown may help students to write about specific suggestions. Keep in mind that some students will support the policy as it stands, and may not (as Bernice Powell Jackson) feel the need to offer alternatives or suggestions for improvement.

Discussing the Unit

Preparing for Class Discussion

1. This question provides students with a "what if?" scenario about affirmative action. Students may come to realize the necessity of such a policy in modern-day America and may make an effort to support the programs. Even if students hold that the world would be "better off" without affirmative action, this preparation question will require them to review their point of view and the support they have for it. Awareness of places where affirmative action has been instituted is also helpful for students to put the policy into perspective: "Does your workplace/school have an affirmative action policy?"

2. The goal here is to encourage students to reinforce and review their own philosophy regarding affirmative action before leaving the unit. Students

should try to formulate, as descriptively as possible, their own stance on affirmative action. Perhaps students can refer back to the articles in the unit to adopt ideas which have been eloquently stated by the authors. If students are undecided, ask them to explain why.

3. Steinberg differentiates between nondiscrimination policies and affirmative action and identifies two versions of affirmative action. At its basic level, affirmative action goes beyond nondiscrimination policies by holding employers responsible for seeking protected groups. In its more controversial form, affirmative action seeks to assure racial justice by requiring that certain "goals and timetables" be met by employers (para. 3). As Steinberg puts it, affirmative action is a term "fraught with ambiguity," partly because it has evolved in a piecemeal way and was "never formulated as a coherent policy" (para. 1). Ask students how affirmative action might be made into a more coherent policy. Who should define affirmative action? How should its effectiveness be evaluated?

From Discussion to Writing

1. Andy Miller and Bernice Powell Jackson take opposite positions in the affirmative action debate. Miller argues that affirmative action should concentrate more on "the section about work experience" on college applications, whereas Jackson (in the words of Jesse Jackson) wants us to push for, "to pursue the dream of an inclusive society." To create a dialogue between the two writers, look at one of the two essays, and then break it down into its main points. After doing this, take the other essay and ask, "How would Jackson respond to Miller's point here?"

2. For the essay entitled "Affirmative Action Helps _____," the group (or groups) that students choose to write about should be common enough that adequate resources are available in the library. Again, urge students to state the reasons why they chose a group: What makes that group particularly in need of this policy?

3. In his essay "Pursuing King's Dream," Benson Cohen reviews some common misconceptions about affirmative action: "Affirmative action does not allow for unqualified individuals to enter educational institutions. In fact, affirmative action was established to ensure admissions were decided on an equal basis from a more varied pool of applicants than the traditionally limited pool of white males." You might put a few books on reserve in the library dealing specifically with affirmative action, or direct students to Internet resources that may aid their research, such as The Affirmative Action and Diversity Project research page, hosted by the University of California in Santa Barbara <http://humanitas.ucsb.edu/aa.html>. (For more research links on this topic, visit <http://www.bedfordstmartins.com/ot/13.html>).

Topics for Cross-Cultural Discussion

1. The purpose of this question is to encourage non-native students to think critically about their own culture and compare it to that of the United States. This will possibly bridge a gap of unfamiliarity between non-native and American students, and improve discussion.

2. Again, this topic is meant to prompt non-native speakers to share ideas with the class about their native countries. This may be a particularly useful one if a non-native student's country does not have an affirmative action policy because then there is a mode for contrast with American culture: Students may see what it is like to live in a culture without affirmative action.

15

Is the Death Penalty Necessary?

Since the days of the Old Testament, people have struggled with the concept of justice. Does "an eye for an eye" always make sense? Should we amputate the hand of those who have stolen? Should we castrate those who have raped? Should we kill those who have killed? What accounts for the support of taking the lives of those who take lives? Some argue deterrence, economics, or social protection. But at the core of the death penalty is the human desire for revenge. Thieves, rapists, and stalkers may spend enough time in prison that their victims and society will feel avenged. But a murder victim, who has been robbed of life, will never see justice, and the murder victim's family will, perhaps, never feel avenged or compensated. The death penalty is a trump card, in this sense. Nothing more absolute can be engineered; even life in prison without parole offers the possibility of the occasional pleasure to those who receive the sentence. A good book, a savored cigarette, a long laugh — these are the privileges of prison inmates that offend the victim's family and friends, and that seem perverse to proponents of capital punishment, for the victim of a murder will never again enjoy even such small pleasures.

Since students will most likely already have opinions on this subject, you might orchestrate an open discussion about all perspectives. On the one hand, the expensive appeals process makes capital punishment more expensive to taxpayers than life in prison; states with capital punishment have not seen a decline in their murder rates; and innocent people have, on occasion, been executed. On the other hand, forensic science makes it increasingly possible to achieve exact convictions for murder cases; the legal process could be streamlined; and rehabilitation for violent capital offenders is a grim possibility. Discuss the legitimacy of each position and encourage your students to look at the logic that governs each position, not merely the emotional weight.

To provide your students with a well-known point of view on the death penalty, have them read this unit's "From the Bookshelf" selection by Helen Prejean, from *Dead Man Walking: An Eyewitness Account of the Death Penalty in the United States.*

Two Voices from Death Row

MICHAEL ROSS, My Name Is Michael Ross

Vocabulary/Using a Dictionary

1. The meaning of *volens* is "to wish."

2. The cursor is a blinking dash that marks one's place. Its role is *cursory* in that what it does is superficial rather than substantive.

3. Land is *degraded* when it erodes, thus lowering its level.

Responding to Words in Context

1. *Ludicrous* (para. 6) lightens the tone of the point that Ross is making, though he may not have intended it. *Pathological, illogical,* or even *insane* might have been better choices.

2. He began to see himself and his actions more clearly, as a "normal" individual would, one assumes.

Discussing Main Point and Meaning

1. Depo-Lupren lowers Ross's level of testosterone, which allegedly reduces his urges to be sexually sadistic.

2. Ross believes that his mental illness — sexual sadism — caused him to commit his crimes, and that with the proper medical attention he never would have committed them.

3. He compares them to having an irritating melody stuck in one's head or an obnoxious roommate one cannot avoid.

Examining Sentences, Paragraphs, and Organization

1. The statement represents the perspective of society in general. Ross, in part, considers himself more a victim of his illness than the "worst of the worst" of perpetrators.

2. The two anecdotes demonstrate the severity of his illness but do not contain criminal acts. Descriptions of Ross's actual crimes would diminish the reader's sympathy.

3. He condemns a society that does not concentrate enough of its efforts on prevention and fails to diagnose and treat sick individuals. This strategy, in part, takes the blame off of Ross himself.

Thinking Critically

1. He does seem to be evasive on the subject of his crimes and victims, but his objective is really to discuss an illness that most people are unfamiliar with, and thus he gives it his full attention.

2. It does seem surprising that Ross would voluntarily be executed, as he was very engaged in fighting the original verdict and sentencing in his case.

In-Class Writing Activities

1. Encourage students to avoid emotionalism — whatever position they take. Good responses will advocate what is best for society as a whole.

2. Good responses will draw on as many specific details as possible (from each case).

TERESA ALLEN and ANDREA HICKS JACKSON, A Voice from Death Row

Vocabulary/Using a Dictionary

1. A *misdemeanor* in a literal sense is an example of bad or wrong behavior or conduct.

2. Nerve, gall, presumptuousness, daring, impudence, brazenness, rudeness, disrespect, and guts are all reasonable synonyms for *audacity*.

3. People might become *institutionalized* in some school environments, in long-term care facilities (nursing homes and mental hospitals, for example), or in military organizations.

Responding to Words in Context

1. Jackson refers to her religious conversion; her commitment to Jesus Christ will "save" her from her sins, she believes, and deliver her to heaven.

2. Yes, this is irony. The motorcade is meant to take Jackson to her death, not to protect her from harm.

Discussing Main Point and Meaning

1. Jackson believes that because she was high on drugs she did not have control. Upon writing this article, she believed that she deserved to be released from prison.

2. Jackson believes she has "a clean slate" because she was absolved by the prison chaplain and by God.

3. Because death-row inmates are theoretically soon-to-be dead, no one cares about the state of their health, Jackson claims.

4. Getting mail is the highlight of Jackson's day.

Examining Sentences, Paragraphs, and Organization

1. Teresa Allen's introductory material helps to place the article within the context of the status and makeup of women in prison, specifically those on death row. Allen provides historical background and statistics to show what may perhaps be "society's new willingness to prosecute aggressively and punish all criminals, regardless of gender" (para. 3).

2. Jackson's statement is based on the assumption that she was not responsible for her crime. If one accepts that assumption, then one could agree with the statement.

3. No, it is not chronological. The piece begins with a description of the day that Jackson's execution was stayed, then describes her conversion and the conditions on death row, and ends with Jackson's argument for her release. It moves from the dramatic to the mundane and then puts forward its argument at the very end.

Thinking Critically

1. One gets the sense that Jackson has little interest in the life she took and little sympathy for anyone but herself, which could be off-putting to a reader. Still, the point of her discussion is to humanize herself to those who believe she deserves to die.

2. Answers will vary. Encourage students not to oversimplify or merely to repeat Jackson's reasoning that death-row inmates, in a sense, are considered "already dead."

In-Class Writing Activities

1. Students might also imagine themselves as Jackson's defense attorney, trying to convince a judge or a jury to stay her execution. Ask students to think of ways that they might defend Jackson and to write a persuasive monologue. Have students read their letters or monologues aloud in class and critique each other's work. Good responses will make both argumentative (logical) and persuasive (emotional) appeals.

2. Encourage students to be pragmatic and to describe an environment that would be legally and logistically feasible. Ask them to explain the particular features of the facility they envision and to provide the reason behind each. Perhaps ask students to describe (if they can) a correctional facility in their area. Does this affect their construction of a prison environment?

Students Debate the Death Penalty

ABBIE GIBBS, Witnessing Execution

Vocabulary/Using a Dictionary

1. The term *morbidity* in medicine measures the rate of a disease in a particular locality.

2. There is obviously much anticipation and/or anxiety associated with trying to catch or grasp something. The object of the catching or grasping has been dropped from the more modern meaning, and a slightly more negative tone has been applied to it.

Responding to Words in Context

1. Gibbs was drawn perhaps to the excitement of the situation, as drivers are often compelled to slow down and to survey a car accident. She may be feeling the rush of adrenaline that comes from anticipating a terrifying event.

2. She wants to show that both she and Long have the choice to feel remorse: she for Long, and Long for his victims. By refusing to feel remorse for Long because Long refused to express it for his victims, Gibbs makes a point about what she views as just punishment.

Discussing Main Point and Meaning

1. Gibbs thought she might change her mind about capital punishment, but she did not.

2. She waits to feel emotion as a result of her witnessing the execution, though she never does.

3. His apparent "eagerness" makes him seem inhuman in a way, and this effect perhaps contributed to Gibbs's response.

Examining Sentences, Paragraphs, and Organization

1. If the piece were written by an inmate in the prison, the details would seem more symbolic of the cold and impersonal atmosphere. In this context they are more symbolic of Gibbs's anticipated activity for the day, and thus seem less permanent.

2. By transitioning from Long's feelings about his approaching death to the feelings of his victim's family, Gibbs sets up a kind of hierarchy of importance: To her, the family's feelings are more important than Long's feelings, and thus she stops trying to identify with Long almost as soon as she starts.

3. Gibbs wants to demonstrate her openness to emotion and the possible change of mind she expected before attending the execution. Thus the reader can experience the event similar to the way she experienced it.

Thinking Critically

1. Perhaps she could have been sympathetic to Long and still felt that his execution was justified. At the same time, to feel sympathy for a person is to identify with or have some investment in his or her life. However, it is surprising that someone of her age could be so dispassionate while witnessing an execution; one might expect more vulnerability.

2. It is difficult to believe that Gibbs was ever ambivalent about the death penalty; her reaction is essentially unemotional. It seems that she may have watched the execution to confirm rather than to test her opinion.

In-Class Writing Activities

1. Look for controlled logic, as evidence to support a plan that has never been tried will be unavailable to students.

2. Answers will vary, but students' responses should be compatible with the text (that is, Long was not overtly afraid, remorseful, or self-pitying).

EDITORIAL BOARD OF THE COLLEGIATE TIMES, Death Penalty Alternatives

Vocabulary/Using a Dictionary

1. People's tempers tend to "explode" during discussions of *volatile* subjects like the ones the authors list.

2. A defendant must be considered mentally capable to participate in his or her own defense to be deemed *competent* to stand trial.

3. *Equitable* and *equal* are similar adjectives, though the former generally refers to situations, actions, or results, whereas the latter generally refers to individual qualities of persons or things (for example, size, number, force, rights, rank, ability).

Responding to Words in Context

1. The authors believe that all murders are essentially equal in a criminal sense and that the small fraction of murderers on death row is symbolic of a great inequity in the system.

2. The graphic language underscores that Tucker's crime was as horrific as any other brutal murder, which suggests that the sympathy she received was unwarranted. The authors are attempting to demonstrate the subjectivity that comes into play in death-penalty cases.

Discussing Main Point and Meaning

1. The authors' position is that the death penalty can never be fairly meted out and is not the most efficient means of punishment for our society. The authors are not overtly sympathetic to murderers, but are rather critical of a justice system that, in their words, is incompetent.

2. The authors think that society should somehow be compensated by criminals who threaten its well-being.

3. Tucker's case received a lot of media attention because Tucker was a woman, and she had gained the sympathy of many important people, though her crime was as brutal as any. The authors illustrate the way that subjective feelings and opinions play into what should be strictly legal decisions. This is evidence, the authors feel, that the death penalty can never serve justice.

Examining Sentences, Paragraphs, and Organization

1. The "gray area" refers to the discrepancy between the number of actual murders in the United States and the number of death-penalty sentences.

2. The contents of the injection are listed to illustrate the calculated coldness of the death penalty. Along with the time and Tucker's last words, the authors include the drug contents to demonstrate the intended efficiency of the sentence; this is ironic as the authors later proceed to describe the inefficiencies.

3. The authors hold back their opinion until paragraph 6, where they point to the inequitable distribution of the death penalty in our justice system.

Thinking Critically

1. The writers of this essay are interested in punishments that serve society as well as punish criminals. The death penalty would not, in the authors' opinion, provide a long-term service to society. They could say something more about the imperfections of the "rehabilitation" model and the problem of early parole for some violent offenders (even murderers, particularly juvenile murderers).

2. Answers will vary. Students should be very specific in making their distinctions.

In-Class Writing Activities

1. This assignment may provide a good opportunity to discuss with students the importance of defining abstractions in argumentative writing. Punishment — like freedom, justice, love, equality, and many other abstract concepts — can have many different meanings for many different people. One must define any key abstractions in one's argument so that the reader follows the logic precisely.

2. These responses should be grounded in the text — quoting, paraphrasing, and summarizing it as much as possible. You might discuss the concept of "close reading" with students.

JOHN LLOYD, The Death Penalty Makes Murderers of Us All

Vocabulary/Using a Dictionary

1. A *gratuity* is a tip for services rendered (on top of the cost). Tips are often standard (expected) and thus are not always *gratuitous*. A *gratuitous* tip might be one given on top of paying a bill that already included *gratuities*.

2. Since *liable* (para. 4) can mean both likely and legally bound, it is fair to say that both meanings apply in Lloyd's use, whether or not he intended it.

3. Impotence, incompetence, inadequacy, insufficiency, and inability are all reasonable antonyms for *efficacy*.

Responding to Words in Context

1. He focuses on the concept of *desert* because proponents of the death penalty so often do (for example, "killers deserve to be killed").

2. Lloyd's accusation is largely rhetorical: A juror who votes for the death penalty in a murder case is not a murderer, just as a murderer's accomplice is not a murderer, at least in the legal sense. Those who carry out death sentences are merely tools of the state, which might be labeled as a *murderer* in Lloyd's sense if the state were a human being.

Discussing Main Point and Meaning

1. If Lloyd's logic were sound, then those who carry out death-penalty sentences would surely have to be put to death. However, his logic is unsound.

2. Lloyd ends with a discussion of conscience because that is what guides most people in formulating their opinions of capital punishment. It is also a way of moving away from his logical argument to a more emo-

tional one, in the event that his reader is not yet convinced of his position.

3. Lloyd agrees with Hamlet's assessment of punishment (which in Lloyd's words is that "all humans are more or less evil and deserve severe punishment").

Examining Sentences, Paragraphs, and Organization

1. The tone of the last line is a bit smug and self-congratulatory, which does not at all serve Lloyd's purpose. It accuses proponents of the death penalty, in a sense, of being without a conscience (amoral, really). Any ambivalent reader or any reader leaning toward support of the death penalty could easily take offense.

2. "What is right to consider" is a bit cryptic. It could refer to Hamlet's point that if *desert* were a consideration of law, then all people should be punished. It could refer to the following point that some might be punished "for what they might do."

3. The claim seems empty considering Lloyd's former hostility toward proponents of the death penalty.

Thinking Critically

1. Fair punishment is, in a way, a timeless human concern. And yet there is something peculiar about twentieth-century American culture, which is a violent and highly murderous society. Answers will vary.

2. Lloyd's real argument, though not explicitly stated, is that the state has no right to commit an act that its individuals are prohibited from committing. To do so would be immoral and hypocritical, setting a poor standard of justice.

In-Class Writing Activities

1. Advise students to briefly summarize the plays and novels from which they have chosen their characters, before describing and analyzing the characters themselves. This would be a good assignment for students to read aloud to their classmates.

2. The best responses will be grounded as much as possible in logical argument — for example, the hypothetical juror might cite other comparable cases in which the death penalty (constitutional in most states) was assigned. He/she might also make an emotional appeal, focusing on the severity of the crime committed (and a possible lack of remorse by the accused) as well as on the suffering of the victim and the loss suffered by the victim's family.

Discussing the Unit

Preparing for Class Discussion

1. Answers will vary. Keep students focused on the specifics of the articles.

2. Once again, try to keep students focused on the specifics of the articles in the unit. Ask them to cite particular passages (and perhaps to point out effective rhetorical strategies) that influenced their opinions.

From Discussion to Writing

1. This is a difficult assignment. Try to familiarize students with the concept of *synthesis* in expository writing. Learning to blend several sources smoothly into one essay/argument is a critical skill for the college writer.

2. This is an exercise in logic or, at least, in considering the reasoning behind both points of view. Students should learn to differentiate between passion and thoughtfulness in their writing. You might accomplish this by showing them that they can advocate for any position — regardless of passions — through logical thinking.

3. Students may do better on this assignment if they work in groups. A sample dialogue among the student writers might go something like this:

Abbie Gibbs:
"Michael Ross deserves to die. Even though he acknowledges his crimes and the pain and loss that he caused his victims and his victims' families, he committed these acts without empathy. It is without feeling that I would watch him die."

Editorial Board of the *Collegiate Times*:
"But Michael Ross suffers from a mental illness which, it is believed, can be controlled by Depo-Lupron injections and therapy. Yes, he should pay for his crimes and remain in jail, but instead of being executed, he might be put to work in a maximum-security factory to offset the cost of living in prison. Also, because Ross is willing to discuss his crime and his mental illness, he shows some signs of rehabilitation. After all, it has been proved that criminals can be corrected. Perhaps Ross is an example of such rehabilitation."

John Lloyd:
"I doubt that Ross can be rehabilitated. As I've said, all humans are more or less evil and deserve severe punishment. However, the problem with capital punishment is not that it's not deserved, it's that occasionally the innocent get executed. Though Ross admits to the murder of eight women, and while he does deserve to die, he should not be ex-

ecuted because capital punishment is neither just nor ethical. It is evil and equal to murder."

Topics for Cross-Cultural Discussion

1. Encourage students to be specific in their comparisons/contrasts. Has there been a court case in students' native cultures which drew national attention? What was the outcome? Do students agree or disagree with the verdict? Why?

2. The focus in this assignment should be on the logical solution that would best promote the good relations between the two countries and the sovereignty of each nation. You may want to cite recent international cases: the caning of the American teenager in Singapore, or the U.S. government's wish to extradite Libyan suspects in connection with the bombing of a Pan Am flight #103.

THE COMPACT READER
Short Essays by Method and Theme
Sixth Edition

NEW!

Jane E. Aaron

JANUARY 1999/PAPER/400 PAGES/$21 NET
INSTRUCTOR'S EDITION

A new edition of a long-time favorite, *The Compact Reader* is actually three readers in one — short-essay, rhetorical, and thematic — now with 34 brief essays, 20 sample paragraphs, and more concrete guidance on reading and writing than any other short-essay reader.

MODELS FOR WRITERS
Short Essays for Composition
Sixth Edition

Alfred Rosa and **Paul Eschholz**
both of the *University of Vermont*

1998/PAPER/556 PAGES/$20 NET
INSTRUCTOR'S MANUAL

Models for Writers combines an excellent collection of 75 short, accessible essays with abundant support for student writers. This popular reader includes chapters on elements of the essay as well as methods of development.

OUR TIMES
Readings from Recent Periodicals
Fifth Edition

Robert Atwan
Series Editor, *Best American Essays*

1998/PAPER/440 PAGES/$23 NET
INSTRUCTOR'S MANUAL/COMPANION WEB SITE

This thematically arranged reader features 51 *very* contemporary selections and 29 "sidebars" from 53 *very* recent periodicals on 15 topics of *very* current interest, with unique apparatus to get students talking and writing right away.

BEDFORD/ST. MARTIN'S

1–800–446–8923 • www.bedfordstmartins.com

Students live in the real world. —
Here's a textbook that does, too.

Already adopted at more than 150 schools across the country

REAL WRITING WITH READINGS
Paragraphs and Essays for College, Work, and Everyday Life

Susan Anker

1998/617 PAGES/PAPER/$29 NET

REAL WRITING
Paragraphs and Essays for College, Work, and Everyday Life

Susan Anker

1998/522 PAGES/PAPER/$26.50 NET

Connecting the developmental writing course to students' real lives, *Real Writing* is the first paragraph-to-essay workbook that gives students a real reason to write — and provides them with the skills they need to succeed in college, at work, and in everyday life. The extensive and thoughtful ancillary package simplifies instructors' and students' busy lives.

"*In my nearly thirty years of teaching, this is the book I have been trying to find. It addresses writing problems visually, simply, and in an orderly way. The added tips for instructors and the appendices are wonderful.*"

— Margaret Montgomery, *Alvin Community College*

Ancillaries for REAL WRITING *Simplify Instructors' and Students' Lives*

FOR INSTRUCTORS

Instructor's Annotated Edition for REAL WRITING

Teaching REAL WRITING
1. **Practical Suggestions**
2. **Additional Resources**
3. **Background Readings**
4. **Classroom Posters**

SOFTWARE

Electronic Supplements for REAL WRITING
1. **Interactive Writing Software**
2. **Interactive Grammar Tests and Exercises**
3. **Additional Resources on Disk**

FOR STUDENTS

Notebook Dividers to Accompany REAL WRITING

FREE

BEDFORD/ST. MARTIN'S

1–800–446–8923 • www.bedfordstmartins.com

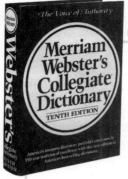
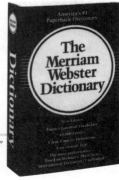